REBELLION

REBELLION

A Novel

MOLLY PATTERSON

HARPER

An Imprint of HarperCollinsPublishers

HarperCollins books may be purchased for educational, business, or sales promotional use. For information, please email the Special Markets Department at SPsales@harpercollins .com.

FIRST EDITION

Library of Congress Cataloging-in-Publication Data has been applied for.

ISBN 978-0-06-257404-6

17 18 19 20 21   LSC   10 9 8 7 6 5 4 3 2 1

For my grandmothers,
VIOLA STILLE AND COLLEEN PATTERSON

REBELLION

Driving, 1999

Hazel is driving and damn her children and damn her eyesight and who cares where she's going. Up to Hamel for a half gallon of milk. Out to the cemetery west of I-55. Into Edwardsville, just to drive past the old high school where she used to cook lunch, serving her own children when they came through the line. Never saying more than hello, you want potatoes? Then turning to the next one: And how about you? There's the brick building, there's where the tiger used to crouch above the doorways. Gone—the place has a different use now; the high school has been moved out to 157.

Back home without a hitch. This time, most times. The stoplights in town are enough to guide her, and she knows these streets. Occasionally, yes, a shape dives into view from the left side or right and she's not quite sure what it is—could be a bird or a tree branch or, Lord, a child on a skateboard—but she keeps her hands steady on the wheel while a fist grabs her stomach and squeezes hard.

Has she got into an accident? Even a little one, even once, in all these years?

No, she has not.

Down Sumner Road, following its jigs and jags. These roads, her roads, are the width of two cars, but they slope just a little to either side, and so gliding down the center she feels, looking ahead, like she's balancing on the blade of a giant knife.

Here it is March; here it is April. Here she is—Hazel—driving, driving.

*   *   *

The house is white clapboard, has damp cellars, has olive green carpets circa 1963. Sits on one hundred fifty acres, including barn and fruit trees, septic tank, dug well, and a garden verdant and terrifying with eight weeks of weeds. All the rest of the land is planted in corn and soy. This still groomed, carefully attended.

In the kitchen, a Christmas cactus points out the closed window. The rooster clock on the wall cock-a-doodle-doos to an empty house.

Flocked wallpaper in the dining room. A wooden hutch. Painting of Jesus and the disciples seated in a row like the head table at a wedding. Jesus is looking down past the bottom of the painting, past the expandable table with all of its leaves stowed away, past the chairs, even past the green carpet to the wood planks below. Hidden there is the impress of an iron stove that once squatted fatly in the center of the room.

The second story wasn't added until 1927. Outside, one can see it and other changes: different siding, seams at the edge of the porch, a garage that hides the cellar door. Before all this, the house was a simple square located just down the road, until the sturdy German forebears put the cabin on logs and rolled it up the hill. No one can explain why this was done.

But here it is.

And there, *there* in the garage: a maroon Lincoln believed by most everyone to have last been driven at a date no more recent than Thanksgiving. Sometime between pie and dishes and Rummikub, the keys were palmed by a devious daughter. Only late the next day was the mother informed—by phone, the daughter safely back in Chicago—that the theft of these keys was "for her own safety."

The spare key had been accounted for: the mother had given it to her son for safekeeping. This fact should have been verified, of course, and was. Only the brother hadn't cared to admit to his sister, when the idea of the key repossession was first proposed, that he wasn't exactly sure where the spare one had gone. When asked, in fact, lied: *Yeah, I have it right here.* What did it matter, as long as the mother didn't have it?

Could the mother have had it?

No.

Well, yes, in fact, but of course she mentioned this fact to no one. Berated her daughter and sulked to her son in the days following Thanksgiving. Still hadn't forgiven them by Christmas. (Grumbling in the kitchen while rolling out dough for the crescent rolls, while boiling and mashing many pounds of potatoes.) But through the winter and early spring she accepted rides to the grocery store and to church, *Oh, yes, thank you so much, oh, I sure do appreciate it*, from various members of the son's family—daughter-in-law and eldest grandson, and once the younger grandson, whose long hair and scowling expression frightens everyone but his grandmother. No need to drive herself anywhere other than to prove a point. Or for the freedom of the road, grown skittering at times, unsteady, but still hers to claim.

In early May a stepladder was dragged out of the garage and set up under the cherry tree. From the kitchen's south-facing window, the Christmas cactus pointed. First step, second step, third step, fourth. The fourth just missed.

The daughter-in-law was luckily coming for lunch that day. Then the ambulance, crunching gravel, pulling up the lane to the house. Out jumped two men, one fat and one skinny. Steady hands and a stretcher, *Easy now, don't you worry.* The querulous reply: *Just a little fall, I don't need all this fuss.* Backdoors slamming shut on *Wendy, you be sure to lock up the house—*

A phone call made from the kitchen—*To the hospital, yes*—then the daughter-in-law, dutiful, closing doors, turning locks. Since then, the house has stayed quiet. Days and weeks, one month, two. From outside come all the normal sounds of crickets, birdsong, and the distant rush of semis out on I-55.

Up the lane now comes a Corolla. A four-hour drive, and she's still here before her brother.

Figures.

*   *   *

Debbie has a long drive from the northwestern suburbs of Chicago and a full-time job, which in her world means sixty hours on a good week (and this was not a good week; this week she had five thousand pages of discovery to review), so Saturdays and Sundays are not exactly free time, especially not with a ten-year-old house that seems to have all the problems of a century-old one: perpetually running upstairs toilet, gutters that won't drain, signs of a carpenter ant infestation in the home office. Also a daughter who is home for only an abridged version of summer, newly graduated from college and joining the Peace Corps.

She's leaving in two weeks for Burkina Faso, and is right now experiencing some very intense anxiety, some very long sessions of crying and unexpected malaise, wandering around the house trying to anticipate (aloud) what exactly she'll miss most about home once she's so far away. For once, she's eager to spend some good quality time with her mother, which hasn't happened in a long time, not since before the teenage years, and because Debbie is not just a hardworking lawyer, but a hardworking single mom, she has been trying her best to indulge her daughter's requests. Including that she, Mal, join Debbie at the farm on Sunday rather than driving down together today. One of her college friends is in town, and she's not going to see him again for two years, Mom, two whole years at the very *least*.

With so much to balance, one might think Debbie would have trouble getting down almost to Edwardsville by ten on a Saturday morning with only this to look forward to: going room by room through the house where she grew up, where her mother has lived all eighty-four years of her life, deciding the fate of the furniture, the pots and pot holders, the cross-stitched pillows, the dusty artificial flowers in stem vases—all the things that won't fit into the three-hundred-square-foot "apartment" in the assisted living center where Hazel has recently been moved.

But here she is. Ten o'clock, and the sun is already barreling down on her head as she stands beside the car, listening to chapter 7 of the latest book-on-tape checked out from the Orland Park Public Library. For two months she's been coming down almost every weekend to see her mother, first in the hospital and then at Golden Valley Retirement Home and Assisted Living Center. That's eight hours of additional car time a week, and most of it in areas without anything better to listen to than country music or Christian talk radio. Ask most people which is the flattest state in the country, and they'll tell you it's Kansas, but those people haven't driven through Illinois. Set a quarter rolling, and it will keep on going all the way to the horizon.

Ten o'clock, and she's been here fifteen minutes. Whereas her brother, who lives less than ten miles away and whose job almost never requires forty hours of work in a week—much less sixty (or eighty!

Try eighty!)—and whose spouse actually puts *real bacon* in a pan and fries it for him every weekday morning (try sitting in Chicago traffic with a plastic spoon stabbed through the foil lid of a yogurt container), who, to the best of Debbie's knowledge, does not have a child preparing to move across the world for what will no doubt be an absolutely life-transforming experience in an exciting and vibrant place, but one that brings with it exposure to malaria and encephalitis, as well as a pretty real risk, it seems clear, of being kidnapped, raped—*he* can't be bothered to leave the house on time.

She sees his truck coming while he's still a ways off. Reaching in through the open window of the car, she takes the keys from the ignition and drops them into her purse, so when he pulls up he'll see her standing in the hot sun, foot tapping, and know that he's been wasting her time.

The truck rolls to a stop behind her car. "How was the drive?" he asks.

"Long."

"No traffic, though. Saturday morning, can't be anyone crowding the roads between here and Chicago." He shrugs stiffness out of his shoulders, as if he's the one who's been behind the wheel for hours. "Where's Mal?"

"I told you, she's driving down tomorrow. One of her friends was coming to town, and she promised him a bed at our house."

He whistles through his teeth. "That's cozy."

"Oh, get off it, Joe. She's twenty-two."

"I'm just saying, her trip might get a lot harder if she gets over there and finds out she's been—" Sweeping a dome over his stomach, he laughs heartily. Debbie rolls her eyes.

Quiet then, and they both glance at the house. Windows closed, it's been sealed since the day their mother fell, breaking her hip and shattering an elbow. Well, not quite sealed: Joe and Wendy came out here once a few weeks ago to take a few things for the new place in the retirement home. Lucky Debbie, she managed to get out of that one. Joe'd driven his wife out here that Sunday morning, pouring rain, mud everywhere, leaving his youngest son—who was grounded after getting caught drinking alone in the parking lot of a 7-Eleven—in the care of the older one, when they all knew goddamn well Travis couldn't do a thing to keep Jesse from going out. And when Joe walked through the door of his mom's house he just thought, Get me out of here. Reminded him of a funeral. In fact, took him right back to—strange—not his dad's death when he was eight, but a visitation for their neighbor, Mrs. Hughes, several years later. The air had that same closed-up, cottony quality, that cemetery quiet. In the house, Wendy had given him a this-isn't-so-bad-now-where-do-we-start? look. It should have made him feel better, but after twenty-odd years her can-do has started to get to him. It's useful sometimes, though; talking to the doctors, for example. He isn't good with hospitals or doctors or any of that. After the second day his mother was there, he spent no more than a half hour in her room at a time, dropping by in the early afternoon and leaving with the excuse that he had to get back to the shop. Wendy, meanwhile, spent most of each day there and didn't seem to even notice the smell that she brought home, something like canned meat, sick-making.

Wendy is good with hospitals, good with nursing homes, good at everything the last two months has thrown at them. She made caring for his mother her full-time job, and he got the reports. Anyway, she's the one who knows how to handle these things. That day in the house, she'd brought along a floor plan of the apartment and a measuring tape, to see whether the sofa and rocking chair would both fit.

Debbie sweeps her eyes now over the lawn. "Hasn't anyone been out to cut the grass?"

"Travis was here two weeks ago."

"It doesn't look that way to me."

"You want to take a ruler to it? Measure it?" Joe shakes his head. "The rain we've been getting, you cut the grass in the morning and by nighttime it's halfway to your knees again." He gives her a look: What does she know, living four hours away? The look she returns: *This*, at least, you could do.

They go into the house, where the kitchen smells of linseed linoleum baking in sunlight. Debbie opens the fridge, notes that the perishables have been removed (surely her sister-in-law's doing), but all the rest remains: ketchup, mustard, barbecue sauce, mayonnaise. A jar of black-berry jam with "1996" penciled on the masking tape. Tub of margarine. Two sticks of butter. An old Tupperware container that, opened, re-veals a half cup of chopped pecans. Her mother's got a microwave and double burner in her little apartment, though she's taking most of her meals in the dining room, where she can sit and be social, ha. When Debbie asked if she was making friends, she turned her head and said tightly, "I don't know these people."

Debbie shuts the fridge and says, "Let's start upstairs with the hard stuff."

"Downstairs is harder. Most of the useful stuff is down here."

She looks at him. "Upstairs is all old junk and papers. You don't think Mom's thrown out any of her *Reader's Digest*s, do you?"

The second floor is an oven, so they retrieve the box fan from the downstairs bedroom, which is the only one their mother has used for the last few years. The husks of dead flies now line the windowsills up-stairs, and when Joe fits the fan into a window frame, sleepy herds of dust wander out over the floor. "Ninety-six degrees," he says, stepping back from the fan. "That's what the weather said for today."

They're already sweating when the first of two closets is thrown open and they begin taking things down from the shelf. There are shoe boxes whose yellowed glue is giving out at the seams, stacks of old calendars, old catalogs, boxes of books with titles both famil-iar and unfamiliar, *Murder on the Orient Express* and *Prayers from the Middle Kingdom, Vol. IV*. Hazel has never been much of a reader, so who knows where these came from. But it's all the same: the exten-sion cords with fabric-covered wires, the ball of panty hose, the hand mixer missing one of its beaters. Stiff hats worn by their mother no more recently than Watergate and purses with cracked handles and rusting clasps. When lids are removed from the boxes, they find un-opened credit card offers, envelopes fat with tissue-paper dress pat-terns, replacement lids for mason jars . . .

"Jesus Christ," Joe says, unearthing a stack of S&H Green Stamp collectors' books. He flips through the pages and finds one partially filled. "When's the last time you saw one of these?"

Debbie pauses in the act of unfolding a torn plastic tablecloth. The memory is of a permed and gum-smacking grocery store cashier dialing up their stamps, tearing along the perforated lines, handing a pile of them to her mother along with the receipt. Hazel tucking them into her purse. "They stopped giving those out—what?—twenty years ago?" she says, taking one from her brother.

"Something like." He twitches his nose. "Wonder if they're worth anything now."

The house has eight rooms, two cellars, a garage, and a barn. They have today and tomorrow, and then Debbie has to drive back to Chicago: no time for reminiscing. "Probably as much as those bank calendars," she replies. Then she takes the other books from her brother and places them in the trash pile.

*   *   *

It's slow going in the morning; they make it through only the first of the upstairs bedrooms. For lunch, they drive into town to eat fast-food burritos in an air-conditioned space. The beans are soupy, the soda flat, but good Lord, the *air*. On their way back out to the farm Joe says, Why don't we stop and get some beer, make this thing a little easier, and Debbie says, Yes, please.

The plan was, the first day it would just be them two, and on the second day they'd bring in the reinforcements. "Why did we want to do this to ourselves?" Debbie asks as they pull back into the drive.

"I don't know what *you* were thinking. Me, I figured I'd only get the boys out here for one day. Might as well be when we're hauling things out."

In one corner of the second bedroom are the Christmas decorations. Old grapefruit boxes filled with ornaments they'll divide. The Advent calendar will go to Joe for safekeeping until December, and the same for the one-foot-high porcelain tree with lights. These can be put up in the apartment at Golden Valley.

Into the trash pile go the artificial tree in parts, a broken suitcase, a musty cooler, all the old folding chairs with rust flaking off.

And then come the boxes of paperwork.

Debbie says, "Look for tax forms, contracts, anything related to the farm."

Joe begins leafing through a pile, dubious. "How far back do we go?"

"Seven years for taxes. Nineteen ninety-two." She sits on the floor and then scoots back to the wall, dragging a box of papers with her. "Any contracts we should look at—receipts and all that—to see whether they need keeping." Thank God she's a lawyer, undaunted by the prospect of spending hours in the labyrinth: small type every way you turn.

But Joe isn't her, and after a few minutes of passing papers over to his sister, asking trash or keep, his head is waterlogged. Everything is slow. With the light through the window and the papers swimming before him, he feels as if he's back in school, staring at chalk dust caught in sunbeams and feeling his butt grow numb on the chair.

He struggles to his feet and declares that he's done.

Eyes raised over glasses, mouth pinched, Debbie puts on their mother's disapproving expression.

"I'll make you a deal," Joe says, putting his hands up in a defensive posture. "You handle the papers, and I promise I'll get all the rest up here done. Every single thing that's not folded up and stuck in an envelope, I'll sort through it."

A pause as negotiations are considered. "Fine," Debbie says after a moment, and goes back to scanning the fading print.

*   *   *

In a narrow closet off the landing, a discovery: six old paintings on canvas, mounted on wood. The paint is cracked, chipped, bubbled, flaked. There are tears in the canvas, furling corners. But the images are still clear enough: each one is a landscape, recognizable by certain trees, fences, and far-off farm buildings as barren winterscapes viewed from one or another of the house's windows. They are not very good paintings. In better condition, they might be sold at a thrift store.

But they are interesting. That night, when they take their mother out to dinner, Joe asks about the pictures.

"Your father painted a little," their mother says, squinting critically at the hot buffet against the far wall. "I burned most of them."

*   *   *

After dinner, in the parking lot, Debbie says good night to her brother and Wendy, and to her mother, who frowns when she tells her that Mal is coming the next day. "You're going to make her go through that house with you?" Hazel asks. This is how she refers to the place now—"that house"—as if it's betrayed her.

"She wants to see it again," Debbie says. "And she can't wait to see you. We'll be out to pick you up in the afternoon when we're done. Tomorrow I thought we could go to Graebner's. We haven't been there in years."

"It isn't open on Sundays."

Debbie is caught short, Joe and Wendy, too. You don't expect to be corrected by Hazel, who is sometimes uncertain of grandchildren's names and can't always remember which year it is.

"Someplace else, then. Anywhere you've been wanting to go, Mom, just say."

Hazel shakes her head. "Any place is fine." She moves to the passenger's-side door of Wendy's car to wait.

Debbie had planned on staying the night at the house, but the prospect of going back out there now makes the back of her neck sweat. Pulling out of the parking lot, she drives to a hotel and checks in, then calls Mal at home. Her daughter doesn't answer, probably out at a bar, which is exactly what she should be doing, enjoying her last nights in America: sweet youth, careless in the summer, in the city, alive.

*   *   *

When Mal pulls up to the house the next day, she still has the taste of spit in her mouth, but all visible signs of her hangover are gone. She sees her mom's car, a moving truck, and a beat-up Chevy with a bumper sticker on the back that reads "Stop Staring at My Rack" beside an outline of deer antlers. Pretty funny, really. Mal has always taken a kind of pride in her country cousins. And her grandma, living her whole life on this farm. Her grandma is so authentic, a stoic German farmer to her core. It's unbelievably sad that she has to live in an old folks' home now. Mal's mother has said the sad thing is that Hazel has never been anywhere else, never been around many people, barely traveled anywhere except for a wedding or funeral, but Mal doesn't agree. She figures her grandmother is the last of a dying breed, truly tied to the land. She drinks *well* water, for God's sake, and has a real cellar, not a basement, but a cellar with a door in the floor, where she used to keep potatoes and onions from the garden. Nowadays you have to go to Africa to find people like that.

Mal parks and crosses the lawn, goes in through the side door onto the screened-in porch. "Hello!" she calls out, and peeks through the window into the dining room, where her two cousins are crouched over the upturned table.

They both look up, and Mal wonders if they knew she was coming. "Hey," they both say, and Travis adds, "The door's unlocked."

She goes in through the kitchen and then joins them in the dining room. "What're you doing with the table?"

"Taking the legs off," Jesse grunts, leaning into a screwdriver, "so we can fit it through the door."

Mal squeezes past to see the living room. The space is empty except for the piano, with indentations in the carpet and brighter spots where the furniture used to sit. She spins around, a slow three-sixty. "God, this is weird. What did you do with everything?"

"Some of it's at Grandma's new place," Travis answers, shaking out his arm as he joins her in the living room, "and some's in the truck. My mom and dad just drove a load of shit to the dump."

"I thought we were going to save some of it."

"They just took the broken stuff, old magazines and whatever."

A few feet away in the next room, Jesse tunes them out. It's taking forever to get the legs off this table because the screws are real tight and probably haven't ever been loosened. It's not the work he minds, but this whole thing is crap: his parents and Aunt Debbie sticking Grandma in a fucking nursing home when she's lived her whole life in this house and probably doesn't even know there's a world outside where kids his age are opening fire on their schools and the president's getting his dick sucked by a fat chick in an ugly hat. And if his grandma doesn't want to know about all that, why is it a problem? If she wants to be quiet and live alone, she should get to do it. She's never done a thing to anyone, never been anything but nice, doesn't get on his case or ask what he's been up to. Pays him twenty dollars to come out and cut her lawn, and afterward gives him a Coke, and if there's a ball game on, they watch it together and they don't talk about anything but the pitching and the hits, and whichever commercials she finds interesting. Not that he cares about baseball, but it's kind of cool that his grandma, who is old as shit, always stays up to watch the games, even when they're on the West Coast and aren't over until eleven or twelve o'clock.

He wouldn't have even come out here to help, except that his dad and Aunt Debbie would probably throw most of her stuff away, and he figures it's his job to try to save as much as he can. When his grandma was over for dinner a few days ago, he'd asked her what she really wanted to keep, and she'd looked at him and said, "I guess it doesn't really matter." Then his mom had interrupted and said all cheerful that they'd keep as much as they could, so one day when Jesse moved out, he'd have furniture for his place. It wouldn't have surprised him if his grandma had gotten offended, since his mom was basically giving away all her stuff without permission, but she hadn't. Instead, that little smile she sometimes got came over her face and she leaned over to ask him if he was planning on moving out soon.

He wishes.

Travis and Mal come back into the dining room, and Jesse's still working on the table legs, but he's almost done. In a minute they'll be able to haul the table out to the truck and clear up some space. The house is feeling so weird now, it's better just to get it done as fast as possible. Mal opens the door to the stairs and calls up to her mom, "I'm here!"

Debbie comes tromping down. "You made it." She puts her arms around her daughter and grimaces. "Yick, sorry, I'm all sweaty. It's about a hundred degrees upstairs."

"What should I work on?" Mal asks.

"Anything you want." Glancing around the room, she nods at the glass-fronted built-in. "You feel like tackling the doodads, that'd be great. There should be some boxes in the truck. Maybe some shoe boxes for those little things. Wrap them up so they don't break."

Mal pulls open the double doors of the cabinet. One side is devoted to scalloped glass plates and coffee cups that she doesn't remember ever using. On the other side is the collection of salt and pepper shakers and a shelf of other knickknacks, everything crowded together so all that's really visible is the front row. As a child, she'd stood on a chair and peered in; everything seemed magical then because she wasn't allowed to touch it. But she hasn't looked in this cabinet in years, and now some of the figurines jolt her straight back to childhood, without any specific memory attached: that shepherd with the sheep, or the one that's a baseball fitted into a glove, where the baseball is for salt and the glove is for pepper.

Jesus, this is sad. Like so, so sad.

"I'm gonna go grab some boxes from the garage," Mal says.

Debbie follows her into the kitchen, takes a glass from the cabinet. Squints at it, pours some water in, and swishes it around before dumping it down the drain and pouring a full glass to drink. "Travis, Jesse, you guys been drinking water?" she calls to her nephews in the next room. "Y'all get dehydrated, you don't watch out." Every time she's around her brother's family, she finds herself affecting a drawl. She and Mal used to make a joke of it. Driving down together they'd practice in the car: *How y'all din? J'eet yit?*

Mal comes back with some boxes, grabs the roll of paper towels, and goes to work on the knickknacks. And where did it all come from, this souvenir cable car from San Francisco, this sculpted ashtray that reads "Beautiful Biloxi!" over painted blue waves? There's a Chinese fan, even, like the one her roommate brought back from her study abroad in Beijing. Mal shows it to her mother, who shrugs and says, "My guess is Aunt Edith." Meaning *her* aunt, Hazel's younger sister, a tall gourd-shaped woman who went to college on the GI Bill and never married, who for years and years owned her own flower shop in town. Who, in the last fifteen years of her life, had suddenly began taking vacations all over with a black woman named Del. Debbie recalls getting postcards and thinking, There's a story there. But never being told.

*   *   *

"So you're off to save the world, huh?" Joe and Wendy have just returned from the dump, and when he sees his niece, he slings one arm around her shoulders, which is the kind of hug an uncle gives a girl once she's older than, say, ten. "Going all the way over to Africa?"

"I guess so."

"Where at, exactly?" Wendy asks. "I know your mother told us, but I can't seem to remember."

"Burkina Faso," Mal says. And then, patiently: "It's in West Africa."

Wendy looks at her, shakes her head, looks at Joe, shakes her head again. He knows she has always been a little unsure about his sister and niece, never quite certain what to do with them. Why, she's asked him, when they're asked to bring a side dish for dinner, do they insist on showing up with something that requires a geography lesson? *They're soba noodles, they're from Japan,* or *Those are kibbeh, they're like Turkish meatballs.* Joe always ribs them for it, but Wendy gets irked. "You think your mother wants to eat all those spices?" she asks when Debbie and Mal are out of earshot. But Hazel has always seemed to take it in stride.

"Well, we're glad you came down to see us before you leave," Wendy says now. "Africa sure is far away."

"Too far," Debbie says, squeezing her daughter's shoulder.

The house is slowly coming apart and in the process becoming crowded: there are garbage bags everywhere, boxes, rolls of tape. It's dirty and hot and still Debbie hasn't finished going through the papers upstairs, and though yesterday she'd resigned herself to putting them all in her car, taking the whole load back home to deal with later, now she declares that maybe she *will* try to get it done today. Who needs that mess? Upstairs she goes, and Wendy and Joe and Mal disperse to various rooms to join the boys in sorting and packing and carrying. And the house continues to get stranger to them all, but it's work now and they're just focused on getting it done.

*   *   *

A few hours later the sun is evil, the sky is white, the air is so heavy it seems you should be able to shake it out like a blanket, see if there's some better, thinner air under it to breathe. In the house, Jesse holds his jaw tight as his mother speculates about whether this lamp is worth keeping. Travis is ravenous, stares blankly at the kitchen sink as he pushes handfuls of chips into his mouth. He's thinking about the summer class he's taking at Lewis and Clark, thinking it's not so terrible to sit in an air-conditioned classroom with his accounting calculator, setting the world right with numbers. Debbie, upstairs, squints at a tax form. Pages through, mouth open. These numbers are a lot bigger than she'd imagined they'd be. Her mother has rented out the land for forty years and never once, she's almost completely certain, never once until now, has Debbie made the morbid calculations: this is how much she'll get when her mother dies.

Meanwhile, outside, Joe and Mal are packing up the truck and have, one way or another, wandered into a political argument about the bombings in Kosovo. He doesn't remember starting the discussion, but he's gotten her angry, and though he's not even sure he quite knows where he stands on the issue, instead of backing off, he digs in deeper. It seems to him that since the Peace Corps is a government organization, she must have some stake in what the United States does overseas. Some bit of pride, maybe. It seems to him like things over in Europe were getting bad and looking worse, and now the United States and NATO have turned it all around. "You know I'm not some rah-rah type when it comes to the military," he says, pushing a dresser against the wall of the truck with a grunt, "but there are times you've got to step in and put a stop to things."

"What does that even mean?" Mal asks. "Because obviously I don't think it's good when people are killing one another, but how is bombing innocent civilians 'putting a stop to things,' exactly?"

"I don't know there's much of that happening," he says, coming back to the front of the truck. "From what I've heard it's some very targeted bombing."

"We hit the Chinese *embassy*." His niece looks up at him, squinting in the sunlight. She has the square jaw and long German nose that are so strong in the family bloodline, particularly in the females. Right now, she could be his mother at a younger age, or Grandma Louisa staring grimly out from her wedding portrait in sepia. "Some of their journalists got killed in the accident. There were protests in China. Like riots, practically. People don't do that for nothing."

He raises his shoulders. "But that's not really civilians killed, is it? And you just said it was an accident."

"It *was* civilians, just not *white* civilians. Which is a pattern I've noticed: we tend to care a lot more about genocide when it's white people being killed." She gives him a look, challenging him to come back with something to prove he's not racist. Once upon a time, it was Debbie leveling these shots when he happened to show some brotherly concern and ask about the neighborhood she was living in, the precautions she was taking, as if there was something not only offensive but totally ridiculous in the idea that a white woman could run into trouble in a black neighborhood, walking home late at night, weighed down by about a thousand pounds of law books. "Like Rwanda?" Mal is saying. "We didn't ever try to stop *things* over there."

And on and on.

He watches her splutter, watches her wipe a hand over her face and leave a streak of dust across her cheek. Mal could never be his daughter, raised in so many ways foreign to him, but right now he's feeling a pang like what goes through him whenever Travis gets carried away talking about football stats, or when he's seen Jesse skate—he's witnessing some passion take over their imagination, sweep them up completely. It's that moment when you realize there's some little spark inside them that makes them a real person, that's just them all alone, formed out of nothing.

When she pauses for breath, he climbs down from the truck. Looks her in the eye, lays a fatherly hand on her shoulder. Her face is flushed with the heat, and it makes her look like an uglier woman than she is. He has a mind to tell her that, but thinks better of it. Instead, he says, "I'm betting you'll do some real good over there."

Through the flush, despite the heat, she blushes.

*   *   *

All those years, the Hughes family has paid Hazel a good rent. Better than they needed to pay, is Debbie's guess. Well, there's some country neighborliness for you. Poor George Hughes—Debbie really should have come down for the funeral last fall, but what could she do? The weather was bad and she was drowning in work, and anyway, Joe and Wendy were here to accompany Hazel to the church and the graveyard after, so it's not like she had to go alone. Still, considering things now, Debbie feels bad for missing it. Especially since Gene apparently hasn't changed the terms of the rental since taking over his father's affairs. Better Gene than his brother Bobby, who last Debbie heard was twice divorced and wandering the world somewhere.

And so here's the money in the bank: Hazel's big secret. Debbie doesn't have to worry any longer about the monthly bill from Golden Valley. She'll be having a talk with her mother soon. Not this trip, but soon. For now, she's staying quiet.

As evening comes on and the lightning bugs begin to blink and hover in the grass, the house offers up another secret. It's six o'clock. Hazel will be down in the lobby of her building, waiting for them to take her to dinner someplace where the cooking's no good and the tab, if she saw it, would make her sick. They're about to head out for the day when Jesse, in the garage, opens the door of the maroon Lincoln and finds a set of keys in the ignition.

At Christmas, there were arguments. The flat line of his grandma's mouth, a hyphen of anger. "I am not a child," she'd said as his parents and Aunt Debbie sighed and cut their Christmas ham and passed the crescent rolls and mashed potatoes. He'd looked at Travis, thinking, Say something, you're the one they want to hear. But his brother just shrugged. Mal might have spoken up, but she wasn't there. He'd hated everyone at the table then except for his grandma. Across the plate of ham, she met his eye. Kept the frown on her face. But just for him, something no one else saw—she winked.

In the house, they're closing windows; outside, they're starting cars. He puts the keys in his pocket. At dinner, he decides, he'll give them back to his grandma. But it turns out that with everyone around, there's never a good moment, and besides, he likes thinking he has something that no one else knows about. A testament to his grandma's refusal to give in. At the end of the night, he hugs her good-bye without returning them.

Next time, he thinks.

And when that time comes, it's next time again.

*   *   *

Years later, on one of Travis's frequent trips back from St. Louis to see his parents and brother—who continue on against the odds in the same ranch-style house, the same old town, after the night when Jesse, a fifth of cheap vodka in his belly, climbed the scaffolding on the side of the old high school and fell backward onto concrete—he decides to drive out to see his grandmother's old place.

Out 143 there's a big hill he used to jump, and then a soft right onto Fox Road, winding out among the cornfields.

Hazel has been dead for a decade and it's been that long, too, since he saw his aunt or cousin. There are phone calls. Twice a year or so, his father hears from Debbie, who has married a tech entrepreneur and moved out to California. Plane tickets are talked about, but never purchased. And Mal? Mal is good, Mal is somewhere in the world, never the same place. Though after Africa, not such exciting places as you might have expected: Ann Arbor, Cincinnati. She is gathering degrees in subjects for which there is no identifiable job market. Or so Travis's dad tells him, in somewhat different words.

He turns onto Sumner and in the near distance is the big house with the silo and barn where the Hughes family lived—friends of his dad's when he was young. Down a bit farther are the new developments, ugly beige and brick houses for people who work in town but want to live in the country. Satellite dishes on every roof. Three-car garages. When Travis asked his brother if he wanted to come along, Jesse shook his head, staring at the television from his motorized wheelchair. Fucked up, he muttered, what it's turning into out there.

He makes the final turn onto the straight stretch, train tracks under his tires for just a moment. The land is flat and the corn is still low, so he can see in the distance the slight rise, almost a hill, where the house had been. It's gone now, along with the barn and septic tank, the fence and all the trees. He'd known the house was razed, but he hadn't realized the place would look like this: so ordinary and blank. Level with all around it. He had thought he might want to get out and walk around, but why walk through a cornfield? The sky is bigger than he remembered it, great white clouds lumbering through the blue, and the corn is pretty in the most ordinary of ways: green stalks, black earth. Zipping down the asphalt, he's quickly past the place where the house used to be. Past it and gone. A car is a beautiful thing in the country. Straight down the middle. He rolls down the windows and smells manure. It's spring, and because he's not a farmer and never has been, he feels only the poetry in it, and none of the work.

Louisa

1

March 17, 1892

Dear Louisa,

This country has offered up a number of surprises over the years, but here's one to beat them all: it rained mud here yesterday. Actual mud coming down from the sky, a grayish-brown sludge that stuck to the buildings and covered everything. We were all inside the house when it happened, but Li K'ang had gone to the market in search of fresh vegetables and when he came back he looked like some sort of monster that had crawled up from the bottom of a lake, covered from head to foot in mud and slime, and his two eyes shining white out of an equally dirty face. He was laughing about it and not at all alarmed. It happens here from time to time, he says, though not all that often. Certainly such an event hasn't come in the last few years—I should think I would have remembered it! But I suppose it's no wonder with the climate here in the north: dust upon dust, and wind upon wind. The one gets hold of the other and makes us all miserable. At least mud raining down makes for a good story.

Other than strange weather events, we are all well. Freddie is toddling around faster every day, and the bigger I get, the harder it is for me to chase after him. This time around has been harder than it was with him; I have to spend part of each day in bed resting. Don't be alarmed, Louisa, it's nothing serious, but I did think it was supposed to be easier the second time. Luckily I have Hsi-yung helping. She came before for a short time, you remember, last year. I like her; she's a quick, smart girl with a sparkle in her eye and it's easy to tell that she's used to caring for small children. Well, she has one herself, though it's not with her here; I guess she's left it at home for someone else to care for.

We're still waiting on the mail package, and I do hope there will be some letters from you when it arrives. It's been nearly six weeks since the last *came, and that one had your letters from Christmas and New Years. Now you must be busy planting, I think. Let's see: beets and peas and radishes, of course, as well as spinach and broccoli and onions and carrots. I'm sure you have other news to tell me, but if nothing else, then simply give me a list of all you are planting and let me imagine the meals you will prepare when it comes in. For now, I suppose you're getting to the bottom of the cellar and pretty ready for spring, like we are here.*

I am eager for more news of you and Bert, and all the folks back home as well, assuming that you've heard from them more recently than I have. But I am always ready for letters from all. You and I are the two prodigal daughters, Louisa, and must look to each other for confirmation that we have made the right choice in leaving a loving home for the more dubious comforts of the wider world.

Much love, of course, from Owen and Freddie, even if Freddie doesn't know he has wished it. I'm locked up in the house now for the next two months, and not able to do much of anything but read and write, so you can count on receiving plenty of letters from

Your loving sister,
ADDIE

So they all went. The letters were written in a small, neat hand that covered every last inch of space on the page, front and back. Over the years, this was how Louisa would come to think of her sister: as an elegant scrawl like frost on glass. She'd look for Addie not only in the words themselves but in the shape of the letters and the spaces between them, the odd curl at the top of the lowercase *d*, the *o* that never quite completed itself. She'd take comfort in the fact that the handwriting looked the same from month to month and from year to year.

For the first year or two, the letters arrived at intervals of eight to twelve weeks. They would come tied up all together in a packet, a month or more of writing that chronicled the adventures her sister was having as a missionary all the way over on the other side of the world, and that put a check on Louisa's thinking of her own life as containing very much excitement. True, her situation was new as well—marriage and a move five hundred miles west to become a farmer, or a farmer's wife. She and Addie had been raised in a fine two-story house in eastern Ohio, two daughters in a family of six, and the family name well respected in town, so for some little while every aspect of life on the farm had felt like an adventure. She had never milked a cow before, never rendered lard. Back in Marietta, she had helped her mother and the hired girl to make jams and pickles, to mix up catsups and to can a variety of vegetables. She knew the elementals of keeping a house clean.

But the house in town was something very different from the one-room cabin she and Bert lived in on the farm. When she first saw their new home, she'd turned to his chest and wept. He had comforted her then: *Come now, Lou, it's not as bad as that.* Maybe it wasn't so bad if you were used to such living. Well, she would grow used to it. The cabin had a packed-earth floor and no ventilation for the stove except through one of the two small windows. One of the first improvements they made was to carve out a hole in the ceiling and move the stove to the room's center. They put wood planks over the floor, and one of the neighbors brought them a rag rug she'd made. A wedding present, she said, flicking her eyes sideways in apology. The gift had made Louisa so happy she lunged forward to grab the woman's hands, kicking over a stool and alarming everyone—herself included, when she felt the calluses on Mrs. Moeller's fingers and palms. "You are simply the kindest," she said, brushing the hardened skin with a kind of morbid fascination. Her own hands were still smooth. They wouldn't stay that way.

Bert bought some wood from their neighbors, and together they constructed an outhouse. Then they built a henhouse and filled it with chickens. With the leftover boards, Louisa tacked up some extra shelves in the cabin and used them to display what Bert called her "historicals": a variety of fossils and arrowheads they'd found in the soil. She liked thinking that the land had been other things to other people before they were here. Bert said he didn't think she would have liked it so well if those other people were still here, and she supposed he was right.

They'd arrived late in the season, too late for planting, and the acres were not yet theirs to farm; they made up a parcel of land belonging to their nearest neighbor, who was moving into town after the season had done. After the outhouse and henhouse were completed, it was harvest time, and Bert went out every day as a paid hand while Louisa went to the neighbors' to help cook for the men. From the women she learned how many bushels of corn they could expect to get from their acres next year, and how little they would be paid for them, as prices had been falling steadily for a decade and continued to go down. From Bert she learned that none of this mattered; as long as they worked hard, they would do just fine.

Back home, she'd been used to reading novels for at least an hour in the evening, either by herself or with Addie. Now, she and Bert went to bed when the sun went down. She would rub his back to soothe his muscles after a long day's work with Prince in the field. Sometimes they'd speak of what had gone on in their separate days, but after spending hours with the neighbors, Louisa was happy not to talk. The silence in the cabin had a thickness to it, a kind of slow swirl. She floated in it; she sank. There was her body, which was a single thing, and there was her husband's body in its various parts—the shoulders and arms that she kneaded and pushed and beat into comfort, and the skin, sticky with dried sweat, whose combination of vinegar and hay was, to her, the most magnificent scent in the world. The heart, whose slow beat pulsed strong in his neck. Often she would drape herself over him, press her chest to his back, and then he would turn around and grab hold of her and give her love quickly.

She was not often alone, but she missed her family. The letters from Addie had not yet begun to arrive and though her parents wrote her, and her sister Flora, too, she longed to see a face that looked like hers. They didn't even have a mirror in the cabin; perhaps that made it worse. They didn't have a mirror as they didn't have many other things that would have made her more comfortable, things she might have thought about if she'd had more time to plan. She was sixteen years old and everything had happened so swiftly. In the neighbors' kitchens, she told her story: how her father had handled the will for Bert's uncle, and when that uncle died, the big black-haired German with clumsy hands and a broken nose had been invited for a cold dinner on a very hot day. Bert was in town for two weeks, and by the end of it, he had an inheritance and an understanding with Louisa. He went back to Illinois to secure the purchase of the farm; a month later he returned and they had a wedding dinner at the house and the very next day boarded a train headed west. Her parents had come to the station to see her off, and her brother Will and sister Flora and a whole crowd of aunts and uncles and cousins. It was the same group that had seen Addie off just two months before.

She told her story, and the women said wasn't Bert a prize, wasn't Louisa a sweet thing, wasn't her sister a brave soul for going off to save those poor heathens who had never heard the name Jesus. They would get the church to take up a collection.

At night Louisa turned to the photographs she'd brought with her from back home. She wanted to check her memory, to make sure she had not already forgotten faces. In addition to her wedding portrait, she had two earlier pictures taken of her family in the studio a year or two before Addie left: one of the family, and one of the three sisters. But they were artificial and flat; there was almost nothing of them there. What was Addie? Only the squarish face, all cheeks and forehead, and the long rectangular nose. The eyes looked too light, the face stripped of expression.

Louisa tried to conjure up other elements, the way her sister walked, the sound of her laugh, but the memories slipped out of her grasp. A quick flash, as if Addie, galloping by on a horse, had turned just for an instant to look at her. *There*—that was her sister, wasn't it? But when Louisa tried to draw up the idea again, it dissolved, and she wasn't sure that she'd gotten any of it right at all.

It was winter when she finally received the first packet of letters. This was her first winter in Illinois, and the house, tiny and cramped, was closing in on her. Bert assured her that the weather had been mild so far, which was little comfort when the wind came howling through the cracks in the walls and the snow came swirling down and she grew convinced that their cabin was just a tiny candle flame in a deep and immense darkness. She wondered, as she untied the first bundle of letters, if it was this cold in China. Did they get snow there? It wasn't like Australia, was it, where the seasons were reversed—winter in July and summer in January?

She didn't get an answer to her question because that batch of letters only went as far as early autumn. There were letters from the train, let-ters from the ship, and from every stop along the way once they hit solid ground. She would read all of them many times and in every possible order, including the natural one. But the first time through, she began with the latest.

September 30, 1890

Dear Sister,

This is my first letter from Lu-cho Fu, so I will attempt to make it a good one as this will have to serve as your introduction to our new home. If you were here in the flesh, I would invite you to our housewarming; or perhaps I should say if you were here I would have a housewarming because there's no one to invite but the Riddells, and it would be silly to have a party in which the guests only just outnumber the hosts. The Riddells are a family of five and Owen and I feel quite lucky to have them here. Mr. Riddell rode out on a mule to meet us as we came down into the town and if it's possible to know that you will like someone when you first see them from a distance of one hundred yards, then that is exactly what happened. We were twelve days altogether crossing the mountains in our litter—nine days to T'ai-yüan, and then the better part of three days going down to Lu-cho Fu—and that's after spending a week in Pao-ting Fu and nearly as long coming downriver from T'ien-chin.

You can imagine how dusty and tired and jostled we were, and how glad to see a friendly face beaming at us from down the road. I didn't even won-der how it was that Mr. Riddell knew we were arriving just then, but we learned later it was a happy coincidence; he was out on the street and heard two locals gossiping about "wai-kuo jen," which, you may guess, is how the Chinese refer to us. I've learnt almost nothing else of the language, but I will have plenty of time to study soon, once my state becomes visible and I am locked up inside.

So her sister was pregnant. Louisa felt it as a metal splinter in her heart: Addie was going on into motherhood without her. She herself had felt, as soon as she arrived at the little house with Bert, that she wanted a child to tie her to the place, to make her a still point on that expanse of land that undulated—wavered—as it stretched toward the horizon. But so far she had had only a hope and then a loss.

Instinctively, she put a hand to her stomach, and it growled as if to show that food was its only concern. Bert was at the stove, frying mush. They had bought the cornmeal and butter and were lucky to have it, but the butter always tasted of ash, no matter what Louisa did to try to keep it apart from the stove. "Put some honey in," she said with a frown, and Bert reached for the jar while Louisa kept reading:

The house—well, suffice it to say that it is nothing like what we are used to. There is a central courtyard and a smaller one in the back, and walls all around that are ten or twelve feet high. The rooms all open up off the court-yards, so that you can't move from room to room without going outside. I am not certain how we will like that in the rain, but for now we don't mind it. However, we are told that it almost never does rain here, and after riding twelve days through dusty yellow mountains, on paths that had cracks six inches deep and two inches wide, I can believe such a thing is true. The advantage is that this gives us a ceiling of bright blue sky over our house, which is rather cheerful. Certainly better than a raincloud.

So here we are in our new home, and we are settling in. The quarters we've been given are quite large and outfitted with all the necessities. I guess the folks at the Missionary Board arranged the purchase of the place, and the Riddells took it upon themselves to buy linens for the beds, as well as a few basic goods for the kitchen, baskets and a cleaver and a few heavy earthen jars that they say we can use for pickling. They also found two boys to work for us. Three dollars a month will suffice to pay them, Mrs. Riddell tells me, which I suppose is good enough wages in China.

As for the town, I can't tell you very much about it, because one hardly goes outside the "house"; indeed, I've ventured out only a few times, as there is an awful lot to do at home. However, from my few ventures I can tell you that the streets are quite narrow and the walls quite high, so that you feel as if you are in a labyrinth with the Minotaur waiting, perhaps, right around the next corner. Just as it is inside the house, too, where you can't see anything but the sky overhead. I imagine that I may come to miss wide open spaces very soon, and that when I think of the times we all went out picnicking in June, and you and I went running over the meadows to watch the grasshoppers leap out of our path, I shall feel very sorry for myself indeed, and start writing you longer letters, even than this one, that are filled with sighing reminiscences of life back in the States. However, I won't despair yet; there must be some open spaces in town. I am curious, but not impatient, as I know there will be plenty of time to get accustomed to every-thing. This is our new home, after all. How strange to write that! But for now I am content to get the house fitted up for us to live in, and to visit with the Riddells every day. Mrs. Riddell is not exactly "my type" of woman, but one can't choose among friends here when the white faces are so few. In any case, it is a delight to play with their two-year-old, Julie, a sweet little girl named for her mother. You can imagine what I feel, playing with that dear baby and thinking of the future.

Lu-cho Fu waits for us outside our gate, and it will still be there tomor-row, and next week, and next month—whenever we are able to explore it more fully. Trust that when we do, you will receive a most faithful account of all its wonders from

Your loving sister,
ADDIE

p.s. Coming over the mountains, we were stuck for the better part of a day be-hind a camel train. Such terribly ugly, mangy-looking creatures, they seem to have no more love for the men driving them than the men have for them. I wouldn't have thought to see camels in China! But I'm sure that won't be the last surprise I'll encounter.

Indeed, it was only one of a great number of surprises, and not the first. The letters in that packet and in the next many that followed were filled with descriptions of bizarre customs and thrilling encounters: ev-erything was new, exciting, frightening, different. Louisa caught a high note of pride in these letters—*Look at me, living through all of this!* It made her proud of her sister, and somehow, at the same time, proud of herself. Hadn't they both thrown away comfort for love, or something like it? For adventure? For faith? It was something to remember. When Louisa read her sister's letters, the world could again be what it had been to her as a child: grand and mysterious and full of wonders. She could write back, giving an account of the day or the week she'd just spent, and she would search out the significance in her mundane stories; she would make an effort for philosophy. On a good day, if she saw a hawk overhead as she went out to feed the pigs, she would set down her bucket to watch it. The swoops and arcs of the bird's flight would become invisible writing on the sky, and the trees the hawk flew over would be whispering to one another using the secret language of moving leaves, and she would feel herself to be a witness to grace. She would save it up, this feeling, and write it in a letter to her sister.

On a bad day, she didn't notice the hawk at all. Or she saw it and hated it, fiercely. Or she saw it and it made her tired.

Good days and bad days. As one year turned to the next, Louisa began tallying them up and found that she didn't have very many that refused this easy accounting—first days, then weeks. Good weeks, bad weeks—Bert called it the weather. "The weather's fine today, is it?" he'd say, and kiss her on the mouth. The good weather was simply good all the way through, but the bad weather was subtler: it had shape and distinction; it was dynamic; it was as if her soul were curdling. Every movement was a struggle, but because there was no languishing in bed (as her mother used to do when she had a headache), she was forced to make the effort. Sometimes her work would bring her from sadness to anger, or from numbness to hurt, and so when Bert and the hired man came in from the fields they might find her sobbing as she peeled potatoes, or muttering darkly to the weeds as she pulled them up from the garden. The men would stay away from her then, taking their dinner outside to eat while seated on the stools by the henhouse, the plates wobbling on their laps. During these stretches, Louisa refused to go anywhere and as a result often missed out on those neighborly gatherings that had a common purpose. She canned tomatoes alone, scrubbed the sheets alone. Five years went by. Several times she was pregnant, but the pregnancies never completed.

Her sister wrote of her two boys growing and gaining personalities. She wrote of a daughter who died within six hours of her birth. She wrote of going up into the mountains in the summer to escape the heat

and the flies, and coming down again in the fall when it was livable
again. She described and described. The trees in the springtime as they
frothed with white and pink flowers, the pall of dust that hung over the
valley. *Today we visited a temple, another ancient one with great urns overflowing with burnt incense and fake money. But dear, don't put anything else
grand into the equation: a few dirty chickens pecking around the courtyard
within, a saffron-robed monk asleep in the sun.*

Louisa imagined her sister holding her pen over the paper, squinting
up at the ceiling, thinking of adjectives.

*   *   *

The letters came steadily. Reading them, Louisa sobbed for the surety
of her sister's daily existence. Addie's concerns were on a higher plane,
even while she moved on the lower one. The doubts she sometimes
expressed—doubts about the mission, doubts about her role as mother,
as wife—Louisa didn't take seriously. Addie was doing good in the
world, and Louisa was patching holes in her husband's shirts.

Sometimes she pricked herself with the needle on purpose. She wasn't
sure why she did it; the act made her feel better, but the bubble of blood
that came after only made her feel worse.

And then came the letter announcing Addie's return. She was coming for a visit of three months, and Owen and the boys were coming,
too. Most of their time would be spent in Ohio, but they would stop at
Louisa's for two weeks on their way back to San Francisco. From there,
they would take a steamer to Japan and then on to China, repeating
their first trip of six years before.

They would be in Illinois by the end of July. No need to entertain
them, Addie wrote; she only wanted to spend time with her younger sister again, to meet her husband and see the farm. Louisa wasn't sure. She
had known her brother-in-law only briefly and she remembered him as
a much older man (though he was not as old as Bert) who wore glasses
(though in fact he never had), and whose mind was so taken up by lofty
religious ideals that he might well be incapable of noticing—much less
admiring—the things that made up her and Bert's entire world. And
they were coming in July. July meant that Bert was in the fields work-

ing from dawn to dusk, and she—in addition to her usual charge of feeding the pigs and chickens, collecting eggs, cooking and cleaning and laundering—was wedded in the mornings to an overflowing garden, and in the afternoons to the kitchen where the garden ended up: canned and pickled and boiled into jams. She tried to imagine what to do with her sister's family. How would they spend their days? Where would they sleep? At least the house was better than it had been before. The previous fall, after harvest time, a crowd of neighbors had put their little cabin on logs and rolled it a quarter-mile up the hill. With help, Bert had added on a room, and they were now out of the damp hollow whose unhealthy location, he claimed, was the cause of Louisa's "bad weather" and the reason for her "difficulties."

It was a kind of superstition, but perhaps it was true. When the letter announcing the planned visit arrived, it was January, and Louisa was pregnant again. She wasn't sure how far along she was, but by May, when she received a letter from Ohio that included a few lines from Addie, her stomach had grown enough that she'd had to let out her dresses. All through the spring and early summer, the weather was good within and without. The fields and gardens were baptized by sun during the day, and in the evenings, storms rolled in purple and electric. Louisa went to sleep with a hand on her stomach and awoke to find her fingers entwined with Bert's.

Oh, how she wanted this child.

The day of her sister's arrival came. It was hot and sultry, the sky an even white, every blade of grass unmoving. Louisa's dress hung like limp curtains over her ankles. They had grown puffy in the past month, and her hair was thick and oily. Several times a day she went to the outhouse white and shaking and could hardly sit down before her bowels unclenched and delivered a foul liquid mess into the hole below. Was this the normal way? she asked the neighbor women. Was this how it should go? Every day, one of them came to help her keep house. They dipped buckets from the well and swept dirt out through the door. They told her there was no normal way, there was only the way you were given. We were made to suffer, weren't we. Put your faith in God.

Louisa wanted to go to the station in town to meet Addie and her family, but Bert wouldn't allow it. He had grown hard with her—not rough, but implacable. So he hooked Prince onto the wagon and drove away, and Louisa lay down and tried to sleep. Then she got up and dragged a chair outside. She watched a dark line of clouds moving in from the west, fingers crooked from their bottoms as if pointing the way. The fingers gestured down to the earth, then seemed to change direction and turn toward her. She felt a black omen and turned and spat.

The rain came so hard it was a single white sheet. Lightning, thunder. Wind shrieking through the walls, shooting straight through the slab of still air in the house. She didn't light the lamp. Inside her body, the baby was turning and turning, and she thought of all the previous times, the countless others that had never gotten to this point, the losses that had happened slowly and with what seemed to her, always, to be too little pain.

She pressed her face to the window, looking for a ghost wagon in the rain. *Come on.*

*   *   *

When the letters stopped coming, Louisa would think back on that moment. More than three years had passed, she was a mother twice over, but her body remembered the sensation of fear vibrating through it as she sat at the window, keeping watch, waiting. She had stayed there because of that fear; she had a feeling that everything depended on her seeing the wagon, on bearing witness to the moment her sister arrived. The storm sputtered out. Hours passed, but still she remained at her post.

There was something in the expectation. If you waited for the worst, then it couldn't happen.

Addie

2

In Lu-cho Fu, the dust was everywhere. It caked the flat surfaces of the desks and tables and dressers, stuck to the sides of the furniture and to the rounded surfaces of the ceramic vases. It built up in the creases and crevices of the scrollwork at the top of the bed so that the designs seemed to be painted in gray to make them more prominent. It powdered the pillows and cushions. At night when she peeled back the top sheet, if Addie put her palm flat on the mattress, she felt the grit that had found its way into the bed between the sheets. And in the morning, once Owen had finished dressing, when she made up the bed again dust rose into the air. This was the worst of all, the dust crawling in at night to settle on them as they slept. It was like waking up in a china cabinet. You felt that a year had gone by in a night. You could feel time passing.

In the morning, before making the bed, Addie washed her face as Owen lay yawning and stretching in bed. It seemed counter to his personality, efficient and decided in everything else, but ever since they'd arrived in Lu-cho Fu, he'd taken to lolling in bed for several minutes in the morning. It was because they were home now, he said. He was comfortable. One leg thrown out from under the sheet and his arms curled under his head, he watched her ready herself at the washstand in the corner until he fell back asleep. Sometimes he dreamed during this time, vivid flashes or long, involved sagas that he told her about once he had woken again. "We were on the ship crossing over, but we were sailing through clouds, orange and pink from horizon to horizon." "We were swimming together, and we could breathe underwater." "You came into the kitchen one morning carrying a dead rabbit at the end of a string, and you set it on the table and told me to bring it back to life." The dreams always involved both of them, never just him. Even in dreams he didn't leave her behind.

There was no mirror at the washstand, so she never knew whether his eyes were open or if he'd fallen back asleep. She liked the unknowing and the sense of solitude it provided. This moment of the day held an odd sort of magic; it was as if she had no name or identity; she was held suspended, and she thought of nothing at all but performed a baptism that made her over anew each dawn. Overnight, the water in the basin acquired a thin film, like the skin on a custard. Still, it was the means of her purification. Pulling the stiff cloth from the rod at the back of the stand, she'd wet it and wipe her face, her chin, her neck all around. She cleaned inside her ears, tugging on the lobes as she ran a finger around the whorls. For a moment, once she was done washing and her skin was still damp, she felt a sense of newness, a fresh gloss like leaves after a rain. Sometimes it made her smile, and when she turned, Owen would open his arms and his eyes would be suddenly and darkly shining. She would go to him then, because in the morning it wasn't unwelcome, as it was when he wanted her at night, at the end of a strange and tiring and hopeless day. Instead, it was satisfying, a hunger that came on quickly and was just as quickly sated. Then, she wasn't bothered by the sheets twisting up around them or the sticky heat of his skin next to hers, and afterward they both separated to wash and dress and begin their day separately. It surprised her sometimes, how he desired her even now, as big as she was with the child in her stomach.

Once they were both dressed and the bed was made, the omnipresence of the dust bothered her again. She wanted the house to be clean, even though the dust kept crawling across the stone floors and blanketing the furniture. Every day she wiped clean the glass over the photograph of her family that she had brought from America, and every day the cloth came out dirty. The faces, fuzzy and gray, seemed dusty anyway, and sometimes it was a disappointment to set the photograph back on the table and see that it looked no different clean than it did dirty. It was a sort of curiosity piece, but no real reminder of home. You didn't think of a person as a still form, unchanged and silent. Addie considered the picture and was often puzzled to find that it did not affect her. The faces were blank. There was nothing of home in the picture to make her long for it.

*   *   *

Every morning she took the horsehair broom and drew it carefully over the floors, making little piles that she picked up with a damp cloth. The broom was an oddity; she'd had to have it made. The ones they sold at market were only bunches of thin branches tied together, good only for sweeping the courtyards of vegetable scraps or chicken droppings. Addie wasn't sure what the Chinese used inside; perhaps they never swept at all, but only mopped every now and then, when the filth was too much to stand.

The broom she'd had made was like a great brush, with an inch and a half of stiff horsehair. She'd explained to the merchant what she wanted by showing him her hairbrush—she'd carried it with her to market— and then holding her hands wide to show how large she wanted it to be. The merchant had given her a dubious look and then turned to Owen. It was their first real adventure in town without the Riddells to help them—there had been some discussion as to whether it was proper for her to go out, but it was cold enough to warrant thick coats and so Owen thought it would be all right—and in the end the excursion had been a success. The man shook his head over and over again, incredulous, perhaps believing that Addie wanted to use the giant brush for her hair in some unimaginable fashion. At last he'd nodded and taken the coins Owen held out to him. When they returned a few days later, he presented the broom, and Addie found that she was to demonstrate its use for the small crowd that had gathered. "I feel like the traveling salesman at a county fair," she said to Owen as she swept the dirty floor of the shop with exaggerated strokes. "I should have you manning a booth where people can line up to buy their very own."

"We'll have to get our friend here in on the project," he said, nodding to the merchant.

She grinned at him over the stacks piled up in the narrow shop, then turned to her audience and gave a curtsy, which made them laugh. Laughter was fine, but it bothered her that no words could be exchanged; it seemed such a simple thing to open your mouth and speak, but she hadn't yet learned more than three words of Chinese. "We must sound so silly to them," she said.

"I imagine we sound about the same to them as they do to us." He paused, and they both listened to the men in the crowd murmuring to one another and gesturing at the broom in Addie's hands. She handed it to Owen. "I'm done with my circus tricks."

As they left the shop and made their way back to the house, Owen said, "Once the prayer books come in, we'll at least be able to put them into their hands."

"That will be a start," Addie replied.

The prayer books had been due to arrive for several months, according to the Riddells. The Missionary Board printed them, but hadn't sent new supplies for half a year. "I'd thought Mr. Douglas would send along a few boxes with you," said Mrs. Riddell reprovingly, in a way that made Addie feel as if it was her fault that their host in T'ien-chin hadn't set them up properly.

In the meantime, they had no way to start their real work. Owen devoted himself to studying the language, and Addie devoted herself to the house. Back home, it hadn't bothered her to leave blouses and skirts strewn on the chair beside her bed, or to find dried leaves in the corner of a room, tracked in from outside. But here, even though it was impossible to keep the house truly clean, still she kept trying. She went from room to room with a pail of water and a cloth. Wei-p'eng, the older of the two men who worked for them, performed the same cleaning routines, regardless of what she did. She was not quite sure where the prescription had come from, but he adhered to it strictly. He swept the courtyards with his own stick broom twice a day, and he emptied the chamber pots every morning. He collected ashes from the small stoves that warmed the rooms and kept water boiling for them to drink. He ran a cloth over the lamps when he trimmed their wicks, but he didn't wipe the tables or the desks that they sat on until the one day a week when he dusted, and this he did regardless of whether Addie had just done it or not. One day when their friends were over, she'd asked Mr. Riddell to point out to Wei-p'eng that dusting twice in an hour was a waste of time, but though he had nodded and seemed to listen, still he had gone on with his task as soon as the American was done speaking. The next time Addie saw Wei-p'eng dusting right after her, she'd made a show of drawing her finger over a table to show him it was clean. He'd nodded and gone on as before.

After a time, she gave up trying.

* * *

She had plenty of time, and so she wrote letters to fill it. She wrote to her family back in Marietta and she wrote to Louisa, and she wrote long dispatches to the various churches that were sponsoring the mission. She tried to include everything—not only the charming and the exotic aspects of the place but the mundane and the dirty and the terrible things, too. There was plenty of the latter. Wretches dressed in rags, some with horrible disfigurements, begging for food. The opium fiends who lay prone along the city walls. The poor tottering women with their bound feet; Mrs. Riddell had explained that the bones were hopelessly deformed early in life, so that a woman never had hope of walking normally ever after. And of course they heard stories of natural disasters: droughts and floods and earthquakes and landslides. They heard of famine that had dug so deep into certain corners of the empire that people's children disappeared—kidnapped and eaten by starving neighbors.

Addie put all of this into her letters. An honest understanding of the place ensured that their mission would continue to draw support, and she therefore gave an account of nearly every action she and Owen performed, nearly every strange circumstance they encountered.

She left out only one. On their journey upriver, when they were headed to T'ai-yüan from T'ien-chin, they had been stopped by a band of thieves demanding payment. They'd been warned by Mr. Douglas and others during their stay in T'ien-chin that such ransoms were common in China, and nothing much to worry about. Even so, seeing the men waiting onshore as if they'd known they were coming, Addie had been so frightened she'd felt her arms go numb. It was too easy to imagine the thieves leaping from the shore onto the boat and holding knives at their throats.

Their captain spoke with the men. After a moment, he gestured to Owen to come over, and Owen had squeezed Addie's hand and then quickly stepped forward. She'd listened to the gurgle of water a few feet away, the idle scrape of one of the boatmen's poles over the rocks. Then, deep inside, she felt a flutter. It was too early to feel her child move, but that's what it was. She wouldn't have the sensation again for another two months, but right then she felt her child turning, swimming through her blood in a panic, and her hand moved to her stomach before she could think. One of the men saw her. He turned his head sharply and shouted and the others turned, too. Addie shook her head rapidly and put up her hands to show them she had no weapon or anything else to hide.

A long moment passed, and then the leader of the group, the one in front, turned back to Owen. He spoke a few words in what seemed an almost kind voice, and Owen went to get some money from one of their bags; they'd stowed their valuables in different places, so it couldn't all be stolen at once. He dropped a few coins in the Chinese man's hand, but he shook his head, so Owen went back and got more. After he'd given them a satisfactory ransom, the men stepped back and waved them on their way.

As soon as they were moving, Addie's whole body started shaking, and she wasn't able to stop for an hour or more. Owen held her and spoke reassuring words that meant nothing, less than nothing. She'd seen that the dangers in this place would not overlook them.

Now several months had passed, and every time Addie felt her child turning inside her, the cold finger of fear brushed her neck. They had escaped the incident unscathed, she told herself. But she'd be glad when that particular reminder was gone.

*   *   *

On Christmas Eve, they gathered at the Riddells' house before the service and sang Christmas carols: "Away in a Manger" and "Good King Wenceslas." Only the two families had gathered together, with walnut cake and pudding to make it feel festive and to remind them of home. They had no tree with candles on it, however, no smell of pine and wax and flame. The service would begin in an hour, and then the Chinese would come. In the meantime, they were gathered in one of the rooms off the main courtyard, and the music filled the space so that they seemed like a choir. When they got to "Silent Night," Addie found that she was crying. It was not homesickness, but something to do with the sky she could see through the window facing onto the courtyard; it was opening up above them, dark and glittering with handfuls of stars strewn like sugar.

She did not feel afraid. When they lay down at night, Owen placed a hand on her stomach and together they thanked God for the child inside. Addie felt as never before an ability to give herself over to God's grace. There was nothing she could do to determine how the birth would go, and rather than making her nervous or afraid, it made her calm. She was in His hands.

Perhaps it was this that made her weep. Not fear or sadness, but simple awe. Julia Riddell, sitting next to her, saw her crying and did not ask what was the matter, but put her hand over Addie's. She was not a person Addie could ever imagine in tears; she might have been trying to stifle her crying, in fact. Would she be like that at the birth, perhaps stuffing a rag in Addie's mouth to keep her from shouting? What Addie wouldn't give to have one of her sisters with her instead—Flora, who had already gone through it herself, or Louisa, who would understand, regardless. But she would have only Mrs. Riddell as a companion, and for that she knew she should be grateful.

And whatever else one could say about Julia Riddell, she was a beautiful singer. She used her voice now to distract the others' attention from Addie's tears, throwing herself into it, taking up the melody in a clear and delicate voice that stood out from the rest.

After "Silent Night," even the children fell quiet and stood still, waiting for direction. Edward, the Riddells' eldest, darted his eyes around the room as if he expected the adults to be angry if he made a sound. Mr. Riddell suggested that they save their voices for the service. "It's always the favorite part," he told them. "The Chinese love to hear our English songs, though you'll barely hear them chime in."

"Don't they ever sing in Chinese?"

"It doesn't translate well," Mrs. Riddell said. "When you hear what passes for singing here, you'll know what I mean. Shrieking songs that are out of tune and seem to come from the nose. My husband likes them. I can't see how."

"It's an acquired taste. I suppose I like the history of it."

Mrs. Riddell shook her head.

"I suspect that's how the Chinese have kept their dynasties going so long," Mr. Riddell went on. "No marauders could stand the sound."

"Is it really that terrible?" Owen asked. "It makes me want to hear a sample. Have the church put on a sort of recital, maybe."

Mr. Riddell, who was reaching into a box on the side table to take out the promised cigars, shook his head. "We'll do better than that. Next time there's a performance, I'll take you two to see it. Mrs. Riddell will have to stay home alone because the children will want to go, too. They have outrageous costumes."

"They do puppets," said the youngest boy, Charles. "They hold them behind a screen at night with lights, and you can't see the people holding the strings."

Mr. Riddell clipped the end off one of the cigars and handed it to Owen. "He's talking about the shadow puppet shows. They put them on down near the market sometimes."

"When you have your baby," Charles said to Addie, "we'll take him to see it."

She laughed, startled that the Riddell boy had so easily decided the gender. That the baby she was carrying was a boy, Addie had no doubt; she had been certain since the beginning. In those first days, when the idea of being pregnant was slowly making itself known, there had kept flashing into her mind an image of Owen with a little boy balanced on his shoulders, and she knew it was a premonition. But she did not count on others having the same intuition. "Do you think he'll like it?" she asked.

"Yes, because they have fights with swords and everything."

"And if it's a girl?" Owen asked.

The boy made a face. "I guess she can watch, too."

*   *   *

In the last two months of her pregnancy, Addie turned in earnest to learning Chinese. Her brain was operating differently than it had before, though she couldn't quite say how. She was unable to do multiple tasks at once or to keep more than one thought in her head at a time, but the one task or thought to which she did devote herself received a sort of clarity and intensity of focus that she'd never previously possessed. It was as if her mind had been reduced to a narrow channel, one that ended with a light shining on a solitary object.

She stopped cleaning so vigorously. It was not really important, after all, to keep every surface gleaming, and it was impossible anyway. This was the first of her capitulations to life in China, and she felt a sort of thrill the first morning she didn't go through all the rooms with a dust cloth in hand, surveying the pall of gray that settled on the furniture overnight. Instead, she just sat at the table eating a steamed bun and a boiled egg, and when Wei-p'eng came in to take the dishes away, she said "Tsao," which meant "Good morning." It shouldn't have been much of a triumph, but for the first time she listened to how she said it, and then how he said it in return, and thought that she heard the difference. He left to go about his work, and she continued to sit at the table repeating the word again and again, trying to match the intonation. It started low and rose up a little, so that it sounded two notes; it was like a little song. "Tsao," she said to the window, to the table, to the cup of tea grown cool and oily before her. She let the syllable dip and rise, as she thought Wei-p'eng had. It was not quite the same, but closer.

"It's a remarkably difficult language," Mrs. Riddell had said when Addie and Owen joined them for dinner one day early on in their friendship, "but concentrated study will do the trick. I don't claim to be fluent. Mr. Riddell, however, spent four hours a day learning it for the first eighteen months we were here."

"There were some days I did less," he said, smiling, as he glanced up from the cooked greens he was spooning onto his plate. It was odd, Addie thought, that here was the only other household besides theirs in a fifty-mile radius that had silverware. She was comforted by the sight of the familiar forks and knives; it still felt alien to see a table set with chopsticks and thin ceramic bowls. Mr. Riddell went on, "I wouldn't call myself fluent, either, but my wife underestimates her own abilities."

Mrs. Riddell shook her head firmly. "I can talk clearly enough about Scripture, but I don't claim to be capable of conversation on a wide range of topics."

"It would be easier," Addie ventured, "if God had seen fit to make English the common language all over the world."

Mr. Riddell laughed, but his wife gave only a tight smile as she looked at Addie, as if to say that joking was not a mode of conversation *she* chose to engage in, herself.

"Do you use a tutor?" Owen asked.

"One comes twice a week to help the boys," she answered, "but really, I believe they pick up as much simply from hearing the servants speaking to one another. Children are sponges that way. Now, Edward," she said, turning to her son, "say something for Mr. and Mrs. Bell."

Edward, who had stuffed a large piece of potato in his mouth, chewed quickly and swallowed. "What should I say?"

"Say, 'Jesus Christ is Lord.' "

"Jesus Christ is Lord," he said in English.

"If it were *that* simple," Owen said, laughing, "I think I could manage it even now."

"No, but I urge you both to start studying as much as possible," Mr. Riddell said. "Nothing can be accomplished with the Chinese until you're able to reach them on their level."

His wife nodded her agreement. "And *you*, Mrs. Bell," she said, looking across the table at Addie, "you must not make any excuses for yourself. It is easy—all too easy—to let household matters take up a large portion of your attention. You must remind yourself that you're here on a double commission: as both a wife and a missionary."

And which is more important? Addie wanted to ask, but she only smiled and replied that she would be sure to take their advice. "Owen and I will both start studying in a more regular way," she vowed.

But she hadn't gotten around to fulfilling that promise. In fact, she'd learned to say almost nothing in the months since they arrived in

Lu-cho Fu. The thought of all those days ticking by, one after the other, and nothing to show for it but a bigger stomach, was embarrassing. Now she was going to make sure that she did something about it.

And so, instead of getting up from the breakfast table to follow Wei-p'eng with instructions to mop the bedrooms or wipe down the furniture in the front sitting room, she stayed seated at the table and made plans for studying. It would be strenuous but satisfying work. From day to day she would be able to see the improvement. Before long she would be able to ask Li K'ang what his favorite game had been as a child, ask Wei-p'eng whether there was a girl he had his eye on to marry. And of course she would be able to talk to them about God, and in that way make them Christians and save their souls. They had not yet been converted, and it worried her to think that these two young men who spent each day under her roof were as ignorant of the punishment that awaited them after they died as all the other people in Lu-cho Fu. It was overwhelming to think of all the heathens in even this one small corner of China that they had not yet approached. And of course it usually took more than one conversation to bring about a conversion; sometimes, Mr. Douglas had said back in T'ien-chin, it could be years before people opened their hearts to the Word. You just had to keep at it, however; you had to whittle down their resistance. That was their business here, after all; they had not come to China except with the purpose of doing some real good.

A plan formed in her mind and quickly hardened: she would study three hours in the morning and three hours in the afternoon, with a two-hour break in the middle to eat dinner and rest her brain. All she needed were her dictionary and a pen and paper to begin.

That first morning, Addie picked up her plate and teacup and walked back to the rear courtyard, where Li K'ang was busy washing cabbage in a pan that sat on the floor. He looked up in surprise when she came through the doorway and immediately stood to take her dishes. Normally, she left them on the table and he came to clear them away himself.

She handed them over and then, pointing at the cabbage, sifted through the handful of phrases she knew, searching for a way to ask, "How do you say that?" She widened her eyes and made her arms into a gesture of wonder, palms upward, like she was carrying a book flat in either hand. The cook glanced from her hands to the cabbage, and back to her. He cocked his head to one side.

"What I want to say is, 'How do you call that?'"

He spoke a few words of Chinese, and they faced each other without understanding. So she pointed helplessly again, and he walked over and picked up one of the leaves. Coming back to where she stood, he tore it down the middle for her to see the stiff white spine.

Cabbage. Leaf. White. Green. She couldn't say any of these words. Simple vocabulary shorn of grammar and context, but it didn't matter; it was so far beyond her comprehension that it might as well have been the *Iliad* she was trying to recite. What about tomatoes? What about peas? *The peas are coming in, which must mean that spring has come at last.* How long would it be before she could put sentences together, before she could express an idea like this, brimming with different states of being, with a leap that makes a vegetable into a symbol of something greater? Her situation suddenly seemed unimaginably constraining, as if she had been locked alone in a cage and only just noticed. Could you even be said to feel something if you weren't able to express it? Now, with no one around who spoke English, was she simply an object taking up space in the house, something the servants bumped into and tried to avoid?

She would have to start somewhere. Taking the torn leaf from Li K'ang's palm, she held it between thumb and forefinger and waved it like a flag. "What do you call this?" she asked loudly. "What's the word for 'cabbage'?"

He said something in response. The word she was looking for was probably tucked into his speech, but where? Addie sighed and dropped the leaf back into his palm. She closed his hand around it and left the kitchen.

Owen was out with their church deacon, Mr. Yang, but she went into the study and examined his desk. There was a pad of paper, a squat bottle of ink, and a brush—cleaned, but still damp, the tip carefully sculpted to a point, and the brush hung by a ribbon on a small rack that sat at the back of the desk. Off to the side was a copy of the Chinese prayer book; the shipment from T'ien-chin had finally arrived. A box holding the others sat on a stool by the wall. They had already distributed over half to those who came to the services and to strangers in town, but there were dozens remaining, a visible reminder of the insufficiency of their accomplishments. Owen carried a few prayer books with him whenever he went out, and gave them away to those he thought might look at the texts. It was a calculation that included not only a certain look of openness in the person, but the ability to read, which was, they had already learned, not at all widespread. Without that ability, you could count on the book being burned for fuel.

Addie bent down to examine the writing on the pad of paper. The scent of ink rose up, tangy and metallic, and beneath it the cottony smell of the paper itself. The paper was thick, roughly cut at the edges and flecked with wood splinters. She didn't remember buying it; it must have been there when they took possession of the house, along with the furniture and linens. The Riddells had thought of everything. She still sometimes felt their hand in the arrangement of the rooms, and she could imagine Mrs. Riddell standing in a doorway, hands on her hips and a scowl on her face, trying to determine the best way to arrange the chairs and tables.

The paper was not the same kind she used to write home—she was still using the stationery she had brought with her from America. This kind seemed like it should belong to a painter or calligraphy artist, the unlined pages sewn together in a little book. But Owen's script was decidedly amateur, uncertain and halting. And it was not the same character written out again and again as someone practicing their penmanship ought to do, but rather a string of several complete sentences. Of course, it was a Bible verse. Learning the language was a means to an end for Owen—it was the vessel in which faith could be delivered to the unconverted. He had made sure to learn the words for "God" and "Jesus" while they were still in T'ien-chin, and Addie had imagined them riding down into town on their mules, singing out these two words again and again. Somehow, she had already forgotten them. There wasn't much call to use these terms while she remained ignorant of the language, illiterate and mute. The only words that had stuck with her were more practical ones: *bread*, *water*, *thank you*, *good morning*.

Owen had set to learning the language with a determination that was simply a part of it all, another way in which he had settled into their new life without any struggle. He went out into town nearly every day, and he carried the place home with him like a scent on his clothes. Sometimes Addie lifted yesterday's shirt to her nose and she would actually detect it: mixed in with the smell of his skin and sweat was an odor like medicine, sharp and piney. He spent his days walking the streets with Mr. Yang, speaking to the people he met. Turning a corner, he might come upon a man sewing shoes and, putting a hand on Mr. Yang's shoulder, ask him to translate. He would ask the man about his work, his family. How many children did he have? How many boys? Wouldn't he like to see his boys get an education? For it was through education that they would reach the greatest number of people. Get the children into a classroom, and you would establish the habit needed for church. And along with mathematics and history they would begin learning religious teachings. It was the children who were the key, Owen told her.

So there it was: he was growing more certain, more knowledgeable, while Addie was a mist hovering over the surface of a lake. She was losing form while he was gaining it. Yet despite his dedication, the results were not very good. Even to her eye, the page on the desk before her looked like a child's hand had written it. The characters were all different sizes, parts of them either underdeveloped or bulging outside an imaginary box. She pictured her husband as she had seen him that morning, bent over his desk with his brows knitted so tightly he looked like he was in an argument with the paper and brush. She'd almost come into the room and put a comforting hand on his shoulder. But she hadn't. Instead, she'd watched from outside the door and then slipped away without interrupting his work.

She spent the rest of the morning paging through the dictionary they'd been given in T'ien-chin. It was a new advantage, Mr. Douglas told them, that previous missionaries hadn't had. She tried to appreciate what felt utterly impenetrable. When Owen returned just before dinnertime and put his head in the doorway, the dictionary was still open on top of her big stomach, but she had given it up. She had quickly exhausted the small store of words she remembered and had turned to looking up new ones she didn't know, but there were so many, an ocean of vocabulary, and each time she scanned her eyes down the page she found another word she absolutely must learn immediately, one even more important than the word she had intended to look up. She'd set the dictionary down on her lap nearly an hour before, and had spent the time since listening to the rush of wind over the roof. A small stove burned at her feet to keep her warm. At some point she'd closed her eyes but hadn't fallen asleep.

"You should lie down for a bit," Owen said from the doorway.

"I'm not tired, not really. It's only that I got dazed, staring at all these characters." She held up the dictionary. "I need to put my mind to it in a real and devoted way, not just limp along like I have been doing."

"You've got plenty to focus on right now. Why wear yourself out studying? There'll be time later for all that."

"But I don't, Owen," she said, sitting up in her chair. The dictionary slid from her lap and, catching it, she set it down on the table beside her. "I don't have nearly enough to do right now. I'm simply waiting, like a big mama cat curled up in the hay. You can't think how stupid I feel."

He leaned against the doorjamb, considering her. "Then of course you should find something to keep you busy and feeling useful."

"And not knitting sweaters for the baby, either. You've seen the drawer; it's crammed full already. One more stocking and you won't be able to close it." She shook her head and glanced over Owen's shoulder. Wei-p'eng was standing a few feet back, in the shadow of the roof overhang, sweeping the handle of a broom up under the eaves. He performed the work of the house in almost total silence, talking only to Li K'ang. She had heard them arguing once. She'd gone to the kitchen to refill the teakettle, and they hadn't known she was there. Listening to their voices rise against each other and not understanding a word, she'd felt like a trespasser in her own home. What were they arguing about? Were they unsatisfied with her or the work they were made to do, perhaps even fighting over whose job it should be to refill the very kettle that dangled from her hand? She had tiptoed back to the sitting room without the water. It seemed important that they shouldn't see her.

Now, catching sight of Wei-p'eng cleaning under the eaves, she tone of their conversation without understanding the words. She and Owen were not arguing, exactly, but her exasperation was evident enough. The servant kept on with his task, his elbows raising and lowering as he swept the broom handle along the underside of the roof. She looked back at Owen and said, "I need to do something useful. I want to feel part of what we came here to do."

Owen stepped forward into the room and crossed over to her chair, pausing a moment before kneeling down. She could see his uncertainty as to how to handle her. He had come home full of his experiences in town and had not expected to be confronted with an irritable wife. This was what marriage was, a sort of tug-of-war, because it was never only what you were feeling but what your spouse felt, too. When you were both happy, it was like you were running in the same direction, the rope held loosely between you. But when you were feeling differently, it was the opposite; you were both terribly stuck. It wasn't anything to do with Owen now, or what he was saying, exactly, that made her so irritable. It was simply the fact that she was alone in this house day after day. They had come across the ocean, crossing a wide world to get here, but now her world was smaller than ever. And it would stay that way until the baby came.

At last he knelt down and put his hand on her knee. "We'll get you a tutor to come in. Will that do?"

She nodded. "You'll be happy with me when I'm making some progress. When I'm *doing* something instead of sitting here stewing and growing duller by the day."

"I'm happy with you now."

"You'll be happier." She looked over his shoulder as he leaned in to embrace her. Wei-p'eng had lowered the broom and was watching them. When he saw her take notice, he turned and passed out of sight.

3

When the first labor pains came, she was standing in the doorway of the kitchen, trying to talk to Li K'ang. She spent most of her time in the front of the house—the back was where the food was prepared, the laundry was washed, and somehow Addie didn't feel welcome there. But it was her house, and she would go where she pleased, and besides, she wanted to be friends with those who worked for her. So she had made a new ritual of talking to the cook during that part of the morning that preceded the arrival of the tutor.

She stood in the doorway of the kitchen now, asking questions. "What do you call this?" picking up a bowl from the row of them laid out on the table next to the stove. "What do you call this?" pointing to the lettuce piled limply in a basket on the floor. *Che ke chiao shenme?* Again and again she recited this same sentence, and Li K'ang patiently responded with the word she'd requested, but it touched her brain lightly and then flew off, forgotten. She hoped there was a place where these words were all congregating, a flock of ducks settled on a lake, and once she'd reached a certain level of proficiency in the language she would suddenly come upon them all together, preening and clucking, too voluble to be tamed.

Her back had been hurting for days, but she hadn't thought much of it. So when the first labor pain came, low in her stomach and deep inside, she grasped the doorframe and stood slightly bent over, swaying, and felt more surprise than pain. Li K'ang didn't notice. He was turned away, mixing dough in a large bowl. At last he turned to see why she had fallen silent, and she looked at him and squeezed her eyes shut. When she opened them again, he had set down the spoon and was standing with his hands pressed together and his eyes wide. He spoke and the hands came forward, she reached out and squeezed, and they stood swaying like dancers as they waited for the first wave to pass.

When the pain subsided, she asked Li K'ang to help her into the other room. He couldn't have understood the words, but he led her to the sitting room, supporting her weight on his arm and pointing out the steps as if she were a newcomer to the house who might trip over unfamiliar ground. Then he arranged some pillows on the sofa and left her there. She was not sure whether she was glad he'd gone. He should not witness anything like this, it was true, and yet it would have been better to have someone with her. She must have miscalculated somehow; another month was supposed to pass before she needed to worry. She thought about this as she waited for the next wave of pain, as Li K'ang went out and a half hour passed and still he did not return.

Owen came at last, and he was breathing heavily. "I ran all the way here. Tell me, are you all right? Is everything going as it should?" Li K'ang came in after him. He had found Owen and brought him to her.

"I'm not sure." She took a shaky breath and attempted a smile. "I've never done this before."

Owen came up to her and, kneeling, put his hands on hers, which were folded on top of the blanket covering her stomach. She was seated sideways on the sofa with both legs straight out on the cushions and a few pillows arranged under her back. Her stomach rose before her. She had never got used to this shape, and now soon it would be gone. The thought terrified her.

Owen raised one hand to her forehead, and she closed her eyes. She was glad of being touched; it made her feel less afraid. For so long she had been tranquil about the thought of giving birth, but now all serenity had fled. Owen's touch stilled the wildness swirling around in her. She felt as a horse must when its eyes are covered to calm it in a storm. "Help me to the bedroom," she said when he took his hand from her head, "and then go get Julia, if you would."

In the bedroom, she lay with pillows piled up all around while Owen left to fetch Mrs. Riddell. She stared out the window at the small patch of sky visible from that angle. It was a bald blue plate, clean and cloudless. An innocent sky that cared nothing for what was going on under it. There wasn't much of a wind, for once, but from the courtyard came the sound of Wei-p'eng pulling a bucket over the stone tiles. He would be mopping now, going from room to room, pulling furniture back from the walls in order to clean behind it. He did his job well. That should mean that he liked her and Owen, but she knew that he didn't.

It was too early for the birth, and she feared that meant something was wrong. The child might have feeble, stumbling limbs, or lungs that were not yet ready to breathe, or a heart that was too weak to pump blood to all his tiny little fingers and toes. Or the birth could be the problem. The baby could strangle himself on the cord or be positioned incorrectly inside the womb. Addie had heard of this happening, the baby turned sideways or feet-side down. Sometimes it came out all right, but often it didn't. There was a long, tortured struggle and in the end the mother died, or the baby did, or sometimes both.

Not that, she thought. Something must come of this. Then the next contraction swept over her and she clutched a pillow in each hand and squeezed her eyes shut. There was the sharp squeeze and then the pain building as it dug in with its claws. She waited for it to let go. Behind her closed eyes was a molasses darkness, and in her hands were the sheets, balled-up and damp from her sweating palms, and all this was the pain, and it was the silence in the room, too, her shallow breaths. It went on and on until it was done. Then she opened her eyes and she was still there, and the room was exactly the same as it had been before.

Twenty minutes passed, and then the door opened to Owen ushering in Julia Riddell. She walked swiftly over the floor and stood beside the bed. "We called in on the midwife on the way and she's coming directly," she said.

Addie nodded. She had never met the midwife, but she had an image in her head of a tiny woman with long white hair swept up in a bun, and bright black eyes, and a bag swinging from her side filled with Chinese herbs and medicines. She didn't know whether she would be comforted or made afraid by her presence. She had never imagined her child being delivered by Chinese hands. And yet Mrs. Riddell had done it, and with the help of this same woman.

"How will I know what to do?" she asked.

"You'll know," Mrs. Riddell said firmly. "We're not women for nothing." She glanced over at Owen, who stood at the foot of the bed, watching the two of them with his hands folded behind him like an officer of the law. "We'll be all right once she gets here," Mrs. Riddell said to him. "There's nothing for you to do now but wait. I'll come out every now and then and let you know how we're getting on."

Owen cleared his throat and pushed his sleeves up to his elbows, then pulled them back down again. Addie fixed her eyes on him and said, "It'll be all right."

"If I send someone now," he said, taking a step forward, "we might have the doctor down from T'ai-yüan in a few days."

Addie shook her head. A few days? If it were still going on then, there was nothing a doctor could do. "No," she said. "Everything's going to be fine."

"I should have had him come down sooner. It's only that I didn't know it would happen so soon."

"It will be all right, Owen, I promise."

Mrs. Riddell stood. "Come over now," she said, "and pray together."

Owen took her place and, grasping Addie's hands in his, bowed his head and said, "Dear merciful Father, watch over us and bless us with Your grace and goodness. Lead my beloved wife through this struggle and deliver to us another servant in Your name. Amen."

It was the shortest prayer she had ever heard him give. He raised her hands to his lips and then left the room.

*   *   *

Hours after the first pain came, little had changed. The contractions were still no less than half an hour apart, and in the time between them she simply lay in the bed feeling the energy drain from her body. "Rest your eyes, and don't try to talk," Mrs. Riddell told her. "You need to save your strength."

The midwife had arrived, and she looked nothing like Addie had pictured. She was so young it was hard to imagine she had ever delivered a baby before. Her face was as smooth as the cap of a mushroom, with a spot of deep red on each cheek, and she had coarse hair, more brown than black, pulled back from her face in a braid. She wore small earrings, but her clothes were those of a peasant, plain cotton worn thin at the elbows and knees. She looked exactly like all the other women Addie had seen when she was still able to go into town, but somehow more concrete, more visible. There was something disappearing about those other women, a way of being soaked up by the scenery of the marketplace, like water disappearing into wood. They stood behind their husbands with arms folded behind their backs; they bent their faces to the piles of vegetables and wares being sold, and when she did manage to focus on one of them for a moment or two, she was never able to meet her eye.

The midwife, on the other hand, entered the room and, from the doorway, immediately fixed her attention on Addie. Then she turned to place her bag on the floor and retrieve a cloth from inside it. Mrs. Riddell greeted her, and the woman came over. Her eyes met Addie's again and quickly ran over her face, examining it. What was she looking for? Addie was aware of being studied rather than seen, studied in the way a pianist considers a sheet of music, reading the notes and hearing them in her head, imagining the position her hands will take on the keyboard to play the difficult passages. In another situation, she might have turned away from such study, but she was tired and frightened, and it was comforting to stare into the face of the midwife and know that she was being read, assessed, that there were signs in the creases around her mouth, in the tone of her skin and the squint of her eyes, signs that could tell the future.

After a time the midwife took her hand and flipped it upward. She traced the deep lines on the palm and then placed two fingers over the blue vein on the wrist. Her hands were cool and dry. Addie felt the blood ticking beneath her own skin, and she waited as the Chinese woman held her fingers there, eyes turned to the ceiling as she counted aloud. She spoke and gestured to Addie's stomach. The next moment, she was bending Addie's knees, and she reached a hand up between her legs, but it was only for a moment. Then she withdrew her hand and wiped it on a cloth.

"I guess that means that everything is all right?" Addie said, looking from the woman to Mrs. Riddell, who was busying herself smoothing the blankets and tucking them up around Addie's waist.

"There's nothing to do but wait. Things are moving along."

Addie pressed her lips together. It didn't seem as if things were moving along. Already it felt like she had been in this state for days, weeks; it was difficult to remember not lying in this bed, waiting for the next twisting pain. How strange to think that the baby was there, really there, just a few hours from arriving in this room with its smell of lamp oil and clean sheets, that in a short time its cries would leak through the walls and reach everyone in the house—Owen, Li K'ang, Wei-p'eng—and perhaps their neighbors, too. She would be a mother then, and she would know what to do. She would know how to nurse and change him, how to quiet him when he screamed. She would have to know because there was no one to take lessons from but Julia Riddell, who might only remind her to do her duty without telling her what it was. But Addie's fear was that she *wouldn't* know. She wasn't intuitive the way she imagined mothers needed to be; she hadn't had an inkling that she would go into labor that morning. She'd started the day planning out what she would study with the tutor. Had he been told not to come? Had the word gone out? She opened her eyes to ask Julia and saw that the room had darkened and she was nowhere to be seen. The midwife was still seated in the chair by the window. She had knitting in her lap, but she was watching Addie, and she made a movement that let Addie know she was alert and had been monitoring her as she dozed.

"How long has it been?" Addie asked, and the woman tilted her head in the direction of the window and responded in Chinese. The sun was out of sight, slipped behind the rooftop. Somewhere in the house, a door opened and closed, and a moment later the door of the bedroom pushed open and Julia came in.

"How are you feeling?"

"I fell asleep. How long has it been?"

"Twenty minutes, perhaps." Mrs. Riddell glanced around the room, at the shadows that had gathered. "The sun went behind the mountains, you know how it is."

Addie put a hand to her mouth and chewed the tips of her fingers.

"Charles took more than a full day and night to come, and I went in and out of sleep the whole time." She came over to the bed and held up a magazine. "The shipment came at last. Owen's already gone through it."

"He could come in and sit awhile."

"I sent him over to dine at my house. It's not good for a man in his situation to sit alone with nothing to do." She ran a hand along the top of the dresser by the door. Everything was being handled, she seemed to say. There was nothing to do but go along. "Here's October's *Godey's*, and you've got a whole stack of them waiting. Shall I read to you?"

Addie turned her eyes to the ceiling. It was plaster and seemed to glow like the moon. "I didn't know the waiting would go on so long."

Mrs. Riddell pulled a stool near to the bed. Opening the magazine, she said, "Would you like to hear about sleeves or learn a recipe for a quince jelly?"

*   *   *

The stars were fading into the predawn sky. Time had passed, and it felt like a moment and it felt like forever. The room was humid and still, the air close with the scent of sweat and blood. Addie's eyes were fixed on the patch of sky visible through the window, but she didn't see it; she was exhausted beyond the point of recognizing anything but the great yawning pain that opened up and up, swallowing her, drowning her whole. She was taking it on like a capsizing ship.

"You're almost there," Mrs. Riddell kept telling her. "Keep on, now, you've almost got it." But Addie could hardly hear her. She was grasping at the edge of consciousness and could see it crumbling beneath her fingertips; she was falling. There had never been anything but this pain, and it was greater than anything that would ever come after.

Pillows. Smudges on the wall. The flickering of the lamp's wick. The midwife's face as she leaned between Addie's legs, both arms extended as if in offering. Addie's damp hair at the back of her neck. She pushed and pushed until she had nothing left, no knowledge but of struggle and pain, no breath, no thought, until finally, suddenly, a wail ripped the air. All other sounds stripped away, and the baby was placed in her arms, trembling and slick. Its eyes were open and dark as the sky. She looked into them and thought, Yes, I will love this thing. It opened its tiny mouth and bleated once, and Addie felt wash over her a wave that was pain and also the opposite of pain. Both at once, a brand-new feeling.

Juanlan

4

She has a live wire inside her, a little burning blue coil. Usually, she can hide it, tamp it down, so that it feels only like the smoldering coals of impatience. But it's always there, and it's not anger and it's not passion—though if she could only have her body crushed by another, that might do the trick—but both these feelings at once, and others besides. Qin Shi Huang, the first emperor, had all the Confucian books burned and several hundred scholars buried alive. She feels like one of those books. Or like one of those scholars.

*　　*　　*

It takes six hours to get back to Heng'an. People say that after the expressway is completed, it will take less than two, but for now that expressway is churned-up earth, flattened in places and crawling with big yellow LiuGong machines. The wet earth opening like a wound. A vision of the future: China's backward southwest catching up to the north, the east.

The last time Juanlan returned to Chengdu after the New Year, her seatmate leaned over her, his elbow digging into the bag of fruit and candy on her lap. "My coworker's cousin had his house torn down to make way for the expressway," he said, pointing. "It was very near here."

When she looked out the window, expecting to see the remnants of a bulldozed house, there were only orange flags marking the place where the expressway would eventually be. "Where did he and his family go?"

"Oh, they were lucky." The man sat back and pulled a pack of cigarettes from his jacket pocket. "The government paid them, and now they live in Chengdu."

This man did not live in Chengdu. He was there on business and seemed disappointed that Juanlan lived in the city and probably knew it better than him. She was only a student and didn't have the money to go to the McDonald's or to go shopping on Chunxi Lu, but she knew the bus lines and bus stations; the going rate for pedicabs around Wuhou

Si; the warren of shops in Yanshikou, an entire row devoted to shoes, another to tape players.

Her seatmate this trip is an old woman who got on outside Shuangliu, hauling on three giant sacks of carrots, one at a time. Two are now stacked in the aisle and the other is crammed beneath their feet. Juanlan's own bags, which hold everything from her four years at the university, are stowed away in the undercarriage. If only they were beneath her feet, where she could touch them and know they were real. Nothing about this trip feels fully concrete. A few hours ago, she was buying a steaming mantou from the vendor outside the campus gates, gazing up through the leaves of the French plane trees at the white sky beyond. From somewhere over the line of shops had come the clanging from a high-rise construction site. Those trees, the strike of metal against metal, the white erasure of smog: nostalgia is a matter of specific combinations. That particular combination was real but already tainted; her friends were back in the dorms, packing, and it had been two nights since Du Xian kissed her good-bye.

The bus bounces along the narrow rutted roads. They pass house after house with corn drying out front on the concrete patio and a tied-up dog at the end of its leash, barking. The woman asks if Juanlan is going home for the summer. She squints and then laughs. "You look like a student."

Juanlan tells her she lives in Chengdu, a lie only by timing. She doesn't mention that she was a student at Sichuan Normal, that she graduated on Saturday, that none of her family was there. "My father's not well," she says, and this, at least, is no lie. "He had a stroke."

"And you're going home to help care for him?"

She hesitates. "Yes."

"He can't be old." The woman moves her tongue over her teeth, judging Juanlan's age.

"No, he's forty-eight."

She shakes her head. "I'm lucky, more than seventy years old and as you can see, I'm still healthy. But you never know: tomorrow I might not wake up at all." She smiles as if the thought brings her some joy and then calls out to the driver to let her off. "I wish your father good health," she says as the bus rolls to a stop. When Juanlan looks back, she sees the woman standing in the sun with the sacks of carrots at her feet, gazing down the road with one hand shading her eyes.

The bus pulls into the station in Heng'an in the late afternoon. Through the window, Juanlan spots Zhuo Ge standing with a few men dressed in uniform, who must be from his danwei. He is round-faced and smiling, waving a cigarette around as he speaks, and when Juanlan steps down from the bus carrying only her purse, he walks over with his arms held wide, asking why did she give all her stuff away? Has she finally decided to become a nun? He cups his hands to make an alms bowl and accidentally drops his cigarette on the ground. Stamping it out, he says, "If a nun comes looking for a smoke, that one's still got a few centimeters left on it."

"Today's your day off?" Juanlan asks. "You're not in uniform."

"Someone had to come. Ba wanted to, but Ma wouldn't let him."

"How is he?"

"Better than before. He's been working the desk a few hours in the mornings." Zhuo Ge steps forward to take the bags from under the bus and nods to the men he was standing with before. They come over to help and a few minutes later, the police car pulls out into the stream of bikes and motorbikes, pedicabs and people walking. "Hey, Shifu," Zhuo Ge says, leaning forward between the seats. "Take us to the Three Springs Hotel, okay?"

The officers laugh. "Sure thing," says the one at the wheel.

"Not a bad way to get home, is it?" her brother asks.

"No," she says, "it isn't." Any way is as good as another.

*　　*　　*

It's been over two months since her father's stroke. That day, she came back to her dorm after a morning class and the niangniang at the front desk gave her a message that read: "Father ill. Call mother at hospital." Juanlan had to go up to her room to get her calling card. She ran up the stairs and then back down again, squeezing past girls carrying books or laundry tubs, almost pushing them down. She was panting when she went to the phone, and the niangniang clicked her tongue. She was knitting a tiny sweater, and the needles kept flying as Juanlan dialed. An operator picked up, and then a nurse and finally her mother, who said Ba had been acting funny that morning. Then suddenly he was garbling words and couldn't smile when she told him to. Her mother sounded tired and put-upon. Juanlan asked if she should try to take a bus back to Heng'an. "Let's wait and see," her mother said.

She didn't end up going home. When she talked to her brother, he told her that Ba's left side was a little loose and he was more tired than usual. And quiet, but he had always been quiet; it wasn't from his father that Zhuo Ge learned to tell a joke. "And what about the hotel?" she asked. Zhuo Ge had found a girl to clean in the mornings for a few days, he said, and Lulu was covering the front desk whenever their mother went to the hospital.

They were getting by. But it was becoming more difficult for Lulu, and when she had the baby she would no longer be able to help at all. And they couldn't afford to keep paying the girl to clean. The hotel is small. It makes just enough money to stay in business with Juanlan's parents splitting the work between them. Even with Ba home from the hospital now, they've been in a difficult position. But jobs are proving hard to come by, so Juanlan is available. Everyone says it: 1998 has been a bad year for graduates, too many people and not enough jobs. Most of her friends have already gotten employment; they're going to be teachers, and therefore placed by the government. But she doesn't want to teach. She'd thought she would take her chances in the free market. Tough luck there are so few openings, but maybe it's for the best.

"You'll come home for a little while," her mother said, "and then we'll see."

*   *   *

When they get to the hotel, the two policemen help them unload her bags and then say good-bye. Her parents are waiting in the lobby, seated in chairs on either side of a table like guests. Her mother stands and helps her husband to his feet. He smiles, and the smile is a little off, as if he's followed directions for how to do it and hasn't quite mastered them. Still, it is recognizably a smile. "You look good, Ba," Juanlan says and steps forward into his stiff hug.

"I'm lucky," he says, pulling away. "But we missed your graduation. I am sorry, Lan'er." He blinks, and it's not quite in sync, the left eye and the right eye not moving in the same way. She wasn't here before to witness the frozen face or the dangling arm, but she is here now to see the slightly crooked smile, the way of leaning a bit to one side. Different, and yet also how her father was before the stroke, too. He's long had the bearing of someone who hides a limp: a deliberate deflection of attention combined with purposeful movement. When she pictures her father, it's always with his hands clasped behind him, standing somewhere close to a wall.

"Come on," her mother says. "Let's go over, and I'll start dinner while you and Ba rest. Zhuo'er, you're going home to get Xiao Lu?"

"Not tonight," Zhuo Ge says. "She had a headache when I left. She said to tell you she's sorry she couldn't make it." This last to Juanlan, who shrugs acceptance. Her sister-in-law's absence is no matter to her.

"She'll come tomorrow, though. Lan'er, you know your uncle is giving us a dinner."

"No," Juanlan answers.

"Of course; you think he wouldn't want to welcome his goddaughter home? The college graduate." She lifts her chin quickly, a gesture of pride. Then she places on the desk a sign instructing honored guests to please ring the bell and, drawing aside the curtain that screens the exit into the alley, leads the way through to the living quarters on the other side.

Over dinner, they talk about the new expressway, to be completed within the year. Juanlan says, "I didn't see any pavement yet; they're still clearing the path."

"They'll get it done, no problem." Zhuo Ge takes a piece of fried pork. "Laying asphalt is the easy part. They had to plan it out first, and then you have to figure out the displacements, compensations, and all that. By now, it's just a matter of execution."

"There's a lot to execute," Juanlan says doubtfully.

"Wasn't Chengdu to Chongqing a lot more complicated? All those tunnels, and they got it done. You need faith, Mei. I'm a traffic cop"—he puts a finger on his nose—"I know what I'm talking about. Pass the ribs."

Their mother pushes the plate toward Juanlan after Zhuo Ge has taken his fill. "It's just a shame the highway wasn't there while you were at school. Think how much easier it would have been to come home. You wouldn't have had to wait for summer break or the New Year. You could go and come back the same day, if you needed to. If there were an emergency, for example, like with your father."

Juanlan feels compelled to tell him she'd wanted to come home before. Messages might have been lost, or confused. He might have wondered, while he lay in the hospital bed, why she wasn't there. "Ma told me not to come," she explains.

Her father nods. "That was right." Slowly, he resumes eating.

"Of course it was right. You think I would have let you stay in Chengdu if your Ba was at death's door? Look at him. He's strong." Her mother thumps a hand on her own thigh for emphasis, then glances at her husband and son for validation. "He's already gone back to working. Maybe too soon, that's what the doctors say, but you just try to stop him. In the mornings, he's out at the front desk before I can get him breakfast. You'll see."

And so she does. The next day, Juanlan's mother comes into her room early and flips on the light. "Get up, you've been sleeping too long. Ba went out to the desk a half hour ago." Her mother stands in the doorway looking around the tiny room, giving a critical glance at the bag still open from last night's search for pajamas and toothbrush.

"I'll tidy up today," she says, yawning. "I was too tired last night."

"No different than before. Messy, messy."

As a teenager, Juanlan tried to be neat, but she would leave her school things out on the bed: books and notebooks and worksheets sliding over each other. When she was studying for the gaokao, she'd often gone to sleep with the corner of a textbook jabbing her ribs, papers bunching up beneath her hip. More than once, she'd awoken to find marks on her skin from a pen that had come uncapped during the night.

"You stayed up late reading. I saw the light under your door when I went to sleep." Her mother plucks a book from beside the bed, a translation of *Pride and Prejudice*. She laughs when she reads the title aloud. "Is it a good book?"

Juanlan shrugs. "We read it in my British literature class last autumn; I wanted to try it again in Chinese. It's a romance."

"Oh, *romance*," her mother says, pursing her lips in a kiss, and then laughs at herself as she leaves the room.

Juanlan puts on yesterday's clothes, folds up her pajamas, makes the bed. The picture on the cover of the book is of a woman and man, half turned away from each other. She barely understood anything when she read it in English, but the characters had struck her as exotic, their world as lovely and delicate as lace. Rereading in Chinese, it is all too familiar. The people are small; they live in a small place; they take, it seems, only the smallest of risks.

She may not go on reading, after all.

Out in the kitchen, her mother is slicing a salted duck egg. Juanlan takes her toothbrush from the windowsill and runs it under the tap. "Have you been to Tasty Spice?" This is the name of the restaurant they're going to tonight.

"When would I get the chance? Do you remember your mother going out for nice dinners, even before Ba got sick? No, of course not. It's some fancy place near the river," her mother says, spooning congee into a bowl. "Chongqing-style hot pot. You and I will have to watch Xiao Lu to make sure she eats only from the clear broth. That girl."

"I doubt she'll get them confused," Juanlan says around a mouthful of toothpaste.

"That just shows what you know. Your brother's wife, she's careless about her health. I tell her she should eat only boiled chicken and plain vegetables, and she says she wants spicy pork. Yesterday at lunch, she asked where I was keeping the lajiao. She wanted to put it on her rice."

"Did you give it to her?"

"Of course not!" Her mother watches as Juanlan spits into the sink. "You tell her, maybe she'll listen. She's going to hurt the baby, eating spicy food."

"Why would she listen to me?" Juanlan asks, putting her tooth-brush back on the windowsill. "We're not friends." She leans into the little mirror by the sink to examine her skin. Her last week in Chengdu, she bought a whitening cream from one of the specialty shops, but she can't tell whether it's made a difference. If only she'd gotten her fa-ther's thin features along with his dark complexion. Narrow eyes, a long chin, cheekbones so wide it seems someone's pulled her ears and stretched out the plane of her face—Juanlan looks just like her mother, unfortunately.

Her mother sniffs. "So you're not friends. Whose fault is that?"

No one's fault, she could say. They're just different kinds of people. Two years ago, she received a call from her brother saying he was go-ing to get married. Lulu was the cousin of one of his old high school friends, and she'd made him dizzy with love by singing "The Moon Represents My Heart" when a big group of them went to a karaoke parlor one night. She sang alone in the dark little room full of smoke. "Picture it," he said. "That old song." Juanlan didn't meet her until a few days before the wedding, when she took Lulu shopping with her mother and immediately resented her for her loveliness, her white skin, her tiny teeth slightly pointed like a cat's. In Feather Beauty, Lulu had tried on different eye shadows. "The blue looks very good on you, Xiao Lu," Juanlan's mother told her, and then remarked, "You can't wear that color so well, Lan'er. Your brother's almost-wife has better skin." In the big mirror on the wall, Lulu had blinked at her innocently; her face was as light and shimmery as onionskin.

Now, staring at her own reflection in the mirror, Juanlan gathers her hair in her fingers, trying to fashion it into the kind of high ponytail Du Xian once told her he likes. Three nights ago, she sat with him by the river, his mouth on her neck, one hand on her back and the other gripping her thigh with a fierce urgency that made her shake. Beneath the dusty leaves of the trees, every bench along the river was filled with young couples. The river was low and sluggish. There was no moon. Tomorrow, she thinks, he will write from Chongqing.

*　　*　　*

Dinner. Three waitresses at the hostess stand call out their welcome: "Huanying, guanglin!" Juanlan recognizes one of them, the tallest. She went to middle school with her. They were one year apart, and she can't remember anything about the girl except that she always wore gloves during morning exercises, even in the heat. Now, Juanlan waits to be recognized in response. The girl blinks and stretches her smile wider, passing her eyes over Juanlan in a way that says, *I am a waitress and you are a customer, now follow me to your table.* She leads them down a short hall with private rooms on either side to the room on the end, where Juanlan's uncle and aunt and a collection of other relatives and friends are gathered.

"Welcome home, you little scholar!" Her godfather laughs, putting one arm around her shoulder. He's wearing a leather jacket so new it squeaks. In the past few years, he and her aunt have become rich, at least by Heng'an standards, and now they always have something new to show off. Last time she was home, they proudly pointed out the color television taking up the corner of their living room. Releasing her, he propels her toward her aunt, who asks about her journey.

"It was all right. No rain, so the roads weren't too bad."

"Your uncle traveled to Chengdu just last week on business. It's too bad you didn't come home earlier. He could have taken you in the car."

Juanlan's mother lays a hand on her arm, a reminder of something, a warning. "Has Uncle Liu already gotten his license?" Juanlan asks.

"No, no," her aunt says, "not yet. His lingdao was driving. But they could have found room for you in the company car."

"She was fine taking the bus," her mother says tightly, and now Juanlan understands that the offer was refused so as to avoid accepting any more favors. Her parents have taken loans from her aunt and uncle, and they're not all paid back. And then there is always something owed. "Do you know how many guests we've had to give a discount to?" her mother asked her earlier that day. "'Friends' of your uncle who we've never even met." Uncle Liu and Auntie Zhang are outgoing people, essentially confident and hopeful, convinced that things are as good as they've ever been and can only get better. Favors are nothing; debts will float away on the air. Juanlan's mother is not of this belief. She thinks disaster is always waiting right around the corner.

"You sit at this table," Auntie Zhang directs Juanlan, pulling out a chair with the other women. Each place setting is tightly wrapped in cellophane to show that it's been sanitized. An additional charge but worth the show. "You're our guest of honor tonight. What would you like to drink? Coca-Cola? Peanut milk?"

Just then, Zhuo Ge and Lulu come in through the door. Juanlan's sister-in-law is dressed in a loose cotton dress so large it forms a tent over her knees, even though she is only halfway through her pregnancy. Her face is swollen and sallow. Auntie Zhang rushes over to take her by the arm and directs her to a chair next to Juanlan and her mother. Then Lulu proceeds to answer questions about how she is feeling and how they got there. Fine, she says. A pedicab, she says.

"Pedicab!" Juanlan's mother presses her mouth into a line and shakes her head. "All that bouncing in your condition, Xiao Lu. You should have taken a taxi."

"We took the river road. It was very smooth."

"Smooth!"

Lulu shrugs her narrow shoulders and reaches for a handful of dried peas from a basket in the center of the table. "If it was dangerous, your son wouldn't have taken us that way."

Juanlan's mother casts a frown at Lulu and gets up to speak with another aunt. Lulu just goes on grinding the hard peas between her teeth. After a moment, her gaze falls on Juanlan and, blinking slowly a few times, she remarks that her sister-in-law has gotten thinner.

"I'm as fat as ever."

"No, you can see it in your face." Lulu sweeps a palm from her forehead to her cheeks to her chin. "Mine is so puffy. But you've lost some fat there. Are you dieting?"

"I've been trying to eat less rice." Juanlan explains that she and two of her roommates started eating this way a few months ago, when springtime came and they went shopping and saw all the new fashions. Lots of girls at the university, she says, have been trying this diet.

"That's good," Lulu says, nodding. "I can't do anything right now, but after the baby, maybe. Zhuo says I'm getting fatter than I should." She raises a hand to her face again, as if afraid that it's getting bigger as they speak. "I used to move around more—I was standing all day, for my job—but now I just sit."

Juanlan's mother passed along the news several months ago that Lulu had lost her job at the snacks counter in the bus station. It's unclear whether Juanlan should acknowledge it now. She settles on remarking, "You don't look fatter than you should be," at which Lulu laughs bitterly. Impossible to believe that she's only a year older than Juanlan, that she's already a wife and will soon be a mother. She says suddenly, "You have to come spend time with me after the baby comes. Four weeks without going outside or showering"—she wrinkles her nose—"it's too long."

Juanlan's mother appears then and, leaning down, whispers that she should get up and greet her cousin, who has just arrived. She leaves without assuring Lulu that she'll come see her, leaves her sister-in-law to be scolded again for riding in the pedicab or to be instructed on what's safe to eat here and what's not. As she gets up, Lulu gives her a desperate look.

Juanlan's cousin and his wife hug her. She tickles their daughter's feet. When they congratulate her on her graduation, she says "Thank you, it's nothing," and means it. Four years of studying have been turned, as if by magic, into nothing.

"Are you glad to be back?" her cousin's wife asks as she jostles their daughter on her hip.

She wills herself to remember that if she had stayed in the city, if she'd gotten a job at a foreign company or gone to work at a travel agency, she would have had to live with her aunt and uncle in their crowded flat outside the third ring road. It would have taken an hour or maybe two to take the bus into the city each morning, and again going back. Remember, she thinks: the sky so dim with pollution that the sun hovering over the horizon is a greasy orange ball you can look at without having to squint. The sleek stores, all windows, too expensive to enter. In afternoon traffic, a man and his bike can slide under the wheel of a bus and the noise only grows.

She wills herself to remember all this. But remembers, too: she could stare at the sun. The noise was a kind of silence. The cold burn inside her was a steady flame. Here, she feels herself flickering.

"I'm only home for a short while," she says and glances at her father, who's sitting with his shoulders against the back of his chair as if he's tied to it. Then she goes on to tell her cousin about her job prospects in Chengdu, talking up the possibility of working at an after-school English program. She grabs its name from a sign that floats up at just the right moment.

"What a great opportunity," her cousin says vaguely. Then the waitresses come in pushing carts, and they separate to find their places and prepare to eat.

When Juanlan returns to her seat, the waitress, her old schoolmate, begins sliding plates of meat and seafood into the broth and naming them aloud in a monotone: "Pig intestine, chicken wings, fish balls, eel." She has burn marks on her hands. When she leaves, Juanlan leans over and tells Lulu about knowing her, about the gloves she used to wear.

"How pathetic," Lulu says, but she doesn't explain whether the girl's sin was wearing the gloves in the first place or letting her hands get scarred. Whether it was the vanity itself, or the loss of something to be vain about at all.

*　　*　　*

The next morning, Juanlan gets up early to cover the morning shift at the front desk. They took a taxi home from the restaurant the night before, and her father, tired from the strain of talking to so many people at dinner, didn't protest when Juanlan's mother said he needed to sleep in. "This is why Lan'er is here," her mother said, and Juanlan told him it would make her happy to help.

The desk is quiet this early in the day. Only two guests are staying at the hotel. They come down ten minutes apart, and each one says good morning and remarks that there's rain, and Juanlan says it's not bad out, only a light mist, and watches them, ten minutes apart, squint at the sky in exactly the same way, as if the gray expanse has it out for them personally. The two are businessmen in town from places smaller than

Heng'an, here for similar reasons and with similar expectations. The Three Springs Hotel caters to provincial businessmen and government workers. No tourists or vacationers. Juanlan was in middle school when her parents bought the hotel, and ten years later, they're still paying off the cost.

A few minutes after the two men leave, her mother comes into the lobby carrying a bowl of noodle soup. "I want you to go to the market later this morning," she says, setting the bowl down carefully on the desk. "Buy some fish. You're going over to your brother's to make lunch."

Juanlan takes the pair of chopsticks her mother offers. "I am?"

"Didn't you see Xiao Lu last night, dipping everything in oil? Your brother says she isn't cooking at home, then she goes out and eats like that." She nods at Juanlan. "Buy a fish and make some clear broth. A little ginger, no spice."

Juanlan takes a ten-yuan note from her mother. After breakfast, she gets on her bike and rides to the market, then on to her brother's flat, steering around the largest puddles. By the time she arrives, her pants are flecked with mud. She locks up the bike and climbs the stairs, then changes into a pair of house slippers on the mat beside the door. Before she can knock, the door swings open. "I heard you walking up," Lulu says, and stands aside to let her enter.

Juanlan holds up the groceries. "I'm here to make lunch for you."

"I know." She glances at the groceries without interest. "Your mother told me."

"When? She didn't tell me until this morning."

Lulu gives her a look. "Last night, she pulled Zhuo and me aside and said you wanted to spend time with me. I figured you knew." She narrows her eyes, considering how to register the offense.

Juanlan raises her shoulders. "I guess my mother wants us to be friends."

"Your mother doesn't care about me or my friendships," Lulu responds coldly. "Maybe she does about yours, but I doubt it. What she really cares about is the grandchild I'm growing in here." She thumps her stomach. "Aiya, your family—" She looks as if she would say more, but instead turns abruptly away. Heading into the kitchen, she says, "Go wash up, if you want," and leaves Juanlan by the door.

They have a sink in their bathroom, a step up from Juanlan's parents' flat, where the bathroom has only a toilet and a showerhead on the wall that no longer moves. But her mother keeps the bathroom clean, mopping and emptying the trash both morning and night. The trash can here is full almost to overflowing with used toilet paper. Juanlan breathes through her mouth as she wipes the bottoms of her pants with one of the damp hand towels hanging on the wall by the sink.

In the kitchen, her sister-in-law is staring down at the contents of the bag. When Juanlan comes in, she says without turning, "I hate boiled fish. I won't eat any soup." She hunches a little as she puts a hand on the edge of the counter.

"Okay, no fish soup. So what do you want to eat?"

"Oh, I don't care," she says after a moment. "You can fry it up, if you want. We have some green peppers and garlic." She nods at the metal baskets hanging from the ceiling; one contains a few fists of garlic, but the others are empty. "Maybe not," she says and then falls silent without explaining whether the peppers were ever there, or if she only thought about buying them and then forgot. Juanlan wonders what her brother has been doing for meals. Has he been cooking for both of them? Or does he go out for dinner, leaving Lulu at home? She feels, standing in this kitchen, as she did as a child when she visited her relatives in the countryside, and had to share a bed with two of her cousins: a sense of being too close, of encroaching on intimacies. One of her cousins was several years older, and she remembers the simultaneous fascination and revulsion she'd felt at the knowledge that her cousin was bleeding, hearing the rustle of a pad as she turned, noticing the metallic tincture in the air.

"Why don't you go sit?" she says. "Listen to the radio. This won't take me very long."

Lulu nods and goes back into the living room. A bright strum of guitar breaks the air, and Juanlan recognizes the song, a popular one by a musician from Hong Kong. For months, she's heard it several times a day, threads of the melody floating in the hall of her dormitory or leaking from the open door of a shop. She is tired of this song.

Turning on the burner under the wok, she waits for the oil to smoke, and because she's already defied her mother's wishes, she tosses in a few dried chilies before adding the fish. "Rice?" she calls when the food is ready.

Lulu calls back, "There's some left over in the cooker." Then she comes in, dragging a blanket behind her. "You put peppers in," she says in a flat tone, as if simply stating a fact. She pulls the bowl of lajiao over the counter and spoons some onto her rice. "I'm sick of eating food without any flavor. 'No oil! No spice! No raw fruits or vegetables!' Like I'm a child and I need to be told what to do." She blinks angrily at the bowl of rice, now drenched in the spicy oil. Even Zhuo Ge, who loves heat, wouldn't eat a spoonful of it. "Oh, fuck," Lulu says, and dumps it into the trash. At the same moment, the blanket slips to the floor. She'll cry now, Juanlan thinks. Any moment, she will burst into tears. But instead she just sighs and asks for Juanlan to pick it up.

They dine together with the music playing at the same volume as before, a little too loud. *Our love is a river that will carry us far from here.* Juanlan says nothing about the volume, or about the fact that Lulu darts her chopsticks to the fish again and again, breaking off small pieces, which she delivers straight to her mouth with a sort of grim determination. When the fish is nearly picked clean on one side, she clamps her chopsticks around its tail and flips it over to expose all the flesh that's untouched. "You're not much of a cook," she says while she resumes eating. "There's not enough salt."

"Maybe your taste is off."

Lifting her bowl to her lips, Lulu shovels in rice and swallows quickly. "I'm a pretty good cook, myself. But not since I got pregnant, because I don't want to cook what I don't get to eat. Zhuo is as bad as your mother. He won't let me have anything good." Setting her bowl down again, she maneuvers the fish head away from the body. "You want it?" she asks but doesn't wait for an answer before depositing it in her own bowl.

With that selfish gesture, Juanlan decides that she likes Lulu. Her sister-in-law was once so smooth she couldn't find a crack in the surface; now she is all rough edges. As Juanlan watches, she pulls apart the fish's skull with her fingers and then burrows the tips of her chopsticks inside. When they're both finished eating, the table is strewn with bones and grains of rice, and Juanlan begins cleaning up. "Don't bother," Lulu says. "Zhuo will do it when he gets home."

"I can do it. He works all day, and I'm not doing anything."

Lulu levels a gaze at her. "Go ahead and judge me. Everyone else does. But you don't really know anything about my marriage."

Juanlan pictures the normal evening scene: her brother parking his motorbike behind the stairs and then climbing the six stories to his flat. Inside, his wife sits on the sofa doing nothing. The table is filthy. Her hands are unmoving in her lap as she mindlessly slaps the heel of one slipper against the tile floor.

Zhuo Ge has too much life in him to bear such quietness. His charm wafts off him like the scent of a flower hung over a shirt button in the spring. It's always been this way. He is someone who wins and keeps on winning. Even when he was a child, every game went his way, and though Juanlan tried to hate him for it, she never could.

Despite her sister-in-law's instructions, she carries the dishes into the kitchen and washes them in the sink. When she's finished, she goes into the other room and finds Lulu in the posture she'd imagined her brother finding her in each night: idle, staring out the window. "I'm going now."

Lulu looks over abruptly. Her face is clouded with something between melancholy and impatience. Juanlan recognizes this combination; it's the way she feels when she's thinking of Chengdu, of Du Xian, of her own shapeless future. "You should stay," Lulu says.

Juanlan seats herself on the other end of the sofa. "Do you want to listen to another tape?" she inquires, but Lulu shakes her head as if offended by the suggestion. A few seconds pass, and then Lulu asks to hear about life at the university. "What do you want me to say?" Juanlan says, and hears the bitterness in her voice. "I was there for four years. Now I'm back here."

"Did you have a boyfriend?" When Juanlan hesitates, Lulu presses her hands together eagerly. "You did, I see. What's he like?"

What to tell her about Du Xian? With her college roommates, Juanlan could sit cross-legged on a bed and recount the date she'd just had, pausing when she got to the part where they'd groped each other on a park bench, give a significant look, and say, "We sat together at least an hour." Then the girls would laugh, and Hualing would remark, "I hope you sat close enough to make that hour worth it," and sway her chest seductively to make them all laugh even more. Hualing was big-breasted and had crooked teeth. She'd had a boyfriend in the chemistry department for three years, and every time she came home from their once-weekly date at a cousin's flat outside the university campus, she reported on what they'd done in bed. She liked to tell stories that made the whole thing sound amusing, like she was playing with a pet rabbit, coaxing it to do tricks. It sounded nothing like Juanlan's own experiences with Du Xian, which were rare and rushed and difficult. Since neither of them knew anyone with a flat, they had to use the storage shed near the recreation room, the one with a loose window the security guards either missed or chose to ignore. Juanlan never told anyone about it, this part of her relationship that seems now like the only part that means anything at all.

Lulu sits waiting for an answer to her question. Juanlan could tell her that she doesn't have a boyfriend. Or she could invent a different one: someone taller and more handsome and more devoted to her, a boy who has made her promises. Somehow, she fears that if she tries to describe Du Xian, she'll get him wrong. She holds her breath for a second, but then quickly decides. "I do have a boyfriend. He's in Chongqing now."

"Chongqing's not so far. Have you heard from him since you've been back?"

"No, but he was starting his new job right away. He said he won't have time to write except on the weekends." She hears how this sounds, but if Lulu pities her, it doesn't show.

"What's his job?"

Juanlan tells her about the company he's working for, how he'll help to design engines for motorbikes. "He was lucky to get a job in the private market," she adds, "and at such a prestigious place."

Lulu chews her lip, distracted. Then she asks if Juanlan loves him.

"I don't know," she says, startled. "I guess I do."

"If you did, you wouldn't give an answer like that."

"We've been seeing each other for seven months. It's not long enough to tell."

For the first time, Lulu smiles. "I'm telling you, you're not in love. If you were, you would have known the first time you touched." She leans back against the arm of the sofa and rubs her belly. "Have you had sex with him?"

"Yes."

"And did you enjoy it?"

"Of course."

A lock of hair falls forward, and Lulu brushes it back with her hand. "If you didn't know before and you still don't know now, then there's no way that you love him."

Juanlan stands and walks to the kitchen. Her limbs are shaking from anxiousness or anger, from the thrill of talking openly and also from the fear. There's a thermos on the floor, and she picks it up to test whether it still holds any water. Returning to the room with two glasses, she sets them both on the table and opens the drawer below. "You keep the tea in here?"

Lulu nods and picks up where she left off: "It's better that you figure this out now, so you don't waste any more time."

Juanlan concentrates on tipping the bag over the rim of each glass, watching the tea leaves scatter on the surface of the water. "What makes you an expert, anyway?" she asks. "How many boyfriends did you have before my brother?"

"I dated one boy," Lulu says as she takes the glass of tea. "He was very sweet, but it was only a high school relationship. We never did anything more than kiss and hold hands." She lifts the glass to the light and looks through it, closing one eye. "I remember his hands were always so sweaty, he'd have to wipe them on his pants every few minutes to dry them off. Poor boy, he was always apologizing for them. Really, his hands didn't bother me that much, but his embarrassment made me think he wasn't really a man."

In the courtyard outside, a motorbike starts up, and the noise of the revving engine echoes off the walls. Immediately, a dog begins yapping like mad. These distractions draw Lulu's attention, her face turning toward the window as if she expects to see the dog right there. "Anyway," she says, turning back, "we were talking about your boyfriend. What do you like about him?"

What floats before Juanlan is a wavering image of Du Xian standing outside her dorm beneath a light, smoking as he waits for her to come down. He has a funny way of smoking: he holds the cigarette between his thumb and his fourth finger, so the index and middle fingers stick up by his eye, and the pinkie stands as straight as a flagpole. But she can't give this answer to Lulu; it wouldn't make sense. Instead she says he has straight shoulders, he likes the same music as she does, and the year he took the gaokao he scored in the top seven hundred in the whole province.

"Oh, a smart guy, huh?" Lulu's mouth is pinched for a moment before she says, "You really should break up with him."

"Okay, fine." Juanlan laughs. "I'll write him a letter tomorrow."

Lulu frowns. "I don't know him, I haven't met him. But I can tell that you're waiting for him because you have nothing better to do. That's not a good enough reason to marry someone."

"Who said anything about marriage? Just because I'm finished with college, I should find a husband right away?" She doesn't say *You didn't even wait this long.*

"I thought you were saying that you'd already found him."

"A *boyfriend.* I found a boyfriend. It's not the same thing."

"And you're not a virgin," Lulu goes on. "It's not going to be easy to find someone else. But twenty-two is still young enough a man will forgive something like that."

Still young enough. And yet already her life is looping back on itself, bringing her back here, when she'd rather be anywhere else.

"Do you want to know what I'm having?" Lulu says suddenly, pointing to her stomach. She explains that the nurse who did the ultrasound was a friend of Zhuo Ge's, and he'd convinced her to break the rules and tell them the gender. "It's a girl. She made me promise to be a 'responsible mother.' Like I might go home and stab myself in the stomach."

"Does my brother know?"

"Of course." Lulu shrugs. "He's happy. He says girls are more reliable and will take care of us when we're old." The corners of her mouth lift in an expression that is not quite a smile.

Juanlan thinks of what her mother said, how she wonders if Lulu really wants the baby. "And what about you? Are you happy?"

Lulu looks right at her. "No, I'm not happy."

"You wanted a boy," Juanlan says carefully.

"It has nothing to do with that." Lulu blinks and shakes her head. "It would be the same either way." A long moment passes, and she adds, almost as an afterthought, "I'm just tired of it."

Juanlan waits for her to go on, to name what exhausts her. But it seems there is nothing to explain; there is only the result. Lulu tells her she's going to take a nap, and Juanlan says that's fine and lets herself out.

5

The letter from Du Xian, when it finally arrives, is disappointing. He writes that Chongqing is an interesting place, and already his legs are stronger from climbing the city's hills; the flat where he is staying with his aunt and uncle is located on a street so steep that it is actually a stairway. Every day, he takes two buses to get to work and it takes more than an hour, but the work is interesting and his uncle and aunt and cousin have been kind. On the weekends, he often plays basketball with some of his friends. "I am glad to be working, not worried about school anymore. Altogether, I am happy with the arrangements postgraduation. Of course, I wish we could be together." His handwriting is neat, not elegant but clear: the characters all the same size and evenly spaced, as if he has used a writing grid like the ones on which children practice their handwriting. Juanlan has never had a love letter before, yet this does not seem to be one.

She writes him back:

My handsome guy,

I am glad your uncle and aunt have been kind, and your cousin, and everyone in your danwei. I'm not as happy in Heng'an. The hotel isn't busy, and it's pointless for me to be here. Every day I put on music and try to imagine I'm back at school with you. When my mother came in and heard "Fenlie" one day, she asked who was singing it and I told her it was Wang Fei, and she said it was not as good as "Xiangyue 1998" . . . so you see, it's true that everyone loves her big hits, but only real fans admire the earlier album. I remember listening to this song over and over together. I miss you and wish we could be together every day.

Giving you ten thousand hugs and kisses,
YOUR "LITTLE MOUSE"

She had been his little mouse when they sat by the river, back in the fall when they first got together. This was before they ever had sex, when they had only been boyfriend and girlfriend for a few weeks. It had stayed warm through October, but then one evening it was suddenly cold and she tried to burrow under his arm as they sat on the bench. "Like a mouse," he laughed, "like a little mouse," and he'd made his nose quiver to demonstrate. The next time he called her a little mouse, she protested that she didn't want her nickname to be a vermin, but the name stuck, anyway. She gave in because it was an endearment. Now she clings to it as evidence of a promise never clearly spoken. It is all she has.

She mails the letter and waits for a response. In the meantime, she helps with the hotel, sitting at the desk when needed, cleaning rooms or refilling thermoses with hot water. Her tasks are menial, and in the long hours she spends mopping the linoleum floors upstairs or hanging sheets to dry in the alcoves at the end of each hall, she tries to clear her mind. There is no joy in thinking about Du Xian and their relationship, about her father's slow recovery, about the in-between state that she's living in now. She is impatient; she sloshes water on the floors and pushes the mop halfheartedly through the puddles, leaving long wet swaths that take hours to dry in the humid air.

*   *   *

One day, her brother comes by while she's sweeping the lobby. He's in uniform, and she wonders briefly if his stopping by the hotel is an excuse to avoid going home to Lulu during the lunch hour. He lights a cigarette, leans against the desk, and tells her he's been busy trying to figure out how the hotel can start accepting foreign guests. "See, Mei, I'm doing what I can behind the scenes."

"Ba hasn't mentioned it."

"He and Ma don't know yet. I'll tell them when it's a real possibility."

In the corner, by the standing ashtray, sunflower seeds litter the floor. She goes after them with her broom. "What do we need to worry about that for? Heng'an has no foreigners. And if there were any, the Friendship Hotel already has the permits to accept them."

"The Friendship Hotel is for businessmen."

"So are we."

"For now, yes, okay. But Western travelers want a different kind of place—a smaller hotel, not so fancy. You remember Radish Head?" He waits for her to remember his old classmate. "He was transferred to Guilin a few years ago, and he says that almost every week, a new place opens up that caters to foreign guests. They're all small places, little hotels like ours." He glances around the lobby at the dingy linoleum, the worn furniture. "We'll have to renovate," he says.

With what money? she could ask. Instead, she says, "Heng'an isn't Guilin. We don't have any Western travelers here."

"Not now, maybe, but once the expressway is completed, we will. There are already a lot of foreigners coming to Sichuan to see the Giant Buddha or Jiuzhaigou. Why not Heng'an? It's only a matter of time. When it takes less than two hours to get here from Chengdu, lots of people will want to come."

She sweeps more sunflower seeds into the dustpan. "You're more optimistic than I am."

"That's because you've been away. Heng'an is changing, every day a little faster." He takes a drag on his cigarette and coughs. Stepping aside so she can get behind the front desk to the trash, he adds, "In another few years, we won't recognize this city."

"A city? I always thought we were a town."

"That's what I'm talking about." He reaches over the desk to retrieve the tin plate their mother uses to hold fruit; Juanlan swats him away and points to the ashtray in the corner. As he's crossing the lobby to stub out his cigarette, she asks what he's done to get the necessary permits.

"That isn't necessary," he explains. Like almost everything, it's all about guanxi—who you know, and what they are willing to do for you, and what will be expected in return. One of the people he knows is Director Wei, leader of both the Department of Tourism and the Department of Tourism's Communist Party. He has a teenage son, a fifteen-year-old who just graduated from middle school and in September will start high school at one of the most elite schools in

Chengdu. But his English isn't good, and his parents are worried he'll be behind his peers. When Zhuo Ge mentioned that his sister had won a university-wide prize in English at Sichuan Normal, Director Wei was impressed. He wanted to know if she would tutor his son.

"You don't have much else going on right now, do you?" Zhuo Ge asks.

Juanlan sweeps an arm around the lobby. It's as quiet as ever. "Ma has me clean in the mornings while she helps Ba with his exercises."

"This place doesn't need so much cleaning." He runs a finger over the counter of the desk and holds it up to the light.

The next night, Juanlan meets Zhuo Ge by the river, and together they walk to the beef restaurant near the mosque for a dinner hosted by Director Wei. When the hostess leads them into a private room in the back, a tall woman in heels even higher than the waitresses' rises from the table. "Policeman Bai! You've brought your sister. We're so happy to see you both. Call me Teacher Cao," she says, taking both Juanlan's hands in her own.

"What do you teach?" Juanlan asks, taking in the woman's stylish clothes, the careful cut of her bangs.

"Oh, I don't teach any longer. I'm in the education department. But I used to teach art. My specialty is calligraphy—"

"Welcome!" Director Wei cuts off his wife. "Please, have a seat. Zhuo Ge, we're drinking Wuliangye tonight. You think you can keep up with me?"

Over dinner, Teacher Cao asks Juanlan about the prize she won. She talks to her about Chengdu. She plucks the choicest pieces of meat from the dishes that keep coming to the table and places them in Juanlan's bowl. Finally, she mentions her son, who is seated across the table and has barely spoken a word since saying hello. "Do you play any instruments?" she asks Juanlan. "Those with musical talents are said to be very good at studying languages. Wei Ke is quite musical—he plays both the piano and erhu—but so far we haven't seen that particular benefit." She glances across the table at her son with pride. "He mastered the Mozart sonatas when he was still an Elementary Four student, can you believe that?"

Juanlan smiles at the boy, but he immediately looks down and goes to work stirring his chopsticks around in the grease accumulated in the bottom of his bowl.

Director Wei's wife spins the moving plate in the middle of the table, bringing close the golden-fried corn. Plucking a single kernel with her chopsticks, she tucks it into her mouth and frowns. "The corn here is a specialty," she says as an aside. She is one of those people whose approval you would do a lot to win. And given her position—a party member herself and married to a man with no small amount of influence—she can reasonably expect to have people try to please her in most situations.

"To be honest, the English teachers at Heng'an Middle School are not very excellent," she declares as Juanlan watches the spinning plate take the corn dish away from their side of the table. "Wei Ke's teacher last year came from the countryside, and I doubt she's even seen a foreigner, much less had a conversation with one. Studying in Chengdu, you must have had many opportunities to improve your conversational English."

Juanlan tells her about the lectures she attended at the US consulate, and Teacher Cao leans forward as if they're sharing a secret. "They're given by expats? What are they about?"

"They're supposed to introduce American culture in order to 'foster the friendship between the American and Chinese peoples.'" Juanlan smiles wryly at her use of the tired phrase. "I went to one called 'The Shopping Mall and Suburban Youth.' Another was about the history of American missionaries in China."

Teacher Cao raises an eyebrow. "I'd rather hear the one about the shopping malls."

Juanlan laughs, but in fact she remembers very little of that talk; the lecture about the missionaries is clearer in her mind. The speaker spent most of his time talking about the Boxer Rebellion, showing old sepia photographs of the missionaries who'd been killed in the uprising up north. Juanlan remembers the strange, serious faces staring out at her from the projections on the wall, their eyes like glass marbles, both cloudy and clear.

"Your brother told us that you speak very well," Teacher Cao remarks. "We didn't realize that you were a cultural expert, too."

Studying English is not like studying engineering. Du Xian could become an expert on motorcycle engines, but Juanlan has no hope of becoming an expert on foreigners. If she were wealthy and could travel, maybe she would have the opportunity to learn what the books can't teach. As it is, true proficiency is a state she can only pretend to have achieved. But she doesn't need to lie to Teacher Cao, in any case. She is doing them a favor, and they will have to be satisfied with what she is able to offer. "I'm not an expert," she says. "Not at all."

"You're too humble." Teacher Cao deposits a piece of beef tongue in Juanlan's bowl and then sits back in her chair. "We are very pleased that you've agreed to tutor our son."

The next morning, Zhuo Ge drives Juanlan on his motorbike along the river to Director Wei's and Teacher Cao's home. The river is high, though not as high as up north, where they've seen flooding since June. On the news each night, the images are of submerged houses and speedboats skimming past. "Here we are!" Zhuo Ge says, stopping in front of a tall building with bigger windows than those surrounding it. The building is new, erected sometime during the four years that have passed since Juanlan left Heng'an. Though what was in its place before, she can't remember.

They ring downstairs and are quickly buzzed up. On the second floor Director Wei stands at the entrance to the flat, holding open the door in welcome. Shoes line a rack in the hallway, and though he insists that Zhuo Ge keep his on, since he is only staying for a few minutes, he relents when Juanlan asks to remove hers. "You have very small feet," he observes as she steps into the pair of plastic house slippers. "Those are my wife's, and look: your feet are swimming in them."

Zhuo Ge laughs. "You should have seen her when she was young. I used to tease her for having feet as big as mine. Then they stopped growing."

Director Wei squints at her. "Is that true?"

"More or less," she says, uneasy under his gaze.

Inside, the floor is immaculate, freshly mopped. The son, Wei Ke, stands beside the piano with the fingers of one hand resting gingerly on one corner. He looks as if he is merely waiting for the signal to sit down and play. His mother comes out from the kitchen, carrying a tray with tall glasses and a bag of loose tea. She greets Juanlan and Zhuo Ge warmly and asks her son if he's said hello. Wei Ke mumbles his greetings. Then he quickly removes himself to another room.

"Sit, sit," Teacher Cao insists, setting the tray down on the table in front of the sofa. She produces a paring knife from one of the drawers. "Eat some fruit," she says, and pushes a basket of loquats toward them.

Zhuo Ge begs off, saying he has to get to work. "At least stay for a smoke," Director Wei says, pulling two cigarettes from a box of Prides.

"Don't tempt me, unless you're trying to get me a bad work report."

"Okay, okay." Director Wei relents. "I know you've already had too many of those." He tucks the cigarette into Zhuo Ge's jacket pocket for later, and opens the door. "I won't walk you out then," he says, shaking hands. "Go safely."

"Go safely," Teacher Cao echoes, following Zhuo Ge out into the hall to watch him descend the steps. "We won't walk you out. Go safely!" she repeats.

A silence swells in the room for a moment. Director Wei, standing by the door, gives Juanlan a baffled look. "Eat some loquats," he urges, and she obediently takes the knife and begins peeling one. When Teacher Cao returns from the hall, she scolds her husband for not pouring tea. "And where is our son?"

Director Wei and Juanlan sit on the sofa and Teacher Cao and Wei Ke on short plastic stools, and the next ten minutes are slowly filled with strained conversation as they sip their tea. Without Zhuo Ge, they are all ill at ease. Even Director Wei and his wife seem awkward with each other.

After a few minutes, Teacher Cao turns to her son and asks if he's finished learning the Schubert piece.

"I've gotten to the end, but I'm not good yet," he says and frowns at his hands.

"Then play something you're comfortable with. Play one of the Beethoven concertos." With one hand, she touches the fabric of her skirt, an ankle-length print whose pattern appears to be modeled on the tiny petals of a chrysanthemum. Rather than the subdued browns and grays that most women her age favor, it is a vibrant green. Somehow this irks Juanlan: the freedom it suggests, the refusal to give up what others get to enjoy.

"I don't know any Beethoven concertos. I only have a book of his sonatas."

Teacher Cao blinks at her son. "Ke'er, don't you know I don't care what you pick? Our guest would just like to hear you play. Wouldn't you?"

"I would love to hear you play," Juanlan says automatically. "It doesn't matter what—I'm not very knowledgeable about Western music."

"He should play some Chinese music, then." Director Wei leans forward to tap his cigarette in the small trash can beside the table. "What do you want? 'Jasmine Flower'? 'Flying Kites'? 'Under the Silver Moonlight'?"

"Anything is fine," Juanlan says, her skin prickling at the sudden attention. "'Jasmine Flower' is one of my favorites." Wei Ke goes to the piano and, without opening any books, sits down and begins playing an ornamental version of the song, full of runs and trills, his hands chasing each other up and down the keyboard. His father sits listening with what seems only half his attention, his eyes roving around to the window, where across the river a construction crane can be seen bending slowly to a half-built wall. Teacher Cao unconsciously echoes the motion, bobbing her head with the tiny motion of a pecking bird.

After the first verse, Director Wei finishes his cigarette and stands abruptly. He has to go to work, he says. To his son, still seated at the piano with his hands paused over the keyboard, he speaks curtly: "Don't waste our guest's time. You're lucky to have such a talented tutor." He shakes Juanlan's hand, and a moment later the door closes and his footsteps echo down the stairs.

"You may find it best to study in Wei Ke's bedroom," Teacher Cao says. "There are fewer distractions."

Wei Ke starts down the hall, and Juanlan rises to follow him. Passing the bathroom, she spots a Western-style toilet and wonders if they bought it in Chengdu. It is a symbol of the family's status, just as much as the large television and the piano in the other room. But unlike her uncle and aunt, Director Wei and Teacher Cao don't point out their luxuries, and it is this comfort with the objects of their own wealth that strikes in Juanlan a mixture of admiration and unease.

"What a big space," she says to Wei Ke in his room. "You must spend a lot of time here."

"I guess."

They sit and find themselves staring at the blank wall above the desk. "Do you have textbooks? Grammar or vocabulary books, or anything like that?"

"Tons." Wei Ke pushes back his chair and crosses to an alcove filled with books. "All this shelf is English texts," he says, running his fingers over the spines.

"Do you use any of them?"

"I hate English. I'm terrible at it, and I hate it." Suddenly his face is dark with anger. "Why should I waste my time learning to say dumb things? 'This is schoolyard. I like play basketball at schoolyard.'" He makes his voice high and whiny for the English.

Juanlan borrows the tone of a patient teacher: "Until you master the basics, you won't be able to say anything more interesting."

"I don't care. If I have something interesting to say, I can say it in Chinese."

She blinks at him, wondering at his anger. "How do you know you'll never need to know English? It's possible that in ten years, we will—"

"We should be building up our own country, not trying to whore ourselves out to the West." He narrows his eyes as he speaks, trying out these phrases to see their effect.

Juanlan waits to see if he has more to say. When he stays quiet, she replies, "Patriotism doesn't require isolation." Then she smiles at the earnestness of the conversation, as if they were two panelists on *Shihua shishuo*, debating China's place in the world at the cusp of the twenty-first century.

Wei Ke opens his mouth and closes it again. He doesn't return her smile. Instead, his face shuts down, all the anger gone, sullenness left in its place. He seems capable of only a short spurt of argument before submitting to the will of his parents.

They spend the next two hours going through the conversations in one of the books, reading them line by line, twice through, then switching roles. By the time Teacher Cao knocks on the door to ask Juanlan if she can stay for lunch, they are both exhausted and glad to abandon their work.

*   *   *

At the hotel she finds her father seated on a stool beside the front door. This is his regular spot, or was, before the stroke. Since she's been home, he has spent most of his time in their flat across the alley, resting or doing stretches. Or else he's been seated at the desk in the lobby with a book on space flight, one of his favorite obsessions. She's glad to see him back at his old post. From his perch on the stool, he can talk to Mr. Wu, who shows up every morning to set up his repair stand on the closest corner, and who comes over often during the day to chat.

"You're back," Juanlan's father says as she pushes her bike up to the entrance. The words come out in a slow march, but they are clear. "Have you eaten?"

"I had lunch at Teacher Cao's." She leans her bike against the outside wall of the hotel, and her father rises to greet her. "Sit down, Ba. Don't tire yourself."

Ignoring her suggestion, he beckons for her arm to help him down the three steps to the sidewalk. The tiles of the sidewalk are broken and uneven, but he shakes off her arm once he's down the stairs and makes his way over to a birdcage hanging on a wire between two trees. Her father has always brought his bird out in the mornings for exercise. Up at five o'clock, he takes the cage outside and walks down to the river to meet his friends, most of whom are retired and much older than him. They all hang their cages on the branches of the trees, and the birds sing to one another while their owners chat or do their morning exercises. "I've never seen you take Duo Duo out in the afternoon before."

"He needed air."

And in an instant, she understands: the walk down to the river is too much for him now.

Her father pokes a finger through the bamboo rods of the cage, and the bird tilts its head to the side, considering him from its perch. Bright, black eyes, an intelligence flickering. "He likes it okay," he says. Tapping the cage to make it swing, he asks how the tutoring went.

"Wei Ke—Director Wei's son—is a good student, I think, but he's not excited to be studying English." She describes the boy's outburst, his rant against the trend for studying the language.

"It used to be Russian," her father observes, "but the world is changing." He coughs and turns back to the bird.

"He's very passionate about the importance of our country standing alone. Lots of ideas for a boy still in middle school." She hears herself talking from a position of supposed wisdom, shaking her head at the young, and understands that she's trying out this voice for her father.

He pushes the cage so it starts swinging again. "Is he a member of the Youth League?"

She considers the matter: he is the child of two government workers in good positions, both party members. It would be unusual if he *weren't* a member of the party's youth branch. "I guess he probably is," she says, watching the cage swing. The little thrush stays still within, clutching its tiny feet around the rod.

"Then he must be practicing speeches." Her father crooks a finger, beckoning her over. They're finished discussing Wei Ke, it seems. She wonders what Zhuo Ge told him about it, whether he suspects that the favor she's performing is in service to her mother and him.

Close to the birdcage now, she leans in to admire the bird. It has a sleek brown coat and its eyes gleam like oil. Her father feeds it a mixture of crushed eggshell, fruit, and seeds; the eggshell, he claims, keeps the feathers glossy. "Whistle at him," he instructs, and she gives a two-note call. The bird twitters excitedly, stepping back and forth on its perch. She tries again, and this time it performs a short song in response. "He likes your voice," her father says approvingly. "You must keep him trained, or he'll forget how to sing."

It is too much: her father's hopefulness, Duo Duo's instinctual reply to a meaningless call. She has nothing to offer the bird but familiar sounds. And yet, if she were to open the door of the cage, Juanlan is certain the creature would remain inside, dubious of what the world has to offer, or fearful of it.

* * *

The next day, and the next day, and the day after that, Juanlan rides her bike alone to the flat overlooking the river. She wakes early to help prepare breakfast and do some of the cleaning, and then leaves after her father's exercises are done. She and Wei Ke plod through *Conversational English for Every Day* and portions of a grammar text. Even to Juanlan, seated at the desk in his bedroom, the blank wall feels like a punishment. Sometimes she considers stopping the practice and telling him to play something on the erhu instead. However, there is a sense of watchfulness in the flat, as if there might be cameras embedded in the furniture. And so they continue straight through the two hours with only a short break in the middle, when Juanlan replenishes her tea and Wei Ke pages moodily through a magazine. "Why don't you get up and move around?" she always asks. The response is a shrug.

While they study, the other rooms in the flat remain open and empty, only wind blowing in through the open windows. One morning, after it's been pouring rain for a solid hour, Wei Ke suddenly jumps up and races out of the room. Juanlan finds him rescuing the clothes hanging on the line outside the window. The shirts and skirts and pants are swaying on hangers, so wet they're dripping. "I was supposed to take them in if it rained," he says miserably, using a hook to pull down the hangers one by one.

"Why don't we squeeze out the wet things?" Juanlan says. "I'll help you."

He retrieves a plastic tub from the bathroom, and they spend the next several minutes wringing out the long sleeves and pant legs, the water dripping loudly into the tub. "It doesn't matter," he says as Juanlan squeezes out one of his mother's dresses. He seems embarrassed by his horror a moment ago, by letting her see it.

She twists the fabric, and the vibrant pattern disappears into creases. "Will your mother be angry?"

"Probably not. She's not very strict with me."

She rehangs the dress on a hanger and takes a pair of gray pants, obviously Director Wei's. It's strange to be handling his laundry when he's never said much more to her than good morning and thank you. She's felt his eyes lingering on her as she entered the flat, an upward tilt of the chin with him looking down on her appraisingly. Something hungry there. Something selfish. "Your father will be angry, though," she suggests.

Wei Ke chews on his bottom lip as he shakes out a T-shirt with the mascot of an American basketball team on the front. "You like Michael Jordan?" he asks suddenly, dancing the shirt in front of her. "You like the Bulls?"

"I don't know. I'm not a basketball fan."

"But Michael Jordan is the best player who ever lived. All the best basketball players are black people. They're taller and bigger than white people." He crumples up the shirt again and pretends to shoot it like a basketball. "Can you imagine if dark-skinned Chinese were the best athletes? Sichuan would be one of the top recruiting provinces."

"Is it patriotic to care so much about an American sport?" she asks jokingly, but Wei Ke takes it as a serious question. "Sports are universal," he replies, shaking out the shirt and hanging it again.

"You have a lot of rules. Learning English is off-limits, but playing basketball is okay? That sounds strange to me."

"Sports are universal because they don't involve language. They're like math. Or music."

He glances through the open sliding doors at the piano against the far wall. It commands attention in the living room, presides over it as a sleeping lion would. "You love music," she says, a statement rather than a question.

He chews on his lip for a moment. "It makes sense to me. And if I'm a good enough piano player, I can compete at the provincial level and win prizes. I want to go to music school after I graduate."

"The Sichuan Conservatory?"

Indignation pulls his brows together over his nose. "No," he scoffs, "I want to go to Beijing. The Central Conservatory is the best in the nation, everyone knows that."

Beijing is several thousand kilometers away to the north, and the national school is an impossible dream. Wei Ke's parents have power in Heng'an, but it doesn't extend outside this tiny corner of the country. "You've set your sights high."

"'The skill is not as great as the heart's ambition'?" He frowns at the idiom. "Is that what you mean?"

"You're very good at piano," Juanlan says carefully. They've finished wringing out the clothes, and she leads the way back into the living room. "And I'm sure if you work hard you'll be able to achieve all your dreams."

Away from the window, the noise of the rain is softened, and her voice rings unexpectedly loud in the space. Wei Ke sits down at the piano and for a long moment holds his hands just over the keys, the silence a rebuke to her false encouragement. Who is she to talk of dreams? Her own have taken her nowhere. She suddenly wishes that he would slam his fingers down and make a terrible noise, an angry cacophony. He is a child, and such an outburst is allowed.

But when the music comes, it is lively and bright, the notes filling the air like a spill of butterflies. Mozart, perhaps—she isn't certain. She is only sure that it is music from a different time and place. The notes fly around her, twirling, fluttering. With her eyes closed, she could be far from here. A pause comes, and she pictures the butterflies settling. She holds out a hand, half expecting to feel the music alight on her palm.

Hazel

6

When George and Lydie Hughes came up the drive in their pickup, I was coming out from the barn. I'd been feeding the pigs and thinking how glad I was that the little ones were finally weaned: one of our sows had failed to nurse after she farrowed, and we'd had to bottle-feed her piglets until early October. Only four from the litter had survived. But they were putting on weight, and now that feedings were easy again and I didn't have to spend so much of my time perched on a stool in the half-dark, cradling a piglet in my lap, I felt almost the same as I had a couple months before when Debbie went off to kindergarten. Relieved, but also just a little bit sad. Now, in the mornings, I got Joe and Debbie ready for school while Karol ate breakfast, and by the time they ran down the lane to catch the bus, I had only dirty dishes to keep me company at the empty table. It wasn't entirely a bad thing to be alone for so much of the day. But it was an adjustment.

George had been driving, and he was still getting out from behind the wheel while Lydie was already stepping forward with her hands clasped at her collarbone. She had bad news written all over her. You didn't waste time during the harvest just to go visiting. And I knew that Karol had gone over to their place a few hours before.

"Hazel," Lydie said when she was still a distance away. She didn't unclasp her hands. She raised them to her chin and let the weight of her head drop onto the knuckles. "Hazel, I'm sorry, but Karol's got sick."

"Sick?" I said and glanced at George as he came up beside his wife. They both stopped a few yards away, as if behind a line.

"Well, no," George answered. "Not sick, exactly."

And that's when they explained that Karol had had a heart attack. He'd dropped to his knees in the soil, and they'd turned him onto his back while Theo Acker went running off to get his truck. George had pressed down on Karol's chest, but he still wasn't taking in air when Theo peeled across the fields, right over the rows of beans (I would see this later, I would go and stand and look at the crushed plants). They'd lifted Karol into the truck bed and then Theo had shot off like the devil to the hospital in town.

"I'll drive you," George said once he finished explaining. The explanation hadn't taken long—most of the details I learned later.

"And I'll stay here," Lydie put in, "in case you're not back by the time the kids get home from school."

I had a flash of Debbie seated cross-legged on the floor listening to her teacher read a story aloud, of Joe making faces at the chalkboard from the back of the room. It was impossible to think that such a place existed or that my children were there going through their day as normal, while here I was already knowing that our lives had just changed, and changed forever. I knew it as I nodded to Lydie and told her the house was unlocked. I climbed in the front seat of the truck. We backed onto the lane and rolled down to the road, and George took a left onto Sumner without saying a word.

If I'd been able to notice it, I would have been grateful for George's silence. Instead my mind was too busy thinking about how, as he'd delivered the news, I heard the pigs snorting and scuffling in the pen on the side of the barn and thought, I will not be able to keep all this up on my own. I'd somehow known at that moment, even as I climbed into George's truck, that Karol would be dead by the time I got to the hospital. He was already gone, and from here on forward everything would be different, and hard.

*　　*　　*

As it was the middle of harvest, I sold only what had to go right then. The cows, the pigs. I called my sister Rena and told her I needed help, and so her husband John Charlie took care of everything. I didn't know how he managed it, but the day before Karol's funeral three transport trucks pulled up the lane and we all stood outside on the lawn watching the drivers load on the livestock. My sister Edith said it was like Noah's ark. No one laughed, but she hadn't been trying to get a laugh. Debbie remained stoic as they loaded the heifers, though when they started in on the hogs, big fat tears started rolling down her cheeks, and

Rena picked her up and took her back into the house. Joe wasn't there; I'd sent him down to George and Lydie's place to play with their son Bobby. All the rest of us stayed watching. John Charlie directed, and I didn't say a word because it was too much to believe that not only was Karol gone forever but all those animals, too. The barn from now on would be quiet as a tomb.

I saw just how quiet when we buried Karol the next day. The funeral was at the same little country church where we'd married, and the coffin was laid down in a grave near my parents'. There were other Baumanns: a brother who'd died when I was too young to remember him and a sister I'd never known. The other graves had familiar last names, every one of them German. Karol would be the only Wisniewski there.

The coffin wobbled a little going into the ground, but then it settled and the silence that followed nearly undid me. For ten seconds it seemed no one moved or even breathed. There wasn't even any wind to stir the last leaves on the trees. Then our preacher recited the psalm about the Lord keeping you from harm and watching your coming and going, and we all turned and went back to the cars, all but four or five of the men, who would stay to fill in the earth with shovels. One of them was George Hughes.

At the hospital, after the doctor told me about Karol, while we were waiting for Theo to go collect my sisters, George had been the one to sit with me. He didn't try to hold my hand or pat my shoulder. Once he said, "I wish Lydie had come," and I understood that he meant he didn't know how to comfort me, but his wife—my closest friend—would. Several minutes passed, and I watched the doctors and nurses passing in and out of the rooms down the long hall, and then I thought of how my husband was lying dead behind one of those doors, and I broke out in a sob so violent it felt like vomiting. George put a hand on my back then, and at the same time he took out a handkerchief from his pants pocket. It was clean and freshly pressed, and his producing it then felt like a bit of magic.

*   *   *

Karol and I married late. I was almost thirty, Karol thirty-three. He'd been our hired man for the past few years, and it was no surprise to anyone when he asked me to marry him. It was wartime, so the wedding was small—small enough that the wedding party and all the guests could fit into the back of a neighbor's truck to drive to the church and back again. I wore my sister's old gown. We had a pancake breakfast when we returned to the farm, and I got syrup on the bodice, so Iris made me take it off so she could wash out the stain before it set. For the rest of the day, I wore a regular housedress, and that about sums up the amount of fanfare the occasion won.

Not all the family was present, because of the war. All around us, men were disappearing. On trips into town, you'd hardly see a man who didn't have white hair, and all the boys wore looks of grim determination as they waited to be old enough to go get themselves killed. My brother Junior had been drafted, and he was about the least combat-ready man I could imagine: he wasn't one for taking directions, and he had trouble meeting a person's eye when he was forced into conversation. John Charlie was old enough he didn't have to go, but a man like him is always waiting for a chance to prove himself, and the smoke hadn't cleared over Pearl Harbor before he was lining up to volunteer. Even my sister Edith joined the WAC. She was spending time in North Africa cutting strips of gauze and mopping the heads of feverish soldiers who suddenly found themselves missing limbs.

But Karol had a 4-F deferral on account of being blind in one eye, and after we married he got a 2-C as well, since he was now considered "necessary agricultural labor." The very day of the wedding, I moved in with him in the tiny house across the lane. There was room for little more than a bed and a table and chairs, and there was no kitchen or outhouse of its own, but I was happy enough with the exchange. My mother told me that it was better than what she'd had when she married my father, leaving behind forever her family and friends in Ohio. The main house, where we still took all our meals, had once been an even smaller shack than ours. I should consider myself lucky, she said. I did.

I was luckier still when, a few years later, Karol and I were able to buy the farm. After my oldest brother Herb became a minister and moved up to Bethalto, it was assumed that Junior would be the one to take over. But he came home from the war touched in the head, silent and strange and given to unexpected rages that left my father bruised from trying to restrain him, and when a few years later he hopped a train and disappeared, my parents moved to Edwardsville, and Karol and I borrowed enough from the bank to purchase the whole property flat-out. There wasn't any argument from my sisters: Iris had married an accountant and lived in town, Rena had the dairy farm with John Charlie, and Edith was enrolled in a college up in Chicago. They'd all moved on, and I had stayed. Now my reward was to know that I could stay there forever. My future was clear: it would be more of the same as far as the eye could see.

As far as the eye could see turned out to be a decade. Then Karol died, and nothing felt certain. Even with the livestock gone, it was too much for one person. Between Karol and me, we'd assumed the regular roles: I tended the chickens; I cooked and cleaned; I kept the house and garden and raised our children. Karol disked the fields; he tilled and planted. He did the buying of seed and fertilizer and pesticides. I had the house and the space right around it to care for. He had all those acres that made us an income.

Now I was on my own.

The day after the funeral, Rena and Iris stopped by the house. They'd both been over separately every day since Karol died, but this time they had business to discuss—I could tell by the way Iris stood looking out the window while Rena took Joe and Debbie outside. I poured coffee and set out on the table every last one of the half dozen coffee cakes that neighbors had brought over during the past few days. Then I sat down and cut myself a piece. The shock of Karol's death had taken away my appetite, but having people in the house all the time made me want to eat.

When Rena came back inside, she nodded at Iris and the two of them sat. It was like this, Rena said: I needed a man to help me run the farm. She looked at Iris. That's right, Iris said.

I took a big bite of the coffee cake and washed it down with some coffee. "I'm surprised you didn't bring Edith, too."

Rena sighed heavily. "What good's she with this kind of business? It isn't flowers, she don't know a thing." After Chicago, Edith had moved back to Edwardsville and opened a flower shop. I wasn't sure she cared all that much about flowers for their own sake, but it was a business and she was making a living. What Rena meant was that Edith wasn't married herself, and so wasn't likely to counsel me on the importance of having a man to run things.

"One day he's been buried," I said and took another bite.

Iris looked at me pityingly. Rena shook her head. "We're not saying you can't grieve your husband, Hazel. Why, hell, if John Charlie were to keel over tomorrow—"

"—or Walt," Iris added.

"—I'd be a mess. Iris would, too. You're handling this better than anyone could expect. Look at you." Rena pointed her fork at me. She still hadn't taken a bite of the coffee cake, but the fork was useful for emphasis. "You've got dry eyes. You're eating real good, your kids are outside playing in the leaves. This is a real victory, Hazel. You should be proud of yourself."

Iris shook her head and sighed. "Just think what Ma would've done in your position. She'd have been weeping in a corner. She'd have torn out her hair by the handful."

I glanced at the corner, as if I might see our dead mother there. "But I need to get a man to sort things out," I said.

"The way I see it," Rena said, "you've got two possibilities. The first one is, John Charlie steps in for a little while. You know he's got a head for this kind of thing, and we're happy to do it. We want to help you any way we can." She paused to allow me to acknowledge the show of charity. "But long-term, now, Hazel, I just don't know. You've got to get someone you trust, that's the idea. Because it's not simply paying someone to bring in the harvest, you've got to consider what's happening market-wise, what and where to plant, all that. And the truth of it is—" She glanced at Iris.

"—you've got chances yet," Iris finished. She tilted her head, pursed her lips in thought. "Forty-three's not so young, but it's not so old, either. You're going to have some fellows knocking on your door, and I know it's early, but you've got to consider the possibility—"

"You just have to stay open to the idea."

The three of us were spaced out around the table, but Iris and Rena both had their backs to the window, so I was the only one who saw my son go zipping by right then with Debbie in pursuit. They were both blurs of motion, knees and elbows whipping back and forth like pistons on one of those new and modern machines that would take us all into the future. It didn't matter that I couldn't see their faces; they were so caught up in their play that I knew they were happy. Even in the midst of their grief, they'd found something to distract them, a thoughtless kind of freedom that was available only to them. The distractions I was being offered wouldn't bring me any happiness: a ragged old bachelor looking for a home ready-made and a deed to sign his name on. And if not that, then I had to figure it all out on my own: selling off the tractor, finding a renter to farm the land, buying groceries and paying taxes and saving up enough for indoor plumbing so we wouldn't be the only place in a ten-mile radius that had an outhouse forever. "I'm going to figure it out," I said, and swept a hand around the kitchen. I intended to say more, but instead put my hands over my face and cried. And my sisters, in the way that was known to us, sipped their coffee and said nothing, and waited for me to be done.

*   *   *

The first Christmas Karol was gone, Lydie phoned me in early December and said that George would help me and the kids get our tree if we wanted to come over and choose it. "That's one thing I don't want you worrying about," she said. "Heaven knows you've got enough else to deal with."

She and George had a couple of acres that were set aside for Christmas trees. Most of the neighbors and a good number of folks from town drove out every year. They'd call ahead and George would come meet them out front to lend them a saw. Then they'd go pick out their favorite tree, pay him five dollars, and that was that.

Our family had gone every year when Karol was alive. The four of us would round the barn in a little clump. Then the kids would zip ahead, Debbie tripping over her own shoes trying to keep up with Joe, who always ran straight to some tree in the distance that looked perfect until you got up close and saw that the back half was all patchy. When we finally found one that was pretty full all around, Karol would lie down on the ground in his big quilted coat and start sawing while Joe or I held the trunk steady and Debbie danced around with glee.

When Lydie called with her offer, I hadn't got around yet to thinking about how I'd manage the tree on my own. It had been less than two months since the funeral, and I was worried about all kinds of things, not least of all money. The tractor was still in the barn, and I was relying on John Charlie to help me find a renter on good terms. A Christmas tree hadn't even figured on my list of considerations, so I was grateful to Lydie for thinking of it. I thanked her and said we'd be over that weekend.

Saturday came, and we piled in the car and went out to their place in the late morning. The weather was warm, more like it had been back in September, not at all like a normal December day. It wasn't sunny, but there was a particular kind of light through the clouds that made every-thing look as if it'd been baked in egg wash. The ground was soft, and I remember thinking that this must be what Christmas feels like in Flor-ida, all swampy and humid and nothing quite as it should be. I wouldn't have been all that surprised to see an alligator waddling over the lawn.

Lydie met us out front and invited us inside for cookies and chocolate milk. "Too warm for hot chocolate," she said. Joe grabbed two cookies and started for the stairs. The two Hughes boys were already thumping around overhead.

"Sit down and eat those," I told him, "or leave them here. I won't have you getting crumbs in the carpets."

But Lydie waved him off. "Let him go play. He won't do any harm that hasn't already been done." She looked at Joe, and he ran off to find Bobby and Gene. Debbie watched him go, trying to decide whether to chase after him or not. The thought of those boys was too much for her, though, and she sat down at the table while Lydie poured her some chocolate milk. "Make yourself comfy," Lydie said, and pushed the plate of cookies my way.

I took a pinwheel for myself and let Debbie choose a big sugar cookie in the shape of a snowman. It was clear that the treats had been arranged on this Christmas platter especially for us, but instead of appreciating the gesture I felt a stab of resentment that Lydie's life was collected enough that she could remember to do such things, whereas mine was so full of money concerns and worry that I hadn't even remembered we'd need a Christmas tree.

"You and your brother both like those sugar cookies, huh?" Lydie said, watching Debbie. My daughter looked back at her with big eyes, like she'd never seen her before. She set the cookie down on the table and put her hands around the glass of milk. Lydie gave a big sigh and turned to me. "The trees don't look too good this year, Hazel. I'm almost embarrassed to have you take one. It's this odd weather. The needles are going brown, not sure what season it is."

"Doesn't matter," I told her. "I'm just grateful for your thinking of us. If you hadn't called, I don't know. I guess we would've put some tinsel on a lamp and called it a tree."

Debbie gave me a horrified look.

"Your mother's just joking," Lydie said, pushing the cookie plate toward her.

I looked down at the one still on the plate in front of me. I felt sick to my stomach, afraid Lydie was going to say something about how awful it must be, the first Christmas alone. People kept saying things like that—*How terrible*, and, *Oh, you poor thing*. Or: *Oh, those poor dears*— talking about Joe and Debbie. The poor fatherless dears. I hadn't once cried in front of them, not even at the funeral. I didn't want to start now.

But Lydie only talked about the weather for as long as it took for Debbie to eat a second cookie, and when we went outside again, George was waiting. He held a saw at his side, its teeth dull in the cloudy light. In his other hand was a cigarette smoked halfway down to the filter. He stubbed it out on the sole of his shoe as soon as he heard the door, and I was surprised by the good balance he had, swinging his foot up to put out the cigarette without needing to lean against anything. There was a natural grace about it, like a squirrel leaping from one tree to another and immediately falling still.

Joe came charging through the door, cheeks flushed, and the three of us followed George toward the hill slanting up behind the house. As soon as we'd gone a dozen yards, Joe was running. Debbie went chasing after him, her legs kicking out to the sides and her arms flying in that awkward way she ran when she was a child, like she had never quite gotten a handle on it.

That left George and me to walk alone over the grass. For a long minute, the only sound was our feet pressing into the earth. There weren't any birds. Joe and Debbie shouted something to each other, and then it was silent again. At last the quiet got too heavy, and I said, "It's kind of you to help us out. I bet Lydie didn't give you much of a choice in the matter."

He shrugged. "It's not any bother. You've got enough else to take care of, this time of year." He squinted at my son and daughter running over the grass. "They're doing all right."

"Yes," I agreed.

We walked on in silence another few minutes. Joe called out that they'd found a good one, and we went over that way. When we got up close, I saw that it had an uneven top and a big empty patch on one side.

"It's kind of ugly," Joe said, "but the rest are, too."

"Joseph Wisniewski," I said sharply.

George was standing with the saw dangling at his side. "We can find you a better-looking tree than that," he said. "Not that you chose a bad one, son, but you're right. These trees here, they're Scotch pines, and they haven't been good this year."

"Have you got better ones?" Joe asked.

George gestured at a stand of trees behind the barn. "There's some young white pines growing back there. They're doing better than the farmed ones. It's shadier, so they're about the only ones that don't look ready to keel over." He glanced at me right after he said that and gave a short nod. It was to acknowledge his mistake in speaking lightly of death. But he didn't go rigid with embarrassment or try to apologize, and I was relieved to have the moment pass by.

"So we can go cut down one of *those* trees?" Debbie asked, sensing adventure.

"Sure you can."

Turning to George, I said, "Won't it bother Lydie? I don't know how I'd feel about someone poaching my woods."

"I don't see why it should bother her any, since it was my idea. Might be different if you went in there with an ax in the middle of the night."

I bit my lip and looked at Joe and Debbie, considering whether or not to accept the offer. It didn't seem quite right—like pulling the boards off the front of someone's house for firewood. But Joe was antsy, ready to tear off into what must have looked like a forest to him, and Debbie had her hands clasped like she was getting ready to beg God for the greatest gift of her life. They knew there was something just a bit outside the law in the idea, and that made it all the more appealing. "All right," I said at last. "But you will wait for Mr. Hughes to point out the tree he has in mind."

The four of us set off down the rows of brown trees. Now that we'd decided to search for something better, the Scotch pines looked even worse, patchy and skinny. I didn't want one of them standing in my living room. My children had gone through enough in the last few months and the least they deserved, I reasoned, was a good-looking tree, one with soft green needles and sturdy branches and a nice straight top to set the angel on.

We walked in the direction of the barn. It looked the same as ours from the outside, a faded red gone to gray around the bottom, with a corrugated tin roof and a big door that slid open on the side. I could picture what was inside, too: the tractors and combine, the harrow and the cultivator and the manure spreader. There would be bales of hay, bags of seed and fertilizer, rakes and shovels, a Pincor push lawn mower.

I hadn't once been in our barn since Karol's funeral, not since the day the transport trucks came and took away all the livestock. Slowly, the children and I had been reclaiming the house, reconfiguring its space for a family of three. But I feared the dark interior of the barn, the crater that was left in Karol's absence.

Now here we were with George Hughes, and if anyone had seen us, they'd have thought we were a family, normal as could be. We trekked back into the little woods and picked out a tree, and George lay down on the ground to work at it with the saw. I was standing above, holding the trunk still, when my glance fell on him and then darted away. But I looked again, at his eyes this time, a long look that held while the children stood dancing around. Something was suddenly different; we recognized it and they didn't. Like burying a seed in the ground and not knowing what kind it is, but knowing for certain that it will grow.

*   *   *

The winter after Karol died was the longest I'd ever known. In the mornings, I'd stand on the porch watching Joe and Debbie as they went down the lane to catch the bus. It was so cold that I could see my breath, but I'd stay out there, anyway, watching them turn onto the road and then disappear from view. A few minutes passed and then I'd see the bus drive by. Even still, I remained there until my teeth were chattering and my toes and fingers had lost all feeling. I liked being on the porch because it was a summer place, a spring and autumn place—standing there in the winter, it was stripped of memory.

Eventually, I'd go in and warm my hands in the dishwater as I cleaned up the breakfast mess. I'd collect dirty laundry from the bedrooms, sweep and vacuum, get some ironing done. I was trying to keep busy because I knew that unless I called Rena or somebody else, I'd be surrounded by silence until the afternoon. Some days, I did call my sister and either she would come down or I'd drive up to her place. Every week or so, we went into town together and that was enough to keep the day from collapsing in on me, to keep the weight of the house settled firmly on its foundations rather than on my chest, as it often felt.

The problem was that winter was always a slow time on the farm, and you had to work to fill the hours. Karol and I hadn't had this time to ourselves for a long while—until this year, I'd always had either Debbie or Joe at home. But we'd still found more hours alone during the winter than in any other season, and so the cold weather had always done for our marriage what spring did for the earth: it renewed us. When the children were young enough to still take naps, Karol and I would find ourselves going to bed at the same time, undressing quickly and jumping under the covers, climbing our feet up each other's legs, the toes frozen under the chilly flannel. We'd make love quickly and then lie together in the warm bed, making use of the hour or two before naptime was over.

We also spent time doing other things we didn't do much in the busier seasons. For my part, I socialized: Rena would come by, or Lydie, or any of the other neighbors, and we would piece together quilts or embroider pillowcases. Karol took up a hobby. One day during the third or fourth year of our marriage, he came home from a trip into town with a set of watercolors he'd purchased. I didn't know what to think. It was spring when he got them and they sat unused for months in a desk drawer, but the next winter, he took them out and began teaching himself to paint. It became a routine: after feeding the cows and hogs, he'd wrap himself up in scarves and don another sweater and then retreat upstairs with his paints and paper. On the coldest days, he'd come down every half hour or so to let his fingers thaw out. Then he'd go back upstairs to continue this work that no one had asked for, work that he did only because there was a part of him that was tuned to the frequency of beauty rather than of usefulness, and this was the only way he had of working it out.

I was interested in his paintings and I wanted to love them, but I never did. He painted only landscapes, and those landscapes were too recognizable for my taste: they were the same views I had out the windows of the house, or standing in the yard looking south or east. I could appreciate the way he captured clouds and weak winter light, but I would have rather seen something less familiar. "Why don't you paint the sea?" I asked him. "Why don't you paint a castle on a hill?" He just shook his head irritably. "I don't know those places," he'd reply. "I can't picture them, Hazel."

Of course he didn't know them, and I didn't, either. But I wanted to see how he'd imagine a place he had never seen, and probably never would. Viewing his latest painting of our farm in winter, I'd feel myself growing impatient at the idea that he didn't use those lonely hours upstairs for some greater purpose. I didn't have any talent for painting or music or anything more creative than needlework, but I was certain that if I did, I wouldn't have wasted it contemplating the same cloudy sky, the same bleached barn, all those things I'd been seeing every day through every year of my life.

The truth was that I was disappointed in Karol's paintings. They were windows into his soul, yet it turned out that what they revealed was completely familiar. I'd asked him about his earlier life, and he always said it wasn't all that different from ours—he'd grown up on a dairy farm in southern Wisconsin, where his mother worked as both dairymaid and cook in the household of a cousin or second cousin, I was never sure which. Karol's Polish father had died after being pitched from a horse. Karol had gone out to work when he was thirteen years old and kept moving for years, doing the same work as he did now, he said—the only difference was that he'd never before owned the land he plowed. To me, it didn't seem the same at all. He'd moved all over Wisconsin and Illinois, and I knew he'd picked up odd jobs in other industries as well. He'd even lived in Chicago for short stretches. Surely his past offered up more exotic things than he was painting.

But if he had images stored up from this previous period, they didn't come out in his pictures. All those hours upstairs, and he managed to produce only a perfect mirror of the view outside the window, just as gray and flat, just as limited. I was in some of them, a tiny figure standing in a bottom corner with her back turned, a vague small shape walking down the road in the middle distance.

*　　*　　*

One morning at the end of winter, George stopped by. It was laundry day, and I had a basket of sheets and towels to hang up on the line. I'd woken Joe and Debbie early that morning to make sure they'd have time to strip the bedding and take it down to the cellar before running off to catch the bus to school. Debbie dumped her clothes by the door on the porch floor and came into the kitchen, where I was frying some eggs. "I can't *lift* it," she whined, and then Joe ran in complaining that she had taken his *Flash* comic book, which she declared wasn't true. I hadn't gotten any plates on the table or put the bread in to toast; I had lunches to gather, and we were out of wax paper; Debbie couldn't find the sweater she wanted to wear, the green-and-white one that didn't itch, the one Iris had given her for Christmas. I was near screaming, and it wasn't yet eight in the morning. "Joe, you help your sister," I told him. "I've got a full day of washing ahead of me, and you'll do your part if you want to have any sheets to sleep on tonight." They went off, grumbling. I slid the eggs onto a plate. I pulled two thin towels from a kitchen drawer and wrapped up the bologna sandwiches. Somehow they caught the bus and I got through the morning.

By the time George peeled off the main road in his truck and came rolling up the lane, I'd already washed the sheets and was hanging them on the line. It was mid-February and somewhere about ten degrees above freezing. The snow that remained in the elbows of trees was melting, leaving darkened streaks down the trunks. No green had emerged, but that melt was the first indication of spring, and it was sunny enough and there was a good enough breeze that I thought most of the laundry would be dry by sundown. In other words, I was feeling good—happier than I had been in months. All the cold days of winter, the silence of the house had been like my mother when she would go into her dark periods; I'd felt as if I were tiptoeing around it, trying not to get noticed in case it turned its anger upon me. Now the silence was something different, and that difference was good.

George and Lydie lived a half mile away down Sumner, on the other side of a small hill with their barn and the stand of trees in between, so even in the winter, their house wasn't clearly visible. But the truck was coming from the direction of town, and I didn't expect it to turn up my lane. When it did, I dropped a pillowcase in the basket and started across the grass.

A moment later George stepped down out of the driver's seat and pulled a cigarette from behind his ear. "Laundry day, is it?"

My hands were cold from handling the wet sheets. I tucked them under my arms and stood back on my heels. "First good-weather day we've had in a while, so I thought I'd make use of it."

"Lydie's telling me we need to take down the storm windows and put up the screens. I told her let's wait and see."

"It's early yet."

"That's right."

We stood quietly for a moment, and I waited for George to tell me his business. I'd seen him several times during the winter, but the two of us had never once been alone since the day we cut down the tree. Once a week or so, Lydie would bring her stitching to my house and we'd work together as we chatted. Or I might go to their place and we'd eat dinner together while the children were at school, and then Lydie and I would watch *As the World Turns* and afterward maybe play a few hands of gin rummy. If Rena was there, she'd talk George into sitting down to play euchre, but he often seemed to have business elsewhere, outside or in the barn. Sometimes the memory of that afternoon in December would come to me, but it was like the flash of light off a mirror when a person's playing tricks, brilliant and bewildering: Joe and Debbie skipping around; the stillness of the woods; the sharp smell of pine resin when the saw's teeth bit into the trunk. If George ever thought about that moment, he didn't let it show.

Now, he felt around in his pocket for matches. "I was driving back from town," he said, and finding the matches, he pulled one from the box and lit it. "Saw you out here from down the road and thought I'd come by and see how you're doing."

So he had no reason for stopping by, after all. I was happy for it, in spite of myself. "Doing all right," I said. "Glad that spring's finally coming."

He nodded. I watched him shake the box of matches and look around, having run out of things to say. The matchbox was dark blue and had the white outline of a running horse, the same kind we had in the house, the same kind that Karol had always kept in his pocket. Watching George tuck it back into his jacket, I saw my husband in his place, saw him pausing for the few minutes it took to smoke a cigarette before heading out for the morning's work, saw myself watching from the kitchen window and wondering what he was thinking about just then, what he thought about all day as he rode the tractor back and forth in even rows over the fields.

"It's been a spell since we've heard from you," George said.

I didn't mention that I'd seen Lydie only a few days before. She'd called ahead—she always called ahead—and then come over in the morning with a plate of cinnamon rolls. We'd talked about Joe's third-grade teacher, a stern and weather-beaten old woman Gene had had a few years before. I was getting notes sent home about Joe acting up in class, and Lydie assured me that it was nothing to get worked up about, that Mrs. Toddy ran a tight ship. I'd been happy in Lydie's company, grateful that she'd pushed all the silence out of the house. I hadn't thought about George at all.

"It feels long because it's February," I said to him now.

"Shortest month on the calendar, longest month to get through." He took a long pull on the cigarette and turned to blow the smoke downwind. "But you made it through all right here? You've got folks to call on you, aside from Lydie and me?"

"My sisters have been out, when the weather doesn't keep them. Rena's close by, you know, and Edith and Iris are right in town. And Herb, he and his family come down every now and then."

"That's good you've got your family around."

"It's a blessing."

Another pause, and I tried to figure out if it made me uneasy to stand there, making small talk with him. Three separate times in the past few months, I'd gotten visits from old bachelors figuring they'd audition for Karol's place, exactly as my sisters had predicted, but this was something different. George wasn't offering anything, or asking for it, either. He just looked kind and curious and a little bashful, as a person not used to paying social visits always appears when they're struggling through a conversation. I believed what he said: that it had simply popped into his mind as he was driving back from town that he should stop off and see how I was doing.

George threw down his cigarette butt and mashed it into the grass. "I won't keep you any longer. If you need anything, you just holler." He turned a half step away, putting one hand on the open door of his truck. "Neighbors want to be there," he said. "You know that, Hazel, don't you?"

I did, I told him.

"But we don't want to push."

I wanted to tell him that I knew that, too. We weren't people who often stopped by unannounced. When we saw lights burning in a neighbor's windows at night, we felt a quiet satisfaction that they were warm and safe in their home, and then we kept on driving to our own dark house. Neighbors were friends, but the love we gave them was not the same we gave to those who shared our same roof. The love between neighbors was like a walnut kernel. Politeness was its hard shell.

I wanted to say all that, but tears were pricking my eyes, and so the thing I wanted most of all was for George to get up into his truck and drive away. "Thank you for stopping by," I said, backing up a step, and then one more. "Tell Lydie I said hello."

"I'll do that," he said, touching a hand to his forehead. His head was bare, his ears sticking out under little tufts of hair. He wasn't wearing a hat, but the gesture worked without it.

7

As winter began to melt into spring, I knew that it was time to deal with the machinery in the barn. The door was padlocked, the key in a drawer in the kitchen. I hadn't taken it out since October, though I saw it often enough, sliding around with the tape and scissors and twine. I'd half expected Joe to sneak it out to have a look around the barn. The cats were still out there: they came and went through the gap between the walls and the ground. Joe would go in and find their shining eyes in the dark and he wouldn't be afraid. He was a nine-year-old boy, ready to climb up into the seat of the tractor and pretend he was driving it, ready to build obstacle courses in the empty stalls.

Or so I figured. But the barn must have seemed to him to be full of ghosts, because the key remained untouched all through the late fall and winter. I was in no hurry to put it to use, either. Selling the machinery was going to be harder than anything I'd done yet, harder even than planning Karol's funeral. In the witching hour of grief, choosing the outfit for burial had been a mechanical act: this shirt, those pants. It was the same with the coffin. Nothing seemed real. Then his body was laid in the dark wood box I chose, and I hadn't even seen it covered with dirt before I let myself be led away, a hand at my back, I didn't know whose.

All through the winter, whenever I looked out over the empty fields, I'd tell myself that they were still ours, and I would believe it. Karol had gone away somewhere, he'd had enough of the cold, but come spring he'd return. The thin light of March would flutter down and from far off I'd see it glinting off his sandy hair, rising like moths into the rain-smelling air. Underground, the seeds would put out their first green shoots, and one night we'd leave the windows cracked and in the morning we'd wake under dew-soaked quilts, and the birds would find their voices again, and the new year would begin.

This was only fantasy, of course, and like all fantasies, it lost its power the more often I imagined it. The truth was that the fields still belonged to me on paper, but they weren't really mine. Just after the New Year, John Charlie had told me Nate Grisham was interested in renting. Nate had too many sons and not enough land, and he lived close enough that he made sense as a renter. So I'd signed the paperwork for a one-year lease, and now that it was spring, in the mornings I'd see one of Nate's boys seated on a tractor, riding right up to within a dozen yards of the house. I could look out the kitchen window at the young man riding his bright green John Deere like a conquering knight, and if he saw me, he might lift his hand and wave. A neighborly gesture, but unsettling.

My own tractor was currently sitting unused in the barn. Nate wasn't interested in purchasing, and he didn't want to get in the habit of using it and then find himself in a bind when I sold it off. I hadn't yet even tried. John Charlie had bothered me about it, but I thought of the conversation I'd had with Rena and Iris and figured I'd reached the end of asking for help. Moving forward, all the decisions would be mine, so it was best to start now. Winter had passed, and the earth was warming. There was some symbolism there, and you didn't have to try very hard to understand what it was.

* * *

I called the office of the co-op and credit union downtown and spoke to someone named Mr. Freese. I didn't ask for his first name, and he didn't tell me. Karol had always handled the business in town. Mr. Freese said he'd known Karol, and he sure was sorry he hadn't made it out for the funeral. The way he spoke made me think he hadn't thought very much about it, that maybe he'd forgotten until now that someone named Karol had once existed and now was dead.

He told me he wanted to come out to the farm to check over the equipment and make sure everything was in good shape—that we'd seen to oiling the chains and keeping the engine clean. I bit my tongue to keep from asking if he thought Karol was in the habit of burning money, which is what a man did when he let his tractor upkeep slip. Come on out, I told Mr. Freese, any day of the week.

He showed up on a Friday morning, driving a red-and-white Ford

Fairlane that looked as if it had never been out of town—the dirt along the bottom was newly applied. "Nice bit of land you've got here," he said as he opened the door and got out. He squinted at the fields that lay bright as silver all around. We'd had a full week of heavy rain, and there were giant puddles as far as you could see.

"Those aren't our fields out that way." I lifted my hand in the direction he was looking. It bothered me the way he was peering around, like all this was for sale, too, and not just the equipment. "Across the road belongs to the Weavers. That's their house you see through the trees over there."

"They talked to you about buying some land?"

"I'm not interested in selling."

"Sure, sure. You've had a lot to deal with this year." It was the kind of thing people often said to me in sympathy, but coming from him, it was flimsy. He thought I was distracted by grief and would come around to reality at some point or another: I would sell off and move out. He wanted this for no reason but that it was the way sensible women might be expected to act. I got the feeling he'd already decided I wasn't a sensible woman. "It was your late husband's land?"

"He did the work on it, if that's what you mean."

Mr. Freese gave me a patient smile. "I was referring to the deed. Did it come down to you from his family, or was it on your side, Mrs. Wisniewski?" He handled the name without any trouble, as if he had practiced saying it during the drive out from town.

"It's from my side," I told him.

"Well, now," Mr. Freese said after a moment. "Should we go on and take a look at that John Deere?"

I led the way to the barn, slid the lock from the iron latch, and pulled back the door. Inside, old hay carpeted the ground, and a fusty smell clung to the air. The cats were slinking silently between the big machines, their pupils wide in the dark.

Mr. Freese started looking it all over. Dipping out of sight behind the planter, he observed, "A piece like this is perfectly fine for what you've got out here. Some of the bigger farms now, they've got these new grain drills. You seen them?"

I told him I hadn't. Didn't have any interest in them, either, though I kept that to myself. I didn't like him, and I wanted him to do the inventory quickly and not talk to me about it. But he took his time, walking up to each piece and then stepping back to peer at it like he was waiting for it to perform some sort of magic trick.

My eyes went back and forth between him and a pair of Karol's gloves. One of them lay on the ground and the other was dangling from the bench above it, somehow not having fallen during all those months. After a minute of silence that seemed to have its own kind of thudding heartbeat, I went over and knocked it from its hold. Mr. Freese turned to give me a curious smile and asked if something was the matter.

"It's just a mess in here, is all." I stooped to pick up the gloves. I had a very clear image of Karol wearing them as he backed out of the barn one spring day—was it only a year ago?—with his shoulders hunched, dragging an eighty-pound sack of seed to fill the spreader.

Mr. Freese turned his head one way and then the other. He was up in the tractor seat now, examining the steering wheel, the clutch, the brakes.

"You're particular," I said.

"It's a particular process." He climbed down carefully and went around the front to look at the engine. At last, he said he guessed he was just about done. Closing his notepad and tucking his pencil into the back pocket of his trousers, he swept his arm toward the door, but I told him to go on so I could lock up. When I met him at his car, he was gazing at the fields across the lane. He turned and smiled. "I'm going to get together some figures and see what kind of deal we can strike for the whole lot," he said. "How's that sound?"

"Just give me a call when you have a number."

"We're going to look out for you, Mrs. Wisniewski. Don't you worry."

I nodded and then stayed on the lawn, watching him go. That's a custom I've always appreciated: the person driving away can only guess whether you're seeing them off as a friendly gesture or whether you're checking to make sure they're good and gone.

*   *   *

That night I had a dream I was a contestant on *I've Got a Secret*. I was scheduled to go up after the man who revealed he had witnessed Lincoln's assassination. I never saw that episode; I only heard about it from Iris, who watched more television than anyone I knew. But I'd seen the show and could fill in the gaps. I stood behind a curtain, waiting my turn, and watched Jayne Meadows and Bill Cullen and everyone sitting in a line behind the desk while Garry Moore interviewed a little boy. Of course, when he was on the show, he was an old man, so old that his skin hung off the bottom of his chin and his eyes were watery. They'd put a picture of him in the paper after the episode aired, and then again a few months later when he died.

But in my dream he was a little boy, about the age he must have been when he heard a loud shot and darted his eyes across the theater to see a mad scramble around the fallen president. Sitting in the seat beside Garry Moore, he swung his legs and twisted his hands in his lap. He sat forward on the edge of the seat, and even then his feet didn't touch the ground. In answer to one of Jayne Meadows's questions, he said he had to go to the bathroom, and everyone in the audience laughed. For shame, I thought, making this little child talk about such a violent event. I was looking right at him and saw how scared he was, how much he didn't want to answer the questions, how he had to think about each one and then come up with a response he thought the host and the panelists and all the people sitting in the audience wanted to hear, all of them craning their necks forward to make sure they didn't miss a word.

I had a terrible feeling that my secret would sound dull after his was revealed. Garry Moore would introduce me and the panelists would ask questions, and I'd sit there knowing it was nothing they would care about. In fact, it was so uninteresting that I'd already forgotten it myself. The panelists kept asking questions, one after another. I could see the smile on Garry Moore's face, so insistent it looked frightening. But I kept watching the boy as he grew more and more anxious, and it gradually dawned on me that the boy was Joe. The moment I realized it, he looked up, cocked his hand at me, and shot a fake gun—one shot: *pow!*—with a firm, small sound like a cherry pit dropping into a tin pan.

I woke up just as quickly as if one of my children was shaking me. It was that time between night and morning, the time you start calling early rather than late, and the sky was that particular shade of dark turquoise that comes a half hour before the sun starts its slow climb over the horizon. It gives lie to the old saying, "It's always darkest before the dawn." I remember my mother telling that to a neighbor when the woman was going through a time. That's what we called it then, as if adding the word *hard* could make it worse. I didn't know then what this neighbor woman had experienced, only that she had hovering around her that particular air that children learn early to consider with awe. It was grief, though that's not what I would have called it then. I didn't know that she had recently lost her third child in the womb; I pieced that together a few years later. But that afternoon she sat on the porch with my mother, neither of them doing anything with their hands— not shelling peas or darning shirts or peeling potatoes—and when my mother spoke those words about the world being darkest before the dawn, the other woman blinked at her and said, "Seems to me that such a point comes right in the middle of the night."

True enough. I lay in bed awhile and watched the sky turn blue and violet by degrees. With windows on two sides, I could turn one way and see night and then turn the other way and see dawn. It was a tame sunrise, the sun pale as pancake batter spreading over the sky. Once the room was half lit, I swung my legs over the side of the mattress and padded to the kitchen in my slippers to start the coffee.

As I measured out the grounds and filled the pot, a sudden quiver of sadness ran through me. I felt as if I had a deep well inside me, so deep that if you hollered down into it, all you'd get back were echoes. It wasn't like those moments when I suddenly missed Karol. The feeling then was more like losing my stomach, a pendulum swing that left me nauseous. This was more deep-rooted and lasting. Usually I enjoyed this time on weekend mornings, knowing that Joe and Debbie wouldn't be awake yet for hours, and I could sit with my coffee and the paper, easing into the morning instead of running at it full force.

But this morning, that sadness opened up inside me, and I suddenly needed to be near someone I loved. While the coffee gurgled in the pot,

I climbed the stairs and crossed the landing to Debbie's room. She was sleeping deeply, her hair bunched around her shoulders and one arm outstretched like a swimmer reaching for the edge of a boat. She looked as if she'd been caught unawares by sleep and might be angry when she woke up and learned of the trick. Next door, her brother was an imitation of Jesus on the cross, arms flung out in a T and head hanging to the side. I thought of the dream I'd had, of his turning to shoot me with his little gun. That wasn't the part that mattered. What mattered was that he was the child who'd witnessed a death, long ago, in another century. He'd seen violence and was coming to tell me what it was.

No, he was my son sleeping with his mouth, his whole face, open to the world. And his sister in the next room, scowling in her sleep. They were vulnerable things. It was a wonder that I was left alone to look after them, that this was the one thing no one would think to contest.

*   *   *

Almost a week passed before I heard from Mr. Freese. He called and apologized for how long it had taken to get in touch. He'd been waiting to hear back from Dewey Henderson, he said—Did I know Dewey? Up near Hamel with close on three hundred acres?—to see whether he really did want the tractor, after all. Dewey thought he might be in need of it, but he wasn't sure what he was willing to pay. "When will he be sure?" I asked.

"When we lower the price, I expect." Mr. Freese punctuated the sentence with a syllable of laughter.

I hadn't realized we had a price to begin with. I'd been left out of the process. This should have made me angry, and I tried to feel that way, but instead I felt a kind of horror at the thought of someone named Dewey coming to drive away that tractor. It was Karol's. Any other year, he'd have been out in the barn weeks ago, getting everything cleaned and oiled. He'd be driving that tractor out of the barn each morning like a train conductor.

I told Mr. Freese that I'd changed my mind—I wasn't ready to sell, not just yet.

He was quiet a moment. Then he asked who I had helping me. These were difficult matters, he said, real tough questions to sort through on my own.

"Don't I know it," I replied, and then hung up the phone.

*   *   *

March came, and then April was over before I knew it, and then, in mid-May, the cicadas came. The regular ones wouldn't start singing until July, but this was one of those years when the sleeping ones crawled out of the ground and took over the world for a while before disappearing again for a decade or two. They'd been out for a week, whizzing through the air, slamming into the screens of all the windows in the house, when Lydie called me up and said she needed some conversation to fill her ears. "I swear I'm going nuts with these dang bugs screaming."

"I'm doing jam today," I told her. "Been putting it off. But I'd be glad for the company." Out on the porch were several buckets of strawberries waiting to be hulled. They'd come in a little earlier than usual—we'd had a warm spell for several weeks at the end of April—and every day I was out in the garden picking them. I'd just brought up the buckets from the cellar, where I'd been keeping them cool until I could force myself to set aside a morning for making jam. I hated doing it on hot days, and the past several days had been hot. The paper said it wasn't supposed to get warmer than eighty-five, so I figured today was the day.

"Oh, goody," Lydie said, and told me she'd come around after a little while.

By the time she arrived, I was standing at a sink full of floating strawberries, slicing off their heads and dropping them into a pan. "Debbie would think you're brave as an Indian," I said as Lydie stepped inside and shut the door behind her. "Walking all that way. She's scared to death one of those bugs will fly in her face."

"Better her face than her ear."

"She's scared of that, too."

Lydie set her purse down on a chair and stepped up to the sink. "I'd have drove over, but George took the truck down to Theo's."

I nodded. I hadn't seen George other than at church on Sundays, and though I thought I was calm enough about whatever quiet signal had flashed between us, I didn't want to talk about him with Lydie. Handing her a knife, I stepped aside to make room at the sink. A cicada thumped off the screen and spun drunkenly away. "This noise," Lydie said, plucking a floating strawberry out of the water.

"Makes you feel a little crazy," I agreed.

"It's been giving me dreams. Takes me back to when I was working at Curtiss-Wright."

During the war, before she married, Lydie had worked at a mechanics factory in St. Louis, making airplanes. I'd forgotten all about it. Now I listened as she told me about her dream. "It's just like it was back then: I'm seated on a tall stool with a container of bolts set on a little shelf that hangs off the side of the conveyor belt. The metal got poked through with holes and then they'd come up to me, and my job was to put the bolts through the holes and then it went on to the next gal to screw it in."

"Just up there above your head," I interrupted when I saw her looking around for a bowl.

"Thanks," she said, retrieving the bowl from the cabinet. "So anyway, I'm working and working and the girl next to me is talking, but I can't make out a single word cause it's so loud. It's all just a buzz and a whir."

"Sounds like a pretty dull dream."

She laughed. "But see, when I turn to look at her, I realize that she's really a giant bug. It's her that's making the noise, not the machines."

"And then the bolts turn into bugs, too, and start flying up out of your hands?"

"No," she said thoughtfully. "The bolts are just bolts." She reached up to wipe the back of her wrist across her face. It was humid in the kitchen and we hadn't even started boiling the strawberries.

"Maybe you miss working there," I said.

She answered with a shrug. "Maybe," she said. "The work was boring, but that's the only time I ever lived in a city, and it was nice. Every day I'd see a person I hadn't ever seen before and probably wouldn't see again. And taking the bus to work, I liked that, too. I even liked the sound of the garbage collection."

I tried to picture Lydie in a blue cotton work suit, a Lydie sixteen years younger than she was now, boarding a bus with a lunch pail in one hand and a purse in the other. I couldn't quite see it.

Once we got the strawberries boiling, we went out onto the porch with some iced tea to cool off. We'd been out there a few minutes when Nate's tractor came into view. It was a long ways away, on the other side of the field that stretched from the clearing where I burned trash and down over a slight hill. I was used to the sight. I saw it every day. But Lydie squinted at the tractor and asked me how things were working out.

"Good enough," I said. "It doesn't startle me anymore to see him or his boys out there. Three months ago I wouldn't have thought that was possible."

"Nate's a man you can trust."

I nodded. "Trusty, but stubborn." I explained that at the end of winter, he and I had sat down to figure out the best crop plan for the season. I wanted him to turn over more of the cornfields to soy. This was what Karol had been moving toward over the past two years because although the price for soy was more variable, the lows weren't that low and the highs were better than the highs for corn. But Nate wasn't sure—he was a corn and alfalfa man—and in the end, I gave in. Now we had more corn than we'd had in our fields for a while, and I figured by the time it reached its full height in the fall, I'd be so boxed in that I'd have to go up to the second floor of the house to see past my own yard.

I told Lydie that part and she laughed. Every woman around could tell you about the summer when she'd thought she was going crazy with the corn closing in. Maybe men felt that, too, but if they did, I hadn't heard about it.

I got up to go stir the strawberries and add in some more sugar. When I came back out onto the porch, Lydie took up the conversation as if there hadn't been a pause. "That's pretty generous of you."

"What is?"

"Letting Nate make a choice like that. You're the one that'll suffer if he's wrong."

"So will he. We've got a split on the profit."

She nodded, though she looked unconvinced.

The tractor had stopped moving, and I saw a figure climb down from the seat. "It's a strange business," I said, "figuring out where I get my say, and where I don't."

She nodded again without looking at me. We were both watching Nate, who was kicking at something with his shoe, nudging it along the ground. It occurred to me that he might have run over some living thing with the tractor. If he had, I hoped it was dead. I'd once come upon my brother Junior in the act of braining a raccoon with a shovel; he'd left it still moving, screeching in pain, and I'd waited until he disappeared into the house before taking up the shovel and finishing it off myself. "He's a good man," Lydie said, and it took me a moment to understand that she was talking about Nate.

She'd already made this declaration earlier in the conversation, and her repeating it made me suspect that she had something else to say. I figured I might as well say it for her: "Good or bad's not the problem. It's whether I listen to him or he listens to me."

"Yes," she said, "I expect that's right."

* * *

In early July, Nate told me he wouldn't be able to pay the other half of the rent. Not on time, anyway. Not until after the harvest. He came out to the house to tell me, and we stood in the yard because he didn't want to track dirt inside. Overhead, an old oak shook its leaves like a tambourine. Cicadas were droning in the trees behind the barn. These were the regular ones—the others had gone back underground to wait it out another thirteen years. I couldn't imagine that far into the future: my children would both be adults, no longer living at home. And what would I do then? What would my days look like when they were spent all alone?

Nate took off his cap and worked at its bill as he told me he was sorry, he'd thought he'd have the money ready, but he hadn't budgeted correctly. "You know me, Hazel," he said. "You know this doesn't sit right.

I'm going to get you paid just as soon as I can. You've got enough to get through awhile longer?"

I told him I'd figure it out, which put a look on his face like he'd just been punched. There was nothing left for him, though, but to turn away.

After he'd gone, I went inside the house to get the key to the barn. Then I went back outside and pulled open the doors, and I stood in the hot, dry stillness, thinking that everything was recognizable and no longer dear. A single bright beam of sunlight was shooting through a hole near the top of one wall, a stick of light that seemed solid enough you might swing from it, if only you could get up there and grab hold.

Back in the house, I looked up the number for the co-op. The phone rang twice, and Mr. Freese picked up. He told me to come down to the office anytime.

The next morning, I dropped Joe and Debbie at Rena's. My children ran inside, and my sister looked me up and down, eyes narrowing behind the lenses of her glasses. "Don't you look nice," she said. She was thinking, no doubt, that I'd dressed up for Mr. Freese, and it was true, I wanted to appear my best. I'd set my hair the night before, which I normally only did on Saturdays. I didn't want to look like a farmer's wife, with stretched-out curls and chapped red hands. I wanted to look like a woman in control of her future. Rena stepped aside to welcome me into the kitchen. "John Charlie," she said, "don't you think Hazel looks nice?"

He glanced up from the sink, where he'd been drinking a glass of water. "She looks pretty as she ever does," he said with a wink at me. "You're not planning on running off to Hollywood now, are you? Planning to turn yourself into a movie star?"

"Not pretty enough for that," I said, patting my head. One of the curlers had come out during the night, and I'd had to pin up the loose strand behind one ear.

"No, I guess not." John Charlie laughed. "Not for the pictures. But maybe you could get yourself a job in a commercial. Be that mother in the Swiss Crème spot, singing in the cardboard kitchen."

Rena sighed and shook her head. This had been their bit from way back: John Charlie making jokes and my sister pretending to feel em-barrassed for him. Rena was nearly ten years older than me but had married young; she and John Charlie had been together so long it was impossible to know what they really felt about each other anymore.

"You sure you don't want John Charlie to go with you?" Rena asked in a low voice.

I nodded. "I'll be all right on my own." Then I said my good-byes and told her I'd be back around noon. "Take your time," she said. "We'll give them some dinner." I went out to the car, but a moment later, she came chasing after me, waving a ten-dollar bill. "Wait," she said, "wait," though I had already stopped backing up. She handed me the money and asked me to stop by the pharmacy for her. "My back is killing me," she said, and told me to pick up some aspirin. Then, as if it were an afterthought, she told me I might as well get a bottle of Early Times, too, while I was in town. It wasn't any secret that Rena had a whiskey and water every afternoon as she did the ironing, but she pre-tended as if it were.

I took the money and drove off toward town. When I passed my house again, I glanced at it with a strange fear that I'd see a figure at the window, my mother or some other ghost. She and my father had been dead eight years, both killed in a car accident way down in Biloxi, Mississippi, but sometimes the house still seemed like theirs. Of course, I didn't see anything but fluttering curtains.

When I got to the co-op, I parked a few spaces down from the en-trance and took out a tube of lipstick. It was part of the effect I wanted: lipstick the color of holly berries, applied with a perfect clean edge. I made sure it was just right before I went up to the entrance. On the pebbled glass door were the words "Madison County Marketing Co-Operative and Credit Union." Their storage facilities were outside of town; this office was only for money affairs. I knocked once on the door and then went in. Mr. Freese was standing before a filing cabinet the size and shape of a dining-room hutch. The top drawer was open, and he had just been riffling through it.

He said hello and held up one hand, his pink palm facing me like a traffic cop's. I stayed by the door as he continued searching through the files. After a moment, he found the one he wanted and took it over to the only desk in the room. "Please," he said, sweeping his hand toward a chair on the other side, "make yourself comfortable."

Obligingly, I stepped forward and took a seat in the chair. My purse felt heavy and awkward on my lap, so after a moment I moved it to the floor.

"You're looking well, Mrs. Wisniewski." He lifted his chin a little, and I thought of my lipstick, my hair, the way I'd had to search through my closet for a skirt with no slit on the left side because the left leg of my stockings was stitched twice at the knee. I folded my hands together in my lap, to keep myself from raising them to adjust any part of my appearance. "Thank you," I said.

The file he'd taken from the cabinet lay on the desk before him, and for a moment he seemed ready to consult it. Instead he folded his hands and began rubbing the tops of them with his thumbs. "I'm glad you came down to see me today. We've got some matters to talk over, and I like to handle things in person. Much more personal than over the phone. You all on a party line out there?"

I nodded.

"All the more reason, then. You wouldn't want your neighbors hearing all your business, would you?"

"I don't suppose it would matter all that much," I said. "I'm only selling a tractor. It's not exactly keeping books for a mobster."

"No, you're right about that." He chuckled and lifted a hand to his face, rubbing the smooth surface around his mouth. He was not quite the same man in the office that he'd been on the farm. This version had a colder eye, a sort of clinical confidence. I preferred it to the other version because it was truer.

I asked Mr. Freese about looking for buyers. "Selling off Karol's tractor," he replied, "is going to take some time."

"*My* tractor, you mean."

"Now, look, you're clearly a woman with a good head on her shoulders. So I'm going to lay it all out on the line. That tractor you've got out there is in decent shape. It did the trick for Karol"—he paused, seemed to make a decision within himself, and then continued—"and for you, too, I suppose. But it's not top-of-the-line, the tractor or any of the hitches. I might be able to sell them piecemeal, but of course the best situation would be to sell them all together. However, I'm not sure that's going to happen anytime soon. Unless—" Here he stopped and sat back in his chair. He was waiting for me to prompt him to continue, but I didn't feel like giving him the satisfaction. So I sat quietly and tried not to fill in the rest of the sentence.

He cleared his throat. "Unless," he said again, "you sell it all together."

"Sure," I said. "I thought that was the goal from the beginning."

"I'm not talking about the machinery only. I'm talking about selling what's in the barn and the barn itself, too. The farm, Mrs. Wisniewski. I'm talking about selling the farm."

I drew in a sharp breath of air, and the next moment I was laughing. "What in the world would make you believe I wanted to do that?"

He raised his shoulders. "Nothing. In fact, I'm betting you don't. Who would? You and Karol lived there happily for—what? Fifteen years?"

"Just about."

"Well, of course you wouldn't want to leave it, then. And I don't want to pressure you here. But I can tell you that a load of equipment like yours has some real use when the land is right there waiting for it. You have children?"

"Two."

"Sons or daughters?"

"A boy and a girl."

He smiled—a real smile. For the first time, it occurred to me that he might have a wife and children of his own. It didn't necessarily make me like him any better. "Two's a fine number," he said. "Back in the old days, it wouldn't have been enough, but there's the wonder of the modern age for you. No need for seven sons and seven daughters when you've got a John Deere tractor and a washing machine." He paused and took out a pack of cigarettes, raising his eyebrows to see if I minded.

"Go ahead," I said as he rooted around in his pocket for matches.

"But the fact is that you still need someone to drive that tractor. You might not need a whole army of men any longer, but you need at least one. How old is your son?"

"Nine."

"That's a long time before he'll be able to take over things. And that's only if he wants to do it, isn't it? These days, you just don't know. Boys decide they want to do something else. Go to college, work at a bank. Work at a credit union." He stopped to laugh at himself. Pointing one finger upward, he drew a ring around the ceiling, encircling everything that could one day be Joe's. "And in the meanwhile, I guess, you rent out your land. Is that the idea?"

"It is."

He grabbed an ashtray at the front of the desk and dragged it toward him. "To Nate Grisham, I take it?"

Clearly, he already knew all about my situation, but he wanted me to verify it. I had to prove the wisdom of his advice, to show once and for all that it was better to let him do the thinking for me. If I'd gotten into a mess with Nate, it only proved the point. I glanced at my hands folded in my lap, and they looked calmer than I felt. "You don't know our terms," I said carefully.

"No, I don't, not precisely. But we're a credit union here, so I do know the size of the loan he's taken out. And that means I happen to know something about his finances in general." He tapped two fingers on the folder he'd taken from the drawer when I came in.

My eyes wanted to linger on the folder, but I forced them upward, to look Mr. Freese in the eye. "Nate's a good man," I said, parroting Lydie's words from a few months before. And just like then, the pause after I spoke made the words seem meaningless.

"Sure, sure." He nodded patiently.

"And we've signed an agreement. A contract."

"For what period of time, may I ask?"

"For the year."

"You were smart not to commit yourself." I saw him wanting to ask whether I'd asked for those terms on my own, but he shrugged and the question evaporated. "Now, what that means, of course, is that after this year you're free. Free, that is, of commitments that are written down on paper. You've got other commitments, don't you—ones you never signed your name to. And if you don't mind my saying it, I think we can agree that those are the more important promises." He was bearing down on the real purpose now. He lifted a finger in the air and twitched it like the needle on a gauge in your car, telling you the speed and how warm the engine is getting. "Look," he said, "that's fine land you've got out there, and I'm sure that Nate knows it. He'd pay you a good rent if he could. But even at the right price, it wouldn't be much, not when you've got two children to raise. Just a little bit coming in every now and then, two or three times a year."

I thought of Nate walking up to the house, that look on his face when he told me he couldn't pay. He'd flicked his eyes away as he said it. A part of it was shame, but there was something else, too. Politeness. He was giving me a moment of privacy, a few seconds to take in the news that when the money ran out I wouldn't have any more for a long while.

Mr. Freese began explaining how easy it would be to negotiate a sale. He happened to know someone interested in the land, and he would handle the whole thing himself. I didn't need to worry. He gave me numbers, so much per acre, the house, the barn, the machinery I'd come here hoping to sell alone. He added it all up and then flattened it into five digits. It sounded like a lot of money and also like not very much at all. "You want me to give up my home," I said.

Mr. Freese sat back in his chair and folded his hands over his stomach. He didn't have much of a gut, but his pants were pulled up so his palms fitted neatly over the belt buckle. "I expect you'd like it here, if you wanted to settle in town. You have family in Edwardsville, don't you?"

I nodded absentmindedly. I was thinking about Nate again, how we'd been standing in the shade of the tree that Joe and his friends used as first base in their ball games. From above came that shuddering sound as the leaves moved in the wind. Bits of sunlight falling through the branches had scattered over the grass like coins.

"Your family will help you," Mr. Freese said.

"Help me," I repeated.

"Help you get settled. Find a place to stay, find a job."

I'd been lagging behind the conversation, letting Mr. Freese drag the conversation in the direction he wanted to go. My eyes had drifted down to the desktop covered in papers, to the little wire racks with stacks of mail. Now I looked up. "I've already started looking for work."

He raised his eyebrows. "Oh?"

I thought quickly. "My sister owns a flower shop. I may start working there part-time."

"A shop here in town?" I told him the name of the place and he nodded, though he looked unconvinced. "So, then, you've already got a foot in the door."

I didn't, of course. I thought of Lydie working in the Curtiss-Wright factory, how she'd told me she'd returned to it in her dreams. I pictured an assembly line, a long plane wing drifting slowly toward her like a ship. Nate would pay eventually, I was sure of that. It was a matter of having a steady source of income in the meantime. "Mr. Freese," I said, sitting up a little straighter in my chair, "I thank you for your advice. If I were going to take it, I'm sure it would all go as smooth as you said. But since I'm not going to take it, I'd rather talk about something else. Selling that tractor—how about we talk about that?"

He blinked at me for several seconds, a tight smile making his face look like a wrinkled grape. He took out another cigarette and lit it. Breathed in, then blew out the smoke and squinted through the cloud. "Sure," he said. "Of course, it's up to you."

*   *   *

As soon as I was out on the sidewalk, even while I was grinning, I felt the hairs on my arms stand on end. For the first time I saw just how completely the future was balancing on my back—I sensed it there, resting on the point right at the top of my spine. I'd told Mr. Freese that I trusted Nate Grisham. But now I saw that trust wasn't going to be enough.

I was too excited to get in my car right then, so I started walking quickly down the sidewalk, my purse clutched in one hand so it wouldn't swing against my side. Where could I get a job? Where should I look? I passed a café, a deeds and titles office, a pharmacy. The door of the pharmacy was open, and remembering the money Rena had given me, I passed under the twisting fly strip and went inside.

I was at the counter buying a bottle of aspirin when George walked in. "Hazel!" he said.

I grinned at him in response, then turned to thank the pharmacist as he handed me my change. I tucked the money into my wallet, and when I looked up again, George was still standing before me. "What are you doing in town?"

"Lydie made me go see a dentist," he said slowly. The words sounded strange. He lifted a hand to his cheek and pressed on it. "They numbed me up."

"What'd you get done?"

"Got a problem with one of my molars. I had it filled and then came over here with a prescription." Reaching into the front pocket of his shirt, George pulled out a slip of paper. He squinted at it with suspicion. "Supposed to make it stop hurting."

"Has it been hurting awhile?" I asked. "Is it bad?"

He shrugged. "Long enough." The *l* came out like an *n*, and he grimaced.

"Don't let me stop you. You're going to need that medicine."

He nodded but didn't make any move to approach the counter. "Something happened?" he asked me suddenly. "You've got a smile like you won the pot."

"Not exactly that," I said, thinking that I couldn't tell him that defiance was boiling in my blood, and this joy was the vapor rising up out of it. Instead I explained that I'd just left the co-op and was thinking some things over. "Things about the future," I added.

George got a strange look on his face. "What about?" he asked, and I realized that Lydie must have talked to him about me. Either that or he knew just by looking that my situation these past months had been shaky, a sort of tryout for the future that hadn't quite gone as hoped.

"Listen," I said, "have you eaten lunch yet, George?"

He shook his head.

"Then let's go grab a bite," I said, and then stopped and reconsidered. "A milkshake, how about. You go get your prescription filled, and I'll wait."

I stepped outside and stood in the shade of the vestibule. My heart wasn't pounding, but its beat felt sure and strong. A few minutes later, when George came out to join me, I almost took his hand to lead him down the sidewalk. "Is Bennie's okay?" I asked, and we both started walking.

Inside the diner, we sat side by side on stools at the counter. It wasn't yet eleven, and most of the downtown lunch crowd hadn't arrived, but there were a few office men sitting there, sleeves rolled up to their elbows, meatloaf sandwiches and tuna melts slowly getting cleared from their plates as they made conversation with one another and with Alice, Bennie's wife, who was standing in her apron behind the counter. George and I ordered two milkshakes, and when they came I watched him try to use the straw and fail. Ice cream dribbled down his chin, and he had tears in his eyes that came before the laughter. "Oh, George," I said, and I thought how I'd never kissed him and suddenly knew that I wanted to.

We talked for a few minutes about this and that, about Gene starting junior high in September, about a loose gutter I needed to get fixed. Then I told him that Nate hadn't been able to pay rent and Mr. Freese had tried to talk me into selling the farm. "But I'm not going to," I said. "I'm not going anywhere."

The relief on his face answered a question I hadn't asked.

One of the men a few stools down was telling Alice about his wife finding a garter snake in the backyard and going at it with a shovel. "She banged that thing to kingdom come," he said, laughing, and Alice shook her head as she cut a hot sandwich in half with a big metal spatula. I could do this, I thought, stirring my milkshake with the straw. I could work in a place like this. George was eating his milkshake with a spoon, carefully tucking a bite into his mouth and then wiping his lips with a thumb to make sure he wasn't drooling. Kiss me, I thought, and see if you can feel it.

Thinking it wasn't enough to make it happen. But the next day, when I was coming out from the henhouse with my basket of eggs, George drove up in his truck. He climbed down and said he'd been thinking about the gutter I'd mentioned, and it wouldn't take him all of five minutes to fix it. He looked right at me and I looked right back at him, and I said, let me show you where it is. Only instead of me leading him around to the back, we went together into the house exactly as if it'd been planned. Debbie and Joe were down at Rena's, and the door hadn't even closed before I set down the basket and turned to him and then we were kissing. The whole length of our bodies was pressed up against each other, and I didn't say *Why*, or *We shouldn't*, or *Hold on*. And neither of us was starting anything, because it had already begun.

Juanlan

8

One day on her way home from tutoring Wei Ke, Juanlan comes upon a commotion just outside the east bus station. The station is the busiest in town, handling most of the buses to and from Chengdu, but it's small and old, only a tiny waiting room whose floor is always littered with sunflower seeds and oily cellophane bags, the air heavy with exhaust. Right before the turn-in for the buses, a small crowd is gathered. When Juanlan stops her bike and gets off, a woman with knitting swaying from her busily moving needles says, "How do you think he ended up here?"

The man standing next to them says, "The bus, I guess."

At the center of the commotion, a red cap appears, and then an up-turned face. It's a foreigner, a white man with the strained smile and wide, blinking eyes she recognizes from other foreigners she's seen on the streets of Chengdu. He bends down to root through a giant pack at his feet and comes up clutching a notebook with frayed edges. Holding it to his chest protectively, he speaks to the man standing directly in front of him. In barely recognizable Mandarin, he says, "Xiexie, buyao." *Thank you, I don't want.* "Xiexie, xiexie. Buyao, buyao, buyao."

"He's odd-looking, isn't he?" the woman with the knitting says.

Under his cap, tufts of hair stick out, seemingly without color. Blond? Gray? His face is partly shaded by the bill of the cap, but Juanlan sees a high nose with a single deep line on either side. His skin is red in places from sunburn. He might be thirty-five, forty—Director Wei's age or a little older. Dressed in shorts and a T-shirt, he has thick, clumping sandals that are lashed to his feet with a series of black bands. "They always look odd," she says to the woman.

"You've met a lot of them?"

"A few." The foreigner is saying something in English now, but she can't make it out. "You see them on the street sometimes in Chengdu."

"Do they all look as helpless as this one?"

"Not all of them. Some live in the city and know their way around. I had one as a teacher at university."

The woman looks at her for a long moment, impressed. "You studied English at university? You must speak perfectly."

"No, I speak terrible English." But this is how anyone would respond, and the woman doesn't hear her. Instead, she asks which university she attended and then taps the shoulder of one of the men standing beside them. "This little sister studied English at Sichuan Normal. She can translate."

Juanlan is reluctantly pushed forward with her bike, the crowd parting, strangers peering expectantly. The foreigner, once they're face-to-face, looks like a child standing on a train platform who sees someone waving from a window and isn't sure if he's supposed to wave back.

Close up, he looks older. Forty-five, maybe even fifty. As old as her father, with small wrinkles that fan out from the corners of his eyes, though he's squinting so narrowly she can't see their color.

"Go on," says a man in the crowd. "See what he's doing here. See if he needs help."

She nods and says, all right, she will. The foreigner notices them talking, and his eyes narrow further, as if he's sure there's a conspiracy mounting against him.

"Welcome to our city of Heng'an." Juanlan holds out her hand and waits for him to take it. "My name is Jenny."

He shifts the notebook to his other hand so he can shake hers. "You speak very good English, Jenny."

"No, it's terrible."

He glances at the crowd, which has fallen silent for their exchange, and then looks back at her. "I'm looking for a hotel someone told me about. The Friend Hotel, I think?" He riffles through his notebook and then thrusts it out so she can look at a page where "Friendship International Hotel" is written in large Chinese characters.

"This is not far away. You can take a pedicab."

"What about walking? Is it too far for that?"

The top of the hotel is visible from here, but directions, she's found, are difficult to explain in English, always more complicated than she thinks they will be. "Maybe you can walk. But your bag is very heavy."

He reaches down to grab one of the straps of his backpack, swinging it with effort onto his shoulders before securing a buckle at the waist and another over his chest. "Will you show me?"

Juanlan leads him through the crowd as people ask where he's going and exclaim at the backpack's size. "Meimei," cries the woman she was speaking with earlier, "come back and tell us what you find out!" Juanlan apologizes to the foreigner as they set off down the street, him with his backpack, her with her bike. "They are curious," she explains. "Many have never met a foreigner before."

He shrugs; he is used to strangers' curiosity, it seems. "I'm Rob," he says. "Jenny, right? You know, you're the fifth or sixth one of those I've met in China. What do they do: hand out a list of names and tell you to pick one?"

"Some people choose. Others are assigned names by their teachers."

"What about you?"

"I had another name, but I didn't like it."

He asks what it was and she tells him, June. This was the name chosen by the Australian teacher she had during her third year at Sichuan Normal. The teacher had seemed young, younger even than some of the students, spoke quickly and unintelligibly, wore shorts that showed lumpy expanses of thigh.

"June," says Rob, giving the name a flat sound it doesn't have in a Chinese person's mouth. There's a certain laziness to the lips speaking English that Juanlan hasn't figured out. Rob moves his head from side to side. "That's not so bad. Why'd you want to change it?"

"In Chinese, this is a boy's name."

He's quiet for a moment, thinking. "When I was a kid, people called me Bobby, but now I go by Rob. So I guess I've changed my name, too."

"Why did you want to change it?"

"For one, Bobby sounds like a little kid. But also, when I went away to college, I didn't feel like the same person anymore. I guess I wanted a new name to go along with my new life."

She'd felt something similar in her English class. Choosing a different name, she'd tried to conjure up a different existence to go with it. Airport corridors with gleaming floors. Giant planes. A passport full of stamps. Sunglasses pushed up the bridge of her nose, chin tilted down, she would be Jenny in Paris and New York and Seoul. She would grow bored with the ocean seen from ten thousand meters.

Juanlan asks where he's from. America, he tells her, which is what she suspected. He has the bearing of one who unconsciously uses up too much space, the expression of one accustomed to looking out over long distances.

They cut over onto a street that runs alongside the river, and she tries to concentrate on what he is saying. Something about a book he's writing. A book about China. "Oh, you're an author!" she exclaims. Well, no, he's not an author, not exactly. It's a travel guide, and he's one of the contributors. He travels, he says, and then writes about what he finds.

"It must be difficult because you speak little Chinese."

"'Little'—ha! I'd say none. But most people who buy our guides don't speak the language, either. What they need is someone who's in their shoes to try it out first."

It occurs to her that his method would not work very well without people like her stepping in to help, but she doesn't say this aloud. "And you came to Heng'an for this reason?"

"We're always looking for new places, little towns and hidden gems. I spent a few weeks up north and went down the coast to Shanghai, but I've gotta say, the southwest of China is my favorite part. But it's hard to know where to go. A guy I met in Chengdu was from near here and he said there's lots of little old villages around. It's on the ancient tea route, and all that. I thought I'd come check it out." He looks out at the river. Often there is just a narrow channel running down the middle and flat gray stones on either side, but now the water is high and fills its banks. "What's the name of it?" he asks, gesturing.

"It is called Duoyu Jiang."

He echoes the words, badly. "Hold on a sec," he says, and stops to flip open his notebook. "*Dwo yoo jang*," he writes, and Juanlan has the urge to laugh. How helpless he is. She is reminded of a child trying to form his characters.

They walk on, passing a man on a flatbed tricycle stacked with coal cylinders, who stares at them and then frowns as he pushes against the slight incline. She wants to explain that things are not what they appear:

she is not a young giggling woman hoping this foreigner will marry her and take her abroad. She's seen such couples on the streets of Chengdu. The women are rarely beautiful, but in their bright clothes they look like delicate exotic birds hopping alongside the men, who are balding or gray-haired, with thick legs and broad bellies that push at the buttons of their sweated-through shirts.

She points out the hotel up ahead. As they approach, Rob tucks his thumbs in the straps of his backpack. "This place looks fancy," he says, and doesn't appear pleased.

The hotel has two stone lions on either side of the glass doors. Inside, a pretty girl stands behind the front desk, her hair pulled back, her face ready to stretch into a smile the moment it is required. The lobby's floor is so shiny that even from the sidewalk it looks like the surface of a pond in sunlight. "It is not very expensive," Juanlan says, and then adds, "for you."

Rob shifts the weight on his back and replies, "The people who buy our guides are backpackers. They don't like to be treated like rich people. Isn't there another place I could go?"

"My family owns a small hotel," she says quickly, before she can think.

"Oh, yeah? Can you—"

"But you can't be a guest there," she follows up, and explains that the Three Springs is not registered to accept foreigners. The Friendship Hotel is the only one in town with the designation.

He turns his eyes to the building rising eight stories above them. The windows are tinted dark gray, not at all friendly. "Then I guess this is where I'm staying."

*　*　*

Juanlan waits for him while he checks in and stows his bag in his room. Before going in, he asked if she was busy for the rest of the morning, and she decided she wasn't. It's not every day a foreigner shows up in Heng'an, after all. "Great!" he said when she said she was free. "Do you mind doing a little shopping with me?"

He comes back down the stairs wearing a different backpack, a smaller one like a schoolboy might wear. "You're like a turtle," she says, gesturing. "You always carry your shell."

"Ha! Traveling, you know. You have to be safe."

"But Heng'an is not as dangerous as Chengdu. There are less thieves here."

"That's good to hear. I lost my CD player waiting at the Chengdu bus station. Set it down on the seat beside me while I was searching through my bag, and I don't know what happened—a minute later it was gone."

She almost asks how he could be so careless with an expensive item, but this is not her business. Perhaps it is not so expensive to him. In any case, he is in need of a new CD player now, so off they go.

Most of the electronics shops are across the river, at the bottom of the hill from which Heng'an Middle School looks out across the town. Juanlan hails a pedicab to drive Rob the distance—it is two kilometers, maybe three—and follows behind on her bicycle. Traveling in tandem but not together, she is able to enjoy the whiplash of bicyclists and pedestrians who turn to stare. They see a white man blithely blinking into the wind as he is pedaled over the bridge, but they don't know that they, too, are being watched.

When they reach their destination, Juanlan jumps off her bicycle to pay the pedicab driver. Rob has already pulled out a handful of bills, but she has the advantage of language and the driver takes her money without bothering to try to communicate the amount to his passenger. Rob is still trying to pay her back as she leads him into a store. "Never mind," she says, flipping her hand dismissively at the proffered bills. "You are a guest in our town."

They turn to the array of portable electronics. This store is more expensive than some others, Juanlan explains, but it has the brand names and they are authentic. Sony, Panasonic. Some of the cheaper stores sell lesser brands with fake labels slapped on them. Those players will likely not work for long.

"I guess I might as well make the investment," Rob says, leaning over the glass counter.

She struggles to describe the various qualities of the items he examines. How to translate "antishock" or "liquid crystal display"? After trying out a few options, Rob settles on a Discman—the same one he lost. It seems to be an older model, he says with a shrug, but should do just fine.

Juanlan buys two bottles of sweetened green tea and they walk down to the river, where the cover of newly planted trees can at least partially disguise them from the curious gazes of passersby. Juanlan locks her bicycle on a lamppost and they walk along, sipping their drinks and talking about music, how necessary it is for Rob while he travels. "What kind of music do you prefer?" she asks, and he tells her the names: Led Zeppelin, Cream, the Yardbirds, the Who. "What I grew up with," he explains. "You know, the stuff that was popular when I was your age. You probably haven't heard of any of those groups."

"I have heard of some of them," she says, and they walk in silence for a minute, both turning their heads to look out over the river. Even with the changes the town has undergone in the years since Juanlan has been away, the shapes are all too familiar to her: two-story buildings with flat tile fronts, gray river, gray sky, far-off mountains wavering through mist. She glimpses the top of the new bridge with its red-painted arches: even this structure, pride of Heng'an, looks like many other bridges all over the province. At university, when she saw pictures of her friends in their own hometowns, she'd often marveled at how similar the photos looked to her own, how similar the streets were to the streets of Heng'an. She watches Rob now and tries to imagine what it is like to see a thing for the first time. She would like to have the freedom to go around as he does, without a plan and without guidance, with only the trust that you will be welcomed wherever you go.

"Have you traveled?" Rob asks, as if he can discern the patterns traced in her mind. "Outside of China, I mean?"

She frowns. "Most Chinese people don't travel abroad. Only the wealthy are able. Even in China, I have traveled to very little places. Very few," she corrects herself.

He seems to take this response in stride. He asks if she's lived in Heng'an her whole life, and she tells him, no, she lived in Chengdu while she attended university. "I've only recently returned," she adds.

"Oh, yeah? What's it like being back?" He glances around, as if what they're passing now is all there is to know of Heng'an.

She could tell him about her father, but he doesn't seem like a person who understands sadness. He is an American, after all, and perhaps has never lost anything that matters to him. Instead she tells him about her brother and Lulu. "This baby will be the first in our family. My brother will be a father. My parents will be grandfather and grandmother. Grandparents," she remembers.

"And you'll be an aunt!" He says the word with a flat *a*, like the word for the insect. "Congratulations!"

In the glow of his grin, Juanlan finds herself smiling, too. "Thank you. I'm happy for the baby." Saying it, she instantly feels that it's true. A baby is coming soon. She will be an aunt. But another moment passes, and she remembers how ambivalent Lulu seems to be about the coming event, and then she is unsure if her joy is a stable feeling. "Is an aunt an important family connection in America?"

"It depends. Me, I wasn't ever all that close to my aunts and uncles." He glances over at her, his brows knitting in thought. Then his face brightens, suddenly earnest. "But we have a thing—I don't know if it's this way here, but in the States, if someone your parents' age is good to you, close to you and your family, you might consider them an aunt or an uncle. My mom, she had a good friend who lost her husband all of a sudden and she had two kids my age. We were all friends. Our two families were, you know—we were kind of mixed up together." He takes a sip of his tea and replaces the lid. "So I'd say she's kind of like an aunt to me."

"She is still living?" Juanlan asks.

"Oh, yeah." Rob laughs. "I told her I'd bring her a souvenir from China."

They walk on, and before long Juanlan's stomach is growling. Back home, her mother is probably putting food on the table, wondering where she is. For a moment, she considers inviting Rob to lunch, but it would be too difficult for her, too strange for her parents and also for him. "I should go," she says, "unless you need to do more shopping?"

He looks briefly startled, but then his face goes easy again, easy and open. "I might just wander around, see what there is to see."

"Heng'an does not have very much. We have very few monuments or scenic places." And she lists them for him: Jinlong Temple, Kongquan Park, Plum Blossom Hill.

Rob nods, unconcerned, and then asks which is closest. He can't read street signs, and half the streets don't even have signs marking them, anyway. She writes down in his notebook the name of the park and tells him to take a taxi. "That's all right," he says. "I'll walk around and maybe I'll stumble across something interesting."

So this is what it means to travel with perfect freedom: you don't care about seeing what everyone else agrees is worth seeing. Such an attitude implies either perfect wisdom or perfect ignorance. Juanlan isn't sure which, but the confusion interests her, and so when Rob asks if she's free again later, or even tomorrow, she decides that she can find the time. After her tutoring session the next morning, she says, she will come meet him at his hotel. They'll go climb the hill together and she will be his guide. "Awesome!" Rob says. "Shee-shee nee!"

They return to where her bicycle is parked, and she gets on and begins pedaling, leaving him to his own helplessness and likely confusion. But when she glances back at the end of the street, she sees that he is gazing serenely up at the sky. He is someone who does not get too caught up in difficulties. A Taoist monk, almost. Funny.

*   *   *

Later, Juanlan sits at the desk of the hotel with a Chinese-English dictionary, trying to recall which words she'd reached for in conversation earlier and come up short. She's very good at listening, taking in unfamiliar words and phrases and filing them away for later, but in the moment she is not always able to speak as precisely as she wants. Paging through the dictionary, she finds the English translation of *ganma*, what she thought of before when Rob was speaking of his mother's friend: "godmother." A beautiful combination of words, she thinks, if a very strange one.

In the afternoon the rain begins to fall and two men come in through the door, shaking their umbrellas onto the tile floor. Juanlan greets them, takes their ID cards, checks them in. They both work for a construction company based in Chengdu. She takes them upstairs to their room, points out that the small cabinet by each bed holds rubber house sandals and a towel, as well as a woolen blanket, not that they'll need it at this time of year. Here is the mosquito coil. Here is the light switch. She pulls open the curtains to reveal tree limbs waving in the rain and then mentions, as her mother always insists she does, that usually the hotel would charge more for a room at the front of the building, but in this case they will charge only the regular rate because their company called ahead to reserve the room.

She leaves the men and returns a few minutes later with a thermos of hot water. The door to the room is open and she hears them complaining about the long bus ride from Chengdu. One of them has kicked off his shoes and is sitting with his back to the wall, his legs stretched out on the bed. She glances away, embarrassed. The other man is busy hanging up clothes in the shared wardrobe. "Xiao mei," the one on the bed says to her, "is there an ashtray in here?"

His friend answers: "It's there on top of the cabinet, you dunce."

He glances at the ashtray without reaching for it. Patting his shirt pockets in search of the pack of cigarettes, he says, "I bet you're looking forward to the expressway being completed. You must want to travel to Chengdu sometimes, spend time in a more exciting place than this."

She does not like having her private dreams described by this man. "I guess," she says.

The man locates his cigarettes and pulls two from the pack. He hands one to his friend. "When the expressway is open, you'll be able to go to Chengdu just for the day. You could do some shopping and visit your friends. You have friends there?"

"Not really."

"You can visit us, then." The man winks and then strikes a flame from his lighter, which flickers blue and orange and makes shadows of his hands on the wall. His friend shakes his head as Juanlan leaves, her face flushed red.

She is back at the desk when she thinks again about what the men were saying: *You could go just for the day.* But of course it works the other way, too. If businessmen can come to Heng'an just for the day, then they won't need to stay at the hotel.

She has been longing for change, but not of this kind, not if it means her family's source of income will dry up. She pictures a road unfurling like a roll of paper. Sees herself holding one end, watching it go.

*   *   *

In the evening, the television blares news about the floods along the Chang Jiang. The rain now is in Hunan, Jiangxi, Hubei. On the screen, the brown water roils and people cry to the camera, their faces stricken with grief. Juanlan and her parents eat dinner and watch the devastation. "Look at all that water," her mother says, shaking her head. On screen is an image of PLA soldiers in a squarish boat, tearing white ruffles in the water as they peel away from the camera. The voice of a newswoman explains that our people's army is fighting bravely against the ravages of nature.

Juanlan's father maneuvers his chopsticks with difficulty. "Ba, let me get you a spoon," she says, but he makes a swatting motion.

She wonders whether they have considered what the future will bring. It's not her place to ask, and that is a relief. She thinks instead of Rob, of their plans for the next day. She has not told her parents about meeting him, sure, somehow, that they would disapprove. "Tomorrow," she says, "I won't come back until after lunch."

"Why?" her mother demands.

A lie comes quickly: "Teacher Cao asked me to stay. She wants to thank me for helping Wei Ke. I think we're going out to eat." She is ready to say where, but then stops herself from speaking. A good lie is a stone that does not need engraving.

"We can manage without you until afternoon. But they should do more than feed you, Lan'er. With all you're doing for that boy."

"It's good practice for me, too," Juanlan replies vaguely. It is enough; her parents are once again engrossed by the television. The news is done, and a comedy program about a set of neighbors in a hutong of Beijing comes on. The old people are always saying funny things. "Here, Ma, let me get those." Juanlan takes the plates from her mother and carries them to the kitchen, where she washes them alone.

The next morning she rides her bike to Director Wei's flat. It is still raining steadily. She wears a biking rain poncho and brings along two umbrellas. The weather is not good for visiting Plum Blossom Hill, but something tells her Rob will be easygoing. Mud splashes up onto her legs so that by the time she arrives at the flat she is almost unfit for the indoors. Director Wei opens the door. His eyes run from her head to her toes, and then he ushers her into the bathroom to clean off.

When she comes out again, he's standing by the table, sorting through a pile of papers. "I'd like to ask you how my son is doing in his study." He holds a paper in his hands, and Juanlan is reminded of times in school when she would be criticized for bad performance on a test.

"He's doing very well," she says, an approximation of the truth. In the weeks they've been working together, the boy has shown some minor improvement in his reading and comprehension. Since the day she helped him take down the wet laundry, they've developed a routine of working for an hour and then taking a break to play music before returning to study. "Where is he now?"

"In his room." Director Wei nods at the hallway. Surely Wei Ke can hear them, so close by, but his father seems unconcerned as he goes on, "I doubt he will be a very strong English student. He doesn't have the talent for it."

"He's trying."

"Trying isn't enough if you don't have the ability."

"Wei Ke is a very smart boy. There's no reason to think he won't keep getting stronger." She is aware of overstepping, of sounding like a teacher or a school administrator, rather than a tutor whose qualifications are only that she herself is good at the language she's teaching. But she feels the novelty of talking like this with Director Wei, the fun of playing at being an authority.

He's shuffling papers into a folder now. She's ready for him to go. Taking a briefcase from the floor, he opens it up so that its insides are splayed like a patient on the operating table. Juanlan thinks of her father, paralyzed at the hands of a doctor, even though his stay at the hospital didn't involve surgery at all. Director Wei and her father are examples of the two kinds of men that exist in the world: one exercises power, and the other obeys it. Reflexively, she thinks of her brother and then revises this conception—Zhuo Ge is a third kind: the facilitator, the actor.

"You made a friend yesterday," Director Wei says lightly. He smiles at her confusion. "I hear you helped a foreign guest who's come to our town."

Juanlan shakes her head. "I didn't—"

"You didn't meet a foreigner?"

"No, I did." She straightens her shoulders. "But I don't know that I helped him very much. All I did was show him to his hotel."

Director Wei nods. "And you spent time together after."

"We went for a walk."

Narrowing his eyes, he says, "You're suspicious of me. All right, I confess: I'm having you followed." He gives her a serious look, then abruptly breaks into a grin. "I'm joking with you. The truth is that I know the Friendship Hotel's owner, and he mentioned that a foreign guest checked in yesterday. It's my business to know about such things."

She waits for more, to hear how he learned that there was a young woman with the foreigner, to hear how he learned that the young woman was *her*. But he seems uninterested in further explanations. He says suddenly, "I assume you've made plans to see him again?"

Surprised, she can only nod.

"It would be useful for my son to have the opportunity to make conversation with a foreigner."

From the bedroom down the hall comes the scraping of a chair over the floor. They both glance in that direction, but Wei Ke doesn't appear to speak up in his defense, either for or against this plan. "I'm not sure how long the American is planning to stay in Heng'an."

"Then we must seize the opportunity. It's best for Wei Ke to go with you the next time you meet him. The *American*." Director Wei stresses this last word as if the descriptor is fantastical.

Since he will no doubt hear of the rendezvous, anyway, she says,

"I'm meeting him today, after the tutoring session. I can ask him then about meeting Wei Ke."

"Why not take my son with you? Unless you were planning a date with this man. That would be awkward." The corners of Director Wei's mouth turn upward. He reaches into his pocket and takes out a wallet without trying to hide the stack of bills inside. Pinching his finger and thumb over the corner of a bill, he removes a one-hundred-yuan note and holds it out to her. "You'll need to eat. You should take the American to Dongpo Zhouzi."

"I wasn't thinking of anything so expensive. Just noodles or fast fry."

This idea is dismissed with a flick of the hand, the hundred-yuan bill flapping after. He waits for her to take it before returning the wallet to his pocket. "I know the couple who run the place. You won't need to order, I'll stop by and arrange it on my way to the office." He walks past her to the door, where he takes his jacket from a hook on the wall. As he slips his arms through the holes, he adds, "I'm sorry I can't host you myself, but I'm driving up to Tao Xu today."

"It's no problem," Juanlan replies automatically. The door closes behind him, and she contemplates the day she has just escaped: a formal meal with Director Wei overseeing everything, talking to Rob with her as translator, alternately praising and scolding his son. She doesn't like him, simply because she is uncomfortable around him. He makes her feel as if she's the fish on his cutting board—he'll do what he wants and use her as he wishes.

Wei Ke is standing by the desk when she enters his room. "I don't want to meet the foreigner. That wasn't part of the deal."

"The deal?" she says. "I don't know of any deal. I come here and tutor you for two hours every morning, and in return—" She stops, raises her shoulders.

"What I mean is that I can practice English with you. But I'm not ready to speak to a foreigner, Jiejie. I can barely say hello." He sinks into one of the stiff chairs in front of the desk. "You heard what my father said. I'm not good at English, and I'm never going to be."

The moment requires her to be either sympathetic or forceful. She's not up to either one. Pulling out the other chair, she seats herself heavily next to Wei Ke. "Look," she says, "I don't really want to do this, either. The foreigner—I've only met him once. We were supposed to go to Plum Blossom Hill today because he needs a guide, but that's as much as I know."

Wei Ke strokes the fingers of one hand with those of the other. He looks at them admiringly, even in the midst of his panic. He is a pianist, after all. "So, go," he says.

"You know your father will find out if you don't come with me."

"I don't care."

"Well, I do. I don't want to be blamed. And besides, he gave me money for lunch."

Wei Ke yawns, suddenly tired of the exchange. "Oh, that doesn't matter." He sits up abruptly and says, "You know what, if we're going to be speaking English all day, I don't want to do it now," and for a moment Juanlan has to think whether that's the language they've been conversing in this whole time. But of course what he means is that he doesn't want to study. He's fifteen, and without his parents here, he can pretend that he controls his own destiny.

"Fine," she says, and they spend the rest of the morning watching television in the main room.

*   *   *

"Hello, who's this?"

Wei Ke stands dumbly beside Juanlan, and she looks from him to Rob and replies, "This is the son of my brother's . . . associate."

Rob laughs. "Sounds like a mobster's introduction. He's not packing heat, is he?" He makes the shape of a gun at his side. "Mobsters? Guns?" He explains the joke to her, but the length of the explanation makes it difficult to laugh. She doesn't bother translating for Wei Ke.

They stand beneath the overhang of the Friendship Hotel's entrance. The rain is still coming down. Inside the lobby, the woman at the desk is watching them with open curiosity, her face turned toward them like a satellite dish. She might be the same woman from yesterday, but

Juanlan isn't sure. They are probably all instructed to report on the comings and goings of the foreign guest.

"The weather," Rob says, looking out at the rain, "is not cooperating with us. Do we try the flower hill, what's it called?"

"Plum Blossom Hill will not be very comfortable. I think we can go to Jinlong Temple instead." She hands him one of the two umbrellas, and he takes it easily. He had one before, he tells her, shaking it open, but he accidentally left it in Chengdu.

She and Wei Ke share an umbrella, and the three of them set out down the street. Wei Ke, silent until now, asks if they'll take a taxi to the temple. "Of course not," Juanlan replies. "We'll take a passenger van." But as soon as she's spoken, she realizes that this is not what Rob would choose to do on his own. A taxi will cost seven or eight yuan, while the van will cost only one yuan per person. It's no matter to him, but Juanlan is at the mercy of her mother, who gives her money every now and then, and not on any regular schedule.

Then she remembers the hundred yuan Director Wei gave her. They don't need to eat so grandly, after all. She'll just tell the waitress at the restaurant to cancel a few dishes, and that will make up for the money they'll spend on a taxi. She flutters her fingers at an approaching cab.

She and Wei Ke slide into the back. As they peel onto the road that leads east along the river, Rob turns around and tries to make conversation with Wei Ke. "How old are you?" he asks in the patient tone of someone who has spoken with shy children before. "He does speak English, you said, right?"

"Yes," she says. "I'm tutoring him." To Wei Ke, she says in the bright clear English of study: "How old are you?"

He blinks at her, and she repeats the question. "I am fifty," he replies, finally. "Years. Old." His voice is so quiet it's nearly swallowed by the sound of the car engine and the air through the windows.

"Fif*teen*," Juanlan corrects. "You are fif*teen* years old."

Wei Ke stares back at her for a moment before turning his face to the window.

They're getting out of the main section of town now, and through the windshield the slopes of the mountains are visible behind the square, flat-roofed buildings that line the road. A big blue truck, its rear stacked high with spools of steel cording, belches smoke in the air. Construction is everywhere. There is a sense of the country being laid over with foundations for new roads, new houses, for the new dams that will make valleys into lakes and bring power to every new factory, every high-rise building. A motorbike pulls up beside their taxi, beeping its horn, and then cuts between them and the truck to avoid a passenger van coming from the opposite direction. Driving is a miracle, as unimaginable as flying with one's own wings.

They ride the rest of the way in silence. The rain has slowed somewhat, and the driver lets the water gather on the windshield before switching on the wipers. At last they reach the temple, and Juanlan tells him they'll pay extra if he waits. He nods and reaches for the pack of cigarettes resting by the gearshift.

The temple is up a hill, its slate roof visible through the green bamboo. The stairs are made of large, irregular slabs of stone, and Wei Ke takes them easily, Juanlan following. "The laowai is really slow, isn't he?" Wei Ke says as they wait for Rob to join them at the top. "What? He can't understand."

"And you can't, either, when we speak English. Do you want me to talk about you? Say things about you without your knowing?"

He shrugs; nothing she says matters very much to him. He is sulky and irritable, and this is her punishment for bringing him along.

At last Rob reaches the top. "Shall we?" he says between ragged breaths, and instead of responding, Wei Ke starts down the path ahead of them.

They are not off to a good start. But once inside the first courtyard a kind of interested stillness comes over the three of them. It is the temple, sleepy with its centuries of history. The stone flags on the ground are blackened with lichen. Even the thin reedy strains of pop music coming from a tape player nearby seem a natural part of the atmosphere. They pass into the Hall of the Heavenly Kings and stand in the gloom to contemplate the statues. When Wei Ke leaves, Juanlan sneaks a glance at

Rob and sees that he wears the expression of someone who knows his own ignorance and is not bothered by it. "Have you seen a Buddhist temple before?"

"I've been to a few." Rob lowers his voice to a confidential whisper. "Bigger ones, mostly—in Beijing, when I first got here. And then I went to one in Chengdu." Looking around the small space with its dusty corners, he adds, "It wasn't much like this. There were a lot more visitors and there were vendors everywhere, in case you wanted a Coke or something. I don't get it. Like going into a church and up on the altar there's someone selling popcorn." He stops and looks up at the statue of the red-skinned Guangmutian with the snake wrapped around one wrist. "Pretty weird," he says.

Juanlan drops a donation in the box, kneels, and kowtows three times. "Would you like to do it?" she asks, but Rob just smiles and shakes his head. Back outside, the rain has changed over into mist, and she holds out her palm to determine that umbrellas are unnecessary. "But this is cool," Rob says. "I like that this temple is smaller and more *real* than the other ones I've visited." It takes her a moment to realize he's picked up the conversation from before. "And it's so old. Several centuries, right?"

"Yes, many centuries old." She considers explaining that after the People's Republic was proclaimed, citizens weren't allowed to worship in temples anymore, that during the Cultural Revolution parts of the temple were destroyed and the building was used for grain storage by the people nearby. The statues they saw inside are new; the patriots broke the old ones and threw them into the river. A simpler version: "China's history is very complex. This temple has existed through many wars."

"Like the world wars?" Rob asks.

"Yes, and others. The 1949 revolution, for example."

"With Chairman Mao, right? The Long March and all that? I've been trying to catch up on my Chinese history."

"Yes, the Long March passed very near here."

Pointing at the faded red characters crawling along the inside of the east- and west-facing walls, he asks what they are. She explains that they're old political slogans proclaiming that religion is counterrevolutionary. Rob takes out his camera and asks, "Do you think it's okay to take a picture?"

"I think it's okay, just a few very quickly."

He sets down his backpack and holds the camera up to take a picture of one wall from several meters away, then walks closer and focuses on one of the washed-out characters. He leans down to line up the character in his shot. The one he has chosen is a preposition, practically meaningless. Juanlan considers telling him to choose one of the others instead, but just then Wei Ke appears from behind the Hall of the Heavenly Kings and stops short. "What's he doing?"

"Taking a picture."

"Of *that*?"

"Why not? He's interested in history."

Wei Ke looks dubious, then a moment later he walks over and stands beside Rob. "Do you know what you're photographing?" he asks in Chinese.

Rob gives him a baffled look. "What's that?"

"He wants to know if you understand what it means."

"Oh, yeah." Rob turns to Wei Ke. "Old political slogans. Very cool. Cool—do you know *cool*?" He says the word again, drawing out the vowel. *Cooooooool.* He is the friendly foreigner, ambassador of the English language.

Wei Ke stares back at him, his face clenched.

"I already explained everything," Juanlan says.

But this seems to rile him. He takes a few steps toward her, leaving Rob watching with his usual incomprehension. "What did you explain? Did you tell him about how China was cheated and stomped on by the West? How it took the revolution for us to stand up tall? I'm sure you didn't explain that it was the people who painted these slogans. Peasants. Workers." He gives a quick jerk of his head, eyes flashing like a mirror caught by a flashlight beam in the dark.

"What do you know about being a peasant?"

"As much as you do," he shoots back. "I understand our history, and I'm proud of it. What does this laowai know about anything? All he can do is take pictures of old slogans he can't even read."

"You've learned history better than you've learned English. But this 'laowai' knows more of the world than you do. He's a man and he's traveled, while you're a child who has never gone farther from his home than Chengdu."

"But I will. Not like you, who's come home forever just to wash the sheets in her parents' hotel."

Here is the sentence that can't be unspoken. They both fall silent, and Rob, sensing the end of the back-and-forth, says, "Should we go check out the rest of it?"

"Yes," Juanlan says, and leads the way without waiting to see whether either of them follows.

9

The next day is Saturday, and she doesn't have to tutor Wei Ke. After her father's morning exercises, he comes into the lobby where Juanlan is mopping the floor and tells her to go out and enjoy the beautiful day. "It's raining," she says, glancing at the closed glass doors. It's not raining hard, but it has been recently, and a curtain of mist shrouds the buildings across the street.

"Even so." Her father gives his lopsided shrug. "I told your ma I want you to have some fun. Every day, you're doing bitter work for free." He pauses, and Juanlan has enough time to wonder if he's referring to the tutoring or to the hotel. Then she feels guilty for having the thought.

"After I finish mopping, I'll go."

"I can do it." He takes the mop from her, and she watches him push it over the floor, dirty water streaking the red linoleum. His body tilts slightly to one side, but he is not falling down, he is not incapable. "I'm fine, Lan'er. Go."

She finds her mother in the flat across the alley, cleaning up the kitchen from breakfast. "Ba is over there," Juanlan says. "He insisted on cleaning."

Her mother nods without turning from the sink.

"He seems okay. Don't you think he's doing better?"

Reaching for a towel to dry her hands, her mother glances up with eyes as darkly bright as a bird's. "You think he'll be able to do the mopping on his own?" She shakes her head. "Hand me that food cover."

Juanlan takes the netted plastic dome from its place on the shelf and passes it to her mother. The table has been wiped clean and the leftovers pushed to the middle: a plate of pickles, a single mantou, half a salted duck egg. Her mother places the dome over the food and says, "I'll go find him in a little while."

"Ma, I'll stay."

"He wants you to go out. You should go out." She glances around the kitchen to make sure she hasn't forgotten anything, and her eyes pass over Juanlan as if she isn't there.

"Do you want me to clean the bathrooms before I go? So Ba doesn't have to?"

"How do you think he's going to get upstairs? Of course he won't do the bathrooms. He won't mop the floors upstairs, either. He'll come back here and lie down or he'll sit at the desk and read one of his astronaut books. I'll do the bathrooms and the floors, and the sheets and towels, and I'll get the rooms ready after the guests check out. I'm used to doing this. You go out and enjoy yourself, like your Ba wants."

Juanlan bites her lip. "I'll go out and come back again in a little while."

"And make him unhappy?" She shakes her head angrily. "He wants you to go have fun—I don't know why, since you had so much time yesterday to play around. I know lunch with Teacher Cao didn't last three hours, and then you came back and didn't say where you had been. I didn't ask—I figured you would tell your parents, and so if you don't, maybe it's a secret you have. Okay, you have your secret. I don't say anything about it. And I don't say anything when your Ba tells you to take the day and play around. You should respect his wishes, too. Go shopping, buy a new music tape or a necklace. You need a little money?" She pats at her pocketless trousers, her anger gone, expelled in one breath.

"I still have some," Juanlan says. "I'll go see Zhuo Ge and Lulu. Maybe they'll want to go walking downtown."

"Your brother is working today. Maybe Xiao Lu will go, but don't wear her out. You know she shouldn't be moving so much."

"Okay, Ma."

"I don't know if you're doing her any good." She squints, as if trying to see her daughter better. "You girls. You don't know anything about how the world works."

Juanlan doesn't ask what she means. But her mother tells her anyway: "You think things should just keep getting better and better."

As she leaves the kitchen, her mother adds, "Tell them to come to dinner tomorrow. I'll get a chicken at the market, and we'll have lotus seed soup. It's good for Xiao Lu's health."

*   *   *

When Juanlan presses the buzzer at the bottom of the building, her sister-in-law calls down from above, "Where is your foreigner?"

Juanlan's neck cranes upward: there is Lulu's face six stories above, shadowed against the white sky. The tops of the buildings around the courtyard all seem to be bent inward like bamboo. "I told you, he's out of town until the day after tomorrow." On the phone last night, she told Lulu all about the trip to the temple and the lunch after, where Rob mentioned that he was going to Kangding for a few days. Somehow her sister-in-law already knew about the foreigner's presence in town, as well as Juanlan's status as unofficial guide.

"I don't believe you," Lulu yells down. "Anyway, wait a minute and I'll come down."

Through the slotted concrete blocks Juanlan sees the shadowed shape of her sister-in-law on the highest landing, and then the one below. When at last she emerges on the ground floor, her face is pale and her forehead has a greasy sheen. It's been several days since they met, and the shape of her stomach is different, protruding more sharply than before. Even under the loose dress tenting around her, the firm outline is visible. "I feel like if I knock your stomach," Juanlan says, "it will make a hollow sound like a watermelon."

Lulu makes a fist with one hand and raps it against her belly. "Thock, thock," she says.

"Do you want to dent your baby's head?"

She reaches up and knocks her own head behind one ear. "Now we're even."

They pass through the gate of the apartment complex. "You decide," Lulu says when Juanlan asks where she wants to go, so they head up to the main street, toward the area with shops and snack carts and people. At the corner they pass construction, a shirtless man sledgehammering the sidewalk while two others watch. The noise keeps them from talking for half a block. Once they're far enough away, Lulu grabs Juanlan's arm. "Tell me about him," she says.

"Who?"

"You know who. The foreigner."

"What do you want to know?"

"What he looks like. What you talk about."

"He's not handsome. He doesn't look like the foreigners you're think-ing of." Juanlan spreads her hands, picturing to herself the billboards all over Chengdu that have pictures of blond men and women, gleaming white teeth crowding their mouths, blue and green eyes looking out over the sprawl of the city with casual approval.

"What does handsome matter? Do you think I married your brother because he's handsome?" A smile flashes over Lulu's face, a sharp edge to it like the lid of a tin can. "I just want to know what this laowai is like. You've been very quiet about him, Juan Mei. I think you're hiding something."

"There's not much to say. He doesn't speak Chinese, and talking with him is good English practice for me."

"What do you call him?"

"Rob."

"Wah-buh," Lulu repeats. Then she tries again with the same result and gives a short laugh. "Why do foreigners have such difficult names?"

"It's not difficult for them. You should hear him try to say something in Chinese. All he knows how to say is hello and thank you. 'Nee how, shee-shee nee,'" she says in a flat tone, opening her mouth wide the way Rob does when he speaks.

"Maybe I could teach him Chinese. Does he want to learn?"

"Your Mandarin is terrible."

Lulu laughs. "No worse than my math!" And Juanlan pictures the high school student she probably was: popular with teachers and fellow students without ever affecting to be anything other than average. Lulu went to a school in Fengquan, an hour away. But at Juanlan's middle school in Heng'an there was a girl like her, someone who put enough effort into academics without excelling in any particular subject. When they compared grades on exams, she would look briefly discouraged but then laugh it off. Lulu used to have the chirpy lightness of a bird. It's only since the pregnancy that she has grown angry, sparks flying under her skin the way a cold fire burns inside Juanlan's stomach.

"You're right, my Mandarin is really terrible," Lulu admits. "That's why I want to teach your foreigner Sichuanese."

"That won't be very useful for the rest of his travels."

"It *will* be useful! He can go on television." She affects the stilted Mandarin of a television interviewer and says, "Comrade, how have you enjoyed your stay in Heng'an?" and then answers in heavy dialect, "Oh, I had a lot of fun last night!"

They walk on for several blocks, Lulu still clutching Juanlan's arm as if afraid she'll drop to her knees without the support. When they pass a woman selling chilled watermelon, Juanlan asks if they should buy some, but Lulu shakes her head and leads the way to a nearby bai-huodian, where she purchases a bag of chicken-flavored potato chips. "Nothing has flavor," she complains as she pushes the chips into her mouth, staring mournfully at her fingers, covered in yellow dust. "Do you know that some women never return to normal after being pregnant? Maybe I'll always want to add extra salt to everything I eat."

"Or maybe your hair will change color." Juanlan tells her about a teacher from the university who had a baby and when she returned had a large white streak on one side of her head.

"It's bad enough I feel ugly while I'm pregnant. Now you're telling me it's going to turn me into an old woman?"

Juanlan tries to explain that though the white hair made her teacher look older, it was in a wonderful way. Teacher Chen was a graceful woman from up north, tall and pale, her skin almost translucent. She'd once been a ballet dancer, and you could see it in the way she lifted her arms at the chalkboard. The streak of white in her hair, Juanlan goes on, only made her more exotic and lovely.

Lulu squints at her doubtfully. "I'm never going to get my looks back."

The lovelier version of Lulu was never her friend. A smeared sort of ugliness has united them, has made them sisters. Juanlan plucks the empty bag from Lulu's hands and looks for a place to toss it.

"Bring me your foreigner," Lulu says as a sudden breeze snaps the bag from Juanlan's hands, just as she's dropping it into a dustbin. It cartwheels a few yards and then settles, but neither of them moves to pick it up. "It's the only thing that will make me happy."

*   *   *

When she returns home in the afternoon, Juanlan finds a letter on her bed. The return address is Chongqing, though the name below it is not Du Xian's but his aunt's. This is the method they use to keep her parents from asking why a boy is writing to her. She has a story ready: the friend was in her English classes and is now working for a private tutoring school in the city. But her mother hasn't asked, even though the letter on the bed undoubtedly passed through her hands. *Okay, you have your secret.* The truth is that a boyfriend is not a problem. If Juanlan wanted to talk about him, she could tell her mother. But then there would be questions, an ongoing inquiry, a repeated demand to meet the young man and a barrage of advice that Juanlan hasn't asked for and doesn't want.

She tears open the envelope, and a photo strip falls out. It's from a photo booth, the kind with a money slot and a little curtain. An arcade near the university campus had one. In the spring she went there with three of her roommates and they all crammed in—afterward, they cut apart the photos and each took one. Hers is still pasted to the inside of her English notebook. She showed it to Du Xian and suggested that they go take a picture together, too, before they had to say good-bye, but he didn't want to do it. Girls like that kind of thing, he said; guys don't. Now, here are four small frames with his head and shoulders facing squarely into the lens and empty space on either side. He's not making faces in any of the pictures, just a straight-on stare. She looks at them all together and then one at a time, and all she can think is that she's missing something.

The letter itself is as restrained as all the others. There is almost nothing of him on the page. In person, Juanlan often felt like she was the one holding back, as if there were a part of herself that had to be protected or hidden away. But also, like that part was out in the open and it was only that Du Xian didn't notice it there. Sometimes he would grab for her hand, and she would shake it off for no reason, simply to be able to walk with nothing but air touching her skin. Was she sure that she loved him when they were still at the university together? Maybe not. She's not sure even now. But in the place of certainty is a hunger that comes from waiting, and she can trick herself into believing that this hunger is love. Glancing at the pictures again, she looks for minor differences in the repetition of Du Xian's face. Here his chin is lowered a half centimeter. There his forehead is wrinkled, a slight crinkle to his eyes.

She has never gazed at his face so carefully before. They were always walking side by side or seated next to each other on a bench. When they fumbled their way around each other's bodies, it was always in the dark.

The closer she looks at the photographs, the less familiar he becomes. And this makes her long for him even more.

*　　*　　*

"Twenty-two hours." Zhuo Ge bends toward his bowl and shovels rice into his mouth. Once he's swallowed it, he sits back in his chair.

"Did they have food?" Juanlan's mother asks. "Or water?"

"Only on the nearer side. There's a village a kilometer down the road, so the people caught on this side could walk down there. On the other side, though?" Zhuo Ge shakes his head. "Nothing. Not even a bathroom. Some guys from one of the villages up that way came down on motorbikes with hot water and fast noodles. They sold them for five yuan each. Good capitalists!" He laughs. "The people used the ditch by the road as a latrine. They're lucky we got the road opened up again today."

The sides of Lulu's mouth twitch down. She's heard all this already, Juanlan thinks. But Juanlan and her parents haven't, and Zhuo Ge is enjoying telling the story of another landslide blocking one of the mountain roads nearby. As a traffic policeman on a motorbike, Zhuo Ge gets a close-up view of these minor calamities; he has tales to tell. He's a good storyteller, too, with an eye for the best characters and a willingness to embellish. In his rendition of events, the people stuck on the mountain for twenty-two hours demonstrated the best and worst of humanity: there were heroes and villains. The heroes in this case were the enterprising villagers who lived nearby, who made money selling fast noodles and packets of toilet paper. The villains were the drivers who tried to get around the barriers and ended up blocking the road so even motorbikes couldn't get through.

Juanlan discovered quickly that the landslide happened on the road to Tao Xu, the opposite direction from Kangding, which means that Rob should be back tomorrow, as planned. She listens with only one ear to Zhuo Ge and watches his wife, whose face is pinched and unhappy again. Lulu picks at the chicken in her bowl, and every few minutes her mother-in-law urges her to eat. "Drink the broth, Xiao Lu," she says when Lulu complains that she can't eat any more. "It's healthy for you; it will make the baby strong."

Zhuo Ge scoops rice into his mouth while their mother lectures his wife, who is wearing an expression of forced patience. He won't come to her defense; she should make a show of sipping the broth, but instead she pushes the bowl away from her with a scowl.

"Wait," Juanlan says, "you said the landslide was on the road to Tao Xu? Director Wei was supposed to go up there yesterday. Do you think he got stuck?"

Her brother glances at her, thinking. "That would explain why he didn't come out last night. We all figured Teacher Cao kept him home." He grins and adds, "'The lioness from Hedong roars.' Ba knows. Don't you, Ba?"

Their father looks at his wife and says, "I don't speak a word."

"Exactly!" Zhuo Ge says, and they all laugh.

But Teacher Cao does not seem to be an overbearing wife. As a mother, maybe: earlier in the week, when she came home at lunch, she'd sent Wei Ke out to buy fruit so she could have a few minutes to speak with Juanlan alone. She'd wanted to know what more her son could do to improve his English. "He has a lot of pressure on his shoulders," Teacher Cao said. "But he must work harder to get ahead. Tell me, what else do you think my son should do?"

Juanlan had grasped for an answer, some action she could point out that was easy to enact. At last, she suggested that he watch English-language movies. Teacher Cao frowned, clearly disappointed in the answer. "Of course. That is one more thing we could try." A perverse

pleasure warmed Juanlan's skin, seeing this woman feeling thwarted by
her son's inadequacy.

Zhuo Ge has gone back to talking about the landslide. Maybe Teacher
Cao caused it, he jokes, to keep her husband from losing all his money
playing mah-jongg. At this, Lulu looks up suddenly and says, "Maybe
it's a ghost that caused it." They all look at her with surprise, but she
shrugs and goes on: "That's what they say in Fengquan. Landslides
happen when ghosts go walking."

"A ghost," Zhuo Ge echoes. His eyes light up and he adds, "It could
even be a 'foreign ghost.'" It's a pun, a joke, but Juanlan feels uneasy
when he turns to her and says, "What do you think, Mei? You think
that's possible?" His face is merry. Of course he knows about Rob.

"Anything is possible," she says tightly. "But I doubt there have been
many foreigners up there."

"Not many," Zhuo Ge says, "but Director Wei knows some stories.
You should ask him."

Juanlan cannot imagine asking Director Wei to tell her a story about
foreigners wandering into the mountains nearby. She can't imagine asking him to tell her a story of any kind. She still has the money he gave
her yesterday morning; at the restaurant after the visit to the temple,
when she tried to cancel some of the dishes that had been preordered,
the owner told her that it was all set, the bill had been taken care of.
Had Director Wei forgotten about the hundred yuan he had given her?
Juanlan doesn't think so. The money remains in her pocket, and she has
already decided not to give it back.

"Maybe we'll even get a foreigner in Heng'an someday," Zhuo Ge
says with a wink.

"There were those professors who came a few years ago." Juanlan
glances around the table. "Remember, they were on the news? They
were doing research."

"Yes, on 'Chinese market culture.'" Their mother sniffs in disdain at
a subject so unworthy of study.

"And more will start coming soon," Zhuo Ge says, and Juanlan is certain she's saved because he's started talking about the new expressway

again and will forget what they were discussing before. But Lulu, as if waking from a dream, cuts him off and declares, "But we already have a foreigner here. Juan Mei met him a few days ago."

Their parents both turn to Lulu, and then to Juanlan with surprise. "Is that true?" her father asks.

"It's not such a big event."

Her mother is still staring at her. "What does he want with you?"

"He wants to be able to communicate. He doesn't speak any Chinese, and he's traveling by himself. He's older. It's nothing to get excited about."

Her father clears his throat. "You should be careful, Lan'er, trusting a person like that."

"A person like what?"

"An older man. Who knows what his intentions are."

"No, it's not like that—"

"And someone who is so alone."

Juanlan just shakes her head. This is none of their concern. Annoyed with Zhuo Ge, who is happily slurping soup, she says, "Why don't you ask my brother why he's interested in foreigners coming to Heng'an?"

Zhuo Ge finishes his soup and sets down his empty bowl. Then he turns to their mother. "We've talked about the future of the Three Springs." He glances at their father, who has finished eating and is sitting with his hands on the edge of the table.

"You think we should try to be like the Friendship Hotel." Their mother makes a face. "We're a small place, Zhuo'er. We don't need to try to do more than we know how to do."

"It will be no problem if Director Wei helps us out. That's why it's important that we do him a favor now."

"It's easy to offer favors when you're not the one doing the work," Juanlan says.

"I don't understand." Their father looks from her to Zhuo Ge. "We have to register every guest."

"Yes, but Director Wei is close friends with the leader of that danwei. They might overlook some things, Ba. It's not very difficult. This happens nearly everywhere now—everywhere there are a lot of foreign tourists."

"So you're buying his favor," their father says, and turns back to Juanlan.

She lifts her hands. "I'm doing what Zhuo Ge asked me to do."

"What would we do with a foreign guest?" their mother asks. "I've never even met a laowai. We wouldn't know how to talk with one."

Their father is still sitting with his hands on the edge of the table. He looks like he is about to push back his chair. Or like he's keeping himself from falling forward. With a slow shake of his head, he says, "We won't survive unless we take a chance."

His wife gives him a sharp look. "And are you going to learn the foreigners' language? Are you going to have our daughter tutor you, like she's tutoring Director Wei's son? Or maybe she is planning on staying here for good. Maybe that's our children's plan for us."

Juanlan doesn't say anything. There is anger in her mother's tone, and desperation, and perhaps also hope. But the hope rests on Juanlan; she feels it teetering on her skull like the elaborate headpiece of a Sichuan opera singer. She glances at Lulu to see whether her sister-in-law looks sorry for bringing this discussion on them all, but Lulu's eyes are closed: she appears to have fallen asleep.

10

On Monday, the day Rob said he would return, Juanlan calls the Friendship Hotel. Rob sounds tired and irritable, a change from the easy personality he displayed last week. The bus ride from Kangding, he tells her, was terrible; he spent half the time vomiting into a plastic bag. By the time she gets to his hotel the next day, he is back to being cheerful. The weather is fine—for once it isn't raining—and they have made plans to go on a bicycle ride outside of town.

They turn down the street toward Zhuo Ge and Lulu's place. Her brother has agreed to let Rob borrow his bike, but this means they have to see Lulu. When they arrive at the apartment complex, they find her in the courtyard, seated on a bench beneath the little trees. "At last," she says, standing. "I've been waiting for almost an hour."

They aren't late, but Juanlan lets it pass. "Rob, let me introduce Lulu. My sister. My brother's wife." She lifts her hand in the manner of a museum guide.

"Sister-in-law," he says to her in a friendly, instructional tone. Then he steps forward to shake Lulu's hand. "Ni hao."

She giggles and remarks that his pronunciation isn't bad at all, looking expectantly at him to see if he understands. But of course he doesn't. "How strange," Lulu says. "It's like having a conversation in front of a dog. He follows whoever is speaking with his eyes."

Lulu's forgotten the bike key upstairs, so Juanlan climbs the stairs to retrieve it. At the door to the flat, she doesn't bother to take off her shoes. The key isn't on the table, as Lulu said it would be; nor is it under any of the magazines or hiding behind the bowl of peaches. She searches the floor, then looks under the sofa before moving on to the shelves. The bottom two are filled with pens and rubber bands and other household goods, but the top shelf is for display: it holds photographs from a shoot Zhuo Ge and Lulu had before their wedding. Juanlan's mother asked her why someone would waste money on such a thing, as if Juanlan herself were the one who had come up with the idea. "Your father and I only had one wedding picture taken, and that was after the ceremony," she said crossly.

Juanlan didn't point out that such customs didn't exist back then, that they'd gotten married in simple clothing—her mother with a short bob in a white-collared dress, her father in a Mao suit buttoned so tightly it looked like he could hardly breathe—and that weddings nowadays are a more elaborate affair. "Lots of people take these photos," she said. "It's a popular trend." She hadn't seen the actual photographs when she was defending them to her mother, but there was a studio near Chunxi Lu that had wedding portraits up in the window, and she'd stopped to look at them every time she was in the area. The portraits stood out be-cause the people staring out from them were clearly not models. They were good-looking in the way of average people, and in each case the woman was more good-looking than the man.

When she finally saw her brother and Lulu's pictures in Heng'an, she was surprised by how similar they were to the ones she'd seen in Chengdu; in the soft light of the camera lens, dressed up in other people's clothing, they looked almost like strangers. At the time, she'd been struck by how mismatched they appeared: Lulu's delicate limbs, pale skin, and black-grape eyes beside Zhuo Ge's square head and tobacco-stained teeth. In Juanlan's favorite of the portraits, the two of them were dressed like for-eign movie stars, he in a white tuxedo and she in a tight-fitting gold and silver dress that looked like it was made from melted coins.

Now, after spending so much time with the Lulu of swollen feet and limp hair, it is not her physical appearance that strikes Juanlan, or the difference between her and Zhuo Ge as a pair. It's the expression on their faces. In each one her brother is staring dreamily at Lulu, and in each one she is facing away.

After a ten-minute search, Juanlan finds the bike key on the floor beside the television and heads back downstairs. Lulu is seated on the bench, and Rob is sitting beside her, angled so Juanlan can't see his face. "Juan Mei," Lulu calls as she crosses the concrete toward them, "wait till you hear what I taught your friend."

He turns to show a wide grin. "Lulu was just teaching me some Chinese."

They speak in parallel, in two different languages, and Juanlan is the only one to understand both. It should make her feel that she's at the center of things. But instead she feels that in her absence the two of them have become fast friends in the way very young children are friends, playing together without words. Rob demonstrates what he's learned: he points above and says the word for sky, points at his head and says head, points at his foot and says foot. Lulu claps and laughs and grins like a baby. "Feichang hao!" she exclaims.

Rob says "xiexie" and then screws up his face, trying to think of another word to show off his learning. He points at himself and says, "Lan."

Juanlan shakes her head. "This is a Sichuan person's way of speaking. It's 'nan,' not 'lan.' Lulu is a bad teacher." She explains the difference, the confusion of sounds. Lulu is watching, trying to follow along, and at one point she protests, but Juanlan holds up a hand and continues speaking to Rob. "People will not understand you in other parts of China. They will think you are saying 'blue,' like the color, not 'male' like a man."

"What do you mean?" he says. "I thought I was saying 'me.'" He points to Lulu and says the word for female. "Doesn't that mean 'you'? No?" He laughs and says to Lulu, though she can't understand, "What have you been teaching me, anyway?"

They are a quick-talking comedy performance, something that would be on the New Year's Day Special on television.

Lulu still has a smile on her face, and it doesn't fade when Juanlan tells her that Rob hasn't learned anything at all, that he doesn't understand the meaning of any of the words she's taught him. She exaggerates the mistakes, even lies about what he got right and what he got wrong. "We're going now," she says when she's done. "We'll see you and Zhuo Ge at the restaurant at six."

Rob follows behind her. "Baibai," he says to Lulu, and Juanlan thinks for a moment that she has taught him that, too, until she remembers that it's originally an English word, something they all understand.

*   *   *

Riding out from town, Rob asks about Lulu. How old is she? Is twenty-three a normal age to have a baby in China? Does she want a boy or a girl, and does she know which one they're having, and is that an even more important issue in China because of the one-child policy?

"I don't know" or "I guess," Juanlan says in response to every one but the first question. Her brother and Lulu are having a girl, of course, but she doesn't pass on this information, thinking of the day Lulu pointed at her stomach and said that when she imagined what was inside, it wasn't a curled-up baby but a ball of twisted white worms. "Like you see in the shit of a sick pig," she'd said. One afternoon a few days later, Juanlan saw a ripple of movement over the globe of Lulu's stomach that made the foot of the cartoon cat on her T-shirt kick. It might have been a knee or an elbow, or even the baby's head. Juanlan wanted to ask what it felt like, but Lulu was staring down at it with a slack expression, as if she felt absolutely nothing at all.

The sun has burned through the thin layer of clouds. The sky is a hazy blue, and the wind blows the hair back over their heads as they ride. It's been weeks since the sun came out. Even here, not close to any river, Juanlan can sense the sodden quality of the ground, and she thinks of the news reports from other parts of the country. The flood is a disaster unfolding over a period of months. It's strange to think that it's getting worse even now, as they pedal their bikes past a field of yellow flowers in the sun. Rob is smiling and loose-limbed and too tall for the bike, and he laughs at this quandary, exaggerating the way his knees rise almost to the level of his chest as he pedals. His face in the sun does not appear young, but the lines at the corners of his eyes make him look kind. After a few minutes, Juanlan asks to stop so she can put her hair back in a ponytail and Rob plants his feet on the ground and walks his way over, still straddling the bike. Then he reaches back to get something out of his backpack. "Say cheese," he says, lifting a camera to his face.

"The scenery is not very good," Juanlan protests. "You should wait until we're somewhere more beautiful."

"I want to capture this moment." The camera lens blinks. "You've got a look on your face like you're going to kill me. Now this time: smile. *Yi, er, san.*"

A prickle in her stomach. "When did you learn the numbers?"

"So I said it right, then?"

Juanlan bites her lip. Yes, she concedes, he spoke correctly. "Did Lulu also teach you that?"

"All the way up to ten, though I can't remember that far." He lifts the camera again, and Juanlan shields her face, unhappy at the thought of her sister-in-law teaching him anything. He is supposed to be *her* foreigner, helpless but eager. She is supposed to be the one to show him the way. "Come on, now, smile!" he says again.

From behind the web of her fingers, she speaks the phrase Rob used when she first saw him on the street by the bus station, trying to tell people he didn't want what they offered. "Buyao," she says, mimicking the tone of a foreigner. *Buyao, xiexie, buyao, buyao.*

*   *   *

They return from the bike ride late in the afternoon, and there is time only to separate and shower. In less than an hour she's back at the Friendship Hotel, waiting for Rob to come downstairs. When he appears, it is without a backpack—he could be a Western business-man preparing for an evening out on the town. "Shall we?" he says, and gives her his arm.

The restaurant is not a fine one; it has smudged walls and plain wooden tables well dented with use. Against one wall is a bar with three large jars of baijiu, one flavored with peaches, one with goji berries, and one with several snakes coiled around one another. "Jesus!" Rob exclaims, and Juanlan assures him they won't have to drink any of that.

A tiny woman in an apron comes out from the back. "Your brother and his wife are already here," she says. "Right back this way." She leads them through the nearly empty restaurant, out a door, and through a narrow alleyway. The walls are damp and mildewed, the sky over-head a small rectangle of white. The woman warns them to watch their step, not to slip. "Tell him to be careful," she instructs Juanlan. "I can't speak the foreigner's language." It's clear that she wants to say more, to explain that she's never had a white man in her restaurant before, but Juanlan is already tired of having this kind of conversation with store owners and restaurant owners and street snack vendors, so she takes the opportunity to speak to Rob. Instead of passing on the woman's instructions to be safe and to watch his step, she asks if he's going to ask Lulu to teach him more Sichuanese.

"Sure. I could write up a section for the guide on the Sichuan dialect," he says, "and include a few useful phrases. My publisher loves that sort of thing—all the regional differences."

As if on cue, a man's voice somewhere nearby shouts a boisterous "Gua hou!" The phrase is purely regional, and Juanlan considers trying to explain it to Rob—*stupidest gourd*—but it's clear he hasn't noticed or heard. It's all the same to him, a blur of sounds he can't recognize or distinguish. When she glances over at him, he gives her a wink.

They pass two rooms, each filled with loud conversation. In the third they find Lulu sitting alone, idly picking through a basket of dried peas. She cracks one with her teeth and then turns and spits it out on the floor. "I'll break my molars with these things," she says. She gets to her feet, her small stomach poking the front of her dress. Juanlan is reminded of a moment early on in her relationship with Du Xian when they were on the bus and a pregnant woman boarded. Juanlan had blushed deeply, suddenly aware in a way she never had been before of the sex that others were having. A man had given the woman his seat, and Du Xian and Juanlan stood swaying over her, grasping the loops that dangled from the ceiling and avoiding each other's eyes.

Lulu pulls out a chair next to hers and gestures to Rob, telling him to sit.

"Where's Zhuo Ge?"

She frowns and flicks a hand at the door. "Some of his friends are in the room next door. They work at the electrical plant; I don't know how your brother knows them. They wanted us to join them, but I told your brother it's too much for Wah-buh." She turns to Rob, as if she has only just remembered him. "His skin is so dark! What's the good of being white if you're going to be out in the sun all day?" She touches a finger to his arm, and he cocks his head in mild surprise. "Aren't you going to tell him what I said?" Lulu asks.

Before Juanlan can translate, Zhuo Ge comes in through the door. "Mei! I'm glad to see you and your friend didn't ride off all the way to Tibet." He glances at Rob and laughs in a familiar way. Even though he can't have understood the joke, Rob laughs, too. "Did you order any drinks?"

"I didn't have time," Lulu says. "These two just arrived."

He shouts for the laoban to come, and she arrives instantly, asking what she can get them.

"Bring six bottles of Snow to start." Zhuo Ge nods at Rob and says slowly, in his best approximation of proper Mandarin, as if that might help, "This guy can drink a lot of beer, I bet."

"He can't speak Mandarin," Juanlan says. "You might as well speak normally."

Her brother takes a pack of cigarettes from his back pocket and flips it open, pushing it toward Rob in offering. Though he's told her he doesn't smoke, Rob takes one and fits it between his lips. "You don't have to accept the cigarette," she says. "I can tell my brother you don't want one."

"It's okay." He leans toward the flame that Zhuo Ge has lit. "Xiexie," he says.

Zhuo Ge turns to Juanlan. "You lied. He *can* speak Chinese."

"That's all he can say. That and 'hello.'"

"Not true," Lulu puts in. "I taught him a few words earlier."

Zhuo Ge looks from his wife to Rob, and makes a joke about her Mandarin being worse than a foreigner's. Rob watches the exchange, his eyes opened wide in readiness for the translation. Juanlan duly repeats her brother's joke, and when she's finished Rob laughs in an exaggerated way and throws back his head, which makes Zhuo Ge laugh again, and Lulu, too.

When the owner returns with the beer, Zhuo Ge rattles off six or seven dishes that he wants her to bring. There is no menu, or if there is one, he doesn't ask to see it. "What does your laowai want to eat? Beef? Americans love to eat beef."

Before she can answer, he's ordered a braised beef dish as well as beef with pickled peppers. "What else should we get?"

"That's plenty," she says, but Zhuo Ge ignores her and asks the owner what else is good. They go back and forth, discussing various dishes and speculating whether foreigners like to eat this or that. When the owner leaves again, he opens a bottle of beer and pours the contents into four small glasses. "For a toast," he tells Lulu. "Just a sip, and when the owner comes back we'll get a bottle of Coca-Cola for you. Or peanut milk. Which do you want?"

Lulu waves a hand dismissively. "I'll drink tea."

"Not tonight," Zhuo Ge says, pushing back his chair and going to the door. "We've got to honor our esteemed guest." He steps out into the alley to call out for a bottle of Coca-Cola.

"Zhuo Ge!" another voice yells from nearby. "You're not giving the laowai Coca-Cola, I hope!"

"It's for my wife! We're having beer."

"Why not baijiu? What, you're afraid he'll drink you under the table?"

Zhuo Ge shouts back that it's true, he's heard legends of the laowai's drinking abilities, and when the man responds that he wants to see how much he can consume, Zhuo Ge steps out into the alley to continue the exchange. Lulu rolls her eyes and, pushing the basket of dried peas toward Rob, grumbles that in a moment there will be a group of men coming to toast him.

As they nibble on the peas, Juanlan asks Rob about his trip to Kangding. He tells her he was lonely, that the town closed down at six or seven at night and there was nothing to do. It was windy, he says, and beautiful, but he wouldn't want to go back by himself. Juanlan thinks of her father's warning about those who are alone. There is a danger, perhaps, in the solitary soul bumping around without a purpose.

Zhuo Ge returns with three men, one of them holding a bottle of baijiu. The laoban follows them into the room with several small glasses and sets them in a stack on the table. "My friends want to toast your foreigner," Zhou Ge says, distributing the glasses among them. The white liquor is poured and one by one the three friends toast Rob, who each time throws back the entire shot. "Gan bei!" they shout, and Rob repeats the phrase to laughter and praise.

"You can just take a sip," Juanlan says, trying to intercede. "Or drink beer instead." She admonishes the men, telling them that he doesn't know the damage that baijiu can do.

"Foreigners have good constitutions," says one of the men. "He'll be fine."

Then it's Zhuo Ge's turn, and he instructs his sister to translate. Sloshing baijiu into Rob's glass and then his own, he looks around, meeting each person's eye as he takes a dramatic pause. "Heng'an is known for three things," he begins at last. "Plum blossoms, coal, and beautiful women. Heng mei, heng mei, heng mei." He speaks slowly, enunciating the different tones. "Go on," he says to Juanlan. "Tell him what I said."

She tries her best to describe the phrase, how it's based on little more than the fact that there is a small coal mine in the most distant county of their prefecture, and plum blossoms that color the mountains pink in the spring, and a claim that the town has the prettiest women in the country, a claim that every locality seems to make. "The three words sound similar in Chinese," she says, "so we call them the Three Heng Mei. Heng mei, heng mei, heng mei."

To her surprise, Rob repeats after her, botching the tones but trying so valiantly that all the men encourage him. He goes on in English, "And I've seen at least one of those three things since I came to town." He raises his glass to Juanlan. "Heng mei," he says. Then he turns to Lulu and addresses her with a little bow: "Heng mei."

The men all break out in enthusiastic cheers. It is a common joke, which makes it all the better.

Juanlan bites her lip as Rob's glass is refilled. He will be ill before long, and so will Zhuo Ge, so will all the men. But not before Zhuo Ge extracts a promise from Rob that he'll write up the Three Springs Hotel in the travel guide. "That would require him to write about Heng'an," Juanlan says, and Zhuo Ge says, of course, no guide would be complete without it. He makes her translate for Rob, makes her obtain the foreigner's assurance that he'll write about their town and their family's hotel, and Rob says, of course, he'd be happy to do it.

"Gan bei!" the men shout. "Gan bei! Gan bei!" Juanlan watches the baijiu spilling into the glasses and turns to Lulu to make the necessary complaints. But her sister-in-law is not looking at her; she's staring down at the bowl of dried peas. On her lips is the faint outline of a smile, meant for no one to see.

Addie

11

One winter night when Freddie was a baby, Addie woke suddenly and went to his cradle. Her son lay on his stomach, arms bent at his sides, hands squeezed into fists by his ears as if blocking out sound. She rarely had to nurse him more than once in the night anymore, but she'd still awaken three or four times between bedtime and morning, and each time she passed from sleep to consciousness it was as abrupt as opening a door. Eyes suddenly open to the dark, she'd listen for her son's breathing, and it was only when she heard it that she could go back to sleep.

Freddie's face was heavy with sleep now, something deeper than peacefulness dragging the cheeks downward. And yet, rather than feeling assured by the evidence that all was as it should be, Addie felt panic like an ammoniac burn. If her sense that something was amiss always turned out to be based on nothing, then what would happen if there actually were some danger? What if Freddie, one night in his bed, stopped breathing and she lay a few feet away, her own chest rising and falling in a dumb, even rhythm?

She stood looking down at her son. The light coming in through the window silvered his shape so he looked like a photograph of himself. People photographed their dead children, propped them up in a chair or laid them flat in a coffin tilted to the eye of the camera. The image came to her quickly—where had she seen it, and when? Years ago, in some neighbor's home; she might have been six or seven years old. She remembered a smell of camphor and the vanilla scent of cake. A breeze stirring curtains, swirling the shadows on a green rug so that it looked like pond water. On a table by the window was a photograph in a frame that showed a young girl crouched behind a tiny sofa, where her brother lay. They were both wearing lacy bonnets, both grasping dolls. The girl gazed at a point somewhere past the camera, but the boy's eyes were closed and his body was arranged as if he had fallen onto the sofa to sleep. Arms curled around the doll, he wore on his face a slight smile. Not a normal smile—Addie had known that even then. She'd turned away, heard her mother telling the neighbor that the road down the hill had been dry, and if Addie hadn't been wearing her new boots, she would have let her run down it. But you can't let them, always, be thoughtless. That boy, Addie had thought suddenly, will never again go running down a hill.

But here Addie was looking down at her son, and couldn't she see the edge of the blanket in the moonlight moving softly with his breath, and wasn't that his face registering the flash of something she couldn't see? She should go back to bed, crawl under the covers, but the devil was in her now. She couldn't sleep. She would only lie awake staring at shades of silver and gray, the shadows on the wall so terribly still, it was as if they had been pasted there.

Taking up her dressing gown, she wove her arms through the sleeves and quietly opened the door. Outside, the courtyard was glossed with moonlight. She shivered in the cold and considered going back inside to get her coat, but something stopped her. The cold felt bracing and clean. For once, the air seemed clear of the dust that often needled her lungs. Of course, it was probably only the dark that kept her from seeing it, but that didn't matter. If she could fool herself, all the better.

Along the opposite side of the courtyard, in front of the covered walkway that circled the perimeter, were the two benches the carpenter was carving for the sitting room. He had told Owen today that he would be done before the end of the week. If the carpenter was honest, that meant that soon they could have as many as fifteen or sixteen women gather for Bible lessons. The thought made her nervous; she pictured her neighbor Hsiu Taitai's face multiplied several times, each one squinting at her without either understanding or belief.

Addie shook her head. It was late—past midnight—but she was wide awake. The moon was bright enough to make every shape in the courtyard visible: the almost-completed benches; the pillars holding up the roof; the four small trees and the potted flowering bushes; the stone urns filled with rainwater, used for mopping the floors. But the night-time shadows were deep. Perched atop the eaves, the faces on the stone creatures could have been those of owls. Addie stared at one, almost daring it to move.

Everything was still—so still it made her restless, and suddenly she found herself lifting the heavy bar from the front gates and pushing open one side. She paused to see whether Wei-p'eng would come out from his room a few yards away. But no sound came to warn her, and, stepping over the threshold, she stood looking down the empty street. It was a long corridor, bleeding into darkness. She pulled the door most of the way closed, leaving an inch-wide gap, and then set off. On either side, the walls of other houses rose. She touched the soft wood of a door and trailed her fingers along its surface. She could have been a ghost, her presence felt but unknown. On the other side of the door were rooms filled with people soundly sleeping, though she couldn't picture them. Did Chinese children have dolls that they hugged close as they slept? Did the women let down their hair or keep it coiled in a bun? Addie had been invited into various houses in town, but there were places you couldn't go, couldn't even imagine.

At the end of the street she turned left and then right, making her way along the wider street that led to the market. When she arrived at the square, she barely recognized it. The empty streets were one thing, but the square, stripped of all occupants, gave her another feeling she couldn't name. She had the awful thought that this was what the first few moments after death might be like: a wandering through deserted streets that were almost recognizable, but made strange by their emptiness.

The square was still and quiet, but gradually she became aware of a soft clicking sound: a dog was trotting along the perimeter, close to the wall. It was mangy and dirty, as all the dogs in town were. Not large, but not small, either, and Addie suddenly felt that she was an intruder. At night the town's streets belonged to other creatures, and she had no business claiming the empty market for herself. The dog swung out toward the middle of the square and then stopped, considering her with its head lowered, as if she had been its object for some time and yet it didn't know what to do with her now that she was found.

For a long moment, she and the dog looked at each other. Then it growled, and Addie took a step backward. She felt a sudden sharp wind at her back, sweeping down the street she'd just taken. All at once the dog leaped forward, crossing the space between them, and sank its teeth into her leg.

She yelped and took a few stumbling steps, but the dog held on. She didn't feel pain. There was the sensation of a foreign creature latched on to her body, but this was oddly familiar: for months she had been teaching her body to allow such an act whenever she brought her son to her breast. Nursing Freddie was uncomfortable in a way that was worse than pain, in a way that made her want to bat away her son's head, to force a separation between her body and his. She never did; she had been continually reminding herself not to fight. Now she looked down at the dog and saw its blurred head joined to her leg and the tangle of her nightgown caught up around its neck and she kicked the leg it was attached to, and still it held on even as it growled again.

She stumbled toward the wall of a house, and when she felt the smooth surface, she braced herself on it and swung her leg so the dog's head connected with the bottom. The dog made a different noise then and released its hold. She kicked a second time and felt a sickening softness as her foot met a space between the ribs, and it yelped again and then swung drunkenly away.

Not stopping to watch it stagger, she set off running in the direction of their house. She wasn't limping at all; the leg still didn't hurt. It was only when she arrived at the gate and went in through the cracked door, only when she heard herself panting in the moonlit courtyard, that she started to feel a stiff soreness. At the sound of a voice speaking nearby, she turned to see Wei-p'eng standing by the door of his room. He had a long knife in his hand that Addie had never seen before. "It's me," she said in English, but Wei-p'eng didn't move. "It's me," she repeated in Chinese. She had learned enough of the language to be able to say that.

The door of the bedroom opened, and Owen came out. "What's going on?" he asked, taking a few steps forward. "What are you doing, Wei-p'eng? What's this?"

"It's my fault, Owen," Addie said. "I went out, and—"

"You went out—you mean, out into town? At this hour, and alone?" He glanced wildly around the courtyard, as if suddenly unsure that it was the middle of the night. "What were you thinking, Addie?"

"I don't know." Her heart was pounding. She leaned against one of the pillars. Everything had happened so quickly. She couldn't imagine now why she'd had the compulsion to go out. She watched Wei-p'eng cross to the gate and push it closed. He pulled the bar down into place and then went back into his room, sliding his own door shut behind him. With a start, she realized he must have been waiting in the courtyard when she came in. He likely left his bed after she first passed through the gate, and then he'd sat up waiting with the knife at the ready, to protect her.

"Owen," she said now, "I've got a dog bite."

"A dog bite!"

"Could you fetch me a cloth and some hot water? I need to clean it."

He didn't move. "This is completely unaccountable, Addie."

"Yes, but my leg is starting to hurt pretty terrible."

He left and came back a few moments later. "What have you got to say for yourself now?" he asked as he helped her over to a bench and sat down beside her. He put her leg up on his lap and began cleaning the wound, which was no more than a few punctures at the front and back of her leg. They were deep and oozing blood, though not very much of it.

Addie squeezed her eyes shut against the pain of Owen's finger probing the cut. "I'm sorry," she whispered. "I guess that's all."

His face was tight and grim and covered in shadow. He didn't say anything in response. After a few minutes, he went to find a bandage. Waiting for him to return, Addie tried not to focus on her leg, which ached deep down and felt larger than it was. She tried not to think about the dog, either, how it had watched her for a moment, head lowered, considering, and then come forward to attack.

*   *   *

The years ticked by as they would have done back home, as they did for everyone, but the changes that were taking place elsewhere didn't reach as far as Lu-cho Fu. There were no bicycles on the streets here. Neither Addie nor Owen could imagine what cornflakes tasted like or why anyone would want to eat them, though letters from home mentioned how this new food had changed breakfast in more than one household.

Addie's letters in response had the advantage of the exotic, but in reality her life felt more or less mundane.

Her days were filled with family and work. She had Freddie and soon after a daughter named Grace, who died so soon after birth that she was hardly more than an idea: an expectation and then, immediately after, memory. The local women whose homes she visited congratulated her on the fact that she had one healthy son. *What's the loss of a daughter?* they asked in the wake of the death. *What have you lost but a burden?* Mrs. Riddell, who accompanied Addie on these trips—or perhaps it was more accurate to say that Addie accompanied her—always immediately corrected the women's views by saying, "We are all blessed in the eyes of the Lord, the girls no less than the boys, though we are intended for different purposes." A woman must consider her husband as her guide through the darkness of female incomprehension, she said, so long as the man were a Christian. To those women whose husbands were resistant to conversion, Mrs. Riddell explained that the women's special mission was to bring their husbands around to the teachings of Jesus, to keep their family from the dire fate that awaited all heathens after death.

No matter where they began, the missionaries' discussions with locals always ended up at the same point. When they went to nurse a woman whose husband had torn her arm from the socket and blinded her in one eye, Mrs. Riddell explained that his anger stemmed from a stubborn unwillingness to know God. It was therefore the woman's duty to lead her husband to belief. She said all this as she dabbed at the swollen face with a wet cloth, though the woman kept up a low moaning throughout the visit. Addie didn't have the words to say what she felt, which was just as well. What she felt was that the violence visited upon this woman was no part of a divine plan. But she did her part by reading aloud several of the Psalms in translation, trying her best with the pronunciation.

Their methods were sometimes effective, but more often they failed. They failed, and then they kept coming back. Repetition was the key, Mrs. Riddell insisted. Repetition and Hard Truth. People needed to hear the meaning of their own experiences presented to them through the lens of Christian faith. They needed to be taught to recognize the Lord's work and not to question His ways. "Yes," Addie said. "Of course, you're right." In the days immediately after her daughter's death, she insisted that Owen keep Mrs. Riddell from seeing her. Though she knew God had taken her own child for what were no doubt good and meaningful purposes, she did not need to hear that she was wrong to mourn. Addie wanted to lie in bed and be alone with her grief. She asked Owen to send Freddie to stay with the Riddells for a few days, to give her that time alone and to keep Mrs. Riddell busy.

She mourned intensely for three solid days, and then, less acutely, for two or three months after. Then, abruptly, she was done. She wasn't like her sister Louisa, who mourned every baby lost in the womb as if it had been born and she had known it as well as Addie knew Freddie. Louisa wrote: *This sadness has teeth and it chews away at me from inside, making the place even meaner to the next one that tries to grow there.* Addie wrote back to her sister to have patience and hope, to put her faith in God. Look at her own loss, she said: she'd never have thought she could get over losing Grace, but she had. "Surely," Owen was fond of saying to her now, "our daughter rests with the angels." And so Addie believed, too, in an abstract way.

*　　*　　*

The mission started holding classes for girls to attend, and Addie and Mrs. Riddell shared the task of instructing them in math and science, in world history and the Bible. Mrs. Riddell remained for some time the better language speaker, and Addie frequently found herself using gestures and drawing pictures. The history lessons were as fantastic as anything the girls had ever heard, especially when Addie acted out Cortez discovering the New World. She raised her hand to her forehead and squinted out at an imaginary distance. She acted out the part of the natives greeting the Spaniard; sometimes she selected a few girls to help her. They had never heard of Spain or America, either. The world outside their little corner of China was as distant as the stars, and like the stars, every one of those places might be the same as any other. The Bible lessons were surely as strange.

Yet they were learning, these students, and this was something new. She frequently failed at minor tasks, but her reward was that here were several girls who could do what none of their mothers or aunts had ever dreamed of doing; they were allowed to be fully human. Sometimes, looking down at a new girl struggling to write her own name on the slate balanced upon her lap, Addie felt that she was doing something very noble and grand. Here was progress. Here was an unalloyed good. Here was civilization spreading light into the vast darkness of a strange land.

Yet it was more difficult to feel triumphant with regards to Lu-cho Fu's grown populace. After the morning lessons in the classroom, Addie generally went out to visit local women in their homes. Early on in her stay, she and Mrs. Riddell had gone on their rounds together. It was after Grace's death that Addie decided she was ready to begin executing these visits on her own. By splitting up, she argued, they could cover more territory. Mrs. Riddell agreed. And while it was true that this was one motivation for the division, it was also true that Addie was eager for time away from the other woman. Between their mornings in the classrooms, the afternoon visits to homes, and the twice-weekly services, the two women were nearly always together. And yet they weren't friends. Mrs. Riddell was severe and full of conviction. Addie, on the other hand, felt less and less sure as the years went by that the small triumphs were anything more than a distraction from the larger failure of the mission. She seriously doubted that the Chinese could be made to be Christian after all.

Only a few citizens of the town had been brought around to belief. Many were hostile to the idea, spreading rumors that the Christians ate Chinese children or that they were trying to take over the land by stealthy means. There was some menace in the existence of these rumors, a promise of retribution. Still, the more discouraging fact was that most of the people simply remained unconvinced. They came to services and tilted their heads at an angle; they narrowed their eyes as they listened. But in the end they went back out into the streets, and maybe they told a few curious friends about the odd things they saw at the mission: the calendar on the wall with drawings of a foreign place

(a calendar that arrived every year in the package from Ohio, though
sometimes not until March or April); the children with light hair like
sunshine; the photograph of all those somber-looking people standing
in a parlor totally unlike any seen in China. They might share tales with
their neighbors, but it was nothing more than a novelty.

"So we are here to keep the people of Lu-cho Fu entertained," Addie
wrote Louisa a few years into their stay. It was late autumn. Freddie
was two and a half and his brother was newly born, and they had both
recently come through a bout of sickness, the telling of which took up
all but the final paragraph of Addie's letter to her sister. It had been a
difficult and uncertain two weeks, with fevers and flushed cheeks and
necks, vomiting and diarrhea. She gave an account to Louisa that high-
lighted all the most harrowing moments—the night that Freddie first
started running a fever, his head damp with sweat as he twisted in the
sheets and then suddenly fell still, his eyes going vacant; the morning
she couldn't get either child to drink water; the tiny infant Henry shaking in her arms, vomiting nearly continually into a towel she held to his
mouth—and there was an almost frantic need to share the experience
with her younger sister, who was still not a mother, yet hoping to be.
There was an element of relief that was not only about the children but
about what the experience meant to Addie. *Do you see what I am? I am a
mother, and this is how it will be for you, too.* She was, for once, certain of
who she was and what she was doing.

Doubt had crept in at the end. She had time in the last paragraph to
turn her thoughts to other subjects, now that her sons were safe and
fully recovered at last. Henry was sleeping. Freddie was seated on the
floor beside her, sorting stones into little piles and counting aloud. Every now and then, he looked up at Addie and frowned. He seemed to
recognize some deficiency in his mother; he sometimes gave her looks
that suggested it. "I suppose," she wrote, "we might count ourselves
successful if we manage to bring a single soul into the light, even while
leaving China's other millions in darkness."

Addie covered the page in slanting print while keeping one eye on
Freddie, to make sure he didn't put a stone in his mouth and choke. She
worried about such absurd and unlikely dangers, when of course it was

the banal ones that actually killed. In China, children dropped away like dried leaves when sickness descended on a household. Somehow her boys had been spared this time, and her exhausted relief was evident even in her handwriting, which seemed to move toward the edge of the page in a stumbling gallop. *Do you think, Louisa, that we're doing any good here?* She held the pen over the paper, thinking. *I wonder sometimes.*

Owen, however, was certain that God had personally appointed the two of them to carry out His mission in China, and Lu-cho Fu would one day be the exact point from which a whole wave of Christianity would spread out over the land. He was equally certain that his daughter had been gathered into the bosom of God for good reason, that his sons would both grow to carry on the mission their parents had begun, and that the Riddells were solid Christians through and through.

He was not quite so certain of his wife's capabilities.

Or at least so Addie sometimes thought.

The Riddells had established the mission in Lu-cho Fu several years before Owen and Addie arrived, and it had continued to expand ever since. The number of converts was nothing great—there were maybe five dozen Christians in the whole area now—but the school was popular. It was small at first, and after the Bells came, it continued to grow: they now tutored twenty-two boys and girls from ages eight to fourteen, and had graduated nearly a dozen more. It was difficult to tell how many were Christians at heart, but there was more than one way to shine a light in the dark.

Yet Owen wasn't satisfied. He'd come to China with the goal of converting large numbers of people, whole towns and villages. The mission performed many kinds of work—they received regular packages of medicines from T'ai-yüan and were able to treat a variety of illnesses and accidents; they held classes; they actively campaigned against the barbaric practice of foot-binding—but all this was secondary to him. True conversion was a matter of the soul, rather than the mind or body. The only real triumphs Owen ever admitted were those few instances when a person was shaken to his very core by the sudden revelation of God's power and grace; the true convert was the person who needed nothing from the mission except the knowledge of Scripture.

Such conversions weren't easy to effect, and they took up much of Owen's attention. He studied the cases in which they'd managed to win over a person simply through talking or by sitting and studying the Bible together. What was the secret? Why was one person open when another was closed? Over the years he had come to think that it was largely a matter of the person's character, he told Addie. It took some amount of bravery to become a Christian in this place because it went against the traditions and beliefs of the population. There were even instances when converts had been disowned by their families, shunned. Not everyone was up to it. But then, conversion of a nation didn't require that every person was courageous. It only required that there were enough brave souls to begin the wave. After a time, the wave took on its own momentum.

One of Owen's favorite causes was music. In reading the dispatches of missionaries in other parts of the world, he learned that the singing and playing of hymns was central to the success of Christians in places like Africa and Hawaii and the Philippines. "What we need," he said, "is to engage the people with methods like these. What we need is more music. 'Make a joyful noise unto the Lord, all the earth: make a loud noise, and rejoice, and sing praise.' So says Psalm 98."

The Chinese were not strong singers; it was the missionaries themselves who carried the hymns during service. Owen had other plans. Over breakfast one morning, he explained his idea.

"An organ?" Addie said, incredulous. ·

"Why not? We could install it in the chapel." The chapel was a small hall at the back of the Riddells' house, behind the second courtyard. They held services in the space, which had six rows of benches, room enough for fifty or sixty people to squeeze in, though they never had that number. There were no stained-glass windows, no pulpit. There was only a cross hung on the wall, and some scrolls written with Chinese translations of short passages of Scripture. "If we knocked down the wall into the next room, there would be space there for a very small organ," Owen went on. "It might not be one to compete with a cathedral, but it would certainly be an improvement."

Addie was accustomed to her husband sounding ideas when they were alone, and she was occasionally useful in asking questions he didn't think of himself. She inquired now whether they wouldn't do as well to get a piano instead. "It's much more manageable, don't you think?"

"Not with the tuning, it isn't. And anyway, the impact is less." Owen shook his head. "People need to be impressed every now and then, and a piano won't do it. But an organ, now that's a sound to inspire. Isn't that right, Freddie?"

Their son nodded solemnly. He had already finished his breakfast, a roll and a boiled egg, exactly what Addie and Owen were eating. Now he was drawing with his finger on the tabletop, content with whatever thoughts filled his head. He had been a mystery to Addie from the beginning, and only grew more foreign to her after the birth of his brother, who was taking up all her attention now. She was trying to feed Henry bites of mashed noodles and milk, but he was restless on her lap, moving his head from side to side so that she had trouble fitting the spoon into his mouth. "Eat up, He Li," she murmured. It was what the locals called him, a translation that she'd found herself using, too. It felt oddly disconnected from the names she and Owen went by in town. They were Cheng Hsien-sheng and Cheng Taitai; Bell, it turned out, was a popular name in Chinese, too.

"What do you think?" Owen said. "Do you think it'll be a draw?"

"A draw?"

"For the mission." He tapped his fingers on the table as he watched her trying to feed their son, bits of noodle falling onto the cloth that she'd tucked under his chin.

From the courtyard came footsteps, and a moment later Li K'ang came in to clear away their plates. Owen's was filled with crumbs and the shells of two boiled eggs, but Addie hadn't managed to have more than a bite of roll dunked in milk. "I haven't eaten to full yet," she said in halting Chinese. "Please leave it for now."

"Should I get Hsi-yung to come help?" he asked.

Hsi-yung, Li K'ang's sister, was living with them now. Addie had formed a sort of friendship with the young woman, who spoke to her constantly, seemingly unbothered by Addie's ignorance of the language. Hsi-yung was nineteen years old, nearly Louisa's age. She had come to stay for several months after Freddie was born, and Addie recalled how the girl walked the baby around the room, stopping by the window to look out on the courtyard. She was thin and very small; in her arms Freddie looked like a bigger baby, a different one. And though Hsi-yung was quiet then, Addie would get the sense that she was conversing with him in some way, and she was left out completely, no longer part of their world.

That was before, when Hsi-yung first came to stay with them. She'd gone back to her home in the mountains after that and had her own baby, a girl, and when Addie was pregnant again with Grace and was nearly confined to bed for the final month, the girl had returned. She'd gone away yet again but returned after Henry's birth to help. Addie thought Hsi-yung might be pregnant again now, following a visit home two months before. It was odd, when Addie considered it, that the girl had a life and family up in the mountains and was here helping take care of Freddie and Henry, to gather up the soiled diapers for washing, or to watch the boys while Addie worked on the endless correspondence that took up much of her time. It was a pity if you thought too much about it, so Addie generally tried to put it out of her mind.

Li K'ang was looking at Addie, waiting for an answer. She waved a hand at him tiredly. "Thank you," she said. "It's all right. Please don't call your sister."

He rearranged the bowls and plates on the table, moving the bowl of eggs closer to her. "Shall I peel an egg for you?"

Addie shook her head. "I'll eat later."

He lifted the teapot, testing its weight to determine whether it needed more water. Owen's bowl was empty, but Li K'ang wouldn't take it away until Addie had finished as well. He made a cup of one hand and swept into it the shards of eggshell beside Owen's bowl. Then he took the teapot in his other hand and went out through the door.

Owen watched him go, and with his face still turned away, said, "I'll write the Missionary Board to make the proposal for the organ. It's just the sort of thing a congregation might want to sponsor."

"Especially if they can't use the money to get another Bible woman into the field," Addie remarked. The reports from the Board frequently mentioned the chronic shortage of female missionaries. Congregations back home sent money to support them, but there weren't enough women to fill the demand.

"It seems to me that you and Mrs. Riddell are holding down the fort."

"I suppose." She paused. "I think the organ's an excellent idea, Owen."

He shrugged and, watching as she attempted to guide the spoon into their son's mouth again, said, "He doesn't want to eat this morning, does he?"

Henry stopped to blink at his father, and his mouth fell open. Addie took the opportunity to deliver the spoonful of mashed noodles. "But, Owen, won't we have to find someone to play the organ?"

"Mrs. Riddell knows how. She played at their church back in Rhode Island."

"You've already spoken to her about it?"

"What," he said, smiling, "are you jealous that I've been talking over this business without you?"

"A little." It wasn't that Owen and the Riddells had been making these plans on their own that bothered her. She was used to being absent from some of their meetings. Julia had three servants to help her, and she seemed able to handle her house and family, in addition to any number of mission concerns, with ease. Other than coming to help teach the girls' classes, she did nearly everything from within the walls of their house, which doubled as the boys' school and the infirmary, as well as the church. The Riddells' home had always been the center of the mission, and perhaps that was the problem: simply by staying at home, Julia remained an active participant in all the major goings-on, whereas Addie, confined to their own house a half mile away, was cut off from everything and everyone, except for Freddie and Henry, Li K'ang and his sister, and Wei-p'eng. How small the world she occupied had become. She had not set foot outside their house for three days. "And Julia is confident she can do it?" she asked. "It's been at least a decade, I should think, since she played."

"Would you like to give it a go instead?"

Addie paused. "I was never very good at music."

"That's right," he said with a little laugh that was not meant to signify anything other than that she had got at the point he was intending her to. "In any case, we have to figure out how to get one here first." He turned to Freddie, who was still kneeling on his chair, drawing invisible shapes on the table. "How about you, son? Would you like to work the keys? Your brother here can crawl around on the foot pedals."

The food had ended up on Henry's cheek again, and when Addie reached up to wipe away the mess, he squawked and thrust his face aside, and she ended up swiping the cloth over his ear. He made the same sound again and then began crying. "All right," she said, lifting him under his arms and turning him around on her knee so he was facing her. His face was wrinkled and turning pink as he cried, his eyes open but thick with tears. She brushed her hand over his head and got up to go into the other room to nurse him. How she looked forward to the time when she would be finished nursing. Then she'd be able to go out again, to leave the boys in the care of Hsi-yung alone. Her body would be hers again. Her mind, her concentration—all of it, hers.

*　　*　　*

She didn't hear anything more about the organ until nearly four months had passed. Then one late spring day, when the first mail packet arrived after some time, she found Owen with a letter in his hands. "They don't see the purpose," he said with a frustrated sigh. He held the letter up to Addie and then took it away again before she could see what was written. "I made a good case, and the Board refused. It took them just two sentences to do it. They don't understand a thing about what works over here." He folded up the letter and tucked it back in the envelope. "We'll have to find another way."

He enlisted Addie to write to every congregation that sponsored their efforts, so at the end of each bulletin she sent describing their latest efforts and victories, she made a plea for funds and help. She didn't know much about organs, but she thought Julia might provide the necessary knowledge if the time ever came. Privately, she thought it an absurd idea—even in America, few churches had organs. She thought Mr. Riddell felt similarly; whenever the topic came up, he got a distracted and faraway look on his face, as if the plan were too difficult for him to comprehend. It was, Addie knew, the same look she showed whenever a conversation in Chinese was taking place—she could understand some of the words, but it was easier to tune it out, to let the sounds wash over her.

"We are in search of support—financial and practical—for procuring a small and modest pipe organ to add to the atmosphere of worship in our chapel here," she wrote, with more enthusiasm than she felt for the project. "It is an undoubted fact that such a gift to our mission would result in dozens more conversions, as the people here are in awe of such marvels as we take for granted." Secretly, she hoped her husband might give up his campaign.

*   *   *

During the sixth year of their stay in Lu-cho Fu, Owen got permission from the Board for the whole family to return to the States for a visit. They'd wanted to go the year before, but the war with Japan had intervened. Now that it was over and the ports were all open again, they arranged passage on a steamship from T'ien-chin. At the end of February, they set off from Lu-cho Fu. They were repeating the trip of six years before, but this time in reverse.

Whenever Addie thought back on this trip in later years, it would seem as if the whole thing were a dream. It took more than two months to get back to the States, but once they were on American soil, it was easy to cross the remaining distance. After the train in China from T'ien-chin to the port, the train they took from San Francisco seemed almost impossibly fast. And then they were at the station in Ohio, and there was a whole crowd of people to greet them, so many faces and voices that both Freddie and Henry were crying within minutes of getting off the train.

It was thrilling and exhausting, hearing English spoken everywhere, noting the different style of dress that she had only seen in magazines shipped across the ocean (all the women, even her mother, wore walking suits during the daytime now, and Addie felt dowdy in her old dresses).

She found that she could no longer abide eating sweets. She was struck by the attention everyone paid to time.

After Ohio they went to Illinois, and her impressions of the visit were only of an immense nighttime darkness and waves upon waves of corn; her brother-in-law showing them all how to milk a cow; Louisa standing with both hands at her back, surveying them from a distance with an unreadable expression on her face. She was not the girl Addie had left six years before. She was a woman now, with a collection of private heartbreaks that she dragged around with her like a sack. Her pregnancy was already much further along than any of the others had been, yet still her worry was evident. At the end of two weeks, when the time came to part, she put her face close to Addie's and said in a voice much louder than the whisper she seemed to have intended, "Don't you dare never come home."

Owen had arranged for them to take the train to St. Louis and then to board the cross-country line that would take them to San Francisco. He had a surprise, he said, and though Addie didn't know what it was, she accepted the plan without question. When they got off the train at Union Station, only opened the year before and now the largest and busiest station in the world, Addie was nearly overcome by the opulence and the size of the crowds. In the Grand Hall, the ceiling was gold leaf. The building seemed to go on for miles. It was beautiful and terrifying, and seemed to presage some great fall, like the tower of Babel. "What a wonderful surprise," Addie said. "I've never seen anything like it." In her arms, Henry had turned his face to her chest and was breathing hotly into the fabric of her dress. Even Freddie was clinging to her skirts, no doubt afraid he would be swept away by the crowds unless he held on.

But Union Station wasn't the surprise. The surprise was some cargo that was waiting for them in St. Louis. Earlier in the summer, while Addie and the boys were in Ohio, Owen had gone up to Philadelphia to speak to a congregation that had supported their mission over the years. In May, a Catholic school had closed down, and included among the items sold off was a small pipe organ that had graced the chapel for the last fifteen years. It was this congregation that had bought the organ, and it was this organ that would make the trip with the Bells all the way across the country to San Francisco, across the Pacific to China, and across the mountains of Shansi to their little town of Lu-cho Fu, where they would never succeed in installing it in the tiny chapel in the Riddells' house—where it would sit in its many parts in a spare room for several more years, until the arrival of a new missionary requiring a room would necessitate that they get rid of the organ at last, without ever once making the sound that was to have inspired so many.

12

When the new missionary arrived, it was as if she had snuck into town. They had known she was coming for months, and had received word in their last letter from T'ien-chin that it would probably be sometime in the middle of April. She had actually been in the area for over a week— though not in the town—before they knew that she had arrived.

Addie was the one to discover her. She had gone down to the market in search of fruit. The mountains were still gray with winter, yet there was a sense of melt in the air, a certain buoyancy, an added thickness rather than the dry air of winter, which felt too thin sometimes to be breathed. Addie wanted to make a dessert because they were having the Chinese deacon, Mr. Yang, and his wife to dinner. She knew they would spend most of the meal speculating about what the new missionary would be like. Mrs. McBride's own mission had recently closed after a large family stationed there left to return to the States. She herself was a widow with no children. Alone, in other words, though it was unclear how long ago she had lost her husband. Addie imagined a stern woman, stoic in her grief.

Owen had left up to Addie the arrangement of this dinner. It was assumed that she could most effectively perform a missionary's duties by presenting to anyone who cared to witness it the example of a civilized American household. Having clean napkins, fresh candles in the candlesticks, and a dessert that she had made with her own hands became the test of whether Christianity would ultimately prevail in the land. And though the napkins might not matter, Addie did find herself wanting to provide for the deacon's wife the example of a capable woman who could join in intelligent conversation. Her husband had, from the first, been exactly the kind of Christian they hoped to make of the Chinese. He was active and capable; he deferred to them on questions of religion but was a sort of cultural guide even now, after nearly a decade in the area. He was not, perhaps, universally beloved in the area—he spent far too much time in their company to avoid suspicion among those who viewed the foreigners' presence with alarm. However, he had a variety of connections that had proved helpful over the years. And he was not like some of the congregants, whom Addie sometimes didn't quite trust. Mr. Luo, for example—there was something suspect about him, a chicken-hawk look, and eyes that were always fixing on objects behind you, barely out of sight.

Mr. Yang was a trim man with graying hair and a calm, low voice. He had a great command of English, and perhaps this was why Addie felt more comfortable with him than with any of the women she had met. She could speak English with him whenever she felt too tired to converse in Chinese, and even speaking the latter, she could count on him to supply the blank spaces in her vocabulary, filling in the missing words, handing them to her one by one as if they were playing a hand of cards. He was an envoy who ferried back and forth between the mission and the rest of Lu-cho Fu, and he was seemingly as comfortable in one world as he was in the other.

His wife, on the other hand, still seemed after all these years to be uneasy in their company. Addie knew this as well as Owen did—more so, because she had been alone with Yang Taitai, attempted to speak with her woman to woman, as mothers and wives, and received nothing but a placid smile in return. Was she like this at home, too? Did she move about in her own house on her tiny slippered feet, reaching for every surface to prevent herself from falling? That she continued this way even with a husband who had long ago adopted foreign ways was a mystery to Addie. But Yang Taitai was like one of those eggs that had had the white and the yolk drained from an invisible hole and was then painted and set on a little stand as an ornament. There was nothing inside. She was delicate in a way that made you want to smash her. Or if there was some sort of depth to her character, Addie had never yet figured out how to reach it. Every time the two families met, she found herself constructing an image of herself that was in direct opposition to the Chinese woman. It reassured her; she was not like that woman at all. She could cook and clean, and lead the women's group meetings, and write letters to be published in the missionaries' reports back home, and go out into town to go shopping, and ride mules or horses, and patch up a dress that had a rip in its sleeve. Though still uncertain of their overall mission in Lu-cho Fu, with the deacon's wife Addie could at least imagine herself an icon of the capable woman, though sometimes she found Owen staring at her across the table with something like disapproval in his eyes.

She made her way through the maze of streets, taking the long way to avoid having to go down the alleys that were only three or four feet wide. She had begun to develop a fear of those areas, though violent events in China seemed mostly to take place out of the way of other people, on lonely mountain paths. Only a month or two earlier, two local men had failed to return from their journey into Chi-li, and rumor attributed their disappearance to thieves. "Do you think there's any truth in it?" she'd asked Owen, and he had looked grave and said he thought it was possible. "These are the risks we live with," he said. "The Lord's will be done."

As soon as she turned into the market, she felt an energy buzzing out of proportion to the number of people there. A pair of vendors looked up as she approached and seemed more than usually surprised to see her. One of them, lifting his chin in her direction, said, "Look, it's the other one," and his friend, watching her, turned and spat.

She walked quickly past them. Down the street was a knot of people, several men standing with their arms folded behind their backs, turning their faces to one another as they spoke. Addie couldn't see what they were looking at, but the group erupted in laughter, and at the same moment moved apart enough to give her a glimpse of a tall white woman in animated conversation with a man holding a birdcage. Inside it, a small bird was skipping back and forth on a slender bar.

The woman's face was flushed along the cheekbones, her eyes bright. Her hands wove through the air in wild gestures as she spoke. From what Addie could hear, her Chinese was boldly inflected. If she closed her eyes, Addie might have been hearing a town native talking.

The woman wore a long dress and ankle boots and a patched cotton jacket, and on her head was a large-brimmed hat. She glanced at Addie with something laughing in her eyes, also a certain sharpness. Addie felt that the woman knew exactly who she was—not only her name or the fact that she was a missionary here, but what she had been doing that morning, and thinking of, and failing to understand. The woman nodded slightly and went on speaking, but many in the crowd glanced over, and suddenly Addie found herself herded into the circle. "You must be one of the missionaries here," the woman said in English.

"I'm Addie Bell," she replied, the blood rushing to her cheeks. "Are you Mrs. McBride?"

"Poppy." The woman glanced around at the circle gathered around them and said in Chinese, "Come, haven't you ever seen two foreign ghosts talking before?" The crowd laughed at her use of the term, rarely heard from the mouth of a foreigner. To Addie, in English, she added, "It doesn't matter what language you speak in, you're bound to shock them one way or another."

"Yes, I suppose that's true."

The woman gazed at her, and Addie felt embarrassed. Her own words sounded too proper; they broke against the other woman's speech like water on a rocky shore. After a moment, however, Poppy smiled. "It's good fun to shock them sometimes. Keeps things interesting. I've certainly shocked my friend with the bird here, and a moment ago we were simply haggling over the price of the thing."

The man with the birdcage was saying to his friend, "There's a ghost for you. This one looks like a white person, but speaks like a Han."

"Uncle, I'm no ghost," Poppy interrupted. "Ghosts and birds don't get along." She tipped her hat at him and winked. The hat was of worn leather and had a wide brim, like what Addie had seen men out the train window in Kansas and Colorado wearing. They were the hats of men who spent their lives outside, the leather tinted by sweat and sun. On the train years before, she and Owen had encountered a man with the same hat, but he wasn't wearing it. He was dressed uncomfortably in a woolen suit, and the hat rested on the table beside him like a pet. He'd glowered at his plate like it might get up and attack him, and Owen had given him worried glances from time to time as the man's glass of whiskey was emptied and refilled again and again.

She had never seen a woman wearing a hat like that, and she had certainly never seen a missionary with one. It was pushed back on her head, allowing her to see out under it easily. She was a full head taller than anyone else in the vicinity, and Addie thought it must simply be the style to which she'd grown accustomed. It lent her an additional air of ease, of casual command. When she tipped the hat at the man with the birdcage, he gave her a surprised look that quickly dissolved into practiced detachment. "One chiao," he said. "That's the lowest price I can offer you for such a beautiful and elegant bird."

"I haven't even heard it sing. It's probably sick or lazy. I'll pay eight fen or not take it." The man met her gaze and, after a moment's hesitation, lifted his chin to indicate the sale. The crowd standing around murmured their satisfaction.

Poppy dropped a few coins in his hand and took the birdcage. She peered in at the creature, which had ceased hopping back and forth on the little rod and now peered back at her, its head turned at a quizzical angle. It was small and mud-colored, with short brown legs and a tuft of white on its head. It did not look particularly elegant, but it had small bright eyes like jet beads that made it seem intelligent.

The woman made a noise with her teeth and tapped the edge of the cage with her finger. She had short, blunt nails with a line of dirt around the edges, the hands of a peasant or a farmer. No telling how they had gotten that way, what kind of work she had been doing before she came to Lu-cho Fu. The letters from T'ien-chin had described Mrs. McBride as "a highly capable lady educator and nurse," and Addie had imagined high-buttoned collars and starched shirts, an efficient manner, a whiff of ink. It was not that she would have preferred this type of character, but she would have known what she was about. Such a woman would stand with her hands folded behind her as she walked. She would be primly disapproving of everything Chinese. She would be stern and unyielding—like Mrs. Riddell.

Such a woman would pay attention to her hands, too, keeping the nails clean and well trimmed, rubbing jojoba oil into them at night to keep them soft. Addie always did this after laundry day to keep her hands from chapping too badly. Now, seeing Poppy's—tapping the thin rails of the cage with a fingernail edged with dirt, the skin at the knuckles red and rough—and how she made no effort to hide them,

Addie felt embarrassed by her own appearance. She was dressed in a neat gray dress, her hair pulled back with two clips that kept the stray hairs in place. The clips were painted with little flowers, and she wore a gold cross at her neck. Altogether, her attire was not exactly grand, but she saw all of a sudden how different she looked from the two Chinese women standing in the shadows of a shop nearby, who looked like every woman she ever glimpsed on the street. They wore straw shoes and layers of cotton with no particular cut to them. And their hands were mostly lined with dirt like Poppy's were, the lines in their palms darkened like roads on a map. She'd been told that Chinese women wore jade because they believed it kept them healthy; the poorest of them had a bracelet, even if it was of low quality. The way they wore the jade was not at all as she wore the clips in her hair. There was something frivolous about her, the same as the wealthy ladies who were carried through town in litters. She wondered whether that was how she had always been seen. How did they feel about her, all these strangers whose faces shifted around like a kaleidoscope as she moved through a crowd? If she were to fall to the ground at this moment, would they merely step over her as they went about their business?

Poppy lowered the birdcage to her side and turned to Addie. "Are you ill, Mrs. Bell? You look pale all of a sudden."

She shook her head. "No, I'm fine, quite fine." She took a step backward and felt the people open up a path to let her through. "It's only that it's a bit close here. I'll go on, I think."

"Shall I join you in your shopping? I assume that's why you're here." Poppy nodded at the empty basket in Addie's hand. "And by the looks of it, you haven't gotten very far yet. What are you shopping for?"

"Fruit," Addie said. "I'm here to buy fruit."

"You want to buy plums, I bet, but I'm going to talk you out of it," Poppy said as they set off down the street in the opposite direction from which Addie had come. "It's still two weeks too early for them. The ones they've got on offer are going to be as hard as walnuts. Not worth your money or your teeth."

"What should I buy, then?"

"Dried persimmons. There's a man selling them down around the corner. Boil them for a few minutes, and they'll be as sweet and flavorful as you could wish."

Addie told her she was making a dessert and then invited her to dinner. She explained it would be a small party, and told her who was invited. "Mr. Yang is the deacon here," Addie explained. "He's been the backbone of the Chinese Christians in Lu-cho Fu since the mission was begun."

"Oh, well, in that case, I most certainly won't come. That would spoil everything."

"What do you mean?"

"Only that it's Mr. Yang whose ideas I'm most going to upset. He knows it, of course, and I'm sure he's counting on this private dinner to guard you against me." She arched one eyebrow and twisted her mouth into a wry smile. "It'd be a terrible joke to surprise him like that, and rob him of the chance to speak ill of me."

"That can't be right. I'm not sure he even knows who you are."

"Oh, he knows, all right. The Chinese deacons always know more about what's happening than any of the missionaries, and they know that a change is no good because it will challenge whatever systems they've put into place. This is the first I've heard Mr. Yang's name, but I'd bet you he's known about me for the past six months, and been planning how to overthrow me just as soon as I came."

They walked on in silence. Several times, Addie opened her mouth to ask when her companion had arrived in Lu-cho Fu, and where she had been staying, and how it had come to be that none of them knew of her arrival. But before she could begin, Poppy turned to her and said, "You're not one of those married women who doesn't speak the language, are you?" She didn't wait for an answer before adding, "Because if you are, then I don't know what you've spent all your time doing."

Addie bristled at the assumption. "I speak as well as possible, I think, for one who didn't grow up speaking it." Then she stopped, remembering how easily Poppy had conversed with the bird seller. After a pause, she asked, "How have you managed to do it?"

"Oh, I don't know that I'm any good. I speak like a peasant. Put me in a room with a magistrate, and they'll give me a look that could turn your blood to ice." She glanced around as if to ensure that none were standing nearby. "I don't speak perfectly, not at all. And the accent here is something else."

"Where did you learn to speak, then?"

Poppy tossed her hand in the direction of the mountains to the west. "Not awfully far from here, but you know how China is. Every valley has its own language. Makes provincialism in America seem like nothing."

"Oh, I don't know about that. Where I'm from, you go a few miles east and it's a whole different world. Language, religion, everything."

"Where's that?"

"Ohio, the southeastern part. East is Appalachia."

"The mountains start rolling upward and the people get odder, is that it?"

"Exactly," Addie said. "Or at least, that's how we always felt about it. But then, that's probably what the people in Peking and T'ien-chin say about this place."

Poppy laughed loudly, revealing teeth crammed too closely together, each turned at an angle to make room for itself. "You're right about that. We're living among the country bumpkins, according to those in the east. But the joke's on them, because this is where it's *at*, Mrs. Bell. This is where it matters."

"Do you mean that the people here are more accepting of the Gospel?"

"Not in my experience. I only meant to say that the people in these parts are far more interesting to talk to. City folk and country folk, they're not of the same breed." She paused and then asked what kind of people the Riddells were.

Was it possible that they hadn't yet met? Addie knew the new missionary was supposed to be living with them, and had even seen the room they had got ready for her. The old organ, never assembled, had been cleared away.

"I came down into town this morning," Poppy explained, "and I haven't been over to meet my hosts just yet. I wanted to get a sense of Lu-cho Fu untainted, so to speak." She glanced quickly at Addie and said, "Don't take any offense. I find missionary folks sometimes have such a fixed idea of the place they live in, and it tends to be contagious."

Addie assured her that she was not offended at all, though she wondered at the way the other woman excluded herself from the category of missionaries.

After a moment, Poppy said, "I understand you and your husband live in a separate compound from the Riddells?"

"Yes, though not far away. We see each other every day."

"So you all get along well then?"

Addie paused before replying, "Quite well, I'd say, considering how very small our circle is here. You must know something of that from your last post."

"Oh, in Lang-jen there were only the Waverlys and myself, in terms of foreign missionaries. Of course, that's why I had to leave. When the Waverlys decided to go back to America, the Board wouldn't let me stay on alone. They closed down the whole operation."

"I thought they'd kept on some people?"

"Only the local church folks. But how exactly do you expect a mission to continue when the Board has sold off the very place that's the heart of it? I tried to convince them to let our deacon and his family move into the compound. Between you and me, Mr. Chao was already doing more of the work than Mr. Waverly when it came to both the church and the school. The Board simply wouldn't have it. They'll only put a foreigner in the post, and since they wouldn't let me give it a go— well." She laughed. "But who knows? Maybe the Christians will flourish there without any help from Boston. It would be a fitting sort of victory."

They walked on in silence for a minute or two. Addie was trying to determine what to make of this woman, who was vastly unlike anyone she'd ever met. She knew that Poppy had been married and couldn't imagine her as a widow, much less a wife. The new missionary seemed totally independent, so wholly on her own. Addie ventured to ask how long she had lived in China.

"Sixteen years."

"And you came here originally as a wife?"

"Ha! Yes, I guess that's the way to put it." But Poppy shrugged and didn't say any more on the subject.

Addie turned toward the Riddells' house without telling the other woman she was taking her there. It was not far, and they talked of other things—mostly of Lu-cho Fu and how different it looked than Lang-jen, which Poppy said had been in a valley alongside a small river whose name changed with every mile you traveled of it. "Where we were, they called it the Bright River, which was probably the most dishonest name they could have found. If you dipped your finger in, you'd lose sight of it altogether."

At last they had reached the Riddells'. Addie said she would leave Poppy there. "You'll come to dinner soon? Tomorrow, how's that?"

"That sounds fine," Poppy said, and, raising her fist, knocked firmly on the door. "Get on, now," she said with a wink at Addie, "before they open up and see you here. I have a corruptible nature, and they might suspect you."

*   *   *

The plan had been to have the Yangs to dinner one day and Poppy the next, but once the new missionary showed up at the Riddells' house, the idea of a single large welcome meal quickly developed. It was a Saturday, and the mission held no classes, and this was generally a day that the two families stayed separate. When the message came inviting the family to dinner, Addie was already mixing up dough for dessert. She'd gone back to the market and bought some dried persimmons, and when Li K'ang handed her the note, she looked down at the bowl of flour in which she'd been cutting in soft yellow lard. She told Li K'ang the dinner was canceled. "Lai Taitai"— this was the name Mrs. Riddell went by in Chinese—"invited us to go to her house. No dinner." She shook her head again with a sharp jerk.

"I've already killed the chicken," Li K'ang said. "Not to worry, we can eat it tomorrow."

Owen and the boys had gone down to the river, which though often dry was running now after some recent rain, to see if they could catch any frogs. When they returned, Addie told them of the change in plans. "The new missionary has arrived," she said, "and the Riddells want us all to come for a welcome dinner for her."

"She's here? In Lu-cho Fu?" Owen asked.

"Apparently."

"Mama," Henry said, "we didn't catch any frogs at the river."

"No, but there were birds," his brother said. "Big ones that had black along the outside of their wings—"

"—and skinny, with a long neck like this." Henry snaked one arm up in front of him.

"No, they didn't, either," Freddie protested. "Their necks weren't that way at all."

Henry ignored him. "And they went flying away in front of us and one was as big across as I am tall. That's what Papa said, anyway."

"How did she arrive so early?" Owen inquired, giving his sons a stern look for interrupting. "We weren't expecting her for another few days—I'd have thought she'd send word ahead from T'ai-yüan. She was going there first from her last post, was my understanding."

Addie thought of what Poppy had said about coming to town in secret, how she didn't want to have her impressions of Lu-cho Fu formed by the missionaries already here. She meant Addie and Owen, in addition to the Riddells. She had reason to mistrust them, simply because they had all been here so long.

Henry suggested that the new missionary might have flown into town on the back of one of those birds, and that was why they didn't know when she came.

"But—," Freddie said.

"It could be," Addie said. "You might be right, Henry."

Freddie glowered and turned away.

"I look forward to meeting her," Owen said. "A new face will liven up our group."

Addie didn't tell him that this was exactly what she had been thinking.

*   *   *

"But don't you think it's as well for Christianity to settle in through the body as it is through the heart? And more likely to stick, too. For myself, I wouldn't be likely to trust a funny-looking foreigner sailing into *my* town with a stack of dusty books, and explaining how wrong all my age-old beliefs really are. But give me a vial of medicine, and I'm much more likely to listen. Turn the tables around, and it looks like a very different situation altogether, Mr. Bell."

Silence had descended around the dining table. There were eight of them altogether; the children had been served and dismissed, all except the Riddells' second-oldest son, who was fifteen and already a young man and expected to make conversation with the adults. He'd been seated next to the new missionary and had, over the past half hour, been looking more and more alarmed by the way she kept turning to him as she spoke, as if he might have something to contribute to the discussion. The current subject was the refuge for opium addicts that Poppy had helped to set up in another town in China—not Lang-jen, where she had been living before coming to Lu-cho Fu, but another place, farther east. It seemed she had lived in a number of towns and stayed at a number of missions in the sixteen years since she first came to China.

"Opium is certainly a great scourge upon this land—," Owen began.

"And you know it's as much our fault as it is the Chinese's," Poppy said, nodding.

"—but I don't know that it serves our purpose to take in every addict sitting glassy-eyed against the city wall."

Owen's mouth had tightened when Poppy interrupted him. For the past several minutes, the Riddells had been asking the new missionary questions about herself and the work she'd done, and Poppy had proven herself an eager speaker. She was enthusiastic about everything: the Chinese temperament, the work of the missions, the colorful idioms she'd made a habit of learning, the many dishes the Riddells' cook had served them this evening (all on the American model; Mrs. Riddell considered the Chinese diet unwholesome), the weather, the town, the bedroom she'd been given, which was comfort itself, she declared. She congratulated her hosts on the good work they had done in Lu-cho Fu and on the wonderful work that had continued since the Bells joined them. It seemed to Addie that her compliments were genuine. But once she began on the subject of the opium refuge, Owen had seemed ready to contradict her. It was clear to Addie that her husband was frustrated at the woman's loud voice and strong opinions, especially those that didn't coincide with his own.

"Of course we can't save every last one of them," Poppy said, "but I don't see why that means we shouldn't try to save *some*. Surely, Yang Hsien-sheng, you agree." She leaned forward to glance down the table, where the Chinese couple was seated. "Or Yang Taitai, you must feel the same," she added in Chinese. "Isn't it true that opium is one of the greatest problems your people face?"

Mr. Yang replied in English, "Opium has had many terrible results for the Chinese people."

"If you could see up close the misery of the addict's existence—"

"I assure you, Mrs. McBride, that we have," Owen said. "The populace in Lu-cho Fu is no less touched by this affliction than elsewhere in China."

"Indeed," Julia Riddell put in, with a sad shake of her head. She glanced at Addie with something like reproof, perhaps for not having shown her agreement as well. "It's as bad here as anywhere."

"But you don't choose to treat it?"

Mr. Yang explained that they had adopted a policy of refusing medical treatment to opium smokers, since it only encouraged use of the drug.

"I know at other missions," Mr. Riddell put in, "they've chosen an opposite path. Direct engagement with the addict is supposed to lead to eventual conversion. Or so they claim."

"Not necessarily," Poppy said. "Those of us who have treated the poor souls have other concerns when it comes to what's good for them— more immediate concerns. The former addict might recognize God's grace in his recovery, but of course, Mr. Riddell, you understand that the word 'former' is the key one. When they're on the drug, they can't be convinced of anything, because nothing matters—it's all sounds and movement, everything slowed down to where it can be beautiful. Nothing matters, everything is as clear as ice. Clarity, beauty—that's the appeal of it."

"You give a sound description," Owen said doubtfully.

"I tried it, of course, long ago." She glanced at the Riddells' son, whose eyes had grown wide at this revelation. "Look, now I've startled the young man."

Addie couldn't help but laugh, too; it was such a strange idea. The rest of the table looked at her—coldly, it seemed, except for Poppy, who caught her eye briefly and went on to explain why she'd taken the drug. She'd wanted to know what they were fighting, she said. It's easier to trick the devil when you know what he looks like.

Mr. Yang cleared his throat. "I hope you did not try it alone," he said.

Poppy shook her head. "My husband was with me."

A general hush fell over the table. The new missionary hadn't mentioned her husband before now, and it seemed necessary to offer a moment of silence in his memory, though none of them had ever met the man—he'd been dead, Addie believed, for at least a decade, perhaps since before any of them had ever arrived in China. She glanced at Owen and saw that his face was impassive.

"We went together to an opium den," Poppy went on. "This was in P'ing-yao, I think, if memory serves me correctly. Yes, it was, because there was a bank house around the corner, and I remember thinking how odd it was that this town known for its banking should also have a great many addicts. And in fact, the man who ran the place said that several of the money men would come by on their way home after they had finished the day's work. We might have been there together with them, I don't know. By that point, I was no longer fully in command of my senses. Would you pass that basket of rolls, young man?" The Riddells' son complied, and then with a shrinking air glanced at his mother, perhaps afraid he had done something wrong.

Mrs. Riddell was smiling frostily at their guest. From down the table, Mr. Yang spoke up again. "You were in China a long time before you went there?"

"Thank you, Yang Hsien-sheng, no," Poppy replied. "Not *very* long—perhaps six months. I was still a—"

"That place is not good for a foreign lady," he said.

"Your husband," Mr. Riddell said with an ironic smile, "must have been an unconventional sort, I think."

Poppy laughed. "Oh, yes. He had this wild hair on his head, and would you believe, he was six and a half feet tall. With the hair, probably seven. When we buried him, the funeral procession was the loudest I've ever heard, banging drums and hollering and all—it was a mixture of Chinese and Christian traditions, which was what he'd have wanted. But so loud! A large number of people turned out in order to take a look at the coffin, you see." She paused to take a bite of the roll, and then went on. "He'd been a doctor back home in Delaware—that's why the opium habit intrigued him. The drug can be quite useful in easing physical pain, and he recognized its usefulness in that area. Of course, useful becomes something else when you take it to excess. He became an addict himself, ultimately."

Everyone at the table was leaning forward, and it seemed to Addie that none of them were breathing. She had never heard someone speak this openly before, particularly upon meeting a group of people for the first time. It was not that they were unaware of the opium problem in China, but they'd taken the approach of ignoring it. Addie hoped this wasn't for selfish purposes; they really did think it was better not to encourage people by helping them when they were on the drug. What they did was provide an alternative to the opium den: they'd started a school and a church and a medical dispensary. If opium was a way for people to escape the difficulties and discomforts of their lives, how much better to offer the greater solace of Christian faith—it was ministering to the spirit instead of to the body.

Yet opium was central to life in this part of China, and no less in Lu-cho Fu than anywhere. Blank-eyed men lolled on tiny stools, barely able to keep their heads upright. Their skin seemed to take on a slick appearance when they'd been smoking. That and the eyes were both indications of an opium habit, though there were easier ways to tell. Only the other day, Addie had seen a mother, perhaps thirty years old, and thus a mother many times over, holding a baby. She was leaning against the wall outside the door of her home, and was very unsteady. Her feet were planted on the ground, and Addie had got the feeling that she couldn't unstick them. The upper part of her body was swaying, eyes roaming vacantly in every direction, very slowly, which was another habit of the opium smoker. Addie wondered about Poppy's description of time slowing down. What would that feel like? If a fly went by your head, would it seem to move as if through sludge? Seeing that mother's unsteady stance, Addie had gone and taken the infant right out of her arms. She was terrified the woman would drop it. The mother didn't even seem to notice, only giving her a look like her eyes were made of marble. Addie had stepped over the threshold into the family courtyard without knocking, which might have been rude under other circumstances, but with such a clear indication that no one was in charge, she wasn't too much afraid of violating the customs of the place. There was a young girl inside the entrance, sorting through a basket of pitiful-looking potatoes. She was ten or eleven years old, one of the other unfortunate daughters, and Addie handed her the baby and told her that her mama wasn't well. The girl had been shocked at the sight of a white woman abruptly delivering her baby sister into her arms. But the shock lasted only a moment, and then the forlorn look of the abandoned child came back over her face. She'd looked down at the baby without any love, but Addie knew she would take care of it, and had probably been doing so ever since it was born. What else could Addie have done? One couldn't save the world. One couldn't save even the smallest part of it.

But here Poppy was saying that they shouldn't give up on the addicts in delivering their message of Christian charity. She was talking now of the first refuge they'd set up, in the town near P'ing-yao where she and her husband were originally sent when they arrived in China in 1883. There hadn't been a mission there at all when they arrived, and they'd had to make it up as they went along. "As you all have done here," Poppy acknowledged to her hosts, and she turned to take in Owen and Addie with a nod. One of their earliest converts at the mission, she said, was a man whose two brothers had both become terrible addicts. They spent their days smoking while their wives took in sewing work to make a little money, and several of their children had died from sickness and infection. The convert was helping to support the families, but he and his own family had little enough money. "This is the dilemma, you see,"

Poppy said. "They lead miserable lives and therefore take opium to escape them. And the opium only makes their lives that much worse. It's a
vicious cycle." She paused to ask Mr. Yang if he'd understood the term.

"I believe I do," he said with a nod.

Poppy smiled and translated the phrase into Chinese, anyway. To
the rest of the table, she said, "It's really from the Chinese that we get
this idea in the first place, you know. 'Virtuous cycles' and 'vicious
cycles'—it's Buddhist theory."

Owen cleared his throat. "Actually, I believe it's from the Latin."

"Oh, no, *circulus vitiosus* really isn't the same thing. That's a question of logic, of argumentation. I'm talking about behavior and its
repercussions—this is why rebirth is a useful concept, though we don't
happen to believe in it." She paused to smile brightly at Owen, who
nodded stiffly in return. "In any case," she went on, "the man wanted
to pull his brothers out of the mire, so to speak, and he asked for our
help. So we pushed some beds together in a room and some blankets
and such, and on our opening day, we took in three men. One was that
man's brother—the younger one refused to come. The other two were
individuals we'd found down the street from our home. Really, it was
that close. From the courtyard, I would sometimes smell that nasty
odor—of course, you recognize it right away when it wafts by."

"I've always thought of it as a mixture of incense and tar," Addie put
in, "with a hint of pickle."

Poppy laughed. "Yes, that's it, exactly. Your wife"—she turned to
Owen—"has a way with words, doesn't she?"

Owen gave a curt nod. "That's why she does her work here so well."

Poppy raised her eyebrows. "Oh?"

"Proselytizing, teaching. These are tasks that require a certain ease
with words."

"Absolutely," Poppy said. She tilted her head in confusion at this
turn in the conversation, though she looked amused, too. "And in another language, no less."

"My wife's skills in Chinese have improved considerably in the
past several years. As have those of everyone at this table—with the
exception of the Yangs." He nodded at the Chinese couple and gave a

small laugh. "Your Chinese," he said, addressing them, "was already up to par." He repeated himself in Chinese, and Yang Taitai, who had not appeared to be following the conversation, murmured that she had no great talent at anything.

"Only English is still difficult," Mr. Yang said.

Owen smiled and then turned back to Poppy. "My point is that there is a great deal of work to be done here that requires something greater than physical strength or medications or—whatever it is that deters an opium addict from the pipe."

"Time," Poppy said. "That is the most important element."

"Then perhaps we can agree on something after all." Owen sat back in his chair and folded his hands over his stomach. It looked to Addie almost like a defensive posture, as if he feared the new missionary might reach over and sock him in the gut.

"What, on the use of time?" Poppy spread her hands wide. "That's the only hope we have of doing any sort of good in this country. Yes, there we can agree. But how we *use* that time is perhaps a matter of debate. For my part, I'd like to try to go at the deeper problems with everything we've got—"

"—and I think it's wiser to focus on what's been proven effective," Owen said.

"We can't agree on everything," Poppy said, "but I hope we'll find ourselves in accord on the most important issues. And in the meantime, I'd be wise to quiet down so that others at the table may have a chance to speak. My tongue gets away from me sometimes, and I don't have the energy to go chasing after it."

"I'd say you have quite a bit of energy," Mr. Riddell said with a wry smile. Raising his cup to her, he took a sip of the cooled tea.

Poppy laughed and lifted her cup in return. "There's putting me in my place, sir," she said. Then, glancing around the table, she added, "Don't you all worry, I'm used to it," and drained her cup as if it were spirits.

*　　*　　*

"You don't like her," Addie said that night when she and Owen were back home and in their room, alone. The boys had gone to bed a few minutes before, though they could still be heard talking: Henry's constant chatter and the punctuations of his older brother contradicting him, or correcting.

"I didn't say that."

"You don't have to say anything. It's easy enough to tell."

Owen continued removing his clothing, layer by layer, as he got ready for bed. His pajamas were laid out on the mattress. He had unfolded the long gown and placed it on the bed, the sleeves lined up straight at its sides.

"You nearly argued with Mrs. McBride," she said, trying to catch his eye, but he wasn't looking up at her. He was methodically moving through the motions of preparing for a night's sleep. He would be doing exactly the same if they weren't having this conversation, if it was him alone in the room while she spent the last few minutes of the evening in the sitting room next door, perched on her chair at the desk in the corner, with the lamp's low flame casting a small circle of light over the desk.

She spent most nights before bed reading one of the magazines from home or writing letters to her family. There were four different households to write to: her parents, Flora, Will, and Louisa. By far, the most numerous of her letters were to her parents and Louisa, since she knew that Flora and Will saw all the letters sent to her mother. They were in and out of one another's houses every day; she always imagined the backdoor swinging open and shut, Will knocking the mud off his boots as he hollered to announce his entrance; Flora coming in by the front door, perhaps with her children in tow, four of them now, and Addie was certain she kept them all in line. She knew that all the family back in Ohio had dinner together each Sunday, and she liked to think that they always spoke of her as they passed the roast and potatoes around the table, that her news was their news, too. In her clearest moments, she knew that this was probably not the case. It saddened her to think that after so many years, she must be fading from their thoughts. She often went days without thinking of them. They were family, but distance and time had had their effect.

Louisa, five hundred miles to the west, received the same intelligence Addie wrote to her mother. And perhaps because she was the other member of the family who was not close to home, Addie felt closer to her sister than she had when they lived together. Writing Louisa, she was honest in a way she was not with any other person. Over the last few years, as Addie's previous life in America receded into the distance, many of the particulars—the planes and angles of people's faces, the smell of cherry pie, the way the bell in the chapel on the hill seemed to crack the winter air when it rang in the mornings—gave way to a general idea of home that made her keep writing half-truths to her family who still lived there. She wanted to keep the place preserved as she remembered it, and the idea of sharing her failures put it all in jeopardy. But Louisa wasn't there, she was no longer part of it, and perhaps it was because Addie hadn't retained much memory of the farm in Illinois where they'd stayed for a short while three years earlier, that when she wrote to Louisa, it was as if she were sending her letters into the darkness.

Early on, she had written to her sister about her love and admiration for Owen. Now she watched him as he folded his vest in half, smoothing the fabric before laying it on the bed, and she found herself wanting to scream. The vest would be hung in the wardrobe as soon as he had finished undressing, so what difference did it make whether he folded it or not? "You were abrupt with her," she said now. "I'm afraid we weren't very welcoming." She was willing herself not to go over and pluck the vest off the bed, shake it out, throw it on the ground, and trample on it. She thought of how he had sat quietly at the table after the argument with Poppy, his fingers laced up like a shoe. He'd kept his gaze level on the new missionary as she spoke, and only occasionally turned to Addie with a slight tilt of the chin and a contraction of the brows, as if to ask, *This is the woman we have to associate with now?*

After the discussion about opium, it had been clear to Addie that he didn't approve of Poppy, that he found her—distasteful. This was the most oppressive aspect of his personality: the quiet implacability of his judgment. For a time, early on in their relationship, it had reassured her. His certainty had drawn her to him at their first meeting years before, up at the college on the hill in Marietta, a gathering of young people swept up in the mania for foreign missions. Other young men had been eager and bright-eyed, but Owen was the only one who seemed utterly solid, who was steady without being dull. Such men were described as being firm as oak, and that was exactly the right analogy; cut him open, and you would find concentric rings going down to his very core, a density of matter, not a hollow space to be found.

Addie was exactly the opposite. She was spongy; she floated about and had no real weight of her own, no center point about which the rest of her was formed. And just like a sponge, she soaked up the substance she floated in. Today, meeting Poppy, she'd had a feeling of being hauled out of the depths, of getting squeezed of all the cold water and set on the shore in the sun and the wind. She felt a lightness that reminded her of an earlier version of herself, though it was not frightening, as it had been before she met Owen—when she had wondered what would become of her, how she could march through her life with eyes held straight ahead. That was what she had thought she required: a steady track, one from which she couldn't stray. But she had learned that the steady track only went around and around; that in fact, it went nowhere.

Owen was frowning, showing he was angered or at least annoyed. It was the pants that were the issue, rather than the conversation she was attempting to have with him. He was staring at them as he unbuttoned the front, as if they posed a problem he didn't know how to resolve. "You said I argued with Mrs. McBride," he said, looking up at her. "I didn't. I attempted to explain to her that we know perfectly well how to run our mission. We know better than her, I should think, since we've been here for nearly a decade, and she has not."

"Whatever our feelings about her," Addie said, "it has to be a fine thing having another missionary here to help us with our work." She took a step into the room from the doorway, where she had been standing with one hand on the doorframe. From the shelf below the basin, she took the hand towel and gave it to Owen.

He nodded and set it on the bed without unfolding it. "I'm sure that Mrs. McBride has much to offer in the way of experience. She's proven her mettle, I suppose, after sixteen years."

Addie nodded, careful not to look eager. It was something, at least, a place to begin.

Hazel

13

After the first time, George didn't return to the house for another five weeks. I saw him at church and from afar, out in the fields or heading out to the barn as I drove by. He'd lift his hand solemnly and I'd raise mine in return. Usually I had Joe or Debbie with me in the car, and I'd be glad for their mindless chatter because it dammed up my heart, kept it from overflowing, kept me from asking myself what that afternoon together had meant and wondering when and if it would happen again.

Then one day after the children were back at school, I was running the vacuum in the living room when I turned and saw George standing by the television, hands resting in front of him, no shoes on his feet. I gave a shout, not because I was startled by his appearance but because I'd been wishing for it so hard I thought I'd made it happen. I took several steps forward and then stopped short of being able to touch him. I still had the vacuum hose in my hand, and the machine was still running. But neither of us was thinking of it, and when he folded me into his arms, the nozzle leaped onto his shirt and clung on. He yelped, I laughed, and that chased away any need for conversation.

We didn't talk or think. The first time had been like that and the second time, too. It wasn't until the third time that I let my brain wake up, and then it was only to hush it and put it to bed again. Because by then it was clear that what we were doing was a choice. Once could be an accident, but twice was an affair. How much more, then, was three times, four times, five and six and ten? After a time, you stop counting. But still a part of you knows the score.

George would let himself inside the porch to take off his boots, balancing on one foot, then reaching down to line them up against the wall. There was deliberation in the act and deliberation, too, in the way that I'd wait in the house, preparing to meet him. It was a form of resistance, every muscle and bone in my body uniting against the mind. Because my mind still insisted on its old authority, saying that this man was my best friend's husband, and what I was doing was wrong. And when George came in, it wasn't so simple as more forces on one side than on the other, passion winning out over loyalty. Passion wasn't the right word, anyway, and loyalty cut in many different directions at once.

What we were—it was there between us like a sleeping dog we had to take care not to trip over. And so we would pretend we were just neighbors visiting; we'd sit at the kitchen table drinking thin coffee with lots of sugar, and I'd make him some toast and hot milk to dunk the toast in, because he always showed up hungry, even if he'd only eaten his dinner an hour before. We'd talk of nothing—about the weather, about how warm or cool it was. I'd tell him about a quilt I was starting. He'd talk about how the corn was looking.

There'd come a pause in the conversation. Then he'd take my hand and lead me to the back bedroom, and a half hour later he'd be back on the porch, putting his boots on again. And I'd watch him with every part of my body alert to his leaving. Which is to say with a kind of emptiness that filled my chest, because that hour between us was quickly becoming the beating heart of my day, my week. It was the center, the part that was alive and true. All the rest was simply getting by.

He only came over when Joe and Debbie were at school, but on occasion someone else would be at the house—Rena, usually, or Iris or Edith from town—and George would take note of the car in the driveway and walk back the way he'd come without knocking on the door. Those days, I'd sit with my heart beating fast, wondering whether this would be the time he didn't pay attention. Maybe he'd come inside the porch and begin taking off his shoes, and it would only be when my guest went out to see about the noise that we'd all be confronted with the truth of what was going on.

But of course he always did notice another car in the drive and the next day when I saw him, he'd ask after the visitor in a sociable way. *How was Iris?* he'd inquire. Or, *How was Rena?* Every now and then the car in the driveway was his, which meant that Lydie was the one who had come by to see me. We didn't talk about those times. When I saw him the next day, we'd pretend that he hadn't tried to come by at all.

In fact, after several months no topic between us remained untouched with the exception of Lydie. If Karol had been alive, I suppose we would have given him the same wide berth that we gave her, but he was gone, and the same rules didn't apply. Anyway, I liked talking about Karol with George. He was a good listener, and it was nice to talk over my marriage now that it was done, the last chapter written. Already it was becoming difficult to remember what it felt like to be a wife, and though I didn't know that I missed it, exactly, I mourned the woman I had been before I was a widow, and this mourning was separate from what I felt about Karol's absence.

One day, I found myself trying to explain this difference to George. It was the middle of November, and we were in the car together because the harvest was done and there was no good reason for him to be away from home for longer than a few minutes unless it was to go into town. So we'd met in the parking lot of the IGA, and he'd left his car while I drove the two of us back to my house. This was the second time we'd carried out a rendezvous this way. We wouldn't be able to do it often, but neither of us had come up with another way to get through the winter.

To distract us both from the fear of seeing someone we knew—George had pulled his cap down low over his face to lessen the risk of recognition—I was talking about the church potluck I was helping to plan. "I think it must be that I'm used to being alone," I said, "because I just don't have patience for the back-and-forth anymore. Dottie has her ideas and I have mine, and I don't feel like trying to compromise."

"Dottie does like her own ideas," George said from under the bill of his cap.

"Yes, and I used to be able to work with her perfectly fine. Every year we do this potluck together." I paused, remembering how I hadn't helped plan it the year before. I had just lost Karol then, and a church potluck hadn't figured into my list of concerns. Twelve months later, I had the energy to get riled up at Dottie Acker's insistence on serving pineapple punch at a Sunday dinner. "Well," I went on, "I'm finding it impossible to deal with her, and I don't think it's because she's changed. It's me. I like making my own decisions and not having anyone question them."

"Was Karol such a dictator?" George said. "You're free now from under his thumb?" He smiled to show that he wasn't trying to offend. Karol had been his friend as well as my husband.

"Oh, he wasn't worse than any man about getting his way. It's only that being married"—I spun the wheel to the right, turning onto Fox Road—"you're two people, but you've got to act as one. With Karol, I got used to compromising. Now it's just me, I've lost the knack."

George was quiet. He might have been thinking of the two of us, how we didn't have to compromise on anything because there were no decisions to be made together. Or he might have been thinking of his own marriage. For my part, I was recalling the biggest compromise Karol and I had come to. It wasn't really a compromise. I'd been afraid to have children, and Karol had been afraid to wait. Junior was my fear—I'd been worried by the idea of my brother, returned from the war a silent and unfathomable man prone to violent fits, being anywhere near a baby. But what if he hadn't disappeared? Was it a compromise Karol and I made, deciding to wait, or was it only that a change in circumstances took away the argument?

We came up around a blind bend. It wasn't usually a problem because as long as you were paying attention, you could spot any oncoming vehicles before you reached the spot where the road cut low between two stands of trees. I wasn't paying attention and drifted left without thinking, and as we came around the curve, I almost clipped a red pickup headed in the opposite direction. In a moment we were past, but my heart was pushing blood against my eardrums in a steady thrum, and several seconds went by before George said in a murmur, "Speak of the devil."

My first thought was of Karol; my second was of Junior. But we hadn't been speaking of either: that was only my own memory churning in silence. "What do you mean?"

"That was Theo's truck."

Theo was Dottie's husband. "Do you think he saw?"

George drummed his fingers on his knee. "Not sure if he saw me, but I saw him: eyes wide as saucers. Probably thought he was about to meet his maker." He breathed out loudly through his nose—almost a laugh, except it was full of worry.

I held my breath as we turned onto Sumner. This was the critical moment: we were passing George and Lydie's house. She wasn't outside, and the house was set back from the road. Even if she happened to glance out their living room window, even if she was able to tell it was my car, she wouldn't see her husband sitting in the passenger seat. "What do you want to do?" I asked.

George was looking straight ahead, not willing to risk any more than we already had. "I want to be somewhere no one can see me."

"Not even me?"

"You're allowed. No one else."

"Well," I said, "we're almost there." And it was true: we were pulling up to my house. I looked up and down the road and didn't spot anyone coming. "All safe," I said, and together we got out of the car, and together we went inside, and even though we weren't really safe, we felt for a short while as if we were.

*   *   *

Getting caught was a worry, but I just added it to the worry I already had. I worried so much I was hardly sleeping. I'd lie in bed watching the moonlight slide across the ceiling and the shadows stretch themselves like cats, even while I tried not to think of any of the things that rightfully made me anxious. I'd pray for sleep to come, though it never did, and I began to grow nervous about the nighttime rituals. Brushing my teeth, I'd feel my stomach twisting, and as soon as I lay down in bed, my heart began to thump. I felt so fretful it made me nauseous. I'd close my eyes, open them, close them again. I'd move from my side to my stomach, then flip onto my back. Nothing worked, but I'd give it a few hours before I threw off the blankets and went out into the living room to see how the night had colored the house, to examine it in the silver light and decide whether it still felt like my own. I didn't smoke, yet those nights I wished I did, only so in the long scraped-out hours of two and three o'clock I would have something to do with my hands and all that useless concentration.

When Karol was alive, he had sometimes wakened in the night. It had always been a strange curse. His work was hard, and when we went to bed it took him no time to fall asleep; I never understood how it was that he woke in the darkest hours and could not drift off again. But as a mother I was used to hooking my sleep onto that of the other resting bodies in the house—I was always ready to drop my feet to the cold floor and go comfort the child who had cried out in the dark—so when Karol woke in the night, I did, too. Sometimes he was sitting up on the edge of the bed, or standing at the window looking out over the yard. Other times, he was simply lying there awake, and even if his eyes were closed I knew by his breathing that he was up and it was my job to get him to fall back asleep. I'd put a hand on his chest and he'd turn to face me. For a few seconds we'd stare straight into each other's eyes. At that distance, in the near dark, we were both laid bare to each other. The feeling was wonderful and terrible and the only way to resolve it was for Karol to climb on top of me and take me, quick. When we did it that way, in the middle of the night, he kept his eyes opened narrowly and locked on my face. Intensity seemed to seep into us from the midnight vapors; we were both present, and yet somehow absent, too—in separate places, far away. What we did then had nothing to do with our normal bodies, our daytime selves.

Now, awake and alone in the night, I would think of Karol, of those times when we'd come close to reaching our moment at the same time, and how we never talked about it afterward, even when the daylight arrived. There'd been an aspect of shame about those nights, a feeling of guilt that always sprang up if I thought of them as I stood at the stove frying eggs the next morning. It was almost as if he and I were cheating on our real selves, the wife and husband we were by day.

With Karol gone now and sleeplessness once again prowling our old bedroom, I remembered those long-ago nights and wondered if instead of being the exception to who we were, they actually represented the truest part of us. I remembered how there was a shade of violence to each instance, how Karol's eyes shining in the dark beside me had kicked at some deep-down fear; they might have been an unblinking pair of eyes suddenly spotted in the woods. You should run, but instead you freeze, and there he is: a bear, a wolf. Not different from my husband, but part of him. Not separate from our marriage: at the very heart of it.

I thought of Karol. I thought of George. I thought of Lydie, and of my children, and of George's and hers. I thought that no one had ever explained to me about love—how many different notes it sounds at once, and how those notes make a chord that keeps ringing and ringing even late into the night, and how even if you want to damp it, that chord won't be silenced and sleep still won't come.

*   *   *

I needed a job. It didn't have to be much, enough to bring in some money while I waited for Nate to pay me at the end of the fall. Taxes came due in the spring, and I hoped by then I'd have got enough from the harvest to pay them over, and to purchase the seeds and pesticides for the next year's planting. All of that was in the future. In the meantime I had to pay for groceries and electricity, school supplies and gas money, and I needed to have a little cushion for a visit to the doctor if one of us got sick or injured, or for a new tire on the car. I had a sum saved up but was loath to touch it: that was the money Karol and I had been putting aside for the past several years to put in an indoor toilet. It was one of the great embarrassments of my life, that in 1959 we were among the last in the area to still have an outhouse. We'd saved almost enough to reach our goal when Karol died, and during the winter that followed, each time I had to take Debbie outside after dark and stand listening to her go—she'd got more scared now that her dad was gone—I swore that I wouldn't dip into that money for anything. I'd get that toilet put in, no matter what.

Now it was autumn again, and I was staring down another winter without indoor plumbing. I made a promise to myself that it would be our last. Come hell or high water, when the ground softened again in the spring, I'd have the septic tank put in and the plumbing installed and our house would finally be like all of our neighbors', no longer an embarrassment, no longer a source of shame. Now, more than ever, I felt the necessity of keeping up appearances. I couldn't bear the thought of whispered condemnation: *Hazel Wisniewski can't keep her house in order.* A house was the measure of a family's well-being: swept floors, clean stovetops. You couldn't allow cobwebs to grow in the dark corners. You couldn't neglect beating the rugs, scrubbing the screens. I recalled from my childhood those small oblong houses we'd sometimes pass on our way into town, where the paint was peeling and the porch was always missing a step. There'd be children standing barefoot in the yard, snot dripping down from their noses, mean, solemn looks on their faces. (Where did those looks come from? Hunger, I suppose, and too many nights without a bath.) There was always a young girl dangling a baby loose at her waist. There was always a mule in the nearby field that looked half starved. Most of those families had eventually quit the farm business in the long hard years leading up to the war, but their ghosts still haunted those of us who'd stayed on. I was determined not to have anyone thinking my house was at all like one of theirs.

I'd already had to borrow a small sum from Rena and John Charlie to make it through the end of summer. They were doing well enough, they had the money to lend, but I didn't want to do it again. Money tends to come with advice, and having the old homeplace meant I already received plenty of that. Even before Karol died, my sisters had liked giving me their views on everything related to the property. I'd learned to resent their interference wholeheartedly and preferred to go see them rather than have them come to the house. I didn't need their opinions on the way the grass had been mowed, or the fact that we'd switched to a different kind of feed for the hogs. So when I went to borrow money from Rena and John Charlie, I insisted on being charged interest so all of us were clear on what was being asked.

The loan wasn't enough to get me through to the harvest. After my meeting with Mr. Freese, I'd started looking for a job and quickly discovered that they weren't easy to come by. First I talked to Edith about working at the flower shop, and she told me she didn't have the money to pay another worker; there was only herself and a colored woman who came in on Saturdays and one or two days a week. Business was good, but not good enough. That was fine because I didn't know that I'd want to work for my sister, anyway. While Edith and I were close in some ways, she had a certain quality that kept her clearly defined and apart from our family, as if in a photograph hers was the only figure that had been outlined in pen.

I moved on to other options. I ventured into several cafés and diners to see if they had need of a cook. They didn't. I went into the library, and when I spoke to the woman at the desk about working for them, perhaps shelving books, she said she didn't recall seeing me in there before. I said I came in sometimes, hadn't for a while, and she said, Would I consider myself a reader? I said, I read. By the end of our conversation I'd decided that I wouldn't work there even if they paid me five dollars an hour, which they weren't by any means offering to do.

Several days in a row, I went downtown and walked through the doors of a dozen businesses. Bells jangled over my head. Heavyset women grabbed pencils out of their hair and potbellied men patted their pockets for cigarettes to light up as they stared at me from the other side of glass counters, squinting one eye and then the other as if they couldn't quite see me. Noooo, they said slowly, sucking in a lungful of smoke, afraid we don't have anything for you right now.

I grew discouraged. I was a woman in middle age looking for jobs that either didn't exist or else weren't intended for someone like me. The whole working population suddenly seemed like an alien race with a secret language I wasn't able to speak. I stopped going into town and knocking on doors. Keep a lookout, I told Iris and Edith. If you hear of anything, let me know. They would, they said, but the end of it was that Iris kept suggesting that I take a typing class so I could get a secretarial position, though there didn't seem to be all that many of those around, either, and Edith never seemed to come across anything at all.

Things went on this way for a few months. I talked to George about it, with excitement at first, and then later with a feeling closer to shame. He always shook his head in sympathy and said something would turn up eventually.

Then one day while we were lying in bed, he told me he might know of a job.

I twisted around so I could see him. I'd been lying on my side, staring at the rain hitting the window. It was the end of November and rain had been falling all week, which had put me in a sour mood. Even George being there hadn't snapped me out of it; I'd felt low all morning, and now it was afternoon and I felt even lower. I didn't know how he had managed to come over, what he'd told Lydie he was doing, and with the humor I was in today, my mind was going through the lies he might have told and resenting all of them for not being the truth. I asked him what job he was talking about.

"My nephew was complaining the other day, saying how hungry he gets in the afternoon. Says the ladies in the cafeteria give them a scoop of mashed potatoes each, and it ain't enough." George fell quiet, as if that were the end of it.

"What's the job exactly?" I asked.

"Oh, well, working in the cafeteria." He took his thumb and stroked it down my arm. "Thought you might check with them to see if they need somebody. I figure Pete might be able to get himself an extra scoop of potatoes if you were the one doing the scooping." He narrowed one eye at me, not quite a wink.

"Are they looking for someone?"

"Could be. I don't know."

"Then it's just an idea. You don't actually know anything about it."

He drew back his chin. For the first time, I saw a shade of annoyance pass over his face. So be it, I thought. I was annoyed, too.

"I know what I just told you. Is that a problem?"

"I thought maybe you had something more certain in mind, the way you were talking."

"If you're asking whether I called up the school and asked them direct if they'd like to hire my neighbor to work in the cafeteria, no, I sure didn't do that."

"*Neighbor.*" I laughed, one of those short, snorting laughs that has nothing to do with being happy. "That's a word for us. Neigh-*bors*, I guess I should say. You're a neighbor, I'm a neighbor. Together, we're neighbors." George had already taken his hand from my arm, and now I pulled away to make sure my leg wasn't touching his any longer. I left a damp spot where my foot had been. The soles of my feet always started sweating when we were together in bed and then afterward grew as cold as stone. I'd been embarrassed about it at first—it was one of those things I'd forgotten would shame me, sleeping with a man who hadn't seen me that way before—but it hadn't taken long for me to grow as comfortable lying with George as I'd ever been with Karol, and it was only now that I once more felt ashamed. A moment later, the shame was replaced by resentment.

I could feel myself taking short, strong breaths. George was breathing evenly beside me. He'd been silent for at least half a minute when at last he said, "What word would you like me to use, Hazel? 'Mistress'? 'Girlfriend'?" He lifted one hand and rubbed it slowly over his mouth in a gesture I knew so well from Karol—it meant, *I don't know, what do you want?*; it meant, *There's not a thing I can do, so don't look at me that way.* It was a particularly masculine gesture that meant having to stay patient with a woman when she was being unreasonable.

"Not 'girlfriend,' for certain," I said, and in that moment decided to take it back down to even. This was George and me; we didn't fight. Ours was an arrangement meant only for pleasure. I said, "Makes me sound like I'm sixteen, like you're taking me to the pictures."

I waited for him to laugh, for the hand to come down from the mouth and reveal a smile. At last, it did, though the smile was sideways-leaning and thin. We were both quiet for a while. The rain outside had gotten heavier, and the sound swelled on the roof of the front porch, which was right next to the bedroom. The front porch was never used—we always went in the side door through the screened-in porch, as did all of our guests—but it had occurred to me that my bedroom was only a few feet from the front door, where a stranger who didn't know any better might stand waiting. Every now and then, it happened: a traveling salesman, a census taker, another old bachelor arguing his case. The door opened right into the living room, and I had to push the rocking chair out of the way to answer it. One day a stranger might come up by the porch and if the windows were open, they'd hear George and me. If it were a stranger, I figured, they wouldn't know that the man wasn't my husband, that I wasn't his wife—and if it was a bachelor, well, then, he'd have his answer.

"I guess it don't matter much what I call you," George said thoughtfully after a minute. "I know what you are to me. You know it, too."

"Do I?" Leaning my head on my hand, elbow on the pillow, I was suddenly aware of how the blanket had fallen, how this short sentence sounded like some cheap flirtation. George's eyes darted down to my naked breast, and I figured he had noticed, too. Maybe this was what I was to him, after all. This was what he knew, and what I knew. And it was good to be wanted; it was enough. I tilted my head down and batted my eyelashes for all I was worth. He moved toward me again, laughing softly, and it was another half hour before he was walking home.

*   *   *

The next morning, I called up the high school to ask about talking to someone in the cafeteria. The operator told me to call back after lunch, about twelve thirty, so I could talk to Mrs. Brainerd, or better yet, go on down there any time after about one. I'd find her either out front or in the back, the operator said, and if I didn't spot her, why, then I should just ask.

When I pulled up to the high school, I found a spot near the back of the lot and walked up to the main entrance. The building's many windows reflected the sky and trees and clouds, and I could picture the images inside, chins resting heavily on upturned hands, heads bobbing sleepily and then snapping up again, longing glances at the same windows I was seeing from the other side.

I'd been to school myself, but long enough ago that it seemed almost like a television show I'd watched in pieces. I remembered certain characters and scenes—smudged, inky fingers curled around the edge of a book; a teacher with a hooked nose and a weary stance, leaning against the blackboard with arms folded over her thin bosom; the steamed windows of a winter classroom and all the world gone gray outside; a fat boy scowling—but these images didn't connect to form any complete stories, and like a television show, the world they came from seemed small and self-contained and beamed into view from far away. I'd gone to a small country school down a lane that ended at the two-room building, and I hadn't attended past the age of thirteen. It was all so long ago—nearly impossible to think that I'd ever memorized a poem or spent a single minute puzzling out the answer to a math problem.

The school in front of me now was the one Joe and Debbie would attend. Not with a handful of fellow classmates they'd known forever, but with hundreds of teenagers, both familiar and strange. And they wouldn't quit school, because there'd be no one telling them they needed to; there would be no farm to swallow up their work. They would continue to take the bus that went out 143, and they would walk the distance back to the house, passing fields that all looked the same to them.

Once inside the school, I found myself standing in the middle of a long hallway, empty except for a lean man in a janitor's uniform peeling posters off the wall. I asked him where I could find the cafeteria, and he pointed the way. "You a parent?" he asked. He had a poster in his hands advertising a basketball game that had taken place the weekend before.

"Yes," I said. It wasn't untrue—I *was* a parent—though I knew that wasn't what he meant. I said it without thinking, because I didn't want to explain that I had come there looking for a job. Suddenly the idea of what I was doing frightened me. I hadn't thought any of this through, really.

"What's your kid's name?" I'd already started to walk away, but I stopped and turned back. The poster was dangling from the janitor's hands, and he had on his face the friendly expression of someone who's in no hurry to get back to work. "I know most of them," he added, "or anyway, I try to."

"I doubt you know my son. He keeps to himself, pretty much."

"What's his name?" he asked again.

"Pete," I said quickly.

"Pete what?"

Just then, the bell rang. The doors of the classrooms were all pushed open, and students began pouring noisily out into the hall. "I'm sorry," I said, turning. "Got to beat the rush."

"Too late for that," he said. I glanced back over my shoulder and saw him considering me with what looked like a mean sort of glee. If I were to get a job in the cafeteria, I'd probably see him every day, and he'd soon know that I had lied when I told him I had a son named Pete at the school. The crowd around me was growing. I made my way to the end of the hall and turned right, in the direction the janitor had pointed. At least, I thought as I squared my shoulders, moving through the throng of jostling students, at least I didn't give him a last name.

The cafeteria, when I found it, was empty but gave off the impression of recent abandonment. The trash cans were filled almost to overflowing, and the smell of cooked food still hung in the air. Balled-up waxed paper littered the linoleum floor. I tried to imagine spending my afternoons here, cleaning up and restoring to order this single large room where several hundred teenagers gobbled down lunch each day at noon; I pictured them descending all at once like a flock of birds on a field of corn, and I imagined myself as a sort of scarecrow waving them away and eventually being covered by all their beating wings. For a moment, I stood soaking up that stillness, and I thought that when the students came in, it must feel like an invasion.

Later, after I had been working there for some time, I would wonder how I'd gotten it so wrong. The cafeteria was itself only when it was crowded and noisy. The students coming in didn't spoil the place, they woke it up. The room sat empty most of the day, and during that time it felt haunted in the way that a house is haunted when the family is gone; the walls seemed to stare at one another, amazed at the vast plains of unoccupied space between them. Every day, when the bell rang for first lunch and the doors were flung open, I would feel the cafeteria taking in the students as a body takes in breath, and I would feel a part of that body, and it would surprise me to think that there had ever been a time when I wasn't.

That day, however, as I stood looking at the sandwich crusts and peas and bits of potato on the ground, a very short but sturdy dwarf dressed all in white, like a doctor, pushed open the doors from the kitchen and came out with a broom in her hand. "Can I help you?" she said, taking a few steps toward me. The broom was at least a foot taller than she was.

"I'm looking for Mrs. Brainerd," I said.

"You've found her." She raised her eyebrows and smiled, close-lipped, in a way that suggested a challenge rather than any goodwill. She was used to meeting others' surprise head-on, I thought. Staking the broom on the ground beside her, she waited for me to speak.

"I hope I'm not a nuisance. I was told this was a good time to come meet you, with lunch finished."

She kept her lips pressed together.

"I'd like to work here. That is, if you have any need. I'm a good cook." I stopped, unsure of how to go on.

"Where have you worked?" she asked.

"At home."

She laughed. "All right. Have you got an army to feed?"

"Just myself and my two children."

I saw her take in the lack of a husband. Perhaps I had thought of getting that very response. She asked my name and I told her.

"The strange thing is," she said, "that I find myself in need of an extra set of hands right now. Strange," she repeated, shaking her head. "We've had one out to have a baby and she won't be back till the New Year. Left a week and a half ago, earlier than she'd thought. Well, what can you do? It's been a madhouse in here ever since." With her free hand, she ticked a finger around the room, pointing at the full trash cans, the dirty floor. "I can't promise you'll have work in the spring, but if you want to finish out the semester, then we'll see what happens. Do you have any professional references?"

I shook my head. "Not unless you want to talk to one of my sisters."

She threw her head back and laughed with her mouth open, and I saw that she had a bridge on her uppers that didn't fit very well. "You had a husband, I guess," she said, closing her mouth.

"Yes. He passed away last year."

"I'm sorry for your loss." She began pushing the broom over the floor, lifting her elbows up to her ears to get enough thrust. "Come in tomorrow morning and we'll give it a try. Seven a.m., sharp."

14

Once I started working, George and I didn't see each other for a time. Only an hour or a little more separated when I arrived home and when Joe and Debbie came walking up the road from the bus drop-off, and George still hadn't hit on any good way to come over in the down season without raising suspicion. We didn't meet and we didn't meet and something cracked open inside me, a fissure down through my very core, a canyon of loneliness that seemed sometimes to whistle with the cold wind that ran through, and other times seemed filled with a hot, wrathful desire. I'd get home from the cafeteria smelling of cooking oil and industrial dish soap, and as I filled the sink with warm water to give myself a wipe-down, I'd try to telegraph my longing to George, to will him to feel what I was feeling. I imagined the door opening, his heavy shoes on the floor. I pictured the cloth dropping from my hand in the eagerness of our meeting. Sometimes I took my own pleasure, thinking of that.

One afternoon when I got home from the high school, I couldn't stand it anymore. I called over to his house.

Lydie answered, and I bit my thumb. "I haven't laid eyes on you except at church," she said. "My nephew says he sees you in the cafeteria scooping peas."

I closed my eyes and replied, "Sometimes I scoop corn. Or I do the meat. I use tongs for that."

She laughed. "I'll bet that's exciting."

"I've got bills to pay," I said, opening my eyes again. It came out sounding harsher than I meant, almost like an accusation.

She didn't take it that way. "You sure do, and you're paying them. You're doing everything you've got to do, Hazel. I hope you know it."

What do you say to a thing like that—kindness where you least deserve it? There's not much to do but change the subject. "What are you doing right now?"

"Just tying up this roast for dinner. Nothing much. Did you want to come down and visit awhile?"

"The kids will be home soon."

"So bring them along. You know Joe's down here most days at some point anyway. And I'd love to see Debbie. Hang on a minute." There was a pause and a little rustling, and I knew she'd set down the phone. A minute later, she came back on the line and said she had plenty for supper. Why didn't we join them?

"You shouldn't go through the trouble."

"What kind of trouble is it? You help me peel a few more potatoes, and we'll thaw out another container of beans. It's nothing fancy, mind you, but I should hope we can figure out how to feed seven people at once. What would our mothers think, worrying like this when they fixed meals for nine or ten every day?"

As she hadn't said anything about George, I didn't know if he was there in the house with her at the moment, or outside somewhere, or maybe he'd gone into town. Even if he were away right now, he'd be home by suppertime. I tried to imagine all of us gathering at the table together. We'd eat in the dining room, I supposed, instead of the kitchen, and Lydie would be seated at one end of the table and George at the other, and I would turn my head like I was at a tennis match to talk to one and then the other.

I thought about all this and then I thought that I would do almost anything to lay eyes on George, even if I couldn't talk to him alone, or touch him in any way. There wouldn't even be a handshake; women didn't shake hands on meeting a friend. Only men did that. Curious— I'd never considered it before, how men wanted that touch and women didn't. "I'll be down in a little while," I said now to Lydie. "Just as soon as the kids get home, we'll drive on over."

"Yahoo," Lydie said.

*   *   *

This dinner would be the first time our two families met, outside of church, since George and I started our affair. Driving the short distance down the road to the house, I got myself into a state, something almost like panic. I gripped the wheel with both hands like it was the reins of a bucking horse. In the backseat, Joe was narrating the events of his day, and they equaled for drama those of a Shakespeare play. The big event in the fourth act was the game of tag he'd nearly won at recess. By the time we got to the Hughes's house—not more than a two-minute drive, though it felt much longer—my heart was pounding hard enough in my chest that I worried a vein must be throbbing somewhere visible. As Joe opened his door and got out, I glanced in the rearview mirror. No throbbing vein, but I was pale. I pinched my cheeks for color, and when I glanced at the backseat, I saw that Debbie was copying me. She grinned, and it made me feel better at once.

Lydie stood in the doorway, holding open the door and letting the cold air into her kitchen. It was above freezing outside, but not by much. The glow of the lights from inside made the afternoon suddenly seem much darker; it was December, after all, and the days were still getting shorter. I thought of the previous year, with its warm weather at this time, and realized with a start that we would need to get another tree soon.

"How was school today?" Lydie asked as we entered the kitchen. She gave me a nod hello and then glanced down at my daughter to wait for an answer.

"We practiced spelling zoo animals and we drew pictures. I wrote 'tiger' and I gave it a long tail and it was purple."

"A purple tiger, my goodness. I've never seen a purple tiger before. Green and yellow, sure. I've even seen a blue and white one. But never purple. What color are the stripes?"

"They're *purple*," Debbie insisted.

"There's two colors," I said, putting a hand on her head. "Mrs. Hughes wants to know what the other color is."

Debbie thought for a moment. "I think it was red," she said at last. "It was purple and red."

"Goodness gracious. And you said you know how to spell the word *tiger*, too? Can you spell it for me?"

"I have to write it down," she said seriously, and then, tipping her face up at me, asked if she could show us how.

Lydie went to fetch a pad of paper and a pencil, and I sat Debbie down at the kitchen table. "Now don't go using up a lot of paper," I told her. "You write small and cover the whole page, and then ask if you need to start another."

She said she would, and when Lydie returned, Debbie set herself to the task of spelling out words with a quiet, determined seriousness while Lydie and I stood at the counter making another pie. She'd already mixed up the crust and had the bottom rolled out when we got there, and she stopped me when I began to protest that she shouldn't go through the trouble. "What did I tell you?" she said. "As if it's such a hard thing to fix a pie. I just need to get some apples from the cellar." She moved to the sink to wash the pie dough off her hands, but I said I would do it. "All right, if you don't mind going down there. I should have done it before I got my hands all covered in flour."

I went out through the door, to the back of the house. Their house had two small cellars, as ours did, and I knew that the one at the side had an electrical cord running down to it to power the washing machine and the chest freezer they'd got a few years back. The one at the back of the house was where the other food was kept. The double doors were directly underneath a set of windows in the living room, and as I reached down to pull the handles on the cellar doors, there came a *tap-tap* on the glass. I glanced up, ready to see George smiling at me through the window, but instead it was Joe. Surprised, I shook my head, and he made a face and disappeared from view.

It was dark in the cellar, the only light coming from the open doors above. Shelves lined the whitewashed walls, and on those shelves were wooden crates piled with potatoes, onions, beets, and carrots. Crumbles of dirt covered the floor all around, and the space smelled of earth and the damp. There were two crates of apples, small knobby green ones, which were good for baking and terrible for eating raw. We had a tree of our own near the old pig shed, but I'd barely gathered any of them this year. The ground around that tree was covered with bruised fruit, and whenever I ventured close to it, I smelled cider vinegar strong in the air.

I hadn't brought down anything to hold the apples, so slipping my arms out of the sleeves of my cardigan to make a bundle, I piled in a dozen or more and then carried them back up the stairs into the winter light. It was maybe thirty-five degrees outside, and I had gooseflesh on my bare arms. Bending down to close the door, I heard a voice behind me: "Someone tell you it was summer?"

I turned around and saw George. He'd just walked up from around the house, the side close to the barn. "I saw you come up out of the cellar," he said, "and thought I'd stop and say hello. Before we sit down for supper."

Words weren't coming at the moment—I was thrilled seeing him right there before me, and at the same time it felt dangerous; anyone might see us, hear us, together. George's breath was coming out as steam on the cold air, and I had to restrain myself from stepping into that cloud. I wanted to be caught up inside it, invisible together.

"Hazel?"

"Hello," I said at last, and that was all I could manage. I'd seen him at church a few days before, but we hadn't spoken because Debbie had left her coat in the car and started complaining about the cold, and we'd ended up leaving quickly. Church was about the only place we routinely saw each other now that it was winter. Every Sunday, I would tell myself I was going to listen to the sermon, that I needed to listen, to be chastised, washed like the inside of a basin, scoured until it was spotless. But the preacher was so dull I never kept to my goal. He delivered his sermons like he was reading a stock ticker; there was nothing holding the sentences together. Every now and then I would tune in and pick up a familiar Bible verse, but just as quickly I'd lose focus again. His sermons often featured a tale from his childhood in Pennsylvania; he'd grown up near Amish country, and their way of life was a constant source of inspiration for him. This should have been interesting, yet somehow he managed to drain it of all drama. And if it wasn't a childhood story, it was something contemporary—a story from the news, or a reference to the season. The change from winter to spring, or summer to fall.

It was winter now, and I was shivering without my cardigan on. George glanced at the sweater I'd fashioned into an apple carrier and said he guessed I should get on inside if I didn't want to catch cold.

"I'm okay," I said. "Really."

"You're shivering."

"Only because it's cold outside and I'm wearing hardly any clothes."

He laughed. "That's just about right, I'd say. How are you?"

"I invited myself over for supper," I said. "You should've heard how I pushed Lydie into asking us to come."

"I did hear. I was there in the kitchen when she was talking to you. Didn't sound like you pushed her into anything. You're always welcome here."

"You don't feel strange?" I asked in a quieter voice. I glanced around to make sure no one was near. I hadn't heard the boys, but they might have come outside while I was down in the cellar.

"Do I feel strange," he repeated, though he made it sound like a statement. He squinted one eye, thinking. "No, I don't believe so. I think if I had to find a word for what I feel, it'd be something like *happy*." He turned his eyes down and suddenly looked bashful as a teenager, working himself up to saying more. I could imagine him as he must have been when he was courting Lydie years before: tongue-tied without even knowing it, because he'd never been asked to put feelings into words, to name what was like soda water bubbling inside his chest. He lifted his eyes again and shook his head. "I have missed this sight," he said. "I have missed your skin."

Now it was my turn to feel bashful, and at the same moment I was suddenly sure that we had been talking too long. I started past him, half expecting him to reach out and touch my arm. But there was a wall of windows behind us, and he wasn't a foolish man.

Back in the kitchen, I dumped the load of apples on the counter. "You found them all right," Lydie said, opening a drawer to take out a couple of paring knives.

I took one and told her that I'd run into George on my way back into the house.

"And he kept you out there freezing without your sweater on?" She gave a rueful laugh. "There's politeness for you."

"I expect it was my fault."

"Well," Lydie said, and the subject was dropped. She wasn't wondering why it had taken me five minutes to get the apples from the cellar, instead of three. She wasn't wondering what I had to say to her husband. She was only thinking about getting the pie in the oven and serving dinner to two families and making her friend, the widow, feel comfortable in her own happy home.

*   *   *

At supper, I found myself seated next to George at one end of the table. Debbie was on my other side. Then came Lydie, and winding around the other side were the three boys. That was one way of looking at it. Debbie pointed out the other way: "All the boys are sitting together," she observed after we'd finished the prayer and begun passing the food. "And all the girls, too."

"Now, wait a minute." Lydie drew back and looked at Debbie with feigned surprise. "Are *you* the one that put us down this way?"

Debbie giggled as she took a slice of bread from the basket. I took it from her and began spreading on the butter.

"She did a top-notch job," George put in. "It wouldn't be right to have girls and boys mix, now would it, Debbie?"

"We have to sit mixed at school," Bobby said. "They won't let the boys sit together in class, like we want to. The teacher splits us up."

"I'd wager that's because you boys get rowdy," Lydie said, "and the girls calm you down."

Debbie was still caught up in the idea that she'd had a hand in the seating arrangements at the dinner table. "I have *my* mom on one side," she said importantly, "and I have *your* mom"—she pointed her fork across the table at Gene and Bobby—"on the other. And there's only one dad."

It was always something like this that did it. Everything normal, and then suddenly there would come a slap and it came from someone who least meant to give it—who was surprised, even, by the words that came out of her mouth. During the silence that followed this observation, Debbie stared down at her plate, and I could sense the possibility of tears.

"You know what, dear?" Lydie said, touching a hand to Debbie's back and leaning down to see her face. "There's actually two dads here, because your dad is here in all of our hearts. Isn't that right?" she said, glancing over Debbie's head at me.

"Sure it is," I replied mechanically.

"That's right," she repeated, and when Debbie raised her face, Lydie took the opportunity to turn the attention away from her by asking Bobby what he'd done in school that day.

The talk went on. Lydie wasn't a chatty woman—among strangers she could be downright shy—but she knew how to draw out others when the situation required it. A regular meal might pass in relative silence, but this wasn't a regular meal. She got her sons to carry the conversation while the rest of us recovered. At some point, I felt George's foot nudge mine and settle there, touching. I didn't risk looking at him, but for the rest of the meal I was aware of almost nothing else. His touch—even through layers of sock and hard leather—was a thrilling fact. I'd never before felt such affection for a foot. It was the truest thing in the room, and no one else knew it.

*   *   *

After the meal was done, while the others retired to the living room to watch television, Lydie and I cleared the table and started on the dishes. The pie had come out of the oven during supper, and it was still cooling on the counter, so we'd agreed to do the cleanup and have dessert after. Lydie was slicing a chunk of cheddar cheese for the pie while the swelling horns from *Laramie*'s theme song rose up from the other room. The strings followed, and then the boys shushing one another as the song came to an end. They were rarely quiet except while watching television.

Lydie asked about my job at the cafeteria, what it was like working there. "Are the others mostly married women," she asked, "or is it younger gals?"

"Neither one, really. There's a couple married women, and there's one other like me. A widow." I laughed at my use of the term, which was formal-sounding and odd; I almost never referred to myself that way, but I'd been introduced as a widow enough times since I started work that it only seemed fitting to use it now. Lydie raised her eyebrows but didn't say anything in response. "Her husband's been gone eight years," I added. The woman I was speaking of was a gal named Rita, whose husband had died fighting over in Korea. She was the only colored person I'd ever been in close contact with before, and I'd been nervous working with her the first few days because she didn't have a car and I worried that she'd ask me for a ride if we got too friendly. I didn't ever go into the colored section of town, and I didn't intend to start now. Rita tended to keep to herself, pretty much, and I'd stopped worrying about getting too close.

Now I described for Lydie the other women I worked with. Mrs. Brainerd and Betty Ann, who knew everyone's business and made a point of sharing it (it was from her that I'd heard about Rita's husband), and the two Marys, and Edith, who was nothing like my sister who shared the same name. The Edith I worked with was thirty-three years old, yet looked twenty-three. She had dimples and beautiful hair the color of a copper penny that she managed to keep styled even beneath the hairnet.

"Sounds like you found a good place, working there." Lydie picked up the stack of plates, carried them over to the sink, and began running water for dishes. "And Joe and Debbie? How are they handling it?"

"They're doing just fine. I drive them down to my sister's, and they have breakfast with her and John Charlie and then Rena takes them down to get the bus."

"I didn't even think about the fact that you'd have to leave in the mornings before they do."

"I didn't, either, until I got the job. It's worked out well enough." We both stood waiting for the sink to fill. The water was yellowish, though not as dark as the water at our house, which was almost the same shade as weak tea. The well made it that way. I hadn't realized how accustomed I was to off-color water until I started washing dishes at the cafeteria and saw it come out of the faucet as clear as crystal.

"Now, listen here, Hazel," Lydie said. "It doesn't make any sense for you to drive three or four miles in the opposite direction every morning just to drop them off at your sister's place. That must mean Joe and Debbie have a longer bus ride, too. Why don't you stop by and drop them here on your way into town? I can feed them breakfast just as easy as Rena can, and you know Bobby's on the same bus, so there's no danger they'll miss it."

It was too much to think of—Lydie taking care of my children five days a week, even if it was only for an hour in the mornings. "We can't trouble you like that," I said.

"I wouldn't offer if I didn't want to do it. Look, it's a whole lot of bother for you to be driving all over the county every morning. I'm already fixing breakfast for George and the boys. It's not any trouble to make a bit more."

"Really, I couldn't ask you to do all that."

"You're not asking!" Lydie said, and I could tell that she had gotten impatient, even annoyed. "I'm telling you it's no trouble, Hazel—I'm *offering.* And to be frank, I wish we'd settle it now so I can stop trying to *convince* you that it's not any trouble." Shaking her head, she plunked a few glasses into the soapy water and began washing them with furious strokes. "My goodness," she muttered when I still didn't say anything. "All this fuss over *nothing.*"

"Well," I began in response to Lydie's grumbling. *I'll think about it,* is what I was going to say. But right at that moment, she knocked the glass she was rinsing against the side of the sink and it broke dramatically: one large piece of glass flew up and pinged off the faucet. The remainder of the glass was still in her hand.

"Damn," she said fiercely, shaking her head. "Clumsy. I don't know what's got into me." She turned to look at me, a strange smile forming on her lips, and then she gasped. "Why, Hazel, what's—"

I flinched as her hand rose to my face. I don't know what I was thinking she would do—slap me, I suppose. I wasn't much used to being hit, but my mother had used to smack me when I was a child, and even as a young woman, when I didn't do what she said, or didn't do it fast enough, or didn't do it up to her standards. She was a moody woman, and when she was in one of her moods she was quick to use her hands rather than put into words exactly what was bothering her. It had been years since that time, and my mother was long gone, but my old instincts returned—I flinched, in spite of myself, as Lydie's hand came up, dripping with dishwater.

"You're cut," she said, patting a finger to a spot just over my left eyebrow. She held it up so I could see: it came away red with blood. "Must be a piece of glass flew up and got you. Now let me see if it's still in there or what." And after dipping her finger in the dishwater to wash off the blood, she took my shoulders firmly in her hands and steered me over into the light. "Sit down," she instructed. She pulled out a chair, and I took a seat. Then she tilted my head down so she could examine the wound. "Bleeding like the dickens."

She went to the counter to get a clean washcloth, and as she opened the drawer, I heard footsteps in the next room and turned to see George standing in the doorway with my daughter beside him. "Debbie here wanted to know—" He stopped. "What in the world?"

"I broke a glass," Lydie explained, closing the drawer she'd been riffling through and coming back over with a yellow dishcloth in hand. She glanced down at Debbie, who had followed George into the room and then, like a shadow, stopped beside him again.

"I'm all right, Debbie," I said, holding out one hand, but she didn't come any nearer. "Just a little cut." I reached the hand up and wiped away a drip of blood that was making its way down to my eye. "It doesn't even hurt," I added, which was true; I couldn't even feel exactly where the cut was on my forehead.

Debbie swallowed hard. Then she was crying. "Now, there," George said. He put a hand on top of her head. "We came in to see about having pie, but looks like you've got more important things to take care of. You need a bandage?" He was looking at me, but Lydie answered yes, and he took Debbie out of the room.

While they were gone, Lydie tilted my head so she could see the cut. She blotted it with the cloth and bent to get a closer look. "What will people think, seeing you at work tomorrow with a bandage on your head?"

"They won't think it's my husband, that's for sure." The words were out of my mouth before I could stop them.

But I could feel her smiling as she said, "Maybe they'll think you've got another man in your life now. A terrible, mean one."

A moment later, I heard the floor squeak behind me, and Debbie came around so I could see her standing just behind Lydie. "We got these," she said, holding up a bandage and tape.

Lydie went to get the scissors out of the drawer. As she taped on the bandage, she said, "There, now you have to agree to let me watch the kids in the morning." I felt her finger running along the tape, making sure it stuck. Then she took a step back and tilted her head, considering me through sharp eyes. "It's the only way I'll know you forgive me."

15

In the mornings now, I dropped off Joe and Debbie a little after six thirty. It was easier taking them to George and Lydie's place rather than to my sister's. We didn't have to leave as early, and Joe and Debbie had more time to eat breakfast. And they liked getting to spend time with the Hughes family—George, especially. Other than John Charlie, he was the closest replacement for a father in their lives, and the fact that he didn't try to fill the role made them love him all the more.

I could tell that Lydie enjoyed having Debbie around, too. She had lived for years in a household of boys, all mud and stink and rough edges. One day Debbie came home from school with her hair in two neat little braids. I never braided her hair; the most we ever did with it was put it in a ponytail.

I would have felt some jealousy, but Lydie was careful not to over-step. The very afternoon Debbie came home with those braids in her hair, Lydie called to tell me that she'd given both my children a cookie to put in their lunchboxes that morning. "I hope you don't mind. I made them last night, and they made the house smell like cinnamon. And I was still getting the boys' lunches together this morning, and Joe asked if I'd made snickerdoodles, so I just thought—"

"It's all right," I cut her off. "I appreciate it. And Debbie's hair looks nice, the way you did it."

"Oh, good, I'm glad you like it. We don't have to rush in the morn-ing, the way you do. We've got time for silly things like braiding hair."

She understood that it wasn't a simple matter for me, having her watch my children in the morning. She thought it was because we weren't fam-ily, and it was because of that, partly. But of course there was another cause. I didn't know how to feel about our two families getting closer like that. It complicated things. It made it harder to think of George-and-me as something entirely separate from the world, a thing all alone.

Meanwhile, days in the cafeteria were mostly the same, and that sameness held a kind of novelty for me, even months after I'd started working there. I liked being around people who weren't family or neighbors or church folk. I liked working with women I'd never have known otherwise. None of the others were from outside town, and they thought I was some kind of special creature for having lived my whole life on a farm, with a barn and a well and fields of waving corn stretching out in every direction. "Isn't that strange," said Betty Ann one day after I'd been telling her about the livestock we had before Karol died, "to think that the milk that shows up on my doorstep might've used to come from your place out there?"

"It sure would be strange," I replied, "since we haven't had a dairy cow since before I was married."

"But you just said you and your husband raised cattle."

"Beef cattle," I said. "They're different things."

She flipped another potato into the giant bowl between us. We'd peeled about twelve dozen and had many more to go. "But surely one can do the other."

"They *can*, but that doesn't mean they should. It's different kinds," I explained. "Different purposes."

"Oh, well." She laughed and made a face. Betty Ann was always one to laugh at her own nonsense.

The job expanded the scope of my world. I was no longer the lonely queen of an empty house, moving through rooms filled with memories and ghosts. There had been days in the first few months after Karol's death when I'd gone through the house and touched various items of furniture one after another, almost as if I were taking inventory: dining table, hutch, television, sofa. I wasn't trying to drum up images from the past, to remember, Yes, *there*, that's the spot Karol showed a five-year-old Joe how to do the two-step, and that's where we were standing that time he grabbed my arm and made as if to shove me, and then stopped, and turned, and strode out of the room. Instead, I believe I was touching those pieces of furniture to reassure myself that they were still there. After all that had happened, despite the big jagged canyon that had opened up in my world the day he died, I could still lay my palm flat against the painted wood dresser and say, *This is mine, this is still here.* Its cool slick surface would comfort me in a way I couldn't explain to anyone. I didn't care to try. It was a thing almost like the act of love, a physical impulse that wouldn't bear being put into words.

*   *   *

In January I was still working, even though it was the spring semester and Mrs. Brainerd had originally said she wasn't sure whether there would be a place for me then. But I didn't feel like I was on solid ground yet. I was filling in for a girl named Kate who'd had a baby. No one seemed to know whether she'd be coming back. Betty Ann, who'd gone over to visit once she was home from the hospital, claimed there was no way: "If you saw her face," she said. "Like the Madonna herself looking down at that child. She won't want to leave him, I'd lay money on it right now."

Betty Ann may have been sure, but there hadn't been any official word from Kate, and though it wasn't like Mrs. Brainerd to leave things up in the air, I figured she put up with it because from what I'd heard Kate was a lovable type who couldn't do any wrong. People made exceptions for her, even Mrs. Brainerd, who normally wouldn't accept one of us so much as taking a bathroom break without informing her first.

Not knowing whether the golden Kate would want her job back, I felt as if I were on probation. I tried to show myself to be a good and reliable worker. I got there early each morning, before any of the other girls. The first thing I did was put my purse and coat in the standing wardrobe near the backdoor. Then I'd tie on a clean apron. The aprons were stacked on a shelf next to the wardrobe, and it made me glad to see them starched and white and folded with precision, the signal of a clean start every day. Putting one on made me switch over, from home to work: I went from being the authority to being the one taking orders.

Next, I'd go find Mrs. Brainerd in the little office in the back, or in the stockroom where the giant bins of flour and sugar were kept, and the giant cans of tomatoes, the peas and the lima beans and the applesauce. We had a big walk-in freezer for the meat, but she was never in there when I arrived in the morning. I suspect she had a fear of getting locked in the cold. Wherever I found her, when she glanced up and saw me she'd give a little nod. "You made it" was her usual greeting. Then she'd put me to work breaking down chickens or chopping onions, and within ten minutes all the rest of the girls would be there, too, and we'd slide into our morning routines, readying ourselves for the stampede of hungry teenagers that came rushing through the doors at eleven o'clock every day. I liked the energy, the loud bursts of conversation, the laughter everywhere. Those children liked to laugh—much more than my sisters and I had at their age. Partly it was for show (the girls giggling behind their hands, the boys jostling one another and shouting across the room); mostly, though, it was the fact that they were living in a different world, and they knew it. They managed a carelessness that never would have occurred to me at their age.

Yet even I had a whole new life now, and I felt as if I were quite literally stretching, using new muscles. Being around other people this often, I felt the need to smile more, even if I wasn't laughing or feeling particularly glad. At the end of the day, my arms would hurt from lugging big trays of food from the counter to a cart. At night, sometimes my hands would go numb, which Mary L. told me was from all the chopping I did during the day. Our hands got so used to curling around a knife, she said, that when we slept they'd automatically go into that position. Hers had been doing it for years. She held them up as if I might see them go into spasms right then. All I could pay attention to was the long white scar across one palm. "Knife accident," she told me, "about three years ago. Had to get thirteen stitches and then it got all infected, blew up to about twice its size."

"How awful," I said.

Mary shrugged. "Coulda been worse if I hit a nerve or an artery. The doctor says I coulda bled to death on the floor right here, or been left a cripple with just the one hand left to use."

It wasn't meant to be a warning, and I didn't take it for one. It was simply something to talk about.

My days were filled now with conversation. The other women talked about their men, and after a while they felt comfortable enough to ask me about Karol. It felt good to talk about him with someone other than George. I told them some truths, some half-truths, and some outright lies. For instance, I'd explain how my husband used to spend his free hours painting, but I lied about the subject of his paintings. Instead of landscapes, I said he painted portraits of me. I told them he made me into different characters: in one I was Cleopatra, and in another I was an Indian princess. That one made the girls laugh.

We talked about our children and our parents, our neighbors, our friends. The other women all lived in town, and I heard the same grievances from them that I heard from Iris and Edith, grumbling about how some people never bothered to pull their trash cans back from the curb after collection, how other people didn't know how to park correctly on the streets downtown. The city needed to repave Troy Road. The post office always had a line out the door, and the side streets needed more lampposts to illuminate all the dark corners at night. One of the major topics of discussion was the new university. SIU had been founded a few years before, without a real home; it was divided in two, part of it over in East St. Louis and part of it up in Alton. Now the state had decided to send some money its way, and the school had purchased land west of town where the new campus was to be constructed. Folks were divided on how the school would change Edwardsville. "What am I supposed to do with a college?" Mary L. asked one day as we were cleaning up after lunch.

"I don't expect *you* have to do anything," the other Mary replied, "unless you plan on becoming the oldest coed ever to enroll at a university."

"Oh, sure," Mary L. said. "I'll sign myself up for some courses."

"Join a sorority, too," Betty Ann said. "Get some nice young man to escort you to a dance." She did a little twist, the rag in her hand flipping back and forth through the air.

"Just you watch, a few years from now I'll be wearing a black robe and one of those funny hats."

"What'll you major in, hon?" Edith asked. "You can't major in home economics, you know."

"Sure you can."

"Not at a university, you can't."

"Regular economics, then. I'll figure out how to print money."

"I could *teach* that class," Betty Ann put in. "Anyone who's figured out how to feed and clothe four boys on what me and Eddie make is a qualified economist, I'd say."

"They're going to need some professors," I ventured. "Better put in your application, make sure you get in for an interview."

"Are you kidding? I'm gonna go over there and run their cafeteria for them. Show them how it's done. Ask for ten dollars an hour and I'll make them promise not to ever have me serve anything that requires onion. I've cried enough tears for a lifetime in this here kitchen."

I laughed along with the other women. I was glad the university was being built. Who knew? Maybe Joe or Debbie would end up going to college. It was a lot easier to imagine this happening when the school was a few miles away. Different futures were possible. You never knew what might change.

*   *   *

I usually left the school shortly after one o'clock. By one thirty, I was home, and George would come by if he was able. It wasn't frequent, but we had grown bolder; we had to, if we wanted to see each other. Once every few weeks I'd hear the porch door open, and that sound would change the whole shape of my day. I'd hear the screech of the door hinge, and suddenly that hour would be jolted into some other category of time, some other way of accounting for the sun moving over the sky. I lived for those days, for that single hour. Our time together was still the one thing that was truest and best in my life.

But we weren't together often enough. "That's just winter," he told me. "Soon as the season starts, I'll be able to get over here more often again."

Things would be back to normal, is what he meant. Normal was simply the way it had been for the first two or three months before I got the job at the high school, before winter swept the landscape clean and locked us all up in our houses with no excuse for going out alone, into the wind and the cold.

Do you ever think about what it would be like for us to go away together?

I never asked him that question, though I thought about it in an idle way. We wouldn't ever do it, of course, but that's not why I stayed silent.

I couldn't ask him because I didn't want to know if the answer was no. I wanted to think that his mind was an open and free place, that things could happen there that wouldn't ever happen in real life. I should have asked him to tell me about the dreams he had—what he saw and felt in them, whether he ever had the same dream twice. I would have listened to him describe landscapes of beauty and nonsense, and maybe I'd have thought, I can't fathom you.

But I didn't ask him about his dreams, either. I didn't ask him many things. We didn't have much time for talking anymore, and though I missed that old bond, I got my fill of talking at work. He came to the door on the side of the house and took off his shoes and then we went right to bed. I loved being touched. I loved every inch of his skin that pressed up against mine. It was cold in the room but warm under the covers, and while we were making love, George would throw back the quilt because it got so hot we were both sticky with sweat. Then, afterward, we would pull the sheets back over us again and for a few minutes we would lie still with our bodies pressed together. He would hold me to him like he was trying to get back to where we'd been just a moment before. And I would wonder, what were we doing, and how long could it last?

These were more questions that I didn't ask.

*   *   *

Nate had got his rent payment to me in the late fall, and I paid off the loan from Rena and John Charlie. I wasn't making a lot at the high school, yet it was enough to cover our basic expenses, and I felt comfortable for the first time since Karol had died. I wasn't rich, but I had a little savings, and I didn't think I'd have to go to them again, asking for money.

At the same time, I wasn't quite happy with the arrangement with Nate. He'd lost me money, I figured, because he had gambled wrong. He was a good man—I didn't think he was trying to cheat me—but he hadn't listened when I told him how I thought the fields should be planted. At the end of the season, when he gave me the check, Nate showed me the receipts marking exactly how much he was paid for exactly how many bushels of corn. He'd got an average of ninety-eight cents a bushel, which was quite a bit lower than the year before. Of course, prices were down all over, and I couldn't blame him for that. But sure enough, while the prices for soy were down, too, they hadn't dropped as much as they had for corn. In other words, I'd been right, and Nate had been wrong. "He's the one renting the land, Hazel," John Charlie told me when I complained to him and Rena. "You have to let a man make his own decisions."

All this was on my mind off and on through the winter. Then one morning in early February, when I was dropping off Joe and Debbie, Lydie came running out to the car to stop me before I pulled away. "Why don't you come down here later," she said, her breath puffing out in a little cloud by her face, "before the kids get home. George and I have got something we want to talk to you about."

She didn't look angry. I figured it had nothing to do with George and me—too late for my heart, which was already pounding. I told her I'd stop by on my way home, and she went back into the house, clutching her sweater over her chest.

When I got to their house that afternoon, I wasn't out of the car before Lydie was at the front door. She held it open for me, even though there was a cold bite in the air. The grass I walked over was wan and sickly looking, and it was hard to imagine that in a few weeks the crocuses would be pushing their way up through the earth. Harder still to believe that it had been a year since the first day George came by to see me, when we had been neighbors making conversation beside a clothesline flapping with sheets. I remembered watching his fingers as he fumbled a cigarette out of the pack. I remembered white, thin light and puddles of mud.

"You've got me curious," I called to Lydie as I came up to the porch. "I don't have a clue what this meeting is about."

"A *meeting*. Come now, it's not that formal." She smiled as I climbed the steps. Lydie and George used their front porch as it was meant to be used; it was the main entrance, which gave the house a grander impression than ours. I always felt it on the approach: the sense of certainty and accomplishment, as if the very walls were made of some stronger substance than ours. Their house remained more or less as it had been ever since its construction, whereas ours was a patchwork job, bits and pieces added on over the years. The place I'd lived in my whole life had been an afterthought in its original conception—a cabin for some long-gone hired man, repurposed as the home my father bought for his new bride—but their house was a symbol of completion, of intention. The front faced away from our land and toward town, and with the little hillside of Christmas trees rising behind, an island of green in the flat bare fields, the house both fit the area and also stood a little apart. It was, in other words, a grand-looking place from the outside. Inside, it looked more or less like ours.

"Were you watching out for me?" I asked as I climbed the steps.

"I heard the car pull up the drive." She tipped her head in the direction of the road. The house stood at the intersection of Fox and Sumner, but neither was ever very busy with traffic. "How was work?"

"Same as always," I replied. "Those children eat like they've never seen food in their lives."

In the kitchen, George was seated at the table with a mug of coffee resting between his hands. He glanced up as we came in, and I thought it was strange that he'd kept sitting there as Lydie came out to greet me on the porch. Everything felt odd, all our poses in the room arranged as if we were in a play or in the movies, one actor already onstage and two others entering from the right. Even George's greeting felt rehearsed.

"Coffee?" Lydie asked, already taking another mug from the cupboard. In the moment she was turned away, I gave George a look, but he only shook his head.

So there we all were, sitting in a little circle around the Formica table with its spindly metal legs. In the mornings, with Joe and Debbie there, the table must have been pretty crowded. I wasn't ever there to see it, though, and I suddenly wondered what I was doing, letting our families get so close.

"George," Lydie said. "Why don't you explain what this is about."

He nodded slowly without looking at either his wife or me. A stab of nerves made my body seize and go cold.

"It's just that spring's coming soon." He glanced from me to Lydie, and when she nodded, he went on. "And it won't be long before it's time to start planting. We've been talking it over, Lydie and me, and we just wanted to know, Hazel, how things are going with Nate. What your plans are for this year. What you've decided."

I wasn't sure what to say. George wasn't looking at me, and the reason was that we had talked about all this the week before. I'd told him about how I wasn't happy with the decisions Nate had made and the fact that he hadn't been able to pay me on time. We'd talked about all of it, but of course I couldn't say that now. "We haven't come to any decision just yet."

"You think he's planning on it? I mean, you think he's already planning to renew for another year?" Lydie shifted her weight in the chair and then said in a softer tone, "I don't mean to make you feel strange, Hazel. We sure don't mean to do that." She put her hand on George's wrist. "Why don't you explain."

For a moment everything seemed bathed in a bright and unnatural light, which is to say both familiar and strange. I was sitting at the kitchen table of my friend and her husband. They were the couple, and I was the outsider who somehow had business with them.

Then George looked me right in the eye. "We were thinking you might consider renting your land to us." He removed his hand from Lydie's and rubbed both of his together, massaging one wrist and then the other as if they ached. Perhaps they did; his joints sometimes made little popping noises as he lowered himself into bed. For that matter, so did mine. "We'd like you to consider it. Think it over."

He wasn't a pushy man. Not much of one for talking, either. Karol had always liked the sound of his own voice, how it could swell a room, make the very air vibrate like a single bass string. He'd liked to stomp his foot when he laughed to make the floorboards squeak. He'd liked telling stories and talking over his plans for our home and family, both in the near and long term, and I'd understood that it was because he loved me and he loved Joe and Debbie. And above all he loved the land that had become his the day we bought it, because before then he'd never owned the things he worked for, or the place where he slept. It was because of this, too, that he'd especially liked explaining how he wanted things done. If I undercooked his pork chop or if I let the feed pail get low in the henhouse, if I put his socks on the left side of the drawer instead of the right, he'd let me know. He'd *tell* me, he wouldn't ask. He made statements instead of asking questions and spoke with a sureness that allowed no pause for consideration.

George wasn't that way at all. I'd known it before, but I was more aware of it now, watching him move his hands around on his knees. He was uncomfortable, waiting for me to answer, tentative in a way that I hadn't previously seen. I was afraid that if I didn't speak right then, he'd keep adding qualifiers. I said the only thing that came to mind: "Can you handle all that land on your own?"

He glanced at Lydie and then turned back and started nodding. "You know we've got J.B. helping out"—J.B. was the son of a neighbor who made some extra money helping out other families during the busy season—"and in the summer Gene's as good as any man now. Bobby, too, he's getting to be a big help."

"The fact is," Lydie said, leaning forward, "we're in a little bind here. See, J.B.'s said he won't be able to do just the fall. He's thinking of going out somewhere to see about factory work. Indiana, I think he said. Lord knows why he thinks there will be something for him in Indiana. But we don't have enough work right now to keep him on until then, not for the whole season. Taking on your land, though, we would. And especially if you'd rent out your tractor, too—then George and J.B. could go at the whole thing double time. So you see, you'd really be doing us a favor."

It was this last bit that made me understand what was going on. If it really would benefit them, she wouldn't have brought it up; they'd have found another way to put it, talked around it some way. They were already helping me out by taking Joe and Debbie in the mornings. That was all Lydie's doing, I supposed; she was the one making breakfast and getting them out to meet the bus on time. This business with the farm wasn't as clear. It struck me that George must have been the one to come up with the idea. I couldn't imagine Lydie explaining to him why he should take on the burden of an additional hundred fifty acres. Maybe J.B. was thinking of leaving, but if that were the case, then George could always find someone else to take his place. Taking him on for the entire season would eat up any profits George made on my land, especially after paying rent to me for the farm and the machinery.

Why would he propose it? And why would Lydie agree to such a thing? Surely she understood that the only benefit to her would be the good feeling that came of doing a kind deed by her friend. I was their charity case.

This realization came quickly, and it made me angry. It was this matter of two-on-one. I didn't like it. I had my relationship with George, and I had my friendship with Lydie, and I didn't like having to face them as a team.

I could tell they were both trying not to study me too closely, to give me a moment to sort through everything. Lydie took the opportunity to get up and retrieve the coffeepot, even though none of us had finished more than half a cup. She warmed us up anyway, and after she'd returned the pot to the counter, she stood for a moment looking out the window over the sink. It was a view of trees: the little hill of Christmas pines that sloped up from the bottom of the lawn. On the other side, a half mile down the road, was my house. You couldn't see it from here. You couldn't see it unless you climbed to the top of that hill or went driving down the road.

After a minute, she turned from the sink and suggested that we take our coffee and go out for a little walk.

George gave her a skeptical look. "Don't you think it's a little cold out?"

"It's not that bad. And anyway, you've got coats."

"Aren't you coming?" I asked. She shook her head. Confused, I glanced from her to George. It was difficult not to communicate anything more with that glance, not to show that we had our own way of looking at each other when no one else was present. He gave a small shrug and turned away.

"It's better for you, Hazel, to talk to George about the business side of things. Hammer out the details, see if it's something you want to think more about." The corners of her mouth turned down, and I wondered what was crossing her mind. Was it a tiny sliver of worry, an instinctive shiver at the thought that she was sending her husband out to walk alone with a woman? Did that concern have anything to do with me?

In any case, a few minutes later, George and I were walking over the front lawn toward the road. I'd thought we would go around back to walk up the hill, but George led us the other way, and then I understood: on the hill, we would have been visible from the kitchen window. Lydie could watch us going this direction, too, but it would take more effort; she'd have to stand in the dining room and sweep the curtains aside to see.

It *was* cold out. I wasn't wearing gloves, and my hands were chilly, clutching a mug of coffee that wasn't all that hot anymore. George had left his inside; his hands were shoved deep in his pockets. He stayed quiet until we were almost to the road. "I didn't expect that," he said at last, and squinted up the way. A truck was coming along, and we both waited to see if we recognized the driver. No one I knew, but we all lifted our hands in greeting, anyway. "No, I sure didn't expect that," George repeated, "Lydie pushing us out the door together."

"Me, either."

A few dozen yards down the road was a narrow stream. As we walked toward it, George asked what I thought of the proposal he and Lydie had made.

"I don't know what to think."

"You're probably wondering why I didn't bring it up before."

I was looking straight ahead, at the creek bed cutting through the stubble of corn harvested months before. There wasn't any standing water at the moment, but a soft fuzz of frost gave the ditch a silvery glint. Yes, I said, I was wondering about that.

"I've never lived with secrets before. Nothing like this. It's made things difficult—" He started coughing and turned away before he could finish.

I waited, feeling strangely distant from the moment, from the conversation, from him. I watched him coughing—shoulders jerking down—and then turned my eyes to the creek again. I wanted to say, *I've never had secrets like this, either.* But I stayed quiet because I knew our situations weren't the same. They could have been only if Karol were still alive, if I had to worry about my husband sensing another man's touch on my skin. I didn't have to deceive anyone in my house except my children, and despite what some people say, children are the easiest ones to fool.

If our affair was to end, it would only be because George had to end it. I'd understood that from the beginning, I realized now.

So be it. I waited.

"Sorry about that," he said once he'd finished coughing. "Got something in my windpipe, I think."

I took a sip of the coffee. Tepid now, it had an acid taste.

"What I was saying—"

"Things are difficult for you," I filled in. "Keeping secrets."

"That's right," he said and gave me a curious look; clearly, he'd heard the sharp edge in my voice. "What I'm trying to explain here, Hazel—"

"Uh-huh."

"—about this idea, where it came from. I'm just trying to explain why I think it would be a good thing for us."

A sudden gust of wind swelled up, and I pulled my elbows in closer, trying for warmth as George explained what I'd somehow failed to see, that if he were the one renting my land, he'd have good reason to be over at my place every day of the week. He wanted to see me, he said, more than he'd been able. It was killing him, he said. It was eating him up inside.

I'd never heard such words spoken before outside of the movies. They didn't sound as I'd have expected them to. George—calm, slow-talking George—was speaking quickly, but in a low voice, almost a mutter. He sounded more frustrated than he did caught up with passion. It reminded me of the first time our family car had broken down, when Karol and I were on our way into town. Joe was in the backseat and Debbie, just a few months old, was settled on my lap when the car had suddenly begun making a shrieking sound and Karol pulled over to the side of the road, cursing. He got out and opened up the hood. With the doors closed and that shield of metal in between, I couldn't hear what he was saying, but I could hear the tenor of his voice change as he discovered the cause of the screeching and determined what was needed to make it stop.

"—because we can't go on like this," George was saying, "seeing each other every now and then. It doesn't make sense. You name the terms, and I'll sign right there on the line."

It took me a moment to remember that we were talking about the rent. "You won't make anything on it."

"I know."

"It's not just your money, either."

A pause. Then: "Lydie wants to help out."

Why? I could have asked, but I already knew the answer. Because she was good. Because she cared for me and Debbie and Joe. Because every day she looked out her kitchen window at a hill of trees, and never suspected that they could hide a thing.

Louisa

16

Between the last letter and the first newspaper report, more than nine months passed. It was long enough that Louisa could believe the two events had nothing to do with each other. Addie was as far away as the moon and yet always seemed close.

Louisa had just given birth to her third child. Herbert was almost four, Joseph was two and a half, Emmaline was a little thing her brothers could hardly believe was human. They asked her about it. "Mama, why's she so purple?"—this from Joseph, who'd stick a finger right into the soft bulb of his sister's belly and then look hurt when she made a squawking cry. Herbert, meanwhile, always stood with his hands behind his back, staring at the infant with something between fear and love. He had none of the bearing of an oldest son; you could sense him sending out his feeling into the world like a lonely chord played in the dark on a fiddle. Once, she'd found him reciting Bible verses to the cows, and when she explained to him that the lowly animals are beloved by God even without any clear knowledge of Him, Herbert had said, "But look how they're all paying attention!" Already she knew he would grow into a wise man.

The last letter from Addie gave no indication of its being the last. It was a letter like any other: Freddie had grown three full inches in the last year; Henry now squatted down on the ground like a Chinaman. Life kept moving along. There was a sense of flurry about the letter, a suggestion that the writer had sat down amid the hustle and bustle because tomorrow would be as busy as today, so one might as well take the time right now for writing.

Louisa imagined her sister's servants coming in and out of the room while she wrote. There had been a Chinese laundry back in Marietta, and she always pictured the couple that ran it when she read Addie's letters. The couple had gone by Sam and Rose. This had never seemed strange until her sister went to China and began writing to her of people whose names had dashes and apostrophes in them. Then Louisa thought of Sam and Rose and wondered what their real names might have been.

Several months passed without any correspondence from Addie, but this was not unusual: sometimes she would receive a packet of letters all together, an entire season's worth or more. The post didn't come often to Lu-cho Fu. And when it did, once Louisa's letters were delivered and Addie's collected, who knew where else those letters might next get held up. Louisa had only a vague sense of China. She knew the names Lu-cho Fu and Peking. She didn't really know how far apart the two places were, and as for the other towns and cities Addie wrote of, they were all a jumble, there was no keeping them straight. Frankly, it was a mystery that one sister ever received a single letter from the other. When you considered the trip those letters took: horseback and train, however many ships and boats. There might be a camel somewhere in that long line; there might be a Chinaman carrying the mail by foot along the edge of a steep cliff. Louisa could picture the man, bent nearly double beneath the weight on his back: he looked like Sam from the laundry back home.

She began to worry when six months had passed. She'd wonder, as she wrung out the shirts she was washing in the laundry tub, why Addie hadn't written. The next moment Emmaline would start crying or Joseph would remind her it was time to feed the chickens, and the day would march on without her thinking of her sister again.

"Addie's got busy, I suppose," she'd say to Bert as they prepared for bed. "She hasn't written for a while now."

"Ah, well, with her work," he'd reply. Or: "She and Owen've got a school to run, don't they?" in a tone that let Louisa know it was selfish of her to expect a letter from a sister busy converting a country full of heathens. At the same time, his tone said that he considered missionary work to be a protracted form of entertainment, not at all like real life, which could only take place on a farm in western Illinois. It was a tone that communicated all kinds of things, none of them of much comfort to Louisa. She'd turn away and sleep with her face to the moon, or the hazy place where the moon seemed to be.

*   *   *

It was early April when the first report came. Louisa was out in the garden, Emmaline wrapped up in a blanket and sleeping in a little cradle on the ground, Herbert and Joseph helping to break up the ground for planting. They'd been at it for half an hour when Herbert, looking up from his work, raised one dirt-covered hand and pointed behind Louisa. "There's Mr. Barnes," he said. Then, after a moment, in a rueful tone: "I wish he would've come on Blackie." Herbert knew all the horses in the area by name.

Sure enough, their neighbor Jeb was coming up the lane on foot. Midmorning was an unusual time for visiting, but he had three strong sons who kept the farm running. Louisa supposed he was able to get away when he wanted. "Morning," she called out as she stood and brushed the dirt from her knees.

"And what a morning, isn't it? Fine weather we've got today. Helping your mother out, are you, Herbie? Getting the garden put in."

"We're planting vegetables," Herbert informed their neighbor, and then watched with patient exasperation as Joseph scooped up a handful of dirt and dropped it into his lap.

"They're a great help, I see," Jeb said to Louisa with a wink. "And the little one," he said, stepping up to the cradle where it sat on the grass. Emmaline was still sleeping, her face turned toward the inside of one arm. "She don't give you no trouble. That's a good girl." He turned his smile from the baby to Louisa and asked if Bert was out working.

"Him and Al are down in the back fields. You want me to send Herbert after him?"

Jeb seemed to waver for a moment. "Oh, no, that's all right. Now I brought out a paper, and this item might make you uneasy, which, I don't want you to feel frightened, but it's news and I thought, well, you ought to know, with your sister and all."

Louisa glanced down at the boys, who were both seated in the dirt, peering up at Jeb with what looked like suspicion, though they might just have been squinting at the bright sky behind him. "Herbert, you take your brother and go get your pa. Tell him Mr. Barnes is here and wants to have a chat."

As soon as the boys were off, Jeb took a newspaper from under his arm. It was already bent to the place he wanted and he thrust a calloused finger at a few sentences near the top of the page, in the section called "The News Condensed." Her eyes fell on the word "China," but then Jeb pulled the paper back toward him. "What it says is that there's Chinese up to no good and they've gone and murdered a reverend over there."

"Where at?" Louisa asked. "I mean, where in China?"

He raised the paper to his face as if he couldn't quite make out the words. It took everything Louisa had not to grab it out of his hands. "It doesn't say, exactly. In China, it says." He lowered the paper again and then abruptly handed it to her.

Louisa read:

Conflicting reports have been received concerning the I Ho Chu'an, a seditious group otherwise known as the "Boxers," terrorizing foreigners in the Shantung region of China. The grisly murder of the Rev. Mr. Brooks of the Church Missionary Society last December may have foretold a growing movement in which numerous villages are now destroyed and countless native Christians killed.

"It's only the one missionary," Jeb said when she handed the paper back to him. "They don't mention any others." She nodded, but she felt queasy and at the same time as if she were looking off down a long road at a figure coming, though she couldn't make out who or what it was. "Where's your sister's mission now?"

"I don't expect you'd have heard of it. It's in a place called Lu-cho Fu."

Jeb screwed up one eye, thinking. "They all sound so similar, don't they. You have Peking and then, what is it, Shanghai. One of them is where the emperors live."

"I believe it's Peking."

They went on like this until Bert came into view, walking over the fields. He was carrying Joseph under his arm, sideways, the way you'd carry a pillow, and Herbert was trotting alongside him. When they got close, he raised his free hand and waved, and then he was with them and telling the boys to scoot off and let the grown people talk.

Louisa let their neighbor explain what was in the paper. The queasiness had gone away and now she didn't feel anything much at all; she might have been listening to the news from Africa or Brazil. She tried to tell herself that her sister might be in danger, but some part of her refused to even consider the possibility. She watched her husband as Jeb read aloud the passage. When he was finished, Bert said, "It's a great big country."

"That's true. It's as big, almost, as America."

"And it says there are conflicting reports."

"That's how it often is. No one's really sure whether anything's going on, but the news have to report on it in case there is."

Louisa listened to them debating and waited to be pulled into the conversation. It was her sister, after all, and she had the greatest knowledge of China. She doubted whether Bert could even remember the name of the place where her sister was living. The two men went on talking and soon enough had moved on from the topic of China altogether. The conversation tended to go where it always did: the farm, the weather. Louisa stopped listening.

*   *   *

The *Intelligencer* didn't devote much room to international events, and what was included was brief enough that it managed to quiet the clamor in the world to a distant calling like that from a flock of lonely geese flying over. A few weeks after the first report, the paper printed another piece about China. This time Louisa didn't get to see it for herself, but Bert told her that Jeb had given him the story at church. Louisa had had to stay home with Joseph, who'd come down with a high fever almost overnight. He lay across her lap, breathing ragged, and every few minutes erupted in a fit of coughing that brought tears to his eyes. Louisa stroked her son's head and sang a song about kittens and cows. He slept for a while and she left him to walk Emmaline around the yard, and then she brought her daughter inside and laid her in the middle of the bed. When Joseph awoke and started coughing again, Emmaline grinned and cooed and crawled around among the blankets so that Louisa had to keep reaching out to keep her from pitching headfirst onto the floor. In the lonely house, with no other sound but her daughter's cooing and her son's coughing, with only a soft rain-smelling breeze coming in through the cracked window and the occasional creak of the house settling, Louisa felt the world collapsing onto this single point; it was almost more than she could bear. Emmaline was a little idiot, oblivious to all the suffering in the world. Joseph coughed and cried, and Louisa wanted to shake him. She wanted to put her mouth to his and suck the phlegm out so he could breathe more easily, but she also wanted to shake him into unconsciousness. Instead, she stroked his head and told a rambling story about Jonah in the whale and how together they went down through a cave in the ocean floor and came out on the other side of the earth. Emmaline began screaming. Joseph wet the bed.

By the time Bert and Herbert returned home, Louisa had had enough time to reach the end of her rope and then climb back up, hand over hand. When they walked through the door, the face she turned to them was blinkingly serene. Herbert took over the care of his brother and Emmaline took a nap. Bert kept Louisa company in the kitchen while she began boiling some peas to go with the roast she'd managed to put in the cookstove a few hours before.

"I stayed and talked with Jeb after service," Bert said. "It's that same business from China. There was a line in the paper about it, talk of some warships being sent over."

Louisa felt her stomach tighten. She dropped a spoonful of lard in the peas. "Is it American ships you mean?"

"American and others. Jeb says England and Germany have got as many people there as we have."

"Yes, Addie's mentioned it." She shivered a little, saying her sister's name. They were talking about China as if it were merely news. In Addie's letters she'd mentioned meeting British missionaries, and German and French—it was all real, it was her life. *Our governments collectively have bullied China for years, and the unfortunate result is that we missionaries are sometimes assumed to be agents for some conspiracy—I am often aware that the people here must picture a man in a suit and hat when we talk of God, and they have been taught by decades of reckless business to resent such a figure, and rather deeply.* Louisa stirred the peas, watching the lard dissolve into the greenish-brown water. There was some excitement in considering violence that threatened someone you loved, but only in an abstract way, only as a kind of story you told yourself to raise the hairs on your arm. The actual possibility of it remained absurd. "But if McKinley is really sending the military, that must mean it's serious."

Bert sat down, took off one shoe, and busied himself unthreading the lace. "Serious somewhere don't mean it's bad everywhere. And if he decides to send a warship—well, I'd say we've shown the world what we can do."

Louisa watched as he pulled the lace from the shoe and released bits of dried mud that fell onto the floor. She would have to sweep up after him. She hated herself for thinking about something as mundane as sweeping the floor when her sister was perhaps at this very moment in danger. And she hated Bert for the careless way he dirtied the kitchen. He ran his fingers along the lace, stopping at the place where the fibers were breaking. It was a habit of his to fix things before they broke. Louisa had often to remind herself that this was a wonderful quality. At times it could feel oppressive. "It would be better if Addie wrote to let us know she was all right," she said, turning back to the stove.

"She probably has. The newspapers get the story telegraphed. How much longer won't it take for one of her letters to reach us?"

"I think I'll write to Mother, anyway," Louisa said, "and see whether they've got word from her recently."

Just then Herbert came walking through the door of the kitchen, carrying Emmaline. He had his arms hooked under hers and was carrying her front first so that her little body held against his was just a smaller version. "I don't think Joseph liked us being in there," he said, setting his sister down on the floor, where she blinked in confusion and then set off crawling toward her father's leg. "He's coughing a lot."

Louisa went quickly into the back room where Joseph lay on the bed. He was turned onto one shoulder, and his breath was coming in effortful gasps. Placing one hand under his chin, she turned his face from the pillow. It was hot to the touch, and his cheeks were red. "Can you breathe?" she asked, and he heaved a little and then started coughing again.

She scooped him up in the blanket and carried him into the kitchen.

It was hot near the stove and Joseph squirmed, so she sat down at the table and told Bert to bring over the honey jar. Joseph had already had a spoonful in the morning and he'd fought against swallowing it then, but now he didn't resist. His skin was white and red, like a marble, and glassy. Once the honey was down, Louisa stuck her pinkie finger up one of his nostrils and again he barely flinched. "He still doesn't have any muck in his nose," she said to Bert. "You'd think if it was a cold he would, by now."

As the day went on, Joseph didn't get any better, though he didn't seem to get any worse, either. Worn out from coughing, he would sometimes fall asleep for a half hour, but then he'd wake up again struggling for breath. That night, Louisa kept him in the bed with her and it was much the same. In the morning, Bert went out to the barn and Herbert went with him; he was old enough now to help with the feeding, though not old enough to do anything out in the fields. When he came back in after his regular chores, Louisa sent him to the henhouse to collect the eggs. Normally, the henhouse was her domain. Today she was busy with Joseph and Emmaline, and she had time only to reflect that it was something to be able to count on such a young child.

Herbert returned from the henhouse with only a few eggs. He'd found several broken ones, and when Louisa went out to check, she was greeted with more squawking than usual. A snake must have got in. She looked around to make sure it was gone and then put Herbert to the task of cleaning up and putting in fresh hay.

She could no longer remember the time before she'd had her son. And yet she had been pregnant the summer Addie and her family came to visit—pregnant and worried that she would lose him, as she had lost all the others. Then Addie went away again and Herbert arrived, and she had thought that she'd reached the end of her losses.

One did not need to look for bad omens, Louisa decided. A snake in the henhouse could just be a snake.

*　　*　　*

By Tuesday morning, Louisa had resolved that they needed a doctor. She sent Bert into town and he came back with a neighbor and the promise that Dr. Reynolds would follow within an hour or two. The neighbor, Mrs. Moeller, was no substitute for the doctor, even though she imagined herself one. She had never once consulted the services of a medical man; it was a waste of money as far as she was concerned. Inside the house, she took off her jacket and hung it on a hook by the door. "You've gave him honey?" she asked, and Louisa told her they had. Then Louisa took her into the living room.

Herbert was standing by the bed where his brother lay. Even from where she stood, she could see that Joseph's lips had taken on a bluish tint, but his fever was high; she'd felt his head only a few minutes before and laid a cold cloth across it that was still in place. She stood now at a distance of six or eight feet, suddenly unwilling to go up to the bed.

Mrs. Moeller squatted down next to Joseph, edging Herbert away. "Go on and cough," she instructed.

Joseph stared up at her with exhausted suspicion. No one was making him better, not even his own mother, and this neighbor was telling him to do the thing that hurt. For a full half minute he wouldn't cough, but then it happened on its own and went on for some time. Herbert had a cloth at the ready and stepped forward to catch the globule of greenish phlegm when it came at last. "He's been bringing up gunk since last night," Louisa said, biting her thumbnail, "whenever he gets a fit like that going."

Mrs. Moeller stood. "No doubt the doctor will know better what to do. But for my part, I'd say you attend to the fever and it will take care of itself."

It was midafternoon before Dr. Reynolds came rolling up the lane in his black carriage with its high, narrow wheels. He was a large man with a bullet-shaped head, who walked as if he were continually stumbling forward and whose eyebrows, naturally angled down toward the nose, gave him a look of disapproval. Children tended to be frightened of him. He'd come out to see the family once before, and poor polite Herbert had hidden his face in Louisa's chest.

Now the doctor took his bag from under the seat and climbed down into the yard. "It's your youngest who's got sick," he said.

"My youngest son," she corrected. "I have a daughter who's younger."

Dr. Reynolds nodded and gazed at her from beneath his bushy brows. "And where's your man now?"

"Working. Do you want me to get him?"

"Oh, no, that ain't necessary. If he's busy, you know." The doctor shook his head and said, "Let's see the boy then." Brusque, but as if it came from kindness. A doctor couldn't afford to be tenderhearted.

As they passed into the house, Louisa told him of Joseph's symptoms. When she mentioned that he'd been ill since Saturday, he said, as if correcting her, "Not four days, yet." Most of the country families didn't call out a doctor for a child who'd been ill only half a week; most of them didn't call out a doctor at all. Louisa had been raised in a town, and she didn't trust the idea that you simply did for yourself. You didn't leave things to chance and the wisdom of farmers' wives. You went into town to get the doctor, and somehow you found the money to pay him for the visit.

Inside the house, the doctor pulled a chair up to the bed and felt Joseph's forehead. He listened to his breathing and when the boy began coughing, he removed from his pocket a clean handkerchief that he used to capture the phlegm. "Has there been any blood?" he asked as he examined the contents. Louisa told him no, not any that she'd seen. He nodded and then reached out and poked Joseph's stomach. The boy yelped and began crying. "Hurts some, does it?" The crying set Joseph choking and then coughing again. Louisa swallowed hard, feeling ill herself.

Dr. Reynolds stood and looked down on Joseph with a thoughtful expression. "It's lung fever, no doubt about that."

Louisa's heart contracted; she felt it like a thin piece of ice beneath her skin. She heard her mother, two decades earlier, saying to Louisa's father, "They say the poor thing had pneumonia. Carried him right off." And Louisa, a child, had gotten it mixed up, pictured the boy they were discussing with a small blocky object in his hands, something cold and bluely glowing, that he clutched to his chest as he ran away.

"What's your thinking for the boy's care?" Mrs. Moeller asked the doctor. But Louisa put a hand on his arm before he could answer. "Won't you come into the kitchen and have a slice of pie? Mrs. Moeller"—she turned to her neighbor—"could you stay here with the boys?"

Mrs. Moeller went to the bed to rearrange the blankets tucked around Joseph's body. There was a hint of accusation in the movement, a suggestion that the doctor had mucked things up. Dr. Reynolds stooped to take hold of his black bag, and Louisa led him through the next room and into the kitchen. Pulling back the cloth from a rhubarb pie, she cut a wide slab and put it on a plate. "I'm shaking, Doctor," she said, pulling back another chair and sitting across from him. "I'm worried for my son."

He took a bite of the pie and nodded. "You can worry, you know, not that it'll do any good. Children get lung fever, and they get better. Most do." He cleared his throat. "Or many do, at least."

Louisa shook her head. "He struggles to breathe. What am I supposed to do?"

"I'll give you some aspirin. That helps with the aches and the stomach pain." The doctor took another large bite of the pie, and then another. He ate somewhat grimly, as if it were part of his job. "But truth to tell, the sickness has to run its course. It may take a little while."

"How long?"

The doctor shrugged. "Hard to say. He's got a fever right now, but you already know what to do about that, and the good news is that the fever, well, it ain't low, but at least it's below the point where we need to get in a panic. You worry when the boy gets delirious." Finishing his pie, he pushed the plate an inch away from him. "No, thank you, I've had plenty," he said when Louisa offered him another piece. "I'm sorry I can't do more to get your boy feeling better. As I said, I'll give you some aspirin. That'll help some. But mother care really is the best treatment; you feel free to use that liberally, Mrs. Baumann."

Louisa was supposed to smile here, and she did. But resented it, a bit.

The doctor left, and Mrs. Moeller stayed on another hour. They fed Joseph some aspirin and Louisa sat by him and stroked his arm. "Have you heard lately from your sister in China?" Mrs. Moeller asked. Louisa waited to hear if she was asking because of some new report. But it seemed her neighbor wasn't aware of any news at all, at least none having to do with a part of the world that far away. Louisa told her she hadn't heard from Addie in months and kept quiet about the reason this was so concerning.

After their neighbor had gone, Louisa left Joseph in the care of his brother and took Emmaline into the kitchen, where she set her daughter down on a rug in the corner and gave her a stuffed rag toy to play with. Somehow the noon meal had been prepared and eaten, but there was supper to think of. Left over from dinner were chicken and gravy, and peas. She would do a meat pie. As Louisa began mixing lard into the flour, she tried to turn her ear from the sound of Joseph coughing in the other room. Out the window, she saw Bert come out of the barn swinging a pail, on his way to the well. He had his head down. Who knew what he was thinking of. Joseph was coughing and coughing, and Louisa could hear it become a cry. She didn't put down her spoon and go to comfort him. Instead, she voiced a silent prayer: *Dear God, take my sister and leave me my son.*

A minute later, Bert crossed back into view, the pail now filled. This time he did glance up at the window. He didn't nod or acknowledge her in any way, and Louisa felt a shock go through her. It was a punishment. He couldn't know what she'd done, the deal she'd made with God in the silence of her own heart—and yet his look was a judgment.

After he'd gone away again, she remembered that the sun was shining on the windows. So maybe he'd looked up only to see the glint of light on the glass.

*　　*　　*

Within a week, Joseph was mending. His cough lingered for some weeks, but he was up and wobbling around, and Louisa knew that the deal she had made with God would be honored. She knew it without feeling it. Once, years before, while peeling a potato, she'd sliced the flesh at the base of her thumb with the paring knife. It was a deep cut, down through the skin to something more elementary. She'd seen the knife go in and come out again. Then came the narrow line of blood that became a gush, but it took a moment for the pain to arrive. Before it did, during that period of shock, she'd experienced a strange kind of relief. You could be hurt without feeling it, at least for a time. And she'd been thankful to her body for the ways it had of protecting her from its own terrible understanding.

The news from China came, but in dribs and drabs, and it wasn't always clear what any of it meant. The *Newark* was sent to Taku under Admiral Kempff. There were other foreign warships at Taku. But where was Taku? Was that near where Addie lived? Louisa never did write to her mother, but her mother wrote to her. She wanted to know if Louisa had heard from Addie any more recently than they had. The last letter they'd received was from last summer, and they were worried, but they put their faith in God, didn't they, and that's exactly what Addie had done as well. The letter swung between worry and complaint. Louisa put it away, telling herself she would answer it when she found the time.

Her mother had become more religious over the years. Because Louisa hadn't been there to see it, she couldn't quite believe in the transformation. Nearly a decade before, when Addie announced that she was going to China on a mission, their mother had been as baffled as the rest of them. They were all good Christians. Still, there was a limit to what was required of them; crossing a distant ocean to an even more distant land, staying among a strange people in difficult and terrible conditions—this was such an extreme demonstration of faith that it seemed almost unbecoming. That was what their mother had felt at the time; now, she seemed to have reversed her thinking. She had grown more religious even while Addie seemed less and less certain of her faith. Well, belief had its basis in distance. Abstraction is almost always better than proof.

Proof—that was what Louisa was waiting for and dreading. Proof that her sister was doomed, killed. The foreign warships at Taku were attacked from Peking. Eight foreigners from a mission in Shansi went missing. Shansi! That was the region where Addie lived. The mission named in the paper was a place called Pao-ting Fu, which sounded familiar but was not the name Louisa remembered. *Did* she remember it? She went to check the letters. Yes, she was right: Lu-cho Fu.

The news that came was horrible, horrible. Priests doused in kerosene and burned alive. Missionaries beheaded with swords. The deaths of native Christians weren't tallied up with the same exactness as those of foreigners. They seemed to be far more numerous and were noted in passing. Louisa felt very little, considering them. It was their country, after all. Christian or not, it was their kind doing the killing.

On his weekly trip into town, Bert now made a point of purchasing a newspaper to bring home. Louisa skipped over everything but the report from China, which was only ever a paragraph or two. When she'd finished reading it, she put the whole paper in the stove and watched it catch fire, glowing and smoldering and turning to ash. Bert never stopped her. Once, he tried to reassure Louisa of her sister's safety by pointing out that some of the foreigners had got out, fled to T'ien-chin, boarded ships. "Addie might be crossing the Pacific right now," he said. Louisa only shook her head. Her sister was not on any ship home. Her sister was in China, waiting for her fate to claim her.

Then came the news that T'ien-chin itself was under attack. Louisa remembered the first letters she'd gotten from Addie nearly a decade before, when she'd been stuck in the coastal city for more than a month, waiting to start the next stage of the journey to her new home. Everything had seemed utterly civilized—too civilized for Addie's taste. Vast portions of T'ien-chin were taken up by foreign concessions. The streets and houses were no more Chinese than Marietta's had been. "It's a strange feeling," she'd written, "to cross from China into Britain only by walking a block." She'd written of the foreign community, how large and prosperous it was, and of the invitations she had for dinners where duck à l'orange was served on white china plates, with red wine and cognac and delicate fruit tarts. There had been performances of Brahms and Italian librettos. Once, she'd been invited to go to the races. The city had a giant dirt track a mile and a half in circumference, built by two German brothers, and they had two seasons for racing, one in the autumn and another in the spring. The British, in particular, Addie said, were mad for horse racing. On race day, the grandstands were populated by any number of white faces, men and women and children, and Chinese as well.

Louisa wondered now about the fate of that racetrack. She imagined a lone horse running over the dirt without its rider, around and around. She imagined the grandstands empty. It was not a comforting image, but it was better than most of the alternatives.

*   *   *

Eventually, the news she was waiting for did come. It was not until the fall, however, when the harvest had begun and she was busy every minute of every day, putting up vegetables, wrapping apples in paper to store in the cellar, taking over nearly all the care of the livestock, since Bert was in the fields from morning to night. Milking was the never-ending chore, and every day she had three large meals to prepare, too, for both the family and the two boys they hired to help. The kitchen was never cool. The house was never clean.

The letter must have come one of these days when she was so busy that she barely had time to sit, a day when it wasn't until she lay down at night that she realized her muscles had been throbbing for hours, that her bones now seemed magnetized to the stuffed mattress. The letter was written and sent on one of these days, and it arrived on just another. She didn't know which one because it was safely tucked into a box at the post office in Edwardsville, where it remained for a longer time than their mail usually did. They were too busy for the weekly trip into town. All their neighbors were too busy to make the trip, either. Two weeks passed. Three.

They ran to the bottom of their supply of soap and then salt, and at last one morning Bert saddled up Prince and went into town. He was back before the morning was out and found Louisa outside digging beets from the ground. Handing her a letter, he said, "You don't have to look at this, you know, just yet." Bert wasn't a great reader, but you didn't need to be a great reader to see that the envelope was edged in black. Louisa glanced at the letter and quickly turned away again. Her hands were covered with dirt, she said. She asked him to take the letter inside and leave it on the table, and as he walked away, she went back to her work.

It took her another half hour to finish the row of beets. When she was done, she tied them up in an old cloth and brought them to the side of the house. She would bring them down to the root cellar later. Now she went into the house. Now she took off her shoes. Now she washed her hands and scrubbed at her fingernails, rimmed with purple as the envelope on the table behind her was rimmed with black. She dried her hands and turned around.

Joseph had come in from somewhere. "Mama," he said, lifting his arms, and she bent down to hug him as he demanded. She picked him up and held him close. She had made her bargain: here was her child with that sour smell coming from his head, the crust behind his ears. In his hair was something dark and matted. She hadn't given him a full bath in over a week. But he was hers, hers, he was alive and hers.

When he had run off again to play with his sister, she took up the letter from the table. It weighed hardly anything—far too light for the news it held. She was steady now. Her fingers didn't shake as she slid them under the flap. "Dear Louisa," her father had written,

prepare yourself, for the news is more terrible than we dared fear: Addie is killed and all her family with her, we don't know by which method. The Missionary Board wrote to inform us and Mother has not left her bed since the letter came. Your sister and brother-in-law and your dear nephews are with the Lord, we are happy for that. But it is a loss from which we will not soon recover.

Louisa read the letter twice through and was ready to put it into the cookstove as she had the newspapers, but then she stopped herself and thought she might need to have proof later. If she mistrusted herself. If hope was still hidden inside her, somewhere, like a cancer slowly growing.

*   *   *

Half a year passed, and she was pregnant again. If the baby was a girl, they were going to name her Adeline. Louisa would put the tragedy behind her. For it was true that though she took the news calmly at first, the loss of her sister had had its effect. The old darkness had gradually crept up on her again, the "weather" she had used to experience years before, in that time before she gave birth to Herbert, in that time when they were still in the little cabin a quarter mile down the lane. Once again, she felt some part of herself curdling. She felt a screw turn inside her chest, a screech like a rusty hinge that sounded in her head and seemed almost to want to be released into the world. Throughout the winter following the receipt of her father's letter, as she sat by the stove patching Bert's clothes and letting out the seams on Herbert's old shirts and pants so that Joseph, bigger than his brother had been at his age, could wear them, as she moved the needle up and down through the cloth, she kept her lips pressed together to keep the sound from escaping. A screech, a screaming. Beneath the cloth falling over her lap, she'd stab a needle into the flesh just above her knee. This helped. Though sometimes she could swear that the baby in her womb felt it, too, and kicked her in revolt. It was too early for that—much too early, she was barely showing at all. The kicking was in her imagination, but it felt all too real.

The baby would quiet the terrible noises inside Louisa's head. It would remind her that a needle should not have your own blood on it.

When Adeline came, there would be four. Adeline and Emmaline, Herbert and Joseph. There were women who became pregnant and cried with sorrow, but Louisa had the memory of those first years of her marriage, when her body had failed and kept on failing, and so she felt satisfied.

For now they had three. Soon it would be four.

She lost the baby halfway through. Almost halfway. She had grown used to losing babies this way, and it was not easier at all. It would never be easier. She would cry for this one even when the next one came. She would keep crying for this one whenever she remembered her own sister. Adeline, Addie. A doomed name.

*   *   *

She was pregnant again, and this time the baby came: a girl with dark hair and red mottled skin and a mouth like a pink snapdragon, perfect.

Louisa, exhausted from labor, told Bert to name her. "Not *for* anyone," she said as she guided the baby's lips to her breast. "I want her to have her own original name."

"How about Rose?"

She watched the baby screwing up her face for a scream. "There, now, Rosie," she said, moving her hand to the back of the head to guide her in the right direction. "There you are." But the baby refused to hold on.

A few hours later, Bert came in to see her again. It was early spring, and he smelled of manure—he'd been dealing with the giant pile by the barn. By the end of winter it was always an impressive size. "What do you think about Violet?" he asked.

"Violet?"

"For a name."

"She doesn't have to be a flower," Louisa replied. Then, seeing his face, she said that of course Violet was a fine name.

Bert frowned. "She could be a Mary. A Henrietta." They went through a long list of names, one after another, but most of them already belonged to people they knew. At last, Bert held up his hands. "If she's going to share someone's name, anyway, why don't we make it on purpose? Why don't we just call her Adeline, like we planned with the other? We never—"

In the end, they decided on Iris. It was a name neither of them much cared for, though it would come to seem the only choice they could have made.

As all names eventually do for the children that live.

*　　*　　*

The children that live—how do you count them? Do you count Emmaline, who died when she was two? The same age her brother had been when Louisa, in a moment, had made her bargain with God. *Take my sister and leave me my son.* With Emmaline, there was no time for such bargains; you hardly knew she was sick before she was gone. One morning, her body suddenly heavy with death. Tiny teeth bared like a rat's. A strange bruised pallor along the side of the body that held her weight, so that it looked like the mattress was the thing that had killed her, a dark mold growing up, seeping into the skin.

Dear God, take my sister and leave me my son—Louisa hadn't been sufficiently precise back then. And, oh, He had caught her on it, He had taught her a lesson. You don't try to make bargains with God or the devil. You don't call something a prayer when it's no more than a transaction.

This for that?

No. Both will be taken, if that's what He wants.

*   *   *

One day in 1904, late January, Joseph came in with a letter. Snow on his shoes, but he ran right in. Rural Free Delivery had come over a year before, and it had become one of his games to watch for the mail carriage—in good weather from outside, in bad weather from within—and to try to get down to the end of the lane before the driver had a chance to put the letters into the box. If Mr. Gifford had anything for them, he would deliver it directly into Joseph's hands. If not, he would ask after the family, and Joseph would give the report. They were always fine, all of them. Well, that was good to hear. Mr. Gifford would give his strange jerking nod, like someone had tied a string to his left ear and yanked it, and then drive away.

"Mama, for you," Joseph said. He was almost six and not yet in school, but as the designated mail carrier for the family, he had come to recognize the distinction between Mr. and Mrs. on the envelope.

"You're tracking snow everywhere," Louisa said, swatting him back toward the door after taking the letter. "You know better than to walk through with your boots on." She had Iris on her lap. She'd been trying to settle her down after digging a splinter out of her foot, and it had worked until Joseph went running and came back again.

One thud and then another as the shoes hit the porch floor. He came back a moment later, wearing only thick woolen socks. "Is it from Ohio?" he asked. "From Aunt Flora or Grandma?"

Louisa considered the envelope. It was from an unknown address in Delaware. She was certain she didn't know anyone in Delaware. She would have asked Bert if he had any idea, but he and Herbert were both out in the barn milking. The name on the envelope wasn't familiar, either. *McBride.* No title before it. And yet—something caught in her memory. Somewhere, sometime, she might have heard the name.

She took out the letter. It was only half a page long. Scanning her eyes down the narrow column of text, she felt her chest seize up as she read. No, she would not—there was no point in—no. After a moment, she folded the paper up again and slid it into the envelope.

"What's it say, Mama?"

"Nothing that concerns you."

Joseph begged to have it read to him. "Please," he said, but his mother refused. Sometimes a letter went wrong, she said, and was directed to another person by accident.

That evening, while Bert was arranging the fire in the stove, Louisa sat with the letter, trying to decide whether to discuss it with him now or after they went to bed. The children were already asleep, and the two of them were alone. She held the letter at her side. It didn't concern him. It was addressed to her. She knew that when she shared it, he would tell her immediately what to do; he would tell her that she must write back to the woman at once.

She sat in the dim light by the kerosene lantern, watching him, and when, a few minutes later, he came to sit beside her, she kept the letter pressed between her leg and the edge of the sofa.

The next day, she took it out again and read it in private. "Dear Mrs. Baumann," the letter began,

I am not sure whether you recognize my name. I was a fellow missionary at Lu-cho Fu in China where your sister and her family lived. We were dear friends for a time. Forgive me for writing you now. The tragedy is still fresh for all of us and you may not wish to have any reminders—I am certain Addie will not. And yet I write to ask you to intervene on my behalf, for I don't know where to find her unless it is through you. It will be four years this July since we parted—or I should say, it will be four years since she left. We had been in Chungking for nearly a year, far from the violence up north. She did not tell me where she was going, but I supposed it was home. No doubt she has begun a new life since then and does not want reminding of the terrible events of the past, but being returned to the States myself now, I decided that I could not help but try. I have an old letter of yours in my possession that she left behind. Forgive me for keeping it, but I am selfish: I have little else of hers to remember her by. She might have had the same inclination, for she took with her when she left a small possession of mine—a hat. If you should be so kind as to give me a way to reach her, I will retrieve it myself.

The letter was signed, "Poppy McBride."

Louisa had not slept at all the night before, and going over the contents of this letter again and again in her mind, she had inadvertently changed the meaning in subtle ways. She had thought the writer was still living in China. She had thought the letter in the woman's possession was one Addie had written.

But she'd gotten the main idea right—*that* she hadn't changed. This woman, this Poppy McBride, thought Addie was still living. Not only thought, but assumed. Addie had not been there when her family was killed. The idea was so strange, so unexpected, so miraculous, that Louisa had not been able to comprehend what it meant. That Addie would come home? That she would see her sister again after all these years? Of course she hadn't slept. It was too much to bear. The possibilities seemed to spread through her mind like spilled water.

Now it was morning, and in the light of the weak winter sun, Louisa had the lucidity that comes from a sleepless night. The possibilities were not endless—there were only two. Her sister had died, as they'd always thought, or she was alive, and she still wasn't coming home again.

Louisa would not write to this woman. She would not write to her family in Marietta. She would not tell Bert.

Iris was sleeping; the boys were both out in the barn with their father. Louisa took this letter from Poppy McBride and put it into the stove, both the letter and the envelope. The paper smoldered and was immediately turned to ash. It was satisfying, but it wasn't enough. She thought for only a moment before going to the bedroom and opening the bottom drawer of her dresser. This was where she'd kept all Addie's letters, not in any sort of order but piled on top of one another, sliding around. The paper smelled old; some of the letters had turned yellow or even had patches of black mold. See: they were consuming themselves, anyway. They would be turned back to nothing, one way or another. Louisa gathered them up against her chest and brought them into the kitchen, where she fed them, one by one, into the stove.

In a letter she'd written years before, her sister had described a custom in which the Chinese went to the graves of their relatives and burned paper money. Not real money, she said, a kind of special currency that served only this purpose—ghost money, it was called. The purpose was to help the dead in the afterlife, to keep them rich and happy. It was both veneration and bribery, Addie explained, because people thought their dead could aid them here on earth, bring them blessings and wealth, protect them from sickness. "You see what confronts us here," Addie had said. "The dead are less dead in China than they are in the West."

Louisa put the letters into the stove and watched them flare orange, and then white. Each one gave her the same satisfaction she got from pricking herself with a needle, a feeling like slapping a mosquito that's landed on your arm. It's not punishing the thing that's caused you pain; it's simply getting rid of it so you're not bothered anymore.

Addie

17

She tried not to think of what she'd left behind. Those first few days, when they were still close to Lu-cho Fu—when the idea still remained, however absurd, that she could go back if she wanted—Addie tried to push away thoughts of her family. Yet sometimes an image would come into her head of Owen setting out from the house, turning before he stepped over the threshold, and then she would get angry; she would have, for a moment, a wild feeling of abandonment. Her stomach would tighten, her fists clench. How dare he leave the mission and all their work; how dare he leave the boys, leave her.

But of course it was the other way around. She was the one who had left, with Poppy.

They were going south, more than a thousand miles, to a mission in Chungking. There were five of them altogether—Poppy, Addie, and three Chinese guides, who would take them through the mountains on this stage of the journey and leave them in the care of a boatman for the next—and they each rode a mule. They had eight other mules besides, to carry supplies on their knobby backs. Addie was accustomed to riding in a litter, but Poppy had determined that it would be better to ride as they were used to doing in the States. It was a caravan, an adventure. Addie thought of the stories she'd read as a child, James Fenimore Cooper and Sir Walter Scott. This was what she had come to China to do. She had not come to stay confined in one house, one town. She had come to do the Lord's work, to save the Chinese people and transform the land.

They each carried a gun. "Have you shot before?" Poppy asked, and Addie was glad she could say yes. Yes, she had hunted. Yes, she had shot and killed—animals. Of course, that was not why they carried these guns. They had rations; they could buy food along the way. And the men with them could hunt whatever was available in the territory they moved into. It was never a good idea to travel through the mountains without protection. The three men were something; having their own guns was better.

Though they were ultimately headed south, for now they were moving to the east and north. It was familiar territory: they'd go by land and then by river to T'ien-chin. From there, it would all be different. They'd take a ship down the coast to Shanghai, and then take another upriver as far as they could go. Then they'd go by land the rest of the way to Chungking. Addie told herself that when she made the journey back again, it would be much quicker.

*   *   *

Things hadn't worked out for Poppy in Lu-cho Fu. She had fought with the Riddells, with Julia, especially. It was impossible, Poppy said, to live with them in the house at the mission, and she spent as much time as possible outside it. For some time after her arrival, Addie had not seen her at the mission house when she came in the mornings to help teach classes. Poppy would be gone, and none of them knew for certain where she was or what she was doing, though it was an almost constant topic of conversation among them. "We haven't seen her these three days," Mr. Riddell would tell Addie with a helpless shrug and something close to a grin; he seemed sometimes to be amused by Poppy, though his wife was not.

"I guess we're to suppose she's gone up into the mountains," Julia added with a sour expression.

"She's got a certain way about her—"

"Oh, she's proud and coarse," Julia said. "And her ideas about the Gospel are something close to heretical. I worry that she's preaching strange notions, and people won't have the opportunity to have their misperceptions corrected."

Addie asked what kind of misperceptions she meant.

"About the Holy Trinity, for one. She doesn't believe in it. Says there's only God up above, or maybe all around. I'm not entirely certain where she thinks He abides."

Addie was intrigued by these notions, and by the woman who espoused them. She waited for the opportunity to see the new missionary again. At last it came. One morning she arrived at the Riddells' and found Poppy in the classroom. With her was a young Chinese woman she didn't recognize. They were busy pushing the benches against the walls. "Oh, Mrs. Bell," Poppy said, giving her a flat smile, as if spotting her from a distance, "and how are you this morning?"

"Very well, thank you." Addie stopped in the doorway, uncertain as to whether she should enter. There was a distinct feeling of intrusion, though it was the room where she spent most of her mornings; they had moved the girls' classes here some months ago in order to turn over space in their home to one of Owen's new projects, training a group of young men to send out as preachers. The students would start arriving in ten minutes. "Are you taking over the girls' lessons today?"

"I'd like to think we could do it together." Poppy glanced around the room. It was slightly more spacious with the benches pushed against the walls, though still not much bigger than the pantry in the house Addie had grown up in. With all three of them standing in the middle, the students would have to turn their knees to the side to let them by. "Perhaps not," she said.

"I don't know—"

"Lili," Poppy interrupted, turning to the other woman, "let me introduce you to Mrs. Bell." She spoke in Chinese.

Addie saw that the woman had a long rosy bruise along her cheek. She shook Addie's hand and looked her in the eye, as if she didn't know that it was something to feel ashamed of.

"Lili's a runaway," Poppy said cheerfully in English. "She has decided that she no longer cares to live in the home of a good-for-nothing man."

"Your husband did this?" Addie asked. She was sorry, but not surprised.

The woman shook her head. "My husband's first wife did."

"She's been taking beatings like this one for the past several years. Who knows how many bones she's broke. I gave her husband some money, though, so he won't come looking for her." Poppy turned slowly in the middle of the room as if seeing it for the first time. "Lili's going to help out at the mission for a while, and I thought the classroom might be a good place to start."

As it turned out, the Chinese woman didn't know how to read or write, yet Addie found her useful helping to teach the history lessons and Bible verses. That day, she stood in the center of the place they'd cleared and turned around and around, drawing shapes in the air with her fingers. The girls were all riveted, their spines pressed flat against the wall, their drawing slates tipping unsteadily on their laps.

Addie liked her. The Riddells, on the other hand, were not at all pleased that Poppy had returned from a trip into the mountains with a strange woman in tow, a woman whose bruised face was evidence that she had difficult relationships of some kind. "We can't go stealing women from their homes," Mr. Riddell argued. "That's only feeding into the false stories they tell about us."

"It's not stealing," Addie protested. "She was beaten badly in her home—"

"As they all are," Julia interrupted.

"—and she willingly left it." Addie clamped her mouth shut, afraid that in her defense of the new missionary, she might speak more sharply to the Riddells than she intended to do. In such a small community, alliances might be as dangerous as enmities. And she would really prefer that they all got along.

"The point," Mr. Riddell said, "is that the young woman wouldn't have had the chance to leave without our friend assisting—some might say *pushing*—her to do it." He shook his head. "It doesn't look good."

Owen agreed. At night, in their room, Addie listened as he tallied up the offenses Poppy had committed in the short time she'd been a part of their mission. She was unwomanly. She preached a lax version of religious doctrine. She had no community spirit. She resisted the leadership of men.

"She's unorthodox," Addie said, pulling back the blanket and settling on her side of the mattress. In their marital bed, symbol of unity, again she thought of alliances—it was pointless, she realized, to try to prevent them from growing. Clearly, Owen and the Riddells had already made their judgments of the new missionary. It was not a matter of everyone getting along, then, but a question of which side Addie wanted to choose.

"You may call it unorthodox," Owen said without looking over at her, "only if you define orthodoxy as being the right behavior of Christians everywhere." He folded his pants and shirt and replaced them in the bureau. Addie felt her skin grow hot, while she forced herself to stay silent. A moment later, Owen knelt beside the bed to say his prayers, and she turned her face to the wall. They didn't talk any more that night.

* * *

When did it happen? When was the moment she realized that she would follow Poppy anywhere, that she would willingly give up every other association she had in order not to lose that one? Was it the day Poppy told her she was leaving the mission?

They were alone in the chapel room, flies drawing figure eights in the light around them. It was midafternoon, and the others were all gone away somewhere. Addie plucked the hat off her friend's head. Her face was tipped upward, the hat grasped nervously between her fingers. "Take me with you," she said, and Poppy put a hand to Addie's forehead as if delivering a benediction. "I do believe," she said, "that you're as remarkable a little woman as I thought." She leaned down and kissed her on the cheek before taking back her hat and settling it again on her head.

* * *

But that wasn't it; that wasn't the moment. Because by then the lines had already been drawn, and it was already impossible to imagine her life without Poppy.

When was it, then? she wondered. As they made their slow way up through the mountain passes, their mules looking forward and Addie trying to do the same—the drop-off was precipitous and not far from the path—she tried to find the instant her whole world had changed.

They had a few days now before anyone would wonder about their absence. She had written a letter to Owen and given instructions to Lili to put it into his hands three days after they had gone. The letter would explain that she and Poppy had not gone on another short trip into the mountains. This would have been their third such trip—Owen thought it was their third—but in fact it was the first of its kind. Because this time she would be gone for many months, perhaps as long as a year. "Let Lili help," she'd written. The Chinese woman spent a good part of every day at their home. The boys had come to like her, and Owen had grudgingly come to accept her. She could fill the role that Addie was absenting—not wife and mother, exactly, but a female presence. She would comfort Henry when he needed it, and remind Freddie to wash his hair. As for the running of the household, Li K'ang and Wei-p'eng needed no instruction. Owen would find his home more or less as comfortable as before. Addie was not that important to his happiness, when it came down to it.

Of course, she was not only leaving her husband. She was leaving her boys, too. It was all temporary; there was nothing that couldn't be mended. And she trusted that Owen would put on a good face for the boys, and for the sake of the Riddells as well. He would not want people to think that his own wife had defied him. He would tell them that he had sent her on the journey in good faith, that she had heard the call and he had urged her to follow it.

This was what she told herself as they rode the first day, and the second, and the third and the fourth. It was July, and travel was easy, though hot. Their Chinese guides laughed and joked among themselves, while she and Poppy talked very little. Addie felt that her silence and her friend's did not come from the same source. For Poppy, it was, perhaps, a matter of contemplation. For Addie, it was wonder and fear at her own boldness; it was gratitude; it was a thrill that kept her stomach turning in knots. It was a search through her memory for that particular moment when the line was cast out and everything changed.

*　　*　　*

For some time after Poppy came back from the trip that brought them Lili, she didn't go off traveling again. Her relationship with the Riddells continued to cool. Julia had arranged for Lili to move in with a Chinese family living near Owen and Addie, and though Lili herself preferred the arrangement, to Poppy it was an affront. The Riddells treated the mission house like their own personal kingdom, she said. It was not right.

Afternoons, Addie met up with Poppy, and they would walk the streets for an hour or longer. They stopped to knock on the doors at those houses where they knew they were welcome: the handful of congregants they'd amassed in the town. Poppy had given over all her teaching duties to Lili, and now she had taken on the role of the mission's doctor. She often spent the day tending children with swollen stomachs or congested lungs, which meant sitting and talking with the mothers in their homes. She had little real doctoring knowledge; the mission relied on infrequent deliveries of medicines for most of its authority.

For a time, it was enough to keep her busy and interested and away from the mission without leaving the town. Then she left without warning and was gone for five days. Addie was angry the whole time she was away. Why should her friend go off without telling her? Why should Poppy see new places while she stayed behind? Wasn't Addie just as intrepid? Or wouldn't she like to be?

Poppy returned, her face tanned from long hours spent riding in the sun. She was tired but ebullient, and when Addie asked with some bitterness if she had spent her time pleasantly among so many strangers, Poppy replied that she had. "Why don't you come with me next time?"

Addie's hand flew to her chest. "I couldn't."

"Why ever not?"

Why not, indeed. Because she had her boys to take care of. Because it was dangerous traveling through the mountains with only a Chinese guide. Because Owen would never allow it.

A few days later, Addie and Lili were cleaning up after the morning class when Poppy came in with her big doctor's bag swinging from the crook of her arm. "I'm going out again very soon," she said, "and I thought you might want to come with me."

Poppy spoke in English, and Addie knew she was addressing her. Still, she glanced at Lili as if there might have been a mistake. Turning to Lili, too, Poppy described her mission: "I'm going up west," she said in Chinese. "And I want to take Mrs. Bell with me."

Lili replied, "It can be dangerous to travel into unknown areas. But maybe not for you." And to Addie she explained that when Poppy arrived in their village, they hadn't known what to make of her; they hadn't been certain she was human at all.

"There, now," Poppy said, laughing, "I'm a magical creature. You heard it from Lili herself. So you have my assurance of safety, and if that's not enough, then you know I always take Mr. Wang with me, and he's capable of fighting off tigers if required. I've no doubt he *has* fought off tigers. Though he's not one to brag."

"How long will you be gone?" Addie asked.

"Three days, I think."

Lili, who had been studying English with them at the mission, repeated, "Three days," and then translated it into Chinese.

"That's right," Poppy said.

"Do you want to go?" Lili asked.

Addie reached her arms back over her head and stretched. She suddenly felt achy and restless, confined. "I am curious—," she began.

"—but she's afraid of her husband."

Lili acknowledged Poppy's interruption with a nod. She had finished cleaning the slates and stacked them neatly on the table at the front of the room. "This is reasonable," she said shortly.

"I have a duty to my family. I have"—Addie searched for the vocabulary in Chinese to express her thoughts—"responsibilities."

"I had responsibilities," Lili said. "And then I left them."

"My situation is not the same."

"True. You are your husband's only wife, and in your household you have servants to help. In my home, I was just a second wife, and no more than a slave." Lili shrugged, as if none of this mattered anymore. She had shed her old life, her old skin. She wore the same clothes as before, but they hung on her differently and she looked now, to Addie, somehow less Chinese. "I could help," she said, "both here and at your home. If you go, I can teach the classes for you."

She could, Addie knew. The girls would probably learn more from Lili than they did from her. But she said she wasn't sure.

"Nonsense," Poppy said. "It's a settled thing."

Of course it wasn't, not yet. If she were to go on this trip, Addie had to ask Owen for permission, and the idea made her feel ill. He would never grant his blessing for her to travel alone. She would remind him that Mr. Wang was to go with them, but this wouldn't matter. Owen didn't know Mr. Wang; he was not a member of their congregation. And besides, Owen would argue, Addie was not like Poppy: she was married, and a married woman didn't travel without her husband, no matter where in the world they were. Never mind that he had taken trips on his own from time to time and left Addie at home with the boys and the servants. This was as it should be. Such an arrangement made sense.

"These are people," Addie said when at last she got up the courage to broach the topic (and here was Owen, staring severely at her from across the small table in the courtyard), "who have never received the good word. The women in these villages—you know they can't talk to you or Mr. Riddell, if either of you were to go. How will such women ever be converted?"

"In all likelihood, they won't."

So she had found it at last: the limits of his belief. She turned away to hide her disappointment.

"In a land of many millions, Addie, it's not strange to consider the fact that we can't reach them all."

From the back courtyard came the sound of Henry shouting gleefully. It was a Saturday and the boys' bath day, and Addie had left Freddie to see to his younger brother's washing. She would take her bath after the boys, and Owen would go next, and when the family was done, Li K'ang would take his. In times of drought, they had gone without a full bath for months sometimes, but now there was plenty of water in the river.

"Of course you're right," Addie said at last. "There are a great many Chinese who will die unbelievers because they were never given the chance to come to belief. But Owen, is this an argument for attempting nothing? Because we can't reach every soul, we shouldn't try for those we can?"

He gazed at her steadily and was silent for a time. Even after he looked away, he didn't speak. Addie was unsure whether she should continue or wait to see whether he would take up the topic again. At last, he cleared his throat and said, "I don't want you to think that I haven't considered your words seriously. What you speak of is nothing short of our mission here, Addie—our mission together. We've spent the last decade of our lives trying to bring the Chinese to God, and if I've heard you correctly, I believe what you're expressing is that we would do better to bring *Him* to *them* instead. They will not come down out of the mountains to hear the good word. They don't even know that the good word exists." He shook his head. "You're eager, Addie, because you don't understand. I've taken trips like this. You haven't. I've ridden up into some tiny village on the edge of a cliff where there's only one family and none of them has ever been farther than a mile from the place. You haven't done this. You haven't seen these people. They have a few goats if they're lucky, and they've chopped a few square feet of land out of the mountain to plant things on, and every few years nothing grows and half of them die from hunger or sickness."

His face clouded over, and Addie thought that perhaps he had lost his train of thought. But she didn't prod him to continue. She knew that this was not what he wanted. "The women stay back when I come," he went on, "though they don't hide themselves away as they do here in town. They are not so impossible to reach as you seem to think. But it's no use anyway, Addie. I've sat down with the old men in the villages and explained that I'm not some mythical creature, that I have no magical powers, that the only magic in this world is the benevolence and grace of God. I've kept it as simple as possible. Only introduce them to God, and you will have planted the seed. And a seed can grow—that's the idea, isn't it?"

Addie nodded. The sky had begun to darken, and she wondered if the boys would be finished bathing soon.

"A seed only grows when it gets water, Addie. It does no good to plant a seed if you won't be back to water it."

He fell silent, and this time she was certain that he had finished speaking. He folded his hands on his knee. The expression on his face said that he had made his point and it was time for her to agree with him. But she felt a dangerous sensation tickling her chest, a dance of knives tracing her skin. "I know you've done all you can," she said, "but what if I do something else, and that something else makes the difference?"

Owen frowned. "You're suggesting that I don't know how to speak to these people."

"No," she said quickly, "I'm saying that I'm a woman. This is why the mission wants us all here, Owen. They know we have different roles to fill."

"Your role is to look after the boys and to run the house."

"What if that's not enough?"

His eyes narrowed. "Enough for whom? Addie, what are you saying? You weren't called here by God to pursue your own satisfaction. You were called here to do His work."

"Yes, and I might do His work better."

"By going off on your own?"

"For three days, Owen. And with a Chinese guide."

Just then, Freddie came through the narrow corridor dividing the front courtyard from the back. "Henry's splashing," he said. "I told him not to waste."

Addie stood and followed Freddie to the back. In the rear courtyard, Henry was standing in the tub, his hair dripping down onto his shoulders. A wet puddle stretched out around him on the stone floor. He was trying not to grin. "Out," Addie said. "Don't you know we're all waiting on you?"

She stayed long enough to dry his thin body. Freddie was in and out of the tub in two minutes, and then it was her turn. The boys left and she stripped off her dress and climbed into the water. A wedge of brown soap sat on a stool beside the tub, and she used it to wipe away a week's worth of sweat and dust. It had been monstrously hot for several days, and it felt good to be able to get clean. She would wash her hair tomorrow or the day after. This she always did in the morning. Sleeping on wet hair was asking for sickness.

The stars were winking down on her by the time she finished. She had forgotten to get her towel from the bureau, so she used the one that Freddie had left behind. For an instant, she pictured the house from above: all the men gathered on one side, and her on the other.

When she went out into the front courtyard, she found only the boys and Li K'ang. "Daddy's gone out," Freddie said. He had an edge in his voice, as if he knew she were to blame.

"I see," Addie said. "Li K'ang, why don't you go take your bath."

"It's not too cool out yet," he replied. "I'll wait."

"And Wei-p'eng?" She glanced around before remembering that it was their other servant's night away; his family lived up the mountain, three hours' walk distant. He left Saturdays at noon and returned in the early evening on Sundays. "Never mind. Boys, come say your prayers."

She put the boys to bed and sat in the courtyard with Li K'ang, who asked her to read to him from the Chinese prayer book. Several years earlier, he'd announced quite suddenly that he was converting to Christianity. He had been living with them for three or four years by then and never shown signs that he was interested. God's power, Owen had said, is greater than anything we can imagine.

Li K'ang was converted, but he couldn't read, and most nights he asked Addie to read to him. He stood with his hands folded behind his back and listened to the Scripture with great concentration. Usually Addie read only a page or two, but tonight she read for almost an hour without stopping and without looking up to see whether Li K'ang wanted her to finish. At last Owen came in through the unlocked gate, and when he saw them there, Addie seated with the prayer book open on her lap and Li K'ang standing several feet away, silence suddenly fell. "Continue," he said, and Addie did as she was told. She read to the end of the passage, and they all said, Amen.

Owen went to take his bath, and when he was finished, he came back into the courtyard, where Addie was still seated. She had been watching the stars. There were so many of them, and sometimes she would see one falling. Tonight they had stayed still. When she heard Owen come up beside her, she closed her eyes and took a breath, ready to apologize. But he spoke first. He'd gone for a walk, he said, so he could pray and discover what God wished them to do. "I received no answer, Addie," he said. From the other courtyard came the soft splash of water: Li K'ang, taking the last bath of the evening. It was fully dark, but the moon and stars were shining so brightly that every shape was visible. They had not lit any lamps. "I received no answer," Owen repeated. "I leave it to you to decide. I'll go to bed now, and I recommend that you stay here and pray until you learn what it is that God wishes you to do."

Hours later, Addie still remained in the courtyard, seated in the chair. The silence was so absolute she was almost convinced that it had its own hollow sound. It might have been the stars singing a far-off note. She strained her ears, listening.

Yes, she decided, she had her answer.

* * *

They started off on this first journey into the mountains early in the morning. It was still dark outside when Addie heard the clatter of hooves on the stone street, and a moment later there was a rapping on the gate. The household was all awake, Li K'ang having insisted on preparing a breakfast for the brave travelers, Owen and Wei-p'eng standing silently together, off to one side of the courtyard. Owen was smoking his pipe and Wei-p'eng held a mug of tea in his hands, which he looked down at every now and then without choosing to drink from it.

Addie had packed everything the night before, but feeling the presence of the two men out in the courtyard, their disapproval, low and white-hot, she had stayed inside on the pretense of gathering a few last items. At the sound of the mules' approach and then the sharp rapid knock, undoubtedly Poppy's, she came out into the courtyard.

"Your satchel is all packed?" Owen asked. He had his arms crossed, the pipe sticking out by his elbow, dragging a thin curl of smoke like a loose thread behind it.

"Yes." She wondered if he would retrieve her bag from the bedroom, but he made no motion to do so. Never mind, she could get Wei-p'eng to do it while they ate breakfast, and she wouldn't let it bother her if he narrowed his eyes when she asked him. Though he had been with them for years, that didn't mean he had earned the right to stand in judgment upon her.

Wei-p'eng opened the gate, and Poppy, lifting her skirts, stepped over the foot-high threshold. Behind her, framed in the doorway, was a squat mule with a gray blanket laid over its spine and bags hanging on either side. It stared into the courtyard with dumb curiosity, attracted by the movement and sound. The sky was still black, and the half-moon was sinking toward the horizon.

"Good morning, Mr. Bell. Good morning, Addie. The whole house is up, I see." Poppy looked from one to the other and pressed her lips together in a wry smile. Turning back to the open door, she said in Chinese, "Mr. Wang, let me introduce you."

The first mule moved forward a few steps, and the one behind it came into full view. Sitting astride the animal was a man in cotton trousers and shirt, and a thick vest lined in brown fur. His queue lay over it, and he had what appeared to be a bowler hat sitting on top of his head. Outside of T'ien-chin, Addie had never seen a Chinese man wearing a bowler hat—certainly, she had never seen a rough-looking man like him wearing one. He climbed down off the mule and eyed them warily, making no move to cross the threshold.

"Please, come in," Addie said, when Owen remained silent.

But Mr. Wang shook his head and declined her invitation. "Thank you," he replied, "I'll stay here and see to the mules."

Addie tried to think how to say, *You don't want to start out on an empty stomach.* "Please, there is plenty," she said instead. "We have eggs and rolls and milk." Too late, she realized that she should have asked Li K'ang to make noodles, a bowl of hot broth, scallions skimming the surface—a meal that would put their Chinese guide at ease in a home filled with foreign objects, foreign smells.

"Never mind about him," Poppy said. "Mr. Wang isn't comfortable inside any house, much less a foreigner's. He's built for the road, and would probably sleep in the saddle before he'd lie down on a soft bed like those you've got."

Owen frowned at Poppy's comment—during a trip to T'ien-chin

a few years before, they'd bought mattresses to replace the hard ones they'd never grown accustomed to sleeping on—but she seemed oblivious to the offense she might have given. Glancing at the sky, which was turning gray by degrees to the east, she said, "Dawn's coming on. What do you say we eat breakfast and get the road under our feet."

A half hour later, their little mule train was snaking through the streets. The sky was already aflame over the mountains, and within minutes they were climbing the road out of town, Mr. Wang at the front, Addie in the middle, and Poppy taking up the back because, she said, she was more used to rough travel than Addie was, and presumably more able to fend off whatever dangers might sneak up on them on the wending mountain paths.

The town, safely contained within its walls, fell away as they climbed, and the mountaintops, rather than growing closer, only seemed to get farther away. Addie tried to make conversation with Mr. Wang, but he answered her questions in blunt monosyllables, offering nothing more than what was asked. "You're from one of the villages, aren't you?" "Yes." "Do you have a family?" "Yes." "How many children do you have?" "I have three sons." "No daughters?" "I also have two daughters."

After a while, she gave up trying to make conversation with him and talked to Poppy instead. Her friend had not joined in her attempts to speak with Mr. Wang. She had seemed only to wait for Addie to give up before she began rhapsodizing about the scenery. They were in the mountains now, with an incline to one side that dropped off just a yard from the mules' feet, the tufts of feathery grass giving way to nothing but air. "I understand the advantages of living in a valley," Poppy said, "but you do forget what it's like to look *down* instead of *up* all the time. Changes your perspective."

"It gives you a feeling like God," Addie said.

"I wouldn't let your husband hear you speak that way. Sounds too much like sacrilege."

Addie smiled, unwilling to worry about Owen.

Behind her, Poppy hollered, and Addie asked what she was doing.

"Trying for echoes." She hollered again, a little louder than before. "I'm building up to it so I don't startle the mules. Hello!"

How long had it been since Addie had done such a thing? Years upon years, not since she was a child. Going up to T'ai-yang Shan, as they did some years when the summer was too hot to bear, the boys would shout and whoop, calling out into the void to hear their voices come back to them, and then shrieking with laughter. They were always amazed that the sounds didn't go on traveling forever away from them but were returned unchanged, as if their exact doubles were standing on the other side of the valley shouting back at them. Addie had played along with this idea, pointing at a spot far away and saying to Henry, "Look, I think I see your twin hiding behind that tree," and he would squint and ask her, "Where, Mama? I don't see him." Freddie would no longer take part in this game, but he didn't ruin it for his little brother, either, and Addie had laughed along, always feeling as they went up to T'ai-yang Shan a swell of happiness, a hope that two months in a different place would make her life, when she returned, more recognizable as her own, and treasured more from the distance.

"Hello, hello!" Poppy shouted, still not quite loud enough for echoes. "Go on, Addie, give it a try."

"Hello!" she called.

Poppy waited a moment, allowing Addie's voice to hang in the air, and then "Hello!" she sang out, and Addie repeated it again, louder.

"Hey, you!"

"Hey, you!"

And then their voices were coming back to them, overlapping one another. They waited until the last hollow sound had been returned, and then Addie released a loud peal of nonsense, a hoot or a whoop that took a whole chest full of air to send out over the valley. A long moment of silence followed as the sound raced through the air and then, bouncing off the steep rock face, sailed back to meet them.

She'd thought that Poppy would give another shout to echo her own, but she didn't, and so Addie's call returned alone, wild and strange. The sound was outside her now and couldn't be captured. Poppy laughed, and Addie was surprised to hear Mr. Wang laugh, too.

They came upon the village of Han-hsing late in the afternoon, an hour after the sun slipped behind the peaks and shadows had darkened their path. The village consisted of no more than two dozen laotung— cave homes built into the mountains, with low doors that were rounded at the top, and two small windows covered with paper to keep out the flies. Outside the one nearest to the road, two women were sorting through a basket of wilted greens. As the three mules approached, the women stopped their hands and stared. Here was a sight. Mr. Wang greeted them, and this snapped the older woman out of her shock. She stood and began speaking, gesturing up the road and then up at the houses above. After a moment, their guide turned and spoke to Addie and Poppy in the familiar dialect of Lu-cho Fu. "You'll go sit with the first wife and daughters of Ku Chieh-shih, until he comes back from the fields." He inclined his chin, and Addie saw that villagers seemed to be appearing from nowhere. They stood in front of all of the houses, and were coming down the paths to greet them.

Climbing down off her mule, Poppy said, "Let's see if we can't get acquainted with some of them before the village leader comes and takes over everything."

And then they were among them and carried along in a snaking line up to one of the homes. Three doors led out onto the same flat entranceway in front, and framing each one were long sheets of faded red paper painted with Chinese characters, torn in places and covered in a fine layer of dust. They were escorted by one of the women to the middle door of the three. Inside the cave, it was cool and dark. The walls were plastered, and a table was pushed against one wall, a set of shelves against the other. At the far end of the room was the stove and the k'ang, which was covered in blankets. In the winter, the stove would feed heat into the area under the bed, but in the summer the stone k'ang stayed cool. Their hostess led them to it, and they sat.

Addie pushed her skirts aside and sat on one hip with her feet tucked under her. Poppy crawled back and sat against the wall with her legs straight out. Only Ku Taitai joined them. She ordered a younger woman to get tea for the guests and then began talking. Addie couldn't follow all of it, but every now and then Poppy stopped the woman and translated. She understood far more than Addie, who grasped short threads of the conversation but couldn't knit them together.

Ku Taitai told them that her husband was the leader of the village. He had three wives and she was the first. Their home was the largest in the area; it had three rooms on this level and another four up the path. The other wives had those spaces. Ku Taitai had two sons and one daughter. She pushed up the sleeves of her jacket and showed them her jade bracelets. They had goats and farmed several plots of land nearby.

Addie drank tea while the woman talked. She abandoned trying to understand and simply listened to the sound of her voice. An audience had gathered around them, half the village crowded into the room and watching the three women seated on the k'ang. There were only a few old women, who stood hunched with their hands folded at their backs, and Addie wanted to invite them to sit, but understood that it was not her place to do so. After a time, Poppy spoke. She explained about God, that there was only one god, and He had sent the two of them here to share this news. That was all—there was nothing about Jesus or sin or heaven and hell. She asked Ku Taitai which were her children, and the woman beckoned to a young boy at the front of the crowd. He crawled up onto the k'ang, put a hand out to touch Addie's hair, and asked, "What is it?" Then he looked at his hand to see if any of the color had come off on his fingers. Poppy laughed—her own hair was nearly as dark as the Chinese's—and said, "Addie, they think you're made of gold."

Later that night they were given that same room to sleep in, and Addie wondered who had been displaced—a whole family, maybe, crowded in with others now to make way for them. Before being sent to bed, they sat outside with Ku Chieh-shih beneath a million stars, the moonlight so bright they could see the mountains all around, and though Addie could not understand very much of the conversation, she gave herself over to the not knowing. Now, lying in a darkness so deep she couldn't be sure whether her eyes were opened or closed, she shifted onto her side and faced the invisible shadow of her friend. She touched Poppy's cheek, felt her flinch and grow still. Then she placed her palm over Poppy's eyes. Remembering this night later—yes, she recognized it as the moment where she tipped forward and fell tumbling into love. She could trace it all back to here: her leaving Lu-cho Fu and Owen, and all that followed.

At the time, she felt only eyelashes fluttering against her palm. Then lips on her skin, whispering. Addie didn't know what had been said, but when Poppy's hand found her own mouth, she put her lips to the rough palm. It smelled of leather and rapeseed oil and peppers and dirt. She couldn't see in the black cave, and she didn't dare move. The seconds fell away like water into a pool. She breathed in and out, concentrating on the sensation of air filling her chest and leaving it again, until Poppy's hand moved away and it was her mouth instead.

18

One week after they left Lu-cho Fu, somewhere west of T'ien-chin, Addie awoke at the tiny, dirty inn where they'd spent the night and felt hovering over her some vague sense of dread. Her heart was pounding. It could have been night, but she heard the twitter of birds: the timid approach of day, not yet arrived.

Her sleep had been full of dreams. She couldn't quite remember them but knew that she had been reliving odd moments of her life, only at different speeds: slowed down and stretched out, or else sped up to a frantic pace. She had traveled across and around the world in these dreams, and there had been armies of strangers crowding at the edges, and she had run through dark, hazy landscapes for hours, days. And throughout all this, she'd felt hovering close to her the souls of people she hadn't seen or thought of in years: the young German woman in Marietta who'd showed up alone at church every Sunday and never spoke to anyone, the Negro couple who came by the house every fall selling mountain medicines. A woman in Lu-cho Fu whose son had died of infection. A blind beggar in T'ien-chin. All these long-forgotten people crowded around, jostling close whenever she was still. Completely absent were those she loved and knew well. Where were her children? Where were her parents, and Flora and Will, and Louisa? Where was Owen?

She remained in bed for a time, back pasted with sweat against the roll-up mattress. She could hear the rustling of insects in the straw, but exhaustion sat heavy on her chest, and anyway, she had slept here all night; there was no point in caring now. Yet she knew she would not fall asleep again. She got up and dressed and put away her nightgown in the satchel that held her few things. It was not yet light, and Poppy was still sleeping. Addie sat down on the edge of the bed to wait for day to arrive, listening to the twittering birds, the mice scurrying along the walls. Outside, the mules were shifting now, their hooves softly knocking the hard ground.

At last, Poppy stirred and yawned. "You're up," she said.

"I've been awake for a while."

"Anxious to get on our way?"

"I suppose." She was still seated on the edge of the bed, watching the tiny points of gray light that were appearing in the holes and cracks in the wall.

Poppy yawned again and rubbed her neck. Her pillow had fallen onto the floor; the bed sat in the middle of the tiny room, and there was no headboard. Addie figured it had been positioned that way so critters wouldn't crawl off the wall and into the bed at night. "I won't shed any tears leaving this place," Poppy said.

"Neither will I." Then Addie smiled because she was no longer alone in her wakefulness, and the uneasy sensation of her dreams was fading.

A few hours later, the two of them were sitting on the deck of a flat boat making its way downriver. The sun was coming down hard, and Addie had a parasol tilted to block the rays. A Chinese newspaper they'd bought in T'ai-yüan lay open on her lap. She hadn't read more than a few of the headlines. It was difficult work, reading Chinese. In the heat, too, her mind seemed not to be functioning as it should—it felt mushy, like soft wet sand that keeps swallowing footprints.

"It will be even hotter down south, won't it?" she said to Poppy at last, the first words either had spoken in a half hour, at least. The boatmen were carrying on a conversation as they maneuvered their poles along the river bottom, but she wasn't trying to listen.

Poppy had another section of the paper flipped open in her hands, and she glanced at Addie over the top of it. "That's a reasonable guess. It probably works pretty much like it does everywhere."

Addie closed her eyes and felt the heat through the darkness. It pressed against her eyelids, and she opened them again. "Like the difference between Ohio and—oh, I don't know—Alabama. Just think how they toil away in the sun down there, cutting cotton and, and, sugarcane, and all that."

"Dear, I don't believe they have sugarcane in Alabama."

"No. My brain's all scrambled." Addie touched two fingers to her forehead. Her hands were greasy with sweat. They were warm, but her forehead felt cool, almost cold to the touch.

Poppy watched her for a moment. "You're brooding. I can see it on your face. You've got a nervous set to the jaw. And that line between your eyes"—she smoothed a finger down her nose—"I do believe that is worry. Either that, or guilt."

"You can see all that, can you?"

"Sure. The shadows from your parasol throw your face into chiaroscuro."

The boat jerked, scuffing the rocks on the bottom of the riverbed. The water was shallow here, which made it difficult; the men might have to get out to tug the boat along from the shore until they bumped and scraped their way into deeper water.

"I don't want to go back," Addie said, "in case that's what you were thinking. I'm just impatient to be farther along. I'm eager to get on to new places."

Poppy looked out at the dusty stillness on the near shore. A haze hung over the cracked and splintered walls of the riverbanks. "It's supposed to be wet, anyway," she said after a moment. "That's something, at least. A missionary I knew who was down south for several years said it's nearly suffocating in Chungking, how much water's in the air."

"I'll take damp air over dry. Only imagine what it will be like to take the wash from the line and not find it painted over in yellow dust."

Poppy lifted her chin to the sky and smiled before going back to reading her paper.

Addie couldn't read. She folded up her section of the paper and handed it to Poppy, who took it without looking up again. Then she stood and crossed to the edge of the boat. The water was only a few feet below the edge of the craft, and she squatted down and reached out her arm. It looked dirty, stirred up by the boatmen's poles, and she pulled back her hand without touching it.

The boatmen had a number of techniques for getting their craft down a shallow river, but none of them was fast. And Addie was eager to get more distance between herself and Lu-cho Fu. She knew she was still close enough that she could be back in the town in a few days if she wanted, and Owen would forgive her because she'd returned to him before any real damage was done.

Standing up, she shaded her eyes with one hand as she peered at the shore. Several houses were gathered in a knot ahead, at a bend in the river. Plots of farmland reached out around the village, and she spotted a few figures squatting in the fields. Then, from behind a line of scrubby trees, she saw a line of men striding toward the river.

It was some time before the boat arrived at the village. The men were waiting. One held a long rifle and the rest stood with their hands at their backs.

The man with the gun shouted for them to stop, and the boatmen stood up, leaving behind the work of digging the poles into the river bottom to scuttle them along.

"They'll be wanting some money now," Poppy said. She stood from her chair and came up beside Addie, whose heart was beating fast. Poppy took her hand. "Don't get upset, and don't show any fear."

Addie's mind went quickly to that first time, years before, when she and Owen had been stopped. She remembered how she'd put her hand to her pregnant belly without thinking how it would look. And she remembered, too, how her whole body had started shaking as soon as the men let them pass on.

They came to a slow stop now before the men onshore. There were seven of them gathered in a sort of triangle, the man holding the rifle making the point at the center. He stepped forward to address the boat's captain. "What are you doing with these foreign devils?"

Addie was standing shoulder to shoulder with Poppy, and she felt her friend tense at the phrase. It was a term they generally only heard used secondhand. Their Chinese congregants had told them how some of the ignorant people in the town—or more often, in the villages— spoke of them this way. But those people told stories to scare each other, too. They claimed that foreigners stole Chinese babies out of their homes to make a meal of them. They said the foreigners poisoned wells, killing off entire villages with ghoulish glee. These were the terrors of peasants who had never encountered a foreigner before and didn't know how to fit them into their world. It was fear that made them speak in such a way.

This was different. The man with the gun had called them foreign devils without either lowering or raising his voice. It was as if Addie and Poppy weren't there, as if they weren't human; he spoke the way someone might address a stranger he met who was standing with a horse, speaking without fear that the horse might understand.

The boat's captain glanced over his shoulder at Addie and Poppy. "The two foreigners are going home," he said. "We're transporting them to T'ien-chin so they can take the ship back to America."

Addie was not sure she'd heard correctly. She wanted to ask Poppy whether she had got it right but didn't want to turn and whisper to her for fear that it would look like they were plotting an insurrection. The man with the gun glanced at them and she saw that his eyes were cold and incurious. She was used to being stared at, appraised. Normally, there would come the moment when she was expected to perform, to speak either in her own tongue or in theirs, and either action would surprise them. This man seemed as if he were incapable of surprise.

"How much have they paid you?"

The captain told him the amount.

"You'll take so little to help these pests?"

"Brother," the captain said, holding up his hands in a gesture that suggested he was only tired and ready to get on his way, "I'm helping to rid the empire of cockroaches. What's wrong with making a little money along the way?"

The man's eyes were spaced far apart, and this gave him the impression of a snake. "If they lose only their wealth," he said, still speaking to the boat captain but looking at them, "it's too little. They run over the empire like dogs, and they tear it apart as dogs will do when they get hold of something good. They deserve no better than dogs." He stared a moment longer before turning away. Then he said to the man next to him, "Take what money they have and send them away. They aren't worth getting our hands dirty."

Three of the men from shore hopped onto the boat. They came up to Addie and Poppy and stood blinking in their faces. Addie's breath came fast, and she thought she might faint. She waited for one of them to speak. Instead, the one in the middle pivoted and spat into Poppy's face.

Addie gasped. She was afraid that her friend would confront the men, but Poppy's face was tight and pale, the skin pulled over her cheeks like a wind-filled sail. The globule of spit had landed on her jaw and stuck there. She didn't move to wipe it away.

The man glared at Addie through narrowed eyes. He had a long knife, she saw now, and he turned it in the sun, catching the light. Then in one quick motion he used the flat side of the blade to knock the hat off Poppy's head. None of them turned to see where it fell, and in the next moment the man had lifted the knife to her neck and he held it there while the other two began rummaging through the bags pushed against the outside wall of the tiny cabin.

Addie had stopped breathing. She couldn't look at Poppy; she couldn't bear to see the knife positioned at her throat. Her heart was racing so quickly she thought it would break through her chest. Then she heard the men calling to their friends onshore to let them know what they'd found, and she knew they were looking through their luggage. She clutched herself in a sort of embrace, her hands grasping her own arms. She would not show she was afraid if she could help it. Beneath her skirt, she felt the sweat slicking the backs of her shaking knees. She had a pouch of money hidden beneath the layers of fabric, and she wondered if the men would search her for it.

But after a few minutes, they handed off all they had taken and the man with the knife lowered the blade from Poppy's neck and put it back in his sleeve. He hopped back onto the shore and joined the rest. "You can go," the man with the gun said to the captain. "But if we meet you bringing these devils back up the river, we won't be as kind as we were today. Not to them, and not to you, either."

The captain nodded and then called orders to the boatmen to push off again. Poppy sank onto her chair as the boat inched toward the middle of the river, but Addie remained standing. She turned and saw that the men onshore had relaxed their formation. They looked now like any group of villagers standing and talking together. When she turned back around, she saw that the color was returning to Poppy's face. Addie retrieved the hat from where it had gotten caught in a coil of rope and fitted it onto her friend's head. Then she squatted in front of her and grasped her hands.

Several minutes passed, and still Poppy didn't say anything. Addie's knees began to hurt, but she stayed there crouching. At last, some time after they had gone around another bend in the river, Poppy suddenly said in a strange, bright tone, "What in the world was that about, do you think?" When Addie didn't respond, she asked the question again, this time of the captain, and in Chinese. "Why did you tell them we were leaving China?" She was almost smiling now and her eyes were shining.

The captain glanced back at them from his position at the front of the boat. "These men don't like foreigners. They have a strong hatred for all of you, and for those of us who associate with you. Chinese Christians, in particular, they hate very much."

"But why did you tell them we weren't staying?"

He shrugged. "You're still alive, aren't you?"

Poppy glanced at Addie crouched before her and laughed. "I guess they wanted to have some fun. And did they give me a scare!"

"You're all right?" Addie asked, looking up into her face. The sun had gone behind a scrim of clouds, but the day was still bright; it seemed as if the light were coming from every direction.

"A little shaken, that's all."

Addie nodded. Then all at once a great coughing wail came out of her and she was crying harder than she ever had before. She was still squatting before Poppy, and she lowered her face into her friend's lap, letting the tears spread out over the cloth. She felt Poppy's hands on her head, smoothing, comforting. "There," Poppy said after a while, "we're moving along much better now."

Addie didn't need to look to know that they had gotten past the shallows. She felt the lift, the slide into deeper water; the river was on their side now, carrying them away from danger.

*   *   *

It was not until early September that they arrived in Chungking. They came upon the city slowly; for an entire morning and afternoon, the guides were telling them that they had arrived, when all that surrounded them were the same mountains with various houses and terraced fields sprinkled over them—nothing resembling a city. And then suddenly they reached a crest and were looking across at the city walls. Behind them were many hundreds of buildings all crowded together on the steep hills, the density of the houses shading the area brown and gray. Stone streets could be seen running throughout. Boats crowded the various docks dotting the riverside below, and a pall of smoke hovered over the scene, indicating that it was indeed a city, the largest in the southwest of China. Even from a distance it was clear it was a Chinese city, more Chinese than T'ien-chin or Peking or Shanghai, no part of it clearly carved out for Americans and Europeans—no great block buildings in the Continental style, no wide avenues lined with trees.

Although it was autumn, the weather was sweltering and wet, as if the city had been built upon a boiling pot. The water was high in the two rivers, rolling and restless, and the boats that navigated the current looked as if they might capsize at any moment. It was a far cry from the shallow riverbeds of Shansi, where the walls were so dry that birds built their nests within the deep cracks, and small dusty whirlwinds went skipping from bank to bank.

They came down a path that broadened and then narrowed again very suddenly just where the stone pavement began. Then they were passing through the city gates. Inside, they followed the wall, which was a street from which steep staircases ascended. The staircases were in fact other streets, and the houses on either side crowded in close. Addie glimpsed the movement of people crossing from one door to another, the glint of water thrown from a pail out onto the pavement.

The guides took them as far as they could go, and then all at once they stopped, and Mr. Yü, the man who had been with them since Shanghai, told Addie and Poppy to dismount. "The mission house is up that way," he said, pointing up a long staircase. This street was quiet and empty, no one standing in the doorways looking out. "We can get some pangpang chün to carry the luggage."

"Pangpang chün?" Addie repeated, and turned to Poppy, who shrugged: she didn't know, either, what this meant.

Before they had time to wonder, several men appeared, carrying thick bamboo poles on their shoulders. The poles were five or six feet long and polished from use, with loops of dirty rope on either end. Mr. Yü nodded at the nearest mule, which had a trunk on its back and side-hanging bags, and two of the men began unloading it. They each secured a bag to one end of a pole, and one side of the heavy trunk to the other. Then they squatted with the trunk between, lay the poles over their shoulders, and with a grunt, lifted the entire heavy burden. As they began climbing the stairs, Mr. Yü turned to Addie and Poppy and grinned. "You understand how they get their name?" He held his hands up in front of his chest and drew the fingers apart, an imaginary pole stretching between them. "Pangpang," he said. "It means 'stick.' This is our name for these men: pangpang chün."

"Pole soldiers," Addie said. "That's what they call them." It sounded like a toy that Henry would play with. She blinked and swallowed. She hadn't meant to conjure up her son. But she had, and just like that, both her children were there with her. There was Henry running up and throwing his arms around her waist; she could almost smell the sour scent of his hair when it was damp with sweat, fresh from some game he was playing with Freddie or the neighbor boys. She could never figure out their games, even when they explained them to her, gasping for breath, bright-eyed after running all over the streets of Lu-cho Fu.

Thinking of her boys, she felt suddenly ill. "Can we go now?" she asked.

"Of course," Mr. Yü said. He glanced up, and Addie followed his gaze. The men who had gone up before them were turning into a doorway, angling over the threshold with the trunk and bags. "The other guides and I will stay here and watch over your belongings."

Poppy began climbing the stairs, with Addie following. When they reached the doorway, a slender white man in a long Chinese coat came out and greeted them. "You must be our new friends from up north." He looked from one to the other, peering at them from over a pair of spectacles that sat precariously low on his nose, looking as if they might fall off. "Evan Wickford. I'm one of the missionaries here. The oldest and the dullest." He gave a short, stuttering laugh at his joke. He appeared to be forty-five or fifty years old, and he had the air, common to older bachelors, of a stage performer after the show.

Poppy shook his hand and introduced herself. Then she took a step up to make room for Addie. "Pleased to meet you, Mr. Wickford," Addie said. "I'm Mrs. Baker."

She had chosen this name because it belonged to an old childhood friend, and she knew she would remember it. Poppy had wondered why she didn't use her maiden name, but they had both agreed she would do better as a widow than she would as a maid, and Addie couldn't imagine calling herself Mrs. Schepp. That was her mother's name, and she was certain that using it would make her feel like a fraud.

"Well, Mrs. Baker, you can't imagine how happy we are to have you here." Mr. Wickford dropped her hand and glanced up at Poppy, who was towering over them both; the addition of the extra step made her into a giant. Mr. Wickford seemed momentarily alarmed by the view. "I expect you're tired," he said quickly, and turned to lead them in over the threshold. The double doors were propped open with stone blocks, and as they passed through, two of the pangpang chün stood aside to let them by before leaving to go down for another load. "Where did you come from today?"

"I believe the place was called Yinglung," Poppy said. "But we left before the sun came up. I guess you could say we were anxious to finish our journey."

"Yes, I can only imagine." He stopped in the middle of a very small courtyard. It was perhaps ten feet square, with room enough only for a wedge of sky to let in the light. "We were so cheered, Mrs. McBride, to receive word of your coming. Cheered, elated—we all were—only hoping for greater numbers." He looked from one of them to the other with a nervous smile. "You understand that missionaries of the fairer sex are quite valuable to our purpose here, Mrs. Baker. The more, the better, and we were quite relieved and happy to learn that Mrs. McBride would be joining us, and only wished she weren't coming alone. Therefore, I'll leave you to picture how even *more* delighted we were when, not one month after that first notice, our prayers were answered in receiving *your* letter"—he nodded at Poppy—"with the happy news that there would be another addition to our ranks." And finishing his speech, he turned to Addie and gave a small bow.

This gesture of old-fashioned courteousness resulted in his glasses slipping off his nose and onto the ground. He didn't seem disturbed by the accident. In a moment, he had stooped down to retrieve them and set them back in place.

"Yes," Addie said when he was standing and facing her again, "it was only uncertain for a time whether the mission could spare us both. I was ready for a change, and in the end it worked out."

"You must be tired," Mr. Wickford repeated. He looked around the courtyard as if he might find a bed to offer them right there. "How long has it been since you began your travels?"

"More than two months," Addie replied. "We left in early July."

"Yes, from Shansi, wasn't it? I confess I know very little of the place. Never been up north, myself; I came to Chungking years ago, and I've stuck here all this time. But I know it's a far distance." He held out his hands as if producing a gift, then grasped one hand in the other and half bowed to Poppy. Addie was nervous for his eyeglasses, but they stayed on his nose this time. "The loss of the sisters," he said without transition, "was a great blow to us here. I confess I was far from certain that the Board would replace them this quickly. Well, not *replace*; they really can't be replaced——" He blinked at the two women; it seemed that he had baffled himself.

"How long were they here?" Addie asked, trying to recall if Poppy had said anything about the women whose places they had come to fill.

"Four years and a half," Mr. Wickford said ruefully. "They came to us in the autumn of '94. Miss Rose, the youngest, was just eighteen at the time, and Miss Olivia was twenty-three. Between them was Miss Margaret, who turned twenty-one the very day they arrived. I remember it perfectly. Some of our congregants gathered to welcome them, and when they discovered that it was her birthday, they insisted that she eat noodles. The Chinese up north have this custom as well, I suppose?"

"We eat a good deal of noodles in Shansi," Poppy said, "and for no particular occasion."

Mr. Wickford nodded, satisfied. "Poor Miss Margaret—no sooner is she over the doorstep of the mission than she's being asked to adopt Chinese customs! But she smiled very prettily and sat down to eat as if it were exactly what she had expected. This was typical of her manner. Every action she undertook was approached with enthusiasm." He trailed off, lost in memory. Addie supposed he must have been in love with the young woman and had his heart broken. Had he ever declared himself? If so, she didn't suppose he'd been able to make a strong case. He had a kind of softness in his manner, but it was the softness of a bruised peach.

Poppy asked what had taken the women from the mission, and he looked surprised at the question, as if he assumed that the sisters were famous all over China. "Sadly, Miss Rose fell ill last winter," he said, "and when she still hadn't recovered by the spring, Miss Olivia and Miss Margaret decided she had better go back to Pennsylvania. They feared it was the wet climate we have here that was preventing her recovery. The lungs, you know." He patted his chest in sympathy. "You can't blame them, though it would have been better if they hadn't all decided to leave. Send her back, by all means, I said. Send her home to get well, but don't deprive us of all your service and your companionship at once." He looked from Addie to Poppy. "It seemed to me that only one of the sisters could have accompanied Miss Rose, and let the other one stay. Just one as a traveling companion would have sufficed. But they were devoted to one another, from the first to the last."

"You must miss them greatly," Addie said.

"Thank you, Mrs. Baker. Their loss was a great blow to the mission. They did much good converting the women of Chungking—but then, the unencumbered female missionaries always do. The wives and mothers have too many other concerns to put their whole hearts into the endeavor." He stopped a moment, and then a look of horror came over his face. "Oh, dear. Please forgive me for speaking so thoughtlessly. Of course you've both lost your husbands."

Addie had been beginning to look around the courtyard expectantly—she was ready to see their room and settle into their new home—but at these last words she felt her heart shivering in her chest.

"Yes," Poppy said. "Sadly, we have."

Mr. Wickford was silent a moment. Then he went on: "And now here you are, and we're certainly very happy to have you both with us in

Chungking." He put his arm out and, gesturing around the courtyard, said, "I apologize that we're in somewhat tight quarters here. The city, as you no doubt noticed as you came in, is built on steep hillsides, which makes more expansive residences a challenge. The church is much grander. It's on flatter land a half-mile distant from here, down closer to the wharves. I'll take you to see it later."

"And how many people are living here?" Poppy asked.

"Right now we have twenty-two foreigners altogether at the mission, including the children, but we're spread out, you know. Here we have five—I suppose it will be seven, now that you've joined us. You'll meet the Gregorys later this afternoon. They're all out at present."

They continued their tour of the building. He showed them two of the rooms that opened off the courtyard; the other rooms on this level were for the servants, he explained. The first was a storage space, filled with barrels and boxes. The room next to it was a study with shelves of books lining two walls. Mr. Wickford pointed out a general system of catalog, which had prayer books and hymnals and Bibles taking up most of one wall, and the other devoted to a mixture of historical and geographical works, biographies, philosophical treatises, and a few collections of poetry. "Of course," he said, "we have several volumes published by the Board as well. Missionaries' accounts from other parts of the world." They were standing in the doorway. He gestured to the left side of the room and went on, "You'll find Africa there, and South America. There are several from the Orient, but few from the Far East."

"Yes, where *are* our writers?" Poppy said. "We've been here long enough that it's rather surprising we're not better represented on these shelves."

"My understanding is that there are two or three in the works as we speak. Reverend Jameson in Fukien—perhaps you've heard of him?"

Addie and Poppy both shook their heads.

"No, you might not have; he writes a good deal, but it's intended for the audience back in America. In any case, he's put together a chronicle of his time in China that I expect will be read rather widely, once it's finally published. He's been writing it for sixteen years, however, so there's no telling when that will be. There's always more to tell, yet at some point you must say: 'Here is where I stop.' That's what I've said to him many a time, and I suspect I'll have to say it many times more before he listens. Of course, I haven't seen him for a decade." He pulled the door closed and they backed out into the courtyard again. "This is the life we've chosen as missionaries, isn't it? You say good-bye to friends without knowing when or if you'll ever see them again."

His words set off a kind of anxious vibration in Addie's chest. No doubt Mr. Wickford had meant nothing by the comment, and yet it felt as if it were directed especially at her. She'd left her own sons, her own husband, and she hadn't even said good-bye.

*   *   *

That night, after settling into their new room, Addie and Poppy stayed up reading books they'd borrowed from the library below. An oil lamp burned on the table between them, and they both lay on the side of the bed nearest to it, books raised to catch the light. Poppy was reading a Chinese tract, something abstruse and impossible that scholars studied and that had somehow found its way onto the mission's bookshelves. She confessed that she was able to understand only a small part. "I do believe I'm like that idiom Old Hsing told me, about the man who rides through a field of flowers and from his height can only see the colors." Old Hsing was an elderly man back in Lu-cho Fu who had gone up through the Mandarin scholars' system when he was young but never passed the exams in T'ai-yüan. After that failure, rather than try again, he had decided to become a tinker. He had spent the nearly five decades since then walking the streets of Lu-cho Fu banging his pot with a spoon, and after she arrived in town, Poppy had sometimes joined him as he walked to hear his discourses on Chinese language, philosophy, history, and literature. Her reference to the old man now made her eyes go glassy.

"I'm not sure I know that particular idiom," Addie said. "You know I don't have a dictionary in my mind, as you do."

"'Riding a horse while looking at flowers'—something like that. The meaning is that you don't take in the details. At least, I *think* that's what it means." She rolled her neck and moved her shoulders. "It's a pity that the language is so different down here. Who knows if they even have that saying in Chungking."

"Surely *you'll* be fine. It shouldn't be too difficult to pick up the dialect here."

"I certainly hope not. But who's to tell."

Ever since they had started inland from Shanghai, Addie had given up trying to understand much of anything that was spoken around them, yet for some reason she'd assumed that once they got to Chungking, they would settle in quickly. China was China, after all—it was absurd to think that moving from one part to another could be like crossing into a whole other country. But the people not only spoke differently here, they looked different, too. They were smaller and darker than they were in the north. The climate was different, and so was the look of the city, with its buildings nearly piled on top of one another and its narrow stair-step streets. She was not only many miles from Lu-cho Fu, she felt as if she were all the way over on the other side of the world—as far from Owen and the boys as she was from her family back home in America.

She glanced down at the page she was reading from an account of a missionary's time in northern Africa. *The winds, so filled with the red sand taken up from the hills, danced under a sky bleached as white as the bones in the butcher yard. The people trod silently under this sky, dressed all in white with their heads wrapped in turbans.* This was almost how she had imagined China years before, just as strange and foreign. And perhaps the accounts she wrote to the home churches and to her family made it seem that way. The feeling was entirely different, living here, belonging here—as much as they ever could belong to the place. She *would* belong to Chungking, she vowed, even more than she had to Lu-cho Fu.

19

Come with me.

This was what she remembered of Poppy's words when she thought back to the conversation about going south. There were reasons, of course. Good reasons. But in the end it was as simple as this: Poppy was leaving, and Addie couldn't bear to go back to the life she'd had before. Where Poppy went, she would follow. And now that they were in Chungking, it was no longer an idea—something without form or shape—but a physical place, a city. It was red mud and slick streets. It was air that was full of soot and water and the stinging smoke of spicy peppers frying in oil.

In any case, it was life, which turned out to be a day-to-day matter with enough distractions to keep one from thinking too much. Most mornings, they awoke early and left before nine. They spent part of the day in the sick clinic, attending to the ill and to opium addicts. The rest of the day was spent visiting women in their homes or setting up such visits. They weren't needed in the school, since two of the other missionaries had taken on the duty of teaching and seemed to have no desire of giving it up. This was just as well. Addie preferred to be out in the city, moving from place to place.

Mr. Wickford had given them a list of homes that were friendly to their visits. They would go out onto the streets, weaving their way among the water carriers and other coolies who seemed to make up most of the pedestrian population, asking directions and getting lost, and finally knocking on the appointed doors, where they were welcomed inside cramped houses so narrow they seemed sometimes to sway in the wind. The interiors were invariably dark, the walls stenciled with mildew. Even inside, the life of the city seemed to penetrate. The calls from coal sellers seeped through the walls, and periodically the dank scent of the river wafted in, too.

One day not long after their arrival, they headed out in search of the residence of someone named Widow Liu. They had been told by one of the ladies they visited that she would like to meet them. She was very rich, the woman informed them, though not a Christian. "Perhaps she's interested in donating to the mission?" Poppy asked, and the woman said, perhaps—though this was accompanied by a doubtful shrug.

The widow's house was partway up a steep hill in the western part of the city. The street that went past it was a narrow stairway with uneven stone steps. One of the students from the mission school, a boy of ten or eleven, had led them there, walking ahead at such a quick pace that several times Poppy had called out for him to go slower. Each time, he turned and grinned, showing teeth turned at terrible angles. When they arrived at the house, he knocked firmly on the door, waited until a servant had admitted them, and promised that he would be waiting to take them back to the mission when they were done. Then he skipped down the stairs again and out of sight.

It was impossible to tell from the outside how large the house was. Rather than entering through a courtyard, Poppy and Addie were admitted directly into a narrow front room that led into a slightly wider and much longer one behind it. Several doors—all closed—suggested more and more rooms beyond, leading off in different directions, like the spokes of a wheel. The ceilings were low, but the furnishings were rich enough to indicate real wealth, all carved and gleaming wood with embroidered silk cushions. The servant, a tiny woman of indeterminate age, gestured toward the back of the room, where a voice called out from the near darkness: "Come in." Addie and Poppy moved forward together, as if down the aisle of a church.

Seated in a wide chair flanked by tables on either side was a large woman whose features were somehow blurred; even when Addie's eyes had adjusted to the dimness, she found it difficult to quite locate her nose and mouth. They'd been told that Widow Liu had been burned badly years before, but Addie hadn't properly prepared herself. It was somehow worse than the injured faces of the two beggars who'd crouched at the entrance to the market in Lu-cho Fu, if only because she was half shrouded in darkness.

"Welcome," she said. "Please, sit. I'm curious to meet the new sisters."

Addie looked at Poppy in surprise. The widow's speech was not quite a northern one, but it was not the dialect of Chungking, either.

"Oh, we're not sisters," Poppy said. Stepping forward, she pushed her hand out toward Widow Liu, who squinted as if she weren't sure what to do with it. "I always shake hands when I meet someone, Mrs. Liu. I hope you don't mind."

"I don't see well," she said in response, and though her voice had a complaining tone, she allowed her hand to be pressed between both of Poppy's. "And you may call me Widow Liu. I don't like this term 'missus,' and I am no longer a wife."

"I apologize," Poppy said and glanced down, flustered. It was not a state Addie was used to seeing her in.

"And what about you? You must shake hands as well."

Addie stepped forward and took the woman's hand. It lay in her own like a ball of dough, the skin cold and smooth, not like skin at all. "Very pleased to meet you," Addie said. "Thank you for allowing us to come see you in your home."

"Where else would you see me?" She laughed without moving her face any more than it moved when she spoke. Removing her hand from Addie's grasp, she explained, "You wouldn't see me elsewhere because I haven't stepped foot over the threshold of this house for twenty years. Do you know what happened twenty years ago?"

"I'm sorry," Addie said. "I didn't understand you. My Chinese is not very good."

Widow Liu laughed again, but this time it was a real laugh; her cheeks moved outward and her mouth opened wider than it had before. "You speak very well. I think you must understand nearly everything. But you're wise to say you don't—that can be very useful." She lifted a hand, and Addie turned to see the servant who had led them into the room, who was now standing against one wall. "Tea," said Widow Liu, and the servant opened one of the doors and went down a dim passageway.

"Sit down. You make me nervous standing there."

Poppy and Addie murmured their thanks and sat side by side on a bench opposite her. It was a small bench with a thin cushion and no back. They both sat stiffly and did not look at each other.

"Twenty-one years ago, my husband died. This"—she raised a hand to her cheek, the fingers fluttering lightly upon it—"this came after. Not very long after: less than a year. I might have left, otherwise—gone out again into the world. It doesn't matter. The world comes to me, here. The world—everyone—comes to see me, to talk to me, to ask me for things. Just like you've come—I'm sure you'd like some of my money for your school or your church. But tell me, where do you come from? Europe or America?"

"We both come from America," Poppy said.

"And you knew each other there?"

"We met at a mission in Shansi."

The servant came in, lugging a tall copper pot with a spout, steam curling out of the end. She set it on the floor near the wall and left again. Addie waited for Widow Liu to resume speaking, but their host pressed her mouth together and closed her eyes. A moment later, the servant returned carrying a tray with a heavy stone teapot, a large bowl, and three porcelain cups. The three of them watched her go about her preparations, pouring the tea and dumping the first cup, which was too bitter to drink. Once she had filled each of the cups again, she covered them and set them back on the tray. Then she resumed her place against the wall.

Only once the servant was out of sight did Widow Liu resume the conversation. "Where was your mission up north?"

"In a town called Lu-cho Fu," Poppy said, "near T'ai-yüan. You've heard of that city?"

Widow Liu blinked at them. "I am not an idiot."

Addie bit her lip, and was surprised to see that Poppy was blushing. "Of course, I didn't mean to suggest that, Widow Liu." She seemed ready to say more, but several seconds passed, and she didn't speak again. Their host continued to stare at them steadily.

"We know Shansi well," Addie jumped in, "but it's far away. Up there, no one is very aware of the whole south of China. It seems you don't have a similar problem here."

"There are as many ignorant peasants here as there are anywhere else. I assumed you would know that I am not an ignorant peasant. I may not go out into the world anymore, but I know what the world is." She leaned forward and took her cup of tea from the small table between them. Tipping the lid away from her lips, she examined it without drinking, then lowered the cup to her lap. "Please," she said, nodding slightly, and both Addie and Poppy reached forward. "This is tsao-pei-chien. It's grown in the mountains west of here."

"It's very good," Addie said, taking a sip.

"Yes, it's one of the finest in all of China. You know, of course, that we are famous for our tea production. All this"—she waved a hand around the room—"is in consequence of tea."

"You mean your husband's business was tea," Addie said.

"Yes, and opium. The demand for each is not equal."

Poppy cleared her throat. "You know, of course, that part of our business in China is to eradicate the population's fascination with the drug."

"How interesting. When the foreigners are selling it to us, opium isn't considered dangerous at all. Yet when we're growing it and selling it ourselves, it's a plague on the land."

"I don't require a history lesson," Poppy said.

"No?" The widow blinked at her, amused. "I might have thought you did." She paused and then went on, "In any case, all this was my husband's, and now I am in charge. My sons help me manage it, of course." She moved her hands together as if clapping, though they didn't make a sound.

"That's a rare case here in China," Poppy put in. "Women aren't often allowed that kind of responsibility, in my experience."

"I doubt that your experience of China is complete enough to speak on the rarity of my situation."

Poppy sat forward on the bench, and Addie could feel the anger rising off her, a sudden heat, a sharp tang. "It's true that I wasn't raised in China, but I've lived here for many years, Widow Liu, and in that time I've seen enough of the way your people treat their women to know it isn't right. I've seen wives made slaves to their husbands, daughters bought and sold as property. Infant girls killed for the crime of failing

332 MOLLY PATTERSON

to be born as boys—drowned, or dashed against a wall so their heads are broken—"

"You've seen this?" Widow Liu interrupted. "With your own eyes, you've seen an infant killed in this fashion?"

Poppy sat back an inch. "No, not with my own eyes. But I've seen—"

"Or drowned? Have you seen one drowned?"

"No, I have not actually been present for such a, a"—she took a ragged breath, and then another, searching for the word she wanted; it was the first time Addie had seen her Chinese fail her—"a pitiable event."

"I should think not. That would be very shocking for a mother to invite an audience to view the murder of her child." Widow Liu shook her head. "And, you know, I would use a stronger word to describe the act. 'Gruesome,' perhaps—a gruesome event. 'Pitiable' is insufficient." She cocked her head to the side. "Don't you agree?"

Poppy didn't respond. When Addie looked over, she saw that her friend had shut her eyes and was shaking her head.

"And you?" the widow asked, turning to her. "Do you agree that 'pitiable' is not a strong enough word to use in this situation? Of course, since she never saw this act with her own eyes, perhaps your friend is uncomfortable using stronger language." She smoothed the skirts over her lap. Her satisfaction with the conversation was evident in every movement of her hands, which she looked at with fondness. "Luckily, I don't have that same reservation. I will say that for a mother to kill an infant is a despicable act, a horrible act, a gruesome and unforgivable and disgusting act." She paused, and a heavy stillness covered the room. "But despite all that, it is an act that is performed every day in China. Countless times, no doubt."

Poppy's eyes, now open, blinked rapidly. "You don't dispute that?"

"Not at all. You think I don't know the Chinese people as well as you do? Better, dear one, better. Our empire's greatness lies in its respect for tradition, but taken too far, this respect is also a weakness. I see you recognize the truth of this statement. Yet I would not have you think you have an understanding of the situation. In fact, you draw the lines too starkly."

"But you agree that women and girls are treated deplorably here?"

"Of course they are—sometimes. Perhaps often. As I'm sure is the case in your own land. What was the name of that woman who was bludgeoned to death by her husband? There was a case in New York not four months ago."

"I haven't heard of it," Poppy said.

"And you?"

Addie shook her head.

"And yet surely you've received letters from home during that time. The news is not worth passing on when the situation is not unique." Widow Liu glanced wearily to one side, and Addie saw that her gaze had fallen on a clock that sat on a table against the wall. Addie recognized it as a Gallet & Co. mantel model. She wondered where it had come from, how it had ended up here.

"Where did you hear this—this story?" she asked.

"Ah." Widow Liu swatted a hand before her face. "I am familiar with several foreign newspapers. I require an adequate translation, of course, but as I said before, everyone comes to see me." She yawned grandly, without bothering to hide it by turning her face. "What is your specific request, by the way? How much money do you require?"

Addie and Poppy glanced quickly at each other. "We haven't come to beg for money," Addie said. "We came at your invitation."

Poppy added, "But it's true that a donation would not go to waste."

"To fund the girls' school?"

"If you wish."

"In general, foreigners have not brought very much of value to our land. It is the opposite: you have taken away a great deal." She stared at each of them in turn, waiting to see if they would contradict her. They both remained silent. "Only in education have you made a positive change. Particularly in building schools for girls. This is something we've lacked." She reached for the cup of tea, but then held it before her without drinking. "Forgive me if I don't thank you for the gift, since we've given you so many gifts in exchange."

"I wonder if you confuse us," Poppy said, "for mercantilists. We are missionaries, Widow Liu. These are two distinct groups."

"Are they?" She laughed, disturbing the cup in her hand. Some of the tea spilled onto the saucer. "I believe that many of us fail to notice the difference. Perhaps you are too subtle."

"Anyone confused by the matter is welcome to come and listen to what we have to say. Our converts are quite clear about our purpose."

"And your converts represent a very, very small sliver of the population. But let us stop arguing. I am tired with the conversation. I am not a Christian, but neither do I see your faith as any kind of threat to me. Your god is no challenge to my gods. They can live side by side."

Poppy and Addie left without any specific promise from the widow that she would give them money. "She certainly doesn't seem interested in being converted," Addie observed as they were following the boy back to the mission. He had been waiting by the door when they came out, as if he knew exactly how long the visit would last.

"Not at all," Poppy said. She laughed, but it was clear that she was unsettled by the widow's treatment of her.

After a pause, Addie remarked that Poppy had been more vehement in her defense of the mission's work than she generally was in other home visits.

"Perhaps Chungking is making me into a strident crusader," her friend replied with a wry smile. "By the end of two months, I'll be like Julia Riddell."

"Or like Owen," Addie said. As soon as she'd spoken, she regretted the joke.

*   *   *

All through the fall and into the winter, Addie was visited by memories as vivid as the trances of an opium smoker. She didn't know where these memories came from, or why they struck her as powerfully as they did. They had the sensation of dreams, a crackle like electricity in the air before the purple lightning comes climbing out of the clouds. But dreams were alloys of accident and imagination that dissolved too easily. Her memories had substance, the weight of truth.

They came to her throughout the day, as she was leading a prayer group in one of their congregants' homes, as she climbed the steep stairs of Chungking's streets, as she lay down beside Poppy in the bed they now shared at night. They delivered themselves to her consciousness wholly formed. An image from when she was eight or nine years old: flinging herself into the stuffed chair in the little alcove off the stairs. An oblong of light had fallen over the page she was reading in the Gospel of Luke. It was summer, and hot. From the kitchen came the sounds of a spoon scraping over a pan and the girl singing softly to herself. A fly alit on Addie's knee, and abruptly she was filled with a feeling of transportation, of transcendence. She was enraptured with all of God's creations: the fly, the hot white light from the window, the scrap of song from the kitchen, the pages of the Bible blotting with sweat from her fingers . . .

This memory visited her in the moment she was filling a cloth bag with oranges to take to a family who lived down the hill from the mission house. She tried to think if there had been a scent of oranges that day years before, in the old home in Marietta. But they couldn't have possibly had citrus at that time of year.

Another day, ducking beneath a sagging clothesline down near the wharf, she suddenly recalled gray shapes moving through the water off the side of a ship almost a decade before. She was carrying Freddie then. She hadn't yet told Owen. But he was standing beside her on the steamer's deck, and he took her hand and used it to point at the dolphins chasing along beside them in the water. "Let's see if they follow us all the way to China," he said, and for half a day it seemed that they might.

One night she'd walked her newborn son around the darkened courtyard for hours. Li K'ang's sister Hsi-yung had come out, just in case Addie wanted to be relieved, and she hadn't said a word, but Addie had been glad for the assurance of her presence . . .

There was a picnic long ago in a field of flowers, a three-legged race whose start she signaled by raising her arms, a little dog snuffling her ankles with its wet nose . . .

And Owen meeting her eye across a crowd that had assembled to hear a reverend from Boston lecture about the Great Call to Foreign Missions. *It is time for the flame of Christianity to burn brightly in every home, whether it be a tent in the Sahara or a house built upon stilts on some tiny island in the Pacific* . . . Rain had beat the windows and run down in rivulets, and inside the hall a cloud of pipe smoke had settled near the wooden beams of the ceiling . . .

All these memories and others descended upon her brain during the months when she was settling into Chungking. There seemed to be no rhyme or reason in the selection; they raised different emotions within her that ranged from regret to longing to joy. "What are you thinking of?" Poppy would ask when she got a faraway look on her face. It was too difficult to explain because the past was the past. At first she said, "Nothing." And then, after a while: "Our future." Which satisfied Poppy, even if it was the opposite of the truth.

Juanlan

20

In mid-August, the river is rising. In town, it has spread like a hand widening its span, covering the banks and sloshing up onto Jiangnan Lu. The road is technically closed, but motorbike drivers still venture down, edging their way past the water, mud squelching beneath their tires. It is something to be this close to a flood. Things are not as bad here as they are in the east, but it is the same water, the same element building its strength. The Duoyu Jiang feeds the Dadu He. Which eventually feeds the Chang Jiang. Trace the watery paths on a map, and they lead east to Shanghai, to the busy coast. But here is where it starts.

On the main bridge, people lean over the railings and toss detritus into the brown waves, just to see the river carry it quickly away. Tissues, plastic bottles. Anything that floats. They drop things into the water and exclaim to one another at how fast they are gone. Juanlan doesn't throw anything into the water. Lulu does. Every evening, they take a walk together and her sister-in-law tosses down whatever is at hand. Tonight it is a handful of sunflower seed shells. "You can't even see them," Juanlan protests.

"Maybe *you* can't."

"But you can?"

Lulu has one hand on the railing. Her belly is larger now, and she has to angle herself sideways. "See? There they are." She is pointing at nothing. There is only the rust-brown water moving swiftly along. Without turning her eyes from the river, she asks how Juanlan's father is doing.

"Better today than yesterday." The day before, he had fallen while trying to descend the front steps of the hotel. She was tutoring Wei Ke, and when she returned for lunch, her parents were both at the hospital. "My mother was really angry with him," she tells Lulu, "because he was trying to hang up his birdcage on the sidewalk, and he's not supposed to attempt the stairs by himself."

Lulu gives her a look. "He's probably really bored. Maybe he just wanted to do something on his own, for a change."

Juanlan frowns. She is ready to remark that her father's condition is not the same as Lulu's, that if Lulu does not appreciate her mother-in-law's concern for her health, that doesn't mean she knows what is best for her father-in-law, too. But Juanlan doesn't want to anger her, and changes the subject: "I heard from Du Xian," she says.

"And?"

"He wants to come visit for National Day."

This is not exactly true. The letter did not say anything about coming to Heng'an. It only said that they should take advantage of the holiday to see each other. Du Xian's company is giving them one day of vacation plus the weekend to travel, which is not very much time, considering it takes twelve hours by bus to get from Chongqing to Heng'an. In his letter he didn't acknowledge this as any impediment.

"Would you introduce him to your parents if he came here?" Lulu asks. "Would he stay at the Three Springs?"

"I don't know how I'd keep him a secret. I guess I'd have to tell them, wouldn't I?"

"No, you could tell him to rent a room and then never let your parents see the two of you together."

Juanlan glances at Lulu, unsure whether she is being serious or joking. Her sister-in-law is wide-eyed, a caricature of naïveté. "So you think I should tell them?"

"Of course." Lulu turns her face to the water again. Her eyes follow the flight of a plastic bag sifting down to the surface, tossed by a little boy held in his father's arms. Juanlan looks at the boy, but Lulu keeps her eyes fixed on the plastic bag. "If you're planning on staying with Du Xian, you should tell your parents about him."

"*If* I'm planning on staying with him?"

"Yes, 'if.'" She looks up from the water, blinking. "You might have another boyfriend by now. I don't know."

She is speaking of Rob, of course. It's the first time she's brought him up since he left a few weeks ago. When Juanlan first told her that Rob had left, Lulu's mouth dropped open. What is it between them, she wonders? The two of them spent no more than ten minutes alone together the day of the bike ride. Rob is nearly fifty years old, Lulu is pregnant, and they don't share a common language. Absurd to think that they might be attracted to each other—except that Lulu's nonchalance, mentioning him in conversation, is unconvincing. Even now, blinking at Juanlan, she seems almost to be offering up her own longing, wanting her to see it.

"I don't have another boyfriend," Juanlan says firmly.

Lulu remains silent for a moment. Then she turns away. "Let's go," she says. "I'm sick of being here."

*   *   *

Zhuo Ge stops by the flat on his way home from work that evening, and they sit in the living room, their mother and Juanlan on the sofa and Zhuo Ge on a tiny stool pulled up to the table. Their father has retired to the bedroom to rest. The doctor said to keep his leg elevated as much as possible until the swelling goes down.

The fruit bowl holds a few apples, and Zhuo Ge goes to work peeling one of them with a switchblade while their mother tells the story of their father's fall. "He yelled when he hit the steps," she says, "and it made my heart stop. Of course, the yelling was really a good thing. He didn't make a sound that other time." She nods, looking from Juanlan to Zhuo Ge, who is eating the apple off the knife.

"I would have been worried, too, if I heard that," Juanlan says.

"Everything was all right here when you came back?"

"Everything was fine."

"And how was Xiao Lu tonight?"

Juanlan glances at Zhuo Ge. He shrugs as if to say that there is only so much a man can do, or know, when it comes to his pregnant wife.

"We took a stroll on the bridge," Juanlan says, noncommittal. "Then she went home."

"You didn't accompany her?"

Zhuo Ge takes another apple from the bowl. "Ma, she's fine. It's only a couple of blocks back to our place."

Their mother narrows her eyes. She is ready to be angry, it seems.

"In two months, Zhuo'er, your wife is going to have a baby. A little, tiny baby." She holds out her cupped hands; between them, a basketball would just fit. "A *baby*, and right now I don't trust her even to take care of herself. I try to help, and she won't take it. I've seen the way she looks at me. I'm her mother-in-law, and when I talk to her she wrinkles up her nose like she's just smelled spoiled meat. Either that or: nothing." She draws a hand across her face, and her features freeze. Eyes glassy, mouth slightly open. Despite herself, Juanlan almost laughs at the impression. "Do you trust her to care for your baby? No, you're having fun, going out every night to gamble with your friends."

He begins to protest, but their mother isn't finished.

"And *you*," she says, turning to Juanlan. "You're the only one Xiao Lu agrees to spend time with right now, but instead of giving her your attention, you're tutoring that boy, you're running around with that foreigner. Xiao Lu is your *family*, do you understand? What is Director Wei to us? What business do we have with a laowai who comes to Heng'an and then leaves again?"

"The hotel—," Zhuo Ge begins.

"The hotel is doing just fine." Their mother glances at the door to the bedroom and lowers her voice. "You think he's ready for some big change? He can't even make it down three steps without falling. Nothing is easy for him anymore. Nothing." She presses her lips together and shakes her head. Then she leans back into the sofa. "It's late," she says. "Lan'er, go check to see if the guests are all back yet." Her face is drawn, tired; she looks older than she is. Or maybe not. Maybe she looks exactly her age. Soon she will have a grandchild, she will be a nainai. And Juanlan's father, in the other room—the baby, when it is old enough to speak, will call him yeye.

She, Juanlan corrects herself. When *she* is old enough to speak. The baby is no longer a thing, but a little girl curled up inside Lulu's body, waiting to come out into the world and give them all new names.

*   *   *

The next morning she wakes early, an hour before her usual time. It's still dark in the tiny room, with its single small window that faces onto the alley. Four stories up, the sky might be navy, turquoise, headed toward dawn or already past it. Down here on the ground level, it takes longer for the light to arrive.

Even so, she knows the time before glancing at the clock. Upon waking, she can always predict the hour. At the university, it bewildered her roommates, who sometimes tested her on it. Hualing, who had the bunk below hers, would appear as a presence beside her, sensed through closed eyes. She would shake her awake, clock in hand, and ask what time it was. Juanlan always got it right, within five minutes. Then Hualing would reply, laughing, "No, benzi, it's time to go to breakfast."

The university seems as far away as the moon. It's impossible to think that her friends from those four years will this morning wake up somewhere perhaps not very different from Heng'an. Preparing for the new school year, their first as teachers. One of her friends got a job at a travel agency in Chengdu. A few, like Juanlan, are not yet employed.

Do they feel as she does? The presence of something in the chest, burning cold. Not dread, but a kind of anxiousness that fuels itself and keeps on burning. It is the feeling of waiting when you don't know what you're waiting for. You could do something dangerous; you could act without thinking.

She swings her legs down over the edge of the mattress. The tile floor is cool beneath her feet. It is August and sticky, and eight blocks away the Duoyu Jiang is rising higher. It is in the air now, too; the whole world is soaked. Heng'an is the world, as much as any place is.

In the kitchen, her mother is scooping tea leaves into a glass jar. Her father carries the jar with him all day, adding water to the same leaves again and again, so that by nighttime what he is drinking is clear, the flavor leached out. The tea they buy is not expensive. Juanlan has tried to convince him that a new scoop of leaves might be added at some point. This is an indulgence he can't bring himself to attempt. "When I was young," he reminds her, "there were times we were so hungry we ate the bark off the trees."

"You're up early," Juanlan's mother says, giving her a quick glance as she folds up the foil bag and places it back on the shelf.

"Just restless." At the sink, she washes her face while her mother takes her father his tea. When she returns, she takes the towel from the hook on the wall and hands it to Juanlan. "You're going to Director Wei's, I guess."

"In a little while." Juanlan blots the towel on her cheeks. "But I can call Teacher Cao and tell her I can't come today if you want me to sit at the desk instead of Ba."

Her mother makes a vague gesture, then shakes her head. "Why don't you go buy some mantou for breakfast. You can get some money from my purse." She nods at the other room, where her purse hangs from one of the hooks on the wall.

Money in hand, Juanlan goes out through the lobby and pauses at the door. This is where her father fell. She pictures him standing and looking out at the leaves in the sunshine, with a mournful expression tugging down one corner of his mouth. He has his birdcage in hand—if only he could hang the cage closer to the door, he wouldn't have to attempt the steps.

Such a stupid problem.

She makes her way down the street to the mantou seller and a few minutes later returns with the bag of steamed buns. The lobby is empty as before, though she can hear the *slap-slap* of plastic sandals on the floor overhead: one of the guests making his way to the bathroom down the hall. *His*, always *his*. She remembers Lulu's suggestion that Du Xian come and stay as a guest. He could come without her parents ever knowing that she was the reason. There is a certain appeal in the idea, the secret of it.

She stands in the lobby, looking out through the open door. There are two trees in front of the hotel, edging the street. The wire where her father hangs the birdcage runs between them. If they could only run a wire up to the door of the hotel, her father could hang the birdcage there. But then people on the sidewalk would run into it. Crossing to the doorway to take a closer look, she runs her hand over the tile on the front of the building. It's smooth—nowhere to hook a wire, even if it wouldn't dip down. Juanlan looks up, but there are only the windows on the second floor.

She retrieves the master key and then climbs the stairs, her shoes squeaking on the linoleum. The hallway on the second floor is empty, though a sliver of light under the bathroom door confirms that someone is inside. At the door of one of the unoccupied rooms she puts the key in the lock. Inside, the bed is flat and tightly made, a pair of plastic sandals tucked beneath it. A musty scent hangs in the air. She crosses to the window and pulls it open on its track. Feels along the outside. But there is no way to attach anything to the outside of the building.

She slides the window shut and turns back to the door. How easily this problem defeats her. As it has defeated her parents, she supposes. But no: they haven't thought to change their ways to accommodate her father's new condition.

She is halfway out the door when her eyes are drawn to the corner of the room, where a coatrack stands empty. She picks it up and leaves the room. In the hall, she is preparing to lock the door when the bathroom door opens and a man comes out, dressed only in a towel. He has a large belly that hangs over it. His hair is wet and sticking up in patches. His eyes take in the coatrack and then move back to Juanlan. "Xiao mei," he says, "there are cockroaches in the shower. You really need to clean better." And having said his piece, he opens the door to his room and disappears inside.

She does not lock the empty bedroom. She does not inspect the bathroom. A wet smell, a smell of mildew, wafts out into the hall. She picks up the coatrack and goes back downstairs, and when she plants it beside the front door, it looks like what it is, a place to hang coats. But she will explain its purpose to her father and maybe it will mean something to him, that she's thought of his comfort. She stands back to consider it and imagines that the coatrack will stay here, serving its purpose, long after she has left the hotel, left home, left Heng'an for good.

*　　*　　*

A few nights later, she is just leaving her brother and Lulu's flat when Zhuo Ge stops her. "Do you have to get home right now?"

She has plans to watch television with their father, she tells him.

"Ba would rather you went out and enjoyed yourself." He glances over at Lulu, who is seated heavily on the sofa, her feet up on the table before her. The television is on, but her eyes are closed and her chin rests on her collarbone. "We're a very exciting household here, don't you think?"

"Lulu can't go out and be crazy in her state," Juanlan says.

"Well, I'm headed out, and I thought you might want to come with me, get some fun out of this night."

Before Zhuo Ge arrived home, Lulu had been walking her fingers over her belly and humming a song that did not sound like any lullaby Juanlan has ever heard. Then the baby started kicking, and the skin on her belly rose like a sea creature underwater. She pushed back with her fingers—not hard, but without any tenderness, either. "It likes to hurt me," she said without looking at Juanlan. "It isn't even born yet, and already it's being a pest."

Now Juanlan glances at Lulu sleeping on the sofa and then turns back to her brother. "Okay," she says at last, "you can take your sister out. As long as you're paying."

The Two Brothers is like every other teahouse along Jiangnan Lu: a storefront with tables set up on the patio overlooking the river, and several private rooms inside. The road runs beside the river, but it is elevated enough here that it is in no danger of being subsumed by the flood. Still, the Duoyu Jiang makes its subtle roar beneath the voices and laughter coming from the people gathered above it.

Zhuo Ge leads the way inside, to one of the back rooms where his friends are already assembled around a mah-jongg table. Juanlan has met all but one of them before, though she doesn't remember every name. Three are friends of Zhuo Ge's from high school. Another is a fellow policeman, part of his danwei, one of the men who met her at the bus station back in June when she first came back from Chengdu. He nods at her, asks how she is. The last man is unfamiliar, but is introduced as a friend from the Tourism Department named Guo Jun. He tips his chin at the other table in the room. "We'll start another one," he says, rising from his chair, "as soon as our leader gets here."

"Director Wei may be your leader," Zhuo Ge says, "but he isn't mine. If I saw him speeding down the road, I wouldn't think twice about slapping him with a fine."

"Sure, sure, you're a real independent thinker. And you"—Guo Jun turns to Juanlan—"do you know Director Wei?"

"I tutor his son."

Zhuo Ge explains that she's recently graduated in English and that Director Wei called in the favor. "By now, my sister probably knows more about him than any of us do. She's at his house every day."

"So you know his wife, too," Guo Jun says.

"Teacher Cao is often there in the mornings when I get there," she replies, ignoring the invitation to say something more. She may resent Teacher Cao's wealth and the ease it affords, but she knows more than to let this show to a stranger.

Yet Guo Jun presses her to say more. "We like to joke with Director Wei because sometimes he won't come out with us, or he'll go home early. I think it's because he's afraid of angering his wife."

"Maybe he enjoys spending time with her," one of the other men puts in, without looking up from the mah-jongg tiles moving rapidly over the table. "He's a happily married man."

"No such thing!" Zhuo Ge proclaims. "You can be married and a man. You can be happily married, but then that means you aren't a man, because of what you had to give up to make your marriage happy."

"What about happy and a man?"

"Then you must not be married."

"Hao fan," the woman at the table snaps. For a moment, Juanlan is unsure whether she's talking about the move just played or responding to Zhuo Ge's joke. Then: "It would have been better if your parents had just taken a walk," she declares, getting a laugh from all the men. She glances around, her eyes dancing. "You all wish it was the old China, when this meimei and I would have no other choice but Wife Number One and Wife Number Two."

"You would have been Wife Number Seven," one of the men says to her, "if you were lucky!"

"And you would have been a eunuch," the woman shoots back. She is a real la meizi, full of biting humor, able to give it as well as she gets. The kind of woman who goes out to play mah-jongg every night. One of Juanlan's university classmates was this type of girl, always visiting barbecue places, drinking beer with a big group of boys, telling jokes at a quick pace, delivering insults. Out with the boys, though never in a way that got her a bad reputation. It was more like she was a man herself, somehow able to play multiple roles at once.

The waitress comes, and Juanlan orders chrysanthemum tea. She sits at the empty table, and when the tea comes she stirs the dried flowers in the glass, watching the goji berries dance. The two red dates settle heavily at the bottom. If she stays long enough at the teahouse to refill the glass three or four times, she will be glad for their flavor—unlike her father, she disdains the weak tea that comes with too many steepings. If he were here, he'd order cheap eagle tea and be glad enough to drink it. Juanlan knows he wouldn't begrudge her the flavorful chrysanthemum, which is not even expensive. But he would never order it himself.

She scoops out one of the dates and pops it into her mouth, just as Director Wei appears in the doorway. He's standing a little back from the door, at an angle that blocks him from those sitting at the other table, and for a moment she is the only one to see his arrival. He sees her, too—leaning over the glass, spitting the date seed back into it—and the corners of his mouth turn upward, a grudging smile. Then he steps forward and is seen, celebrated, welcomed into the room. Within a few minutes, he is seated next to her.

"You like chrysanthemum tea?"

They are all busy pulling mah-jongg tiles from the drawers on the sides of the table. Zhuo Ge and Guo Jun are engaged in conversation with the others, weighing in on the last round, which the woman squarely won. She has a pile of money before her and is grinning like a fox.

"I don't know," Juanlan replies. "I guess I do."

"Young women always like flower tea," Director Wei says in a decided tone. Some element in his voice is different, strange. Perhaps it is only that they are meeting under different circumstances than usual. He takes off his jacket and rolls up his sleeves. Then he reaches his hand into the drawer in front of him, searching for any tiles he's missed. "And children, too. They like it above other teas because of the sugar."

Maybe, she thinks, she is a child trying to act grown-up.

"Are we ready?" Zhuo Ge asks, turning back to the table. "I'm ready to earn some money from all of you. I've got a baby coming, I have responsibilities."

"I'll send you a gift when it comes," Guo Jun says, "but you're not getting any money from me tonight."

"Sure I will. You and Director Wei, too. Now you"—Zhuo Ge cocks his thumb at Juanlan—"you don't have to lose so much, Mei, since you're playing with my money." He pulls out his wallet and begins to peel off one- and five-yuan notes. When he's finished counting, he hands Juanlan the small stack of bills. "There, a rich man like me doesn't have to mind the loss. But don't go losing it to these jokers, either."

"I'll try to make you proud," Juanlan says drily.

The game begins and she is not as quick as the others; she isn't as used to playing. During the New Year holiday, her family always goes out to the countryside to stay with her father's relatives, and they spend hours every day at the mah-jongg table. Then, too, she is often outmatched. Her aunt and uncle like to play in the cold winter air from morning until noon, and then again after lunch, and after dinner, too.

Zhuo Ge wins the round, and Director Wei, who was East Wind, must pay him double. Zhuo Ge sweeps the money from the center of the table with an exaggerated motion. "What did I tell you?" he says, thrusting the money into the drawer. "I'm not leaving here tonight until I've emptied all your wallets. I'm off to a good start with you, Director Wei."

"How much did you lose yesterday?" asks the other policeman.

"Who can remember? That was yesterday. Today is a different day."

Director Wei smiles and leans toward Juanlan. "Your brother is eager to make up what he lost." To Zhuo Ge, a little louder, he says, "Another night like that, and you'll pay for my son's first year of gaozhong."

In response, Zhuo Ge pulls open the drawer he's just closed. "What's that?" he says, leaning down so his ear is close to the drawer. "Wait, these yuan are trying to tell me something. What is it? Speak a little louder. I think they're saying, 'Zhuo Ge, you're our master now.'" He points his finger at Director Wei. "Maybe you should practice saying that, too, old man."

"Don't get too sure of yourself. An arrogant army is sure to lose."

"Please," Zhuo Ge says, putting his hands up in front of him, "don't quote chengyu at me." He pushes the drawer closed amid laughter from both tables. "Now let's go. You're East Wind, Mei," he says to Juanlan. "Go easy on your brother, okay?"

They play on for an hour, then two. Bills are tossed back and forth with each round, the amounts tallied up so quickly by the others that Juanlan doesn't even bother trying to calculate how much she owes. Only rarely is she the one to collect money from the others. She is not a terrible player, but she's not as fast or nimble. She has to concentrate, has trouble keeping up with the conversation as they play.

It is easy to tell that they all love Zhuo Ge. He is the heart of their group, the one who has brought them all together. And so they tease him more than anyone else and turn to Juanlan for fresh ammunition. When she calls him "Frog" during one of the rounds, they're all eager to learn where this nickname came from. "He looked like one when we were young. Big eyes far apart." She raises her hands to her head and flicks a finger out from each temple. "Our mother was afraid he would never grow into a face like that."

"And now look at me," Zhuo Ge says. "I'm the best-looking guy here."

"Shuai ge," says Guo Jun, his voice raised high like a girl's.

In the laughter that follows, Director Wei leans close to Juanlan and says, "Here I was hoping that *I* was the handsomest man in the room."

Despite herself, she smiles.

They call for the waitress to come refresh their tea, cigarettes are presented and passed around, and abruptly, the conversation breaks up into smaller groups. Juanlan and Director Wei are seated next to each other on the far side of the table, separate from the others. "I'm glad you came here tonight," he says.

She reaches for her glass of tea, needing something in her hands. "Why is that?"

"Because you're having fun. I haven't seen you have fun before. I've only ever seen you doing your duty." These last words he pronounces sharply, as if he has put something sour into his mouth.

"Tutoring, you mean."

"You don't enjoy it, even though you're good. You don't want to be a teacher?"

"No." She stirs the straw in her tea. It's gone cold, and she doesn't want to drink it anymore.

"What *do* you want to do?"

She thinks for a moment. "Work in a private company, I guess, as a translator."

"You're not going to find many jobs like that in Heng'an."

"No." She laughs harshly. "I won't."

"Maybe in the future, our town will have companies working with overseas clients, but that's still several years away. Too long for you to stay here, waiting."

She feels Director Wei's eyes on her as she says, "I'm not planning to stay here long."

"Do you have connections anywhere?"

She shakes her head.

"I do, but that's one of the benefits of being my age. Established, I mean. Do you have a boyfriend?"

She glances quickly at Director Wei and then back at her glass. "He doesn't live here."

"Where, then?"

"Chongqing."

"Ah. And you'll go live there, when you can." He doesn't seem to be asking a question.

"If I could get a job in Chongqing, that would be convenient."

"'Convenient' is not a very strong word to use. If I were your boyfriend, I would feel upset by that word."

"What word would you prefer?"

"If I were your boyfriend?" He is speaking quietly now; they are both speaking quietly. The others in the room are nearly shouting, telling some story about the other night. Director Wei lowers his voice even further, and leans toward Juanlan to be heard. "If I were your boyfriend," he says, and taps his finger on her arm so lightly she almost doesn't feel it, "I'd hope being together would be more than 'convenient.' I'd hope it would be . . . thrilling. Something that you demanded."

There is no time for her to respond before they are pulled back into the general discussion and the game is resumed. But she is breathing quickly, can feel the pulse in her neck. Earlier, when Director Wei walked into the room, the air shifted; she sensed it then without understanding what had changed. Now she knows.

"Time for the accounting!" Zhuo Ge shouts at the end of the night, and they all tally up their money to see how they've done. It is as expected: Director Wei has won the most. Zhuo Ge is not far behind. Juanlan has lost more than any of the others, but it doesn't matter, since the money wasn't hers to start with. And in any case, it's all for fun.

*   *   *

She awakes early again the next morning, dresses, and slips on the plastic sandals at the side of her bed. In the living room, she takes the birdcage from its place on a table near the window and carries it through the kitchen, across the alley, and into the lobby. The coatrack is still standing by the door; yesterday, when she showed it to her father, he'd nodded and thanked her for thinking of him.

The birdcage has an odd weight, uneven and shifting; Duo Duo might be moving back and forth on the rod inside. She sets it on the floor of the lobby while she opens the front door. Outside, yellow light sifts down like the mist from a cut orange. The air is damp and fresh. In her stomach is a fluttering feeling.

She picks up the coatrack and sets it outside the door. Then she peels back the cover from the cage, and before she has even hung it, the bird begins singing.

21

One day the phone rings, and when she answers there is a pause and then a male voice, in English, saying, "Hello? Juanlan? Can I—is there someone—"

The idea of his calling her, reaching her here, is somehow funny. So instead of responding in English, she says in clipped, rapid Mandarin, knowing he can't understand, "This is the Three Springs Hotel. Would you like to make a reservation?"

"Juanlan?" His pronunciation of her name is terrible. He has always called her Jenny. "A girl—her name is Juanlan?"

"How can I help you, please?" she asks in Mandarin.

Another pause in which she can hear him breathing. "I'm sorry, wrong number," he says, as if he is the one who has received the call, instead of the one who placed it.

*   *   *

He calls back, and this time she replies in English. In the minute that passes before the phone rings, she has time to feel guilty for fooling him. When he hears her this time, Rob's relieved laughter comes down the line. He tells her of calling before, baffling some poor girl with his foreign speech.

"That was Lulu." She doesn't know where the lie comes from, but there it is.

"I'm surprised she didn't guess it was me. You said you don't get any foreigners at the hotel."

"She knew—that's why I answered this time."

A pause, which could mean he is thinking of Lulu, picturing her standing there beside Juanlan. She is suddenly sorry for him. Whether it is love or infatuation, there is no hope for it. "Yeah, well, here I am." And he goes on to tell her that he's coming back to Heng'an. In the weeks since he left, he's traveled down through Yunnan to Kunming, then Dali, then Lijiang. He wanted to hike Tiger Leaping Gorge, but parts of it were closed, he said, because of recent landslides. Now he's back in Chengdu.

"You want to come here?" Juanlan glances around the lobby of the hotel. Dull reflections on the floor, the curtain hanging limply over the door to the alley. Du Xian hasn't yet come to visit, hasn't made any real plans to. Yet here is this foreigner coming twice in less than a month. "Why?"

"Because I want to see all of you again," he says simply. "I'll be there tomorrow, and I'd like to take your family to dinner, if you're free."

"It will be difficult for my parents to come." She doesn't explain about her father's fall, that he is practically housebound for now. Rob has not met her father, and she realizes that she doesn't want to present this version of him, slow-moving and slow-speaking, his words slightly garbled. She'd rather Rob didn't meet her mother, either, though for different reasons. Her mother, she is sure, would be disapproving of him. "My parents don't go out in the evening often. I will see whether Zhuo Ge and Lulu are available."

"Excellent," he says, "I'll see you tomorrow."

*   *   *

"Wah-buh! Hel-lo!" Lulu giggles and holds out her hand for Rob to shake. Her other hand is at her back, supporting it or straightening it, the way pregnant women do. In the past few weeks, her stomach seems to have grown by double. She still has more than two months to go, but she stands the way a woman nine months along would stand, and she is wearing the loose housedress that makes someone in her state look even bigger than she is.

"Ni hao." Rob raises her hand and pretends to kiss it. "How's my Chinese?" he asks Juanlan.

"Your pronunciation is better, but you do not speak the tones as you should."

"Well, I'm trying." He winks at Lulu and asks Juanlan about Zhuo Ge.

"He will join us later," she explains.

They enter the restaurant—a small plain one Juanlan chose for its reasonable prices—and sit at a table near the wall. Rob picks up the laminated menu and hands it to Lulu. "You decide," he says. He nods at Juanlan. "Both of you. Order whatever you want."

She explains to Lulu that Rob wants to pay for dinner, but that they should pay instead.

"Why should we stop him," Lulu asks, "if he wants to treat us?"

"Because he's a guest. Do you think if Zhuo Ge were here that he would allow him to pay?"

Lulu shrugs. "Your brother isn't here. And Rob is a man. Let him feel . . . manly." She glances down at the menu and runs her finger down the first column. The dishes are nothing special, the same ones that can be found anywhere in town.

The laoban comes to take their order and then disappears into the back. "I hope you ordered lobster," Rob says. When Juanlan doesn't understand, he explains that in the United States, lobster is expensive. Then he explains what it is because she doesn't know the word. The explanation is difficult, and afterward she has to translate everything for Lulu, who lifts one hand and snaps it like a claw at Rob as she laughs.

As they eat, he tells them about his travels through Yunnan, how beautiful Dali and Lijiang were, how the air was clear and the mountains rose in the distance, covered in snow. He explains about the Naxi people who live in Lijiang, how they have an ancient system of writing that's—he stops, searching for a way to describe it. Like the Egyptians, he says at last, and then introduces a new word: *hieroglyphics*. Juanlan calls the laoban over and asks for a piece of paper and a pencil, and she makes him write it down as she translates for Lulu.

"Who cares about Lijiang?" her sister-in-law says. "I want to know what it's like where he comes from. Ask him."

So she plays interpreter again as Rob explains that he lives in Minneapolis, in the north part of the country, but he travels so much of the time that he's hardly there. He was married for a while but isn't any longer. "After the divorce, I rented a room at the top of this house in a neighborhood where all the people speak Spanish. This little tiny room with slanting ceilings. I'm banging my head all the time there—" He slaps one hand against the side of his skull, just above one ear. Lulu bursts out laughing, and laughs so hard that he suddenly looks sheepish.

"I had this office job, great benefits, all of that. But I don't miss it at all. This job lets me see the world. I feel really free," he says, taking a bite of chicken. Because he's no longer married? Lulu asks, and he doesn't laugh as Juanlan expects him to. Instead, he sets down his chopsticks and thinks for a moment. Yes, but it isn't because the marriage was terrible. It was the routine that ground him down. "In my old life, I woke up every morning knowing exactly how long I would spend eating breakfast, and I'd get in my car at the exact same time, and I'd sit in traffic on my way into the city. Then in the evening, I'd come home, and my wife and I had nothing to say to each other."

"Does he have children?" Lulu asks. Her eyes narrow suspiciously; this is a secret he's been keeping.

No, Rob says, he never had any children. His second wife had kids from her first marriage, but they were older. He squints at Lulu. "About your age, I guess." Then he turns to Juanlan with an embarrassed look.

She would like to ask more. She wants to know how you can have two lives, an old one and a new one that you live back to back. It is, she thinks, a very foreign idea—the kind of thing only a foreigner can do. It seems that he is done talking about his ex-wife, his stepchildren, this family that no longer exists, and the conversation moves on to other topics. At some point, she gets up to go visit the bathroom and asks if Lulu needs to go, too, but her sister-in-law waves her away.

There is no bathroom in the restaurant. The laoban gives Juanlan a key and says she can use one in an alley down the block. Stepping out into the street, she senses a difference in the angle of light; the sun is poised slightly above an apartment building down the street, like a fat bird perched on top of the roof. She squints at it—the sun low enough and orange enough that she can look right at it without going blind—and is instantly struck, for some reason, with sorrow. She thinks of her father, his feebleness. No. That's not it. Something else: a slipping away. This day that is ending. It will soon be gone forever, and then another day will begin and end, and another. She will get older during a series of days exactly like this one, days in which she does nothing significant.

She finds the gate that the laoban described and uses the key to open it. The bathroom is filthy, a trench toilet with a pile of used toilet paper on the ground. She squats to pee quickly, breathing through her mouth the whole time.

When she gets back to the restaurant, Rob and Lulu are seated on the same side of the table. His hand is on her stomach, and he has a starry look on his face. When he glances up he looks so guilty that Juanlan wants to laugh. Then his face relaxes and he says, "Have you felt this thing? That baby's got a *kick* . . ."

"Yes," Juanlan replies. "I have felt it." She settles herself into the chair left vacant by his move to the other side of the table.

"The miracle of life," he says, shuffling an empty teacup between his hands, as beside him Lulu smiles serenely like a pet cat.

*　　*　　*

After dinner, they walk down to the bridge. The river has crested and gone down again, but it is still much higher than usual, still covering the dancing square and Jiangnan Lu. Coins of light bounce off its surface as if the citizens of Heng'an, standing on the bridge above, have tossed down all their pocket change in exchange for wishes.

They stroll until it's time to meet up with Zhuo Ge. He is waiting for them at the row of barbecue stands along the river. He greets Rob warmly, says "Hel-lo" in English, and then laughs at himself. They are getting ready to sit down at one of the low tables outside when Lulu declares that she doesn't want to stay. They have just eaten dinner, she says. She does not want to eat again. "I need to use the bathroom. The baby is pressing on my bladder." Her face is pale, her hair pasted to her temples with sweat.

Zhuo Ge frowns. "We can find a toilet around here." He glances up and down the darkened block. After a moment, his face brightens. "Deng Liyan lives nearby, just up the street. You can use the bathroom there. Maybe he and his wife will want to join us."

Lulu shakes her head. "I don't want to use some stranger's bathroom."

"You've met Liyan. Remember—"

"I don't *want* to stay and watch you eat. I don't want to sit around with some people I don't even know. And these stools are awful to sit on, anyway. I'm pregnant, remember?"

Zhuo Ge glances at Juanlan. "What do you think, Mei? Am I being unreasonable? She has to go to the bathroom, and I offered her a place to do it. Now she's making a fuss because she doesn't want to invite some friends to join us." He reaches into his pants pocket, producing a pack of cigarettes and a lighter. Shaking one from the pack, he pinches it between two fingers and uses it to gesture at Lulu, punctuating each word: "She. Can. Not. Be. Satisfied." Then he puts the cigarette between his lips and lights it. His hands free, he sweeps them away from his body, ridding himself of the whole thing.

Lulu jerks her head, as if she's been hit. "I'm going home. Wah-buh," she calls to Rob. He's moved over to the barbecue to survey the offerings, sticks of various foods piled high on a plastic shelving unit behind the smoking grill. "I'm leaving." Then, to Juanlan: "Tell him, please." She moves away from them, back in the direction from which they came.

Zhuo Ge twirls a finger by his head. "She's crazy right now." He glances at Rob, who wears an expression that he's trying to disguise as ignorance. But it's clear that there's been an argument. Zhuo Ge says, "You should sit down and order some food. I'm going to go see if Liyan wants to come join us. He'll get a kick out of eating barbecue with a foreigner." And with that, he heads in the opposite direction of Lulu, up the street toward his friend's flat.

"Looks like we've been abandoned," Rob says with an uncomfortable laugh.

"I'm sorry. My family loses face acting this way."

He shrugs. "I guess marriage is pretty much the same everywhere."

It's embarrassing, and she wants to explain. But what should she say? "Lulu," she begins, and Rob cocks his head. "She is not very happy. For many months, she has not been happy."

"Depressed, you mean?" He explains the term, and she agrees that it sounds like the right word. He rubs his cheek in a gesture of deep thought. "Maybe she's just tired. I mean, she *is* pretty pregnant."

"That may be one reason for her bad temper," Juanlan concedes. She is not convinced, but Rob seems eager not to continue the conversation. He's provided an answer and is satisfied with it.

When Zhuo Ge reappears, he has his arm around a skinny man who looks like a teenager. "My friend Deng Liyan!" he proclaims as they come up to the table. "Deng Liyan, this is my sister and her foreign friend, Wah-buh. Wah-buh?" He screws up his face and makes his voice like a cartoon character. "Eng-guh-luh-shuh?"

They eat and drink, the argument with Lulu forgotten.

The night is fine: the smell of meat in the air, smoke swirling up through the trees, the thumbprint of a moon somewhere overhead. Perhaps Juanlan is wrong: it's not Lulu's company in particular that Rob likes but simply being around those who include him. She joins the three men in a toast, then another, and another, and the warm beer strikes the back of her throat like a bell.

*   *   *

The next day they take a taxi fifteen minutes outside of town to a nong-jiale, an old country house that has been converted for the purpose of entertaining those who don't live in the country. This one's main attraction is a swimming pool, and Director Wei and Teacher Cao have invited them for the afternoon. "Someone's always treating me here!" Rob had remarked when Zhuo Ge told them of the plan over barbecue. Juanlan didn't explain that this is because he is a prize to be shared, that this excursion is part of an ongoing negotiation of favors. "Bring a swimsuit," she said, and he promised he would.

When they arrive, Director Wei and Teacher Cao are already seated in plastic chairs at the shallow end of the pool, though they're both fully clothed. They stand as the rest of them come in through the gates. "Welcome," Director Wei says. "Take care you don't fall into the veg-etables." He points to the bamboo baskets, one filled with potatoes and the other with carrots. Later, they will eat dinner in the open courtyard beyond, but for now it is afternoon, and though the sun is hidden behind a scrim of clouds, it's warm enough for swimming. "Wel-come," Teacher Cao says in labored English, extending her hand to Rob. "Thanks for inviting me," he says, and in response she gives a tittering laugh. "I don't know what he said!" she exclaims, turning her head from side to side.

Wei Ke and another boy—his cousin, Teacher Cao explains—come running just then, both red-faced, with muddy feet and legs. They were searching for frogs in a rice paddy, Wei Ke says. He looks happy and relaxed. Juanlan has never seen him smile this broadly before. He is fifteen years old, but right now he could be nine or ten. He pulls off his shirt, preparing to dive into the water, but his mother points at a spigot on the side of the building. "Ke'er, you're filthy! Clean yourself off." Then she gestures to a row of doors on the opposite wall and explains to the rest of them that they can go change into their suits there, if they want to swim.

Juanlan is the only woman who has brought her suit. Lulu is too pregnant, and Teacher Cao demurs with a wave of the hand. "My hair," she explains. "I've just had it curled." But the men are all willing, and by the time Juanlan emerges in her one-piece with a towel wrapped around her shoulders, Director Wei and Rob are already in the water, along with Wei Ke and his cousin. A moment later, Zhuo Ge belly flops into the middle, spraying water all the way over to where the other women sit. "Hao fan!" Lulu cries, frowning at her husband.

While everyone else is distracted, Juanlan shrugs off her towel. It is an effort not to announce her self-consciousness, revealing herself like this before Rob, before Director Wei and Teacher Cao. She sits on the edge of the deep end and eases herself in. She is not an adept swimmer but wants to avoid walking around to the other end with everyone's eyes on her. Once submerged, she stays close to the edge and paddles to shallower water. "Your sister is the only brave woman here," she hears Director Wei say to Zhuo Ge. "The others won't even come in." He pauses while his son and nephew do handstands. Then he sweeps his eyes around the pool. "Who's willing to race me?" He nods to the opposite side. "There and back."

Zhuo Ge takes him up on the offer, and at the signal from Teacher Cao, the two men take off. But Zhuo Ge is no swimmer. He flails and sputters in a comic manner, and as Director Wei reaches the other side and turns around, Zhuo Ge is already walking back to the start line, splashing as he goes. "I've been finished for ages," he declares when Director Wei comes up beside him. "Didn't you see me lap you?"

Director Wei smiles, thin-lipped. He is proud of his swimming, Juanlan thinks, and wants a real rival to show it off. After a moment, he turns to her, brushing water from his eyes. "Will the foreigner give it a try?"

"I can ask," she says doubtfully.

Rob makes his way to the spot on the wall beside Director Wei, and when Teacher Cao gives the signal, a new race begins. This time it is a real competition, the two men swimming furiously, hands knifing the water. "Jiayou, jiayou," Juanlan and the others all cry, not saying who they're cheering for. Though the American is taller, his arms longer, Director Wei keeps up with him until they reach the far wall. Then Rob does a flip and pushes off without lifting his head above the surface. In this way, he gains the lead and finishes a meter or two ahead of Director Wei.

Wiping the water from his eyes, Rob extends his hand and congratulates the other man on a good race. "You had me until the flip-turn at the other end there," he says, and looks to Juanlan to explain. Teacher Cao and Zhuo Ge both assure Director Wei that the race was neck-and-neck for the first length of the pool, but he just frowns. "Our foreign friend is a very fine swimmer," he says curtly. "Faster than I had expected for a man his age."

At this, Lulu laughs. "He's not a *grandfather*," she says, and lumbers to her feet. Crossing to the edge of the pool, she squats down on the edge—her legs planted wide apart—and extends an arm. For one nervous moment, Juanlan thinks she is going to pat Rob on the head. His blush says perhaps he expects something similar. Instead, Lulu trails the tips of her fingers in the water. "It's very cool," she says to no one in particular. In response, Rob flicks a few drops at her, and with a squeal, she reaches down to splash him back. Everyone watches the two of them, the moment suspended like a balloon.

Then it bursts, and with almost no sound, Lulu tumbles into the water.

*   *   *

Ten minutes later, as Juanlan helps her sister-in-law towel off in the changing room, she admonishes her for her carelessness. "You could have been hurt. What if you had hit your stomach on the bottom of the pool, or on the wall?"

"It's not like I meant to fall in," Lulu says with a shrug.

"Look at you, you shouldn't even be squatting down in your condition."

"Thank you, *Ma*, I'll be more careful next time. But you heard what Director Wei said about—"

At a knock on the door, they both fall silent. "I came to check on you," Teacher Cao says, stepping inside and pulling the door shut behind her. Her eyes go straight to Lulu standing in her sopping dress, water pooling on the floor beneath her. "We have to get you out of those clothes immediately. You'll catch a cold."

"But I don't have any others."

"Right, you hadn't planned on falling in, had you?" Teacher Cao cocks her head, thinking. Then her face brightens and she says, "You can wear her clothes for now. You don't mind wearing your swimsuit through dinner, do you, Juanlan? With a towel wrapped around?" Her eyes move from one to the other, sizing them both up. "It might be a tight fit, but even with your belly, you're a very petite person, Lulu. It's a good thing your sister-in-law wore baggy clothes today!"

Juanlan feels suddenly ill, her body on display like this, comparisons made. She hadn't thought she was thin, exactly, but it's embarrassing to be lending clothes to a woman in the last third of her pregnancy. She looks to Lulu for some signal that they will find another solution, but Lulu only yawns and lifts her arms over her head. "Help me off with this, will you?" she says.

As Teacher Cao peels the dress from Lulu's body, she talks inexplicably about the village of Tao Xu. "The planned flooding will begin in the spring, so the relocations must be finished by winter," she explains.

"What relocations?" Juanlan asks.

"For the dam. Surely you've heard about the Longjia Hydroelectric Project?"

"Of course," she mumbles, crossing her arms over her chest. For years now, the government has been building this dam. It has been going on for so long that she had forgotten all about it. It's at last getting close to completion. Some villages will be drowned, and the government is rebuilding those villages farther up the mountain: new buildings, new everything.

As Lulu tugs on the shorts that Juanlan had been wearing earlier, Teacher Cao rambles on, talking about how the dam will provide power for the whole province, power that will aid Sichuan's march into the future. What does this matter? Juanlan wonders. What does this have to do with them? But then Teacher Cao comes to the point. "Director Wei has business up there. They've got some relics in Tao Xu that might be useful. In fact"—she nods at Juanlan—"he has a favor to ask."

"I can't button them," Lulu cuts in, referring to the shorts. It's unclear whether she's been listening to anything Teacher Cao is saying, but Juanlan is grateful for the interruption.

"Just leave them unbuttoned," she says, handing Lulu her shirt.

"He's going up there with some members of his danwei tomorrow," Teacher Cao goes on. "There are some foreign documents or something of that nature, some writing that was left behind long ago. It would be helpful, he said, to have someone who speaks English." She pauses before adding, "Your brother is driving them."

"Zhuo is driving?" Lulu narrows her eyes. "He didn't mention it."

"Well, they'll be back by evening."

"And what is the foreigner supposed to do? If Juan Mei is gone all day, how will he entertain himself?"

Teacher Cao taps her fingers on her collarbone. "Why doesn't he come to our flat?" she says after a moment. "Wei Ke and his cousin can take him out into town."

"I could come," Lulu offers. "I could show him how to get to your place." She turns to Juanlan, her eyes bright as a bird's. "That sounds okay, doesn't it?"

Juanlan pauses before replying. Lulu is dressed now, and she feels suddenly vulnerable, standing in her swimsuit in the little room. The idea of going out into the courtyard this way, of sitting down to eat across from Director Wei—she shivers, feeling Lulu's eager expectation and Teacher Cao's smug confidence turned toward her. The older woman is holding two towels draped over her arm. When Juanlan still doesn't speak, she steps forward and winds one about her waist. The other she wraps around her shoulders. "There, that's better," Teacher Cao says, rubbing her hands up and down Juanlan's arms over the towel. "Now, what shall we tell Director Wei? Will you help him tomorrow?"

"Of course," Juanlan says, nodding. "I'm happy to help."

Teacher Cao beams at her as she takes a step back, then another. Glancing from Juanlan to Lulu, she says, "How lovely you are." But it's not quite clear which of them she's talking about.

22

Juanlan's mother does not approve of the trip. "Why do they need *you?*" she asks, and because the implication is that Juanlan could not possibly be of use, she defends the excursion with more passion than she actually feels.

"There are some old documents," she explains, "and they need me to translate them."

"What kind of documents?"

"Something to do with tea."

Her mother gives her a doubtful look. "And if you find something interesting, they're not going to build the dam? Or what?"

Juanlan lifts her hands. "I don't know."

"Huh. It sounds like a whole lot of nothing to me." Her mother glances out the hotel door. "Here they are," she says, nodding at the car pulling up.

Zhuo Ge and Director Wei are in the front. The back holds two other men, Guo Jun from the mah-jongg night, and another man Juanlan doesn't recognize. Guo Jun steps out of the car to allow her to slide into the middle seat, and soon they are driving off down the street. The other man introduces himself, but she forgets his name because no sooner is it out of his mouth than the others all tell her to call him Baozi. He is soft and white like a steamed bun, his skin glossy in a slightly sickly way. "And he's stuffed with cabbage," Zhuo Ge says. "That's why he stinks!" The men all laugh and Juanlan smiles, though she is busy trying not to knock her knees against the men beside her as Zhuo Ge turns onto the road out of town, accelerating past the trucks that belch plumes of black smoke.

She has never been in a car with her brother at the wheel, and she thinks of Lulu with her large belly, glad she isn't here, getting knocked about. Then she thinks of her sister-in-law meeting up with Rob, taking him over to Director Wei's flat, and is anxious again.

There is an odd energy in the car. A feeling of escape. Guo Jun and

Baozi are both from the Tourism Department, both junior members, and whenever Director Wei says something, they laugh riotously. Everyone seems jangly and animated, as if they're headed out on a long journey, leaving behind their regular lives, instead of a day trip for business. Cigarettes are passed around, and the four men each take one. The breeze from the open windows whips the smoke through the car and sucks it outside almost violently.

Up into the mountains they go, careening through villages where people walking on the road leap out of the way at the sound of their approach. *Slow down*, Juanlan wants to tell her brother. No one else seems bothered, and so she says nothing. She looks out the window. On one side is a drop-off, and below it the muddy river rushes over the rocks. They're lucky it hasn't rained much in the last few days. "The last time we drove up," Baozi says, "we got caught in a landslide. We played Beat the Landlord for twenty hours and Director Wei won all our money. If they hadn't gotten the road cleared at last, I would probably have had to throw my wife into the pot."

Guo Jun thumps the back of the front passenger's seat with his knuckles. "You'd like that, wouldn't you, Director Wei? Multiple wives."

In the side mirror's reflection, Juanlan catches him smiling.

"I hear the People's Congress is debating a new law," Zhuo Ge puts in, "stating that all department chiefs get to take two wives if they improve their department over a five-year period."

"That's the way to do it," Guo Jun says. Then he turns to Juanlan. "Don't you agree?"

"I don't think it will work as well for the female department chiefs."

Zhuo Ge grins at her approvingly in the rearview mirror: she's joined in the fun.

"You can have two husbands," Director Wei offers, turning to look at her in the backseat.

"No, thank you. I'm not married yet, but from what I can tell, one is enough."

The men all guffaw at her response, and Director Wei turns back around to face the front. But not before meeting her eye and smiling—a smile that she knows is meant only for her.

* * *

They arrive in Tao Xu after three hours of winding road. Juanlan feels ill from motion sickness and cigarette smoke, and when the door opens she slides out like a dropped sheaf of paper. They've parked in front of the Tao Xu government building. Before they can enter, a man with a birthmark on his cheek the size and shape of a peanut shell comes out to welcome them. "Director Wei," he says, clapping one hand in his palm, "how was the drive?"

"No trouble. The section that got washed out last month looks good."

"We had a crew up here right away to get it done." The man nods at Zhuo Ge, acknowledging his help. Pulling out a pack of cigarettes, he passes them around.

"Mayor Hu," Director Wei says, "this is Policeman Bai Juanzhuo's sister, Bai Juanlan."

"Ah, so you're our 'language expert.'" The mayor looks her over quickly. "We're very glad to have your assistance. Please, everyone, come in."

Zhuo Ge begs off; he's going down to the police station to visit some friends.

Inside, the mayor and another man, a tense-looking underling, pull a few chairs together around a table. Director Wei takes the opportunity to step close to Juanlan. "I'm very glad you could come today," he says.

The air is thin, and her lungs feel too tightly squeezed inside her chest. She takes a shallow breath. "I'm not sure how helpful I'll be; I will try my best."

"You're very obliging."

Mayor Hu calls them over, and they all sit and make small talk while the tense-looking man fixes them tea. Juanlan wants to ask about the documents. She's not sure how much there will be for her to translate or how difficult the task will be; the paper might be old and faded with antiquated language, or spotted with mold. Beside her, Director Wei smokes three cigarettes, one after another. It is several minutes before Mayor Hu suggests that they go look at the house.

"What house?" Juanlan asks.

"Up the mountain," Director Wei says, as if that is explanation enough.

The mayor distributes bottles of water as if for a long hike, grabs a few umbrellas, and leads them outside. "We've had two days without rain," he says, glancing up at the sky, "but I don't think we'll make it through a third."

The air has gotten thicker, and a breeze has picked up. Their destination is only a short distance away, so they walk. They go a few blocks down a small street that runs perpendicular to the river before veering abruptly onto a staircase of rough slabs shoved into the ground. Juanlan slips on one and hits her knee hard on the stone. She gasps, but only the tense man from the office notices. "Are you all right?" he asks. Yes, she says, she's fine. Using the water from her bottle, she cleans off her bare leg.

A moment later, Director Wei also loses his footing. In an instant he is down, fallen hard on one hip. The mayor, ahead of him at the front of the line, stops. "I'm fine," Director Wei says, shaking his head. He bats away the mayor's offer of help and gets to his feet. One side of his body is covered in mud.

"I have some clean clothes you can change into," the mayor says quickly. "Or Ru Dan"—he glances at his underling—"since you're closer to Director Wei's size . . ."

"Of course," the man says. "I'll go—"

Director Wei cuts him off. "There's no need right now. Please, I want to continue."

They make it to the top without further incident. At the end of the staircase is a small house, unremarkable in every way except that its entryway is partly collapsed and part of one wall has fallen in. "As you can see, the building is not in very good condition," Mayor Hu says apologetically, standing aside to let the others pass.

Director Wei stops before the entryway, and the rest of them stop, too. There is going to be some preamble before they go further. Down the hill, a thread of smoke rises from a house, and Juanlan considers the distance from there to here. Well over a hundred meters, maybe two. And yet not only that house but this one, too, will be underwater once the flooding begins. She imagines a wall of water advancing steadily down the valley. But no: it will take some time for the water to reach this point, and by then the house with the smoke rising from its chimney will be abandoned; the people will have moved up to the new town currently being built. Who will miss the old Tao Xu? It's a poor place; most of the houses, the mayor told them, are old and damp and have no indoor plumbing. People will be glad to have new flats to live in.

The mayor gestures to the house and explains that it was built sometime in the late 1800s for the Chungking Tea Export Company. "Of course, our Zaobeijian tea was very popular then, too," he says, "but the cultivation and transport was very disorganized." After the wars with Britain, he tells them in an official tone, Chungking Export set up office in Tao Xu and everyone sold exclusively to them. He waves his hand vaguely, as if the hills all around are planted with tea. Juanlan sees only bamboo and trees.

The men pass around cigarettes and seem content to smoke and allow her to take on the burden of listening. "Was this the office?" she asks Mayor Hu politely.

"No—that building is gone now. It was likely in town, right along the river." He pauses, allowing her to envision the town as it might have looked back then. No motorbikes, no radios, no cellophane wrappers clogging the streams. She thinks of Rob's fascination with little villages "off the beaten path," when he was telling Lulu and her about his visit to Yunnan. Places that time doesn't touch—that's how he'd described it. A poetic expression. But it's not true that time doesn't touch these places: it's selective in what it changes. Time runs over these places like a river over its bed, and the land is shaped by what it takes up and what it leaves behind.

Mayor Hu is still talking, his hands clasped together as he explains that in the house they'd found some papers stored in a chest, some documents that were a mixture of Chinese and English. They'd found an English prayer book as well.

"A missionary?" Juanlan frowns. "That seems unlikely, all the way up here."

"Unlikely, maybe, but not impossible. Ru Dan's own grandfather . . ."

The tense man blinks suddenly at the mention of his name, and he blinks even more rapidly when he sees that they're all waiting for him to speak. "My grandfather," he begins, "said that his grandmother used to tell him about a foreigner who came through here. He thinks so, anyway—it was a long time ago."

"And he was alone," Mayor Hu offers.

"Yes, alone."

"So you see," the mayor says, turning back to Juanlan, "this is what we think we know about him. It's not very much, but—"

"He wore a hat."

They all turn again to look at Ru Dan. He presses his lips together and ducks his head, bashful at having their attention turned on him again. After a few beats of silence, he explains: "That's what my grandfather remembers. He says his grandmother used to tell him about a foreigner with a big hat."

"A foreigner with a hat," the mayor says, smiling nervously. He glances at Director Wei as if afraid that this new piece of information will disturb him. But the director is stamping out a cigarette on the ground, indifferent. "Let's go in," he says.

They step through the crumbling entrance gate into a courtyard overgrown with weeds and bamboo. The old stone floor is broken up, and some of the tiles are turned almost perpendicular to the ground. Two headless lions, their remaining features softened by more than a century of rain, stand guard on either side of the central room.

The plan is to salvage all that they can. During the drive up, Director Wei had explained that his danwei is considering a few small villages around Heng'an to designate as gucheng. These "old towns" are starting to take off as tourist attractions in other parts of China, and there's no reason Heng'an can't have them, too. Once the new expressway is completed, all the new tourists will want special sites to visit. The mayor calls her into a room off the corner in the back. A pile of rubble stands in the middle, and along one side is a broken ladder leading up to a loft. "I thought you would like to see this," he says.

"Is this where you found the chest of documents?"

"No," he says with a laugh. To Director Wei, who has just entered the room behind them, he says, "She thought the chest was up in the storage loft."

"Comrade Bai hasn't been in the countryside very often," Director Wei explains. Then, to Juanlan, he says, "You see the old stove?" He kicks a stone back into the pile of rubble. "This was the kitchen."

It seems she has been brought here not to explain anything to these men but to have things explained to her.

"And the loft was for storing grain," the mayor says. "It would have been crawling with rats. Not a good place to stash things you're hoping to save."

"Can I see them?" she asks. "The letters?"

The mayor frowns. "Oh, they're only records and receipts. Director Wei might have use for them; I'm not sure they'd interest you."

"But I thought there were letters. Letters in English. That's why I'm here . . ." She looks from the mayor to Director Wei, who are sharing a look—she has proved herself stupid—and then the two men turn as one to the doorway. She sees and a moment later hears the rain. It is a silver-white sheet, a waving shroud, a brimming bucket turned upside down over the roof, which is full of holes.

Mayor Hu shakes opens an umbrella and hands it to Director Wei. "I'll give out these others," he shouts over the sound of the rain and, ducking his head, goes out through the doorway into the courtyard to find the other men.

Before she can look around for a better place to shelter, Juanlan finds herself standing beneath the umbrella with Director Wei. "Let me show you," he says.

"Show me what?"

A touch on her back, and it is his hand, guiding her, pushing her toward the far wall. "Over here," he says, leading her to the place where a person would once have sat to feed the stove, to a place in the corner that even now is still dark.

Her heart is beating fast. This is the moment everything changes: Director Wei will kiss her. And she will let him do it, without knowing why.

But instead of bending his face to hers, he points to a wooden beam in the wall. "Here," he says, leaning toward it, "look."

Two words in English, and they are clear enough even now, surviving a century or more. *Forgive me*, she reads.

She pictures a knife at the wall, a hand clenched tightly around the handle. The knife is moving slowly, intently, in ragged lines.

Director Wei asks what it means, and for a moment, she does not have the words in Chinese. She shakes her head, clears her throat. She puts her fingers to the lines, rough slashes in wood, to conjure up the person who carved this message into the wall. But it's no use: the room offers up no ghosts. "Forgive me," she says in Chinese.

Director Wei cocks his head. "Forgive you for what?"

*   *   *

The rain lightens during lunch, and Mayor Hu decides that they should drive up to see the construction on the dam. Progress has been made since the last time Director Wei saw it, he says. "And you"—he nods to Juanlan—"you have not ever had the chance to see it."

They pile into two cars, the group from Tao Xu in one and the group from Heng'an in the other. Director Wei is seated in the passenger seat again, dressed in Ru Dan's clothes. His own muddy pants were handed over to Ru Dan's wife to wash. They were assured that the clothes would be waiting for them back at the office before their return. She thinks of Lulu, who still has her shirt and shorts from yesterday. But of course she will get them back, whereas Ru Dan likely will not.

They take the winding roads, slick with mud. Juanlan watches the green blur of landscape through the windshield, and her mind turns to the day's discovery. *Forgive me*. The words hover a little behind her vision, imprinting themselves on the glass before her. She doesn't speak them aloud, yet she hears them: an insistent refrain running under the men's conversation. *Forgive me, forgive me*. The rhythm of a heartbeat.

Sleep overtakes her in the warm, humid car, and her eyes are closed when they roll to a stop. She blinks rapidly as the doors are pushed opened and the others climb out. Seated in the middle, she waits her turn. They have arrived at an area that feels eerily open, a wide, flat space covered in gravel that could easily fit five or six more cars. After the narrow roads they've been driving, the extra space is unnerving. This is not a place that naturally allows for it.

The gravel expanse prevents her from seeing for a moment the more dramatic sight, but then the construction reveals itself: a giant wall that has replaced half of the opposite mountain slope. A massive concrete blankness, the whole area white and beige, and too bright. Juanlan turns away as if from some image of violence.

Mayor Hu is as proud as if he were in charge of the project, and he goes on and on about spillways and generators and hydraulic heads. As he winds down his speech, they walk the edge of the gravel lot, looking down at the smooth walls of the dam below. Juanlan finds herself strolling beside her brother and Director Wei, who suddenly brings up their morning's work. "Your sister was a great help earlier," he says to Zhuo Ge. "I'm glad you were able to convince her to come along."

"It was only a few words carved into the wall," Juanlan says, blushing. "I thought there would be more. I brought my English-Chinese dictionary." This makes the two men laugh, though she hadn't meant to be funny. The dictionary has been a weight in her purse all day.

"And what did it say?" Zhuo Ge asks.

She tells him what was carved on the wall at the house, and he speculates about the man Ru Dan's grandfather described. Who was he? Where did he come from? And what did he do that made him ask for forgiveness? "He must have murdered someone," Zhuo Ge declares.

"Our friend here"—Director Wei gestures to Ru Dan, walking ahead—"says his grandfather was always told that the man wore a hat. If a detail like that made it into the story, don't you think he would have heard if the man was a murderer, too?"

"Only if he was caught."

"My own belief," the mayor, who has suddenly appeared beside them, says, "is that the man was a trader doing business with Chungking Export. He was probably cheating his Chinese friends."

Director Wei laughs. "That's not such an interesting story, though. No, on second thought, I like Policeman Bai's idea better."

"But you still need to figure out who the laowai murdered."

"I think it must have been about a woman." Director Wei catches Juanlan's eye for an instant before turning his face to the dam.

Zhuo Ge says, "A love triangle. The foreigner stole away some rich man's wife, and had to kill him to keep her from going back."

"Why rich?"

"Because that makes the crime worse."

Director Wei nods. "But the foreigner—let's agree that he was young and handsome. Not like our friend. We have a foreigner in Heng'an right now," he explains to the mayor, "but he's an old man. He's not sweeping any young girls off their feet, is he, Comrade Bai?"

Everyone turns to Juanlan, and she feels the blood rush to her cheeks. But Zhuo Ge answers for her: "I sure hope not! He's spending the day with my wife."

The conversation spins on, all nonsense theories to explain the presence of a foreigner, so long ago, in this place. Juanlan doesn't join in. She thinks of the words, the knife, the hand. She tries to imagine a foreigner, a man in a hat, walking up the mountain to the house they'd visited. Behind his stooped frame are the green slopes rising into mist. Down below is the river. There is no guessing what he might have come here for.

*　　*　　*

There's been a landslide fifteen kilometers south of Tao Xu. A small one, but the road is washed out, and it might be a day or longer before it's repaired. They only learn about the event once they've returned to the village. The rain has started up again; it was falling in sheets all the way back down from the dam. "A landslide?" Juanlan says, uncomprehending. She glances out the window of the government building as if she might see mud sluicing down onto the streets.

"We got lucky this time," says Baozi. "At least we're not stuck somewhere on the road."

"But we're supposed to be back in Heng'an this evening." She finds herself addressing Director Wei, as if he has the power to change the situation.

"What is it, Mei, have you got some big plans or something? A date? Who's it with?"

Juanlan blushes at her brother's questions. "No one. Nothing. It's nothing like that."

"Your sister should not be going on any dates in Heng'an. Her boyfriend lives somewhere else, you know."

Zhuo Ge looks momentarily surprised. To Juanlan he says, "You've been confiding in Director Wei instead of your brother, huh?"

Her cheeks are burning as she shakes her head.

"So it's true?"

"Of course not," Director Wei says easily. "I was only making a joke. But I think your sister has had enough of our humor. Let's turn our attention to the rest of the day. Mayor Hu, I hope you can show us a good time."

The mayor is eager to oblige. He makes a call, and very soon they are checked into a small hotel down the street. Juanlan and Director Wei are given their own rooms, and Zhuo Ge and Baozi share another. Guo Jun has a second cousin he can stay with, he says. He hadn't planned on seeing him this trip, but since they have the time—

They meet up for dinner at six o'clock. On their way to the restaurant, she asks Zhuo Ge if he's called Lulu yet, to let her know they won't be home tonight. "No answer," he says, searching his pants pocket for cigarettes. "She's probably still out with your foreigner."

Juanlan bites her lip. "Probably."

"Anyway, Ma answered at the hotel. If Lulu gets worried, she can call them and find out why her husband's not home."

Dinner includes the same group that went up to the dam, plus several other men and women besides. They are various local party members. Juanlan doesn't try to remember their names. There are not enough women to make up their own table, so the group divides evenly into two. When the beer and the baijiu come, a glass is set before her. The other woman at the table is the laughing wife of one of the Tao Xu men. "Come on," she says to Juanlan. "Let's show these guys that we can hold our own."

"Beer, please," Juanlan demurs, but the others convince her to have a single toast of baijiu before switching to beer.

Director Wei toasts the mayor, and the mayor toasts Director Wei. The tables toast each other. The group from Heng'an toasts the people from Tao Xu. They all drink to the landslide, to the crew that is fixing the road, to the new town up the mountain that will be a new and better Tao Xu.

They drink and drink, and after a while Juanlan thinks that perhaps it would be wiser to stop. But the damage is done. She looks at the table of food and finds that it is difficult to keep any of the dishes from wandering out of her field of vision. Looking up, she sees that Director Wei, too, is sliding away. "Forgive me," she thinks, or maybe she says it aloud. He raises his glass, and she has no choice but to do the same.

*　　*　　*

After dinner, the world slips out of time. Her brother and Director Wei walk her back to the hotel, supported between them. Walk now, Mei. There we are.

Everything is slow—objects right in front of her eyes make smears on her vision, not moving fast enough. Or maybe they are too quick and already ahead of her. She is left alone in her hotel room, where she lays herself carefully on the bed and rolls onto her back.

Fast, faster. With her eyes closed, she's inside a dark tunnel and can feel the rush of speed at her face. Not wind but speed, and it's a terrible sensation. Those tunnels they passed through earlier—only this morning? Dark tunnels through mountains and the mountains might fall on top of them, the rock might crumble, they will all be crushed. A car racing through darkness and men on either side of her, too close, too close.

Ten minutes later, she's crouched on the wet tile in the bathroom, vomiting into the squat toilet. Her hair is hanging down into her face, but she doesn't tuck it behind her ear because the hair is a curtain that keeps out her surroundings. Beneath her plastic slippers, the floor is damp and streaked with dirt. A pail of water with a scoop stands at the ready for flushing, but she is not ready for it yet. She squeezes her eyes shut and takes a shuddering breath.

There's a knock at the door: two short raps. "Juanlan?"

A male voice. Her brother's? She runs her tongue over her teeth. It feels twisted, like a towel being wrung out to dry. She addresses the closed door: "It's me."

"I came to see how you're doing. You're sick?"

Not her brother. Director Wei. She stays quiet, hoping he'll go away. It would be bad enough for him to see her like this—drunk, swaying—in a better environment. But the bathroom, with the vomit at her feet and the trash can close by, makes the indignity much greater, something not to be accepted.

"Can I get you anything?" comes the voice through the door. "They sell bottles of water at the desk. It would be no trouble."

"Thank you, I don't need anything." Her own voice comes out much softer than she intended, and she repeats herself, forcing volume into the reply. The sound seems almost to stick to the tile walls. For a moment, she feels as if she is sealed off from the world, and this bathroom is simply an extension of her body: her creaky voice, the smell of her, the swirl of acid in her stomach.

Then she is vomiting again. A horrible retching and, even worse, the sound of the vomit splashing onto the tile. She feels her toes bathed in warmth and knows that she has thrown up on them, too. She heaves, coughs. With one hand on the damp wall for support, she stands shakily and waits to find her balance. Then she bends to scoop water into the toilet basin.

Opening the bathroom door, she finds the hallway empty. A few doors down, outside the room where she is sleeping alone, a bottle of water stands on the floor. She picks it up and takes it into the room. The water tastes like spit, but she drinks as much as she can. On the bed, she tries closing her eyes again and finds that it is possible now.

Feeling a little bit better, at last she slides into sleep.

*   *   *

The room is darker when she awakens. She has to use the bathroom, but the thought of that toilet, the wet tile, the trash can—no. She shakes her head, and instantly her skull is filled with a bright, vibrating pain. It arranges itself into waves, and the waves move through her brain. And still her bladder is full.

Outside, swooping bats chatter in the night. A breeze from the window meets the side of her cheek. Outside. That is where she'd like to be.

She goes into the hall. At one end is a glass door that leads onto a veranda; ghostly white sheets have been hung there to dry. At the other end are the stairs going down to the first floor. She heads toward them and then descends like a ghost herself, slow and silent, uncertain of the ground.

A clock on the wall reads eleven fifteen. She finds the front door unlocked, which means that the others have gone out somewhere, to keep drinking or to play cards, to do whatever it is that men do when they are gathered in a small town in the mountains and their wives and girlfriends and children are not there.

Juanlan sets off down the street. It's darker out than she'd expected, but the mist has its own kind of incandescence, the small amount of light from people's houses dispersing among the water molecules in the air, and anyway it's not so thick that she can't see several meters in front of her. The turnoff is close by—she remembers that from earlier in the day. A baihuodian on the corner, with a red sign over the door. Turn left, and one block down is the river.

Immediately she can sense the open stretch ahead, though she can't hear the river's sound.

It's even darker down this street, which has only a few shops, all of them closed. Just before she reaches the wall separating the end of the street from the river, she encounters a pile of iron rods on the gravel. She squats behind them and urinates on the ground. When she's finished, she pulls up her pants and goes to the wall, lays her palms flat on the top, leans out and looks down.

All fog. The river is somewhere below; she remembers how high the water appeared earlier in the day, fewer than two meters from where her toes now touch the concrete. She closes her eyes, opens them again. Black versus gray, nothing else to be seen, but suddenly she is certain that the buildings she passed coming down this street only a moment ago are gone. Disappeared into the mist, they are no longer there. And the hotel, the post office, the two-story block buildings that have shops on the bottom floor and flats on the top—they are gone, too. The motorbikes and the white vans, the single small bus that makes the journey down to Heng'an once a day—none of them exists any longer. All that remains is the place with its elementals: the flat sedimentary lines turned up at sharp angles on the mountain slopes; the water in the air, the water in the river.

A hundred years ago, there would have been a small collection of houses and the office for the tea company. Not much more. Up the mountain, the house held a person from some far-off place, in the kitchen, crouching. Hand shaking as it carved a message in the post.

She pulls her head back from over the wall. It's time to go back.

At the baihuodian with the red sign over the door, she hears voices approaching. Men's voices. She doesn't have time to decide whether she wants to be seen before she hears a shout—"Xiaojie!"—and then the forms condense out of the fog, and they are her brother, Director Wei, and Baozi, all walking in a jagged line, laughing. Zhuo Ge's arm is around Director Wei's shoulders. "Xiaojie!" one of them shouts again.

She stops and waits for them to stumble up. Seeing them, she is suddenly aware that her vision is no longer wavering; her head is clear enough, only aching.

"What in the world are you doing out here?" It's Zhuo Ge's voice, but somehow the question seems to come from Director Wei. The men are a three-headed figure, a creature that has stepped out of the mist and recognized her.

"I wanted to go see the river."

"The river?"

"We found a river, too," Baozi sings in a high-pitched voice. "A river of baijiu!"

The three-headed creature is beside Juanlan now, and the part that is her brother puts his free arm around her. Baozi splits off, and she takes his place in a line. With Zhuo Ge in the middle, anyone coming upon them would think that he was the drunkest one, and Juanlan and

Director Wei were holding him up. But it is clear that Baozi is much drunker than any of them. He's singing the national anthem, the words slurred by a heavy tongue. *We millions have one heart! Arise, arise, arise!*

They reach the hotel and file in through the door. Baozi is still singing, and Zhuo Ge good-naturedly tells him to shut his mouth. The hotel owner comes out, smiling and squeezing his hands, and asks if they all had a good evening. "I put fresh thermoses of water in your rooms," he says.

Director Wei glances around idly. "I might have a cup of tea before bed," he says. His eye catches Juanlan's for a moment before moving on. "It's good for settling the stomach."

"You can do what you want in your room, old man," Zhuo Ge says, "but I'm planning on getting some sleep, if this joker lets me." He thrusts a thumb at Baozi, and they all climb the stairs.

Back in her room, Juanlan turns on the lamp and considers her reflection in the mirror. Her eyes are wide and bright, her hair frizzy from the mist. She sweeps it back in a ponytail with her fingers, holds it there at the top of her head. Du Xian always liked the way this looked, but he isn't here now. She tilts her chin, purses her lips. The sight of her bare neck makes her proud, makes her want someone to see it, admire it, kiss it.

*   *   *

Two short knocks, so soft they can hardly be heard. Juanlan doesn't breathe.

A lock clicks, and the door swings open. Director Wei tilts his head, an unreadable expression on his face. A half hour has passed. He's still wearing Ru Dan's clothes, but his feet are bare. He seems surprised to see her, and for a moment she worries that she has misunderstood, that he had no intention of inviting her here. But then he takes a step back, sweeps his arm inward.

Once inside the room, Juanlan isn't sure what to do: where to sit, what to do with her hands.

"Have a seat, please," he says, and gestures to the still-made bed. He pulls out the lone chair and sets it at an angle, indicating that he will sit there. They will not rush things. He turns to the table by the wall and begins to fix tea.

She perches on the edge of the mattress, but this is too awkward. Scooting back until her spine is against the wall, she puts her legs straight out in front of her. She tries to admire them, but they are shaped like a stalk of wosun, the calves and thighs all in a line. When Director Wei turns back, he nods slightly—something like approval in the gesture—but his face looks almost stern. "Be careful," he says as he hands her the cup. "It's hot."

She remarks on the tea. It's not what she has in her room.

No, he says. He brought his own from Heng'an. He nods at the little foil bag on the table and she sees that, yes, it's the same kind she's had in his home.

He sits back in his chair and gives her a wobbly smile, but that smile is enough to let her know that he is still somewhat drunk, too. The thought is reassuring. She extends her foot and nudges his knee with her toe. "Why did you ask me here?"

Director Wei stares at her foot as if he's never seen anything like it before. It is a wonder, a mystery, the first foot ever discovered. "Because I'm not tired," he replies without looking up.

"No"—she pulls back her foot, crosses one leg over the other—"why did you ask me here, to Tao Xu?"

Now he does look at her, and his voice is light. "Because I'd like to know you better."

"Why?"

"Why," he repeats. And then: "Why not?"

She frowns, and this seems to amuse him. He puts a hand on her ankle and strokes the top of her foot with one finger. The sensation makes her leg a live thing, separate from the rest of her; every nerve in her body quivering and turning toward his touch. The awareness of sex embeds itself between her thighs and she is reluctant to acknowledge it, but she feels it and yes, it's what she has come here for. She tilts her head to the empty space beside her on the bed.

But Director Wei just smiles and continues stroking her foot.

Now they are no longer two people but a single accumulation of parts, and one by one, each part draws attention it never has before. His ear, for example, she is considering his ear. It lies close to his head and is lightly pink, perhaps from the alcohol he's drunk. And there is his hair: still mostly black, only a few strands of white. He is not so old, after all. His status used to make him seem older to her, but that same status is what makes him attractive now. The leader of a danwei, he is accustomed to taking charge. His finger is working around to the inside of her ankle now, circling the bone and trailing up the inside of her calf. He has to lean forward to reach her knee, so he tucks her foot under his arm, and this is a relief for the skin that has been stroked for what feels like forever. But now all the nerves are waking up in her knee and the feeling is too much. She puts a hand on Director Wei's to stop him. She should have worked it out ahead of time, decided what she would say, what she would ask for. This is the revelation that has been working itself out in her mind all day, while they were driving up through the mountains and while they were in the crumbling house, during dinner as she was tasting wild mushrooms and greens and tossing back burning baijiu, after dinner as she walked back through the streets with the others—all this time, she was working out an idea that has only now become clear: she can make demands. She is a woman and she is young, and Director Wei wants something from her. She should get something in return.

"What would you like?" Director Wei asks, and at first she thinks he's read her mind. But he goes on, "I want to please you," and reaches his other hand, the one that is free, up between her legs so he is touching her through her shorts and underwear. His touch is not as light as he perhaps intended; the action is awkward, like a dog shoving its nose up there.

"Wait," Juanlan says.

He pulls back but maintains contact: his thumb resting lightly on the crotch of her shorts.

"I want to talk."

"Oh," he says. "That's not what I was thinking." He twitches one finger, brushing the fabric of her shorts. "That's not what you were thinking, either."

"No, I want to discuss this. We should know what we're doing. I should know what I'm getting into."

He sighs and sits back in his chair. "Negotiations." He looks tired, and his eyes are red. His face is red, too: the alcohol is working itself through his system. Not a handsome man, but handsome doesn't matter when it comes to attraction. Someone told her that recently. Lulu.

Juanlan moves her neck, not quite a shrug.

"All right," Director Wei says, and now he is pressing down on his thighs with his palms, impatient to get through all this as soon as possible. "Tell me what you'd like to know."

"What happens when we get back to Heng'an?"

"That depends on what happens tonight."

She swallows her embarrassment. Wills it away. "We go to bed," she says simply, using the usual euphemism.

A smile plays at the corners of his mouth. "We've already gone there." He thumps the mattress. "See?"

"You're still sitting in a chair."

"Only because you won't let me sit next to you."

They are being coy with each other, flirting the way actors flirt in romantic films, but the script is not right, or else they haven't learned it correctly. Instead of hot tension, there is a cool slackness. She shouldn't have stopped him. The moment for talk is not before, but after, because there will be too much time then and they will need to fill it somehow. Tilting her head down, she purses her lips, makes a pout. "Come sit next to me," she says. Even as she's speaking, she twists her body so she can lie down against the wall. The ceiling sweeps up into her vision, and then she feels rather than sees Director Wei rise from his chair. She twists her neck to look at him. His back is to the bed; he is taking off his shirt.

When he turns around again, she laughs because his pants are tented comically over his erection. He frowns. It is an effort, she can see, for him to refrain from covering himself.

"I'm sorry," she says, stifling the laugh, biting it back. "I'm nervous."

"You're not a virgin."

It's not a question, but she answers, anyway. "No."

"That's all right. It's better, really. You have some experience."

He's still standing beside the bed, looking down at her, not moving to join her on the mattress. It's punishment for her laughter. She has to make it up to him, reassure him that the laugh had nothing to do with him. "I'm not a virgin," she says, and feels the blood rush to her cheeks, "but I don't have much experience. I've only been with—the one."

Director Wei nods, satisfied. "Well, you know enough to understand—" He stops, brushes a hand over his face, pushing his hair up at odd angles so that, for a moment, he resembles a much younger man. Then he sits down abruptly in the chair again. Reaching a hand toward her on the bed, he tells her to stand.

She rises before him, and his hands move to her waist. Then he is pulling her shirt up over her head, kissing her stomach, and she thinks, Yes, all right, this. A half hour earlier she stood before the mirror in her room wanting admiration, wanting a man's eyes to fall on her and not be able to look away. So she lets her weight fall against him, waiting for him to pull her the rest of the way down onto his lap. Instead, he pushes her lightly away and tugs on the waistband of her shorts. He is pulling her down so she is on her knees before him. Then she understands.

She unbuttons his pants, pulls the zipper down. With Du Xian, it was always dark when they met in this way. They had to keep quiet, too, and so she often felt when they had sex that they were not who they normally were with each other. But with the lights turned on and Director Wei's hand on the back of her head, she feels exactly the opposite: the thrill of recognition. The assurance that whatever goes on between them will come back to this.

Hazel

23

One spring day, a year after she and George began renting my land, Lydie called me up and asked if I was busy. She had something she wanted to discuss, she said, and she wanted to do it in person. It was afternoon, and I'd gotten home from work a half hour before. Now I was standing in the kitchen, staring at the calendar on the wall, a free gift from the Bank of Edwardsville that featured pictures of various buildings downtown—shop fronts, two or three churches, a historic house on St. Louis Street. The picture for March was of the high school, taken at a steep angle from down the hill. I was staring at it and thinking that my worlds were crossing over—a photograph of my workplace hanging right here in my kitchen—as Lydie repeated that she wanted to talk to me, alone.

She'd found out about George and me, I thought. I imagined her standing at her kitchen phone, just as I was; I could see the phone line stretched out between us, leaping from pole to pole.

I told her to come on over.

As soon as I hung up the phone, I began busying myself in the kitchen. I brewed a pot of coffee and got out two mugs and saucers, the sugar bowl, a little pitcher for milk. The sugar bowl was half empty, and I thought I'd fill it. But then there was a crust around the rim, so I dumped it all back into the bag and washed and dried the bowl before filling it again. I got two spoons and set them beside the mugs on their saucers, and I got out a fresh package of saltines and arranged them on a plate beside some sliced cheddar cheese, and I poured some potato chips into a bowl, and I put some brownies on a glass platter. I stood looking at it, thinking that it wasn't enough. But I knew, too, that whatever Lydie had to say to me would be better said over an empty table. So I removed everything but the brownies and the things for coffee. Then I heard the crunch of tires on gravel and knew she'd arrived.

The storm door was unlocked, and she pulled it open and came up the steps to the door that led into the kitchen. I saw her shape through the thin crepe curtain over the glass. She knocked once and came in.

Glancing around the kitchen, her eyes lit on the table. Her face was tired and drawn.

"How about some coffee?" I asked.

"Just a half cup. I had plenty at breakfast." She gave me a distracted smile and sat. Right then I understood that although there was something heavy in the room with us, it wasn't the thing I'd feared. It was unrelated to me; she had come as a friend, to see if I could unburden her of it.

There was a summersweet bush outside the north-facing window and the birds liked to land on it and peer in with curious, cocked heads before flying off again. A redbird was perched there now, and Lydie and I both watched it watching us. Its eyes were shining black, full of some kind of intelligence it wasn't sharing.

"Have a brownie," I said when the redbird flew off. I pushed the plate toward her.

She took one and set it on her saucer without tasting it. "Do you know what I did the other day?" she said suddenly. "I was downtown and bought myself a copy of *Life* magazine, and then I went into Bennie's and ordered a piece of cherry pie. I sat at the counter reading this long article about Paris. It was all about how the city has come back from the war."

I nodded, not sure where this was going.

"The article said that Paris is like it was back before," she went on, "only better. They were describing a street, rue de la something or other, that leads right down to the Eiffel Tower, and there were pictures, one of them of an outdoor café. A lady in a dress, so pretty and elegant, you wouldn't believe, she was sitting alone at a table with her ankles crossed. She had a glass of wine and you could tell by the light that it couldn't be much later than one or two o'clock, bright light everywhere. Her handbag was sitting on the other chair at the table, and the tables were pushed close together, but they were all empty; she was the only one sitting there, and she was staring off somewhere." Lydie was in a sort of reverie, speaking the way you do when you're telling someone your dream. She'd get to the point eventually, I figured, and I was willing to be patient. "Go on," I said.

"That Frenchwoman was sitting there, having a glass of wine. Sitting all alone somewhere across the world, and I don't know why, but I swear I felt like I was looking at *me*. It gave me the shivers."

"You mean she looked like you?" I squinted at Lydie. She wasn't a bad-looking woman, but she was no model, either; she was thick and sturdy and had the same folds in her neck as I had. We were women who'd spent long periods of time under the sun, crawling down rows of lettuce or strawberries, or shaking out wet laundry and throwing it over the line. We were neither of us the kind of woman who'd catch a photographer's eye. I tried again: "In the face, you mean?"

She gave me a wry smile and shook her head. "No, it wasn't her looks. She looked French. You know—" She narrowed her eyes and pursed her lips. It was such a girlish move that I laughed out loud. "What, can't I pass for a Frenchwoman?"

"Could be. Just probably not the type who spends her afternoons at some café, looking off into the distance and drinking wine."

Lydie leaned forward over the table with both hands flat on the Formica. "That's what I'm saying to you, Hazel. It's like this woman—she was me, but she was living a different life. Like if I'd been born somewhere else, grown up some other place. I kept looking at that *light*, and thinking it looked better than it does here, and I'm telling you it made me feel . . . angry, I guess, because I won't ever see it shining down that way, hitting at just that particular angle."

She's found out, I thought: this story about Paris was simply a distraction, so when she hit me with the accusation, I'd have all my defenses down. It was one of those moments when you know something terrible is coming, when you hear its tiptoes down the hall and you feel only that you don't want to know what it is. "What time of year was it," I asked, "when that picture was taken?"

A breeze had started up outside, and it was stirring the curtains over the window above the sink. Lydie had lapsed into a brooding kind of thoughtfulness, and my question yanked her out of it, back into the kitchen with the clock ticking on the wall. "I don't know. What does it matter?"

"If you ever get there, you'll want to go when the light is exactly like it was in that photograph. You'd be disappointed if you didn't."

"If I ever get there," she repeated. And suddenly she smiled, shaking away the gloom that had settled over her. "We're not likely to be running off to Europe anytime soon. You or me, either one." She took a sip of her coffee. "Doesn't it seem strange to you sometimes, how they saw all those places? France and Belgium and way over there in the Pacific, and they hardly talk about it."

"Who?"

"George," she said, "and—well, I guess Karol didn't go, did he?"

"No," I said. "Never even got called for home duty or anything."

Lydie nodded sympathetically. "He was doing his part, though. People had to eat, after all."

I thought about how, in the years after the war, Karol would always laugh about what a bad soldier he'd have been. There was a desperate glint in his eye when he said it, despite the laughter. No one but me ever seemed to notice. "He was ashamed," I said. "He thought he should've gone with all the others."

"Really?" Lydie said. "Karol always seemed so casual about it. I'd never have thought he minded."

"I remember when the war news used to come on the radio," I said, moving my coffee cup in a little circle on the tabletop, "he'd get this look on his face. Sometimes he'd point to his eye, the blind one, and ask me what I was doing with a man who couldn't go and fight for his country."

"How'd you answer him?" she asked, leaning forward.

But suddenly I didn't want to tell her. It felt too personal. I thought of the time not long after she and George had started renting my land when I'd ask him things about her. The barrier was gone, somehow: talking about her suddenly seemed like fair game, and I had a fascination with their marriage, wanting to know things about her that no one else knew: Did she make the bed first thing in the morning or wait until after the kids were gone? Did she fold the towels lengthwise or widthwise? Did she kick her legs when she slept? I wanted to know if she had chin hairs to pluck, and I wanted to know the worst thing she'd ever done, whether she'd told George about it, whether it seemed that bad to him.

He answered some of my questions. Not all of them. There was a line somewhere that I hadn't bothered to look for then. But I saw it now, and it lay right in front of the soft spots. You didn't reveal vulnerabilities, not when they were real.

I told Lydie I couldn't remember what I'd said to Karol. "It's all so long ago," I said.

She nodded and sat back in her chair. Then she blinked and looked at me and said, "Hazel, I've got a favor to ask."

There was a hitch in the air. "What's that?"

"I went to see Dr. Anderson about a pain I've been having." She fluttered her fingers about her chest. "Tuesday—I saw him on Tuesday. He said he thinks I might have a cancer and should get a test. I've got an appointment next week, over in St. Louis, and I was hoping you'd be able to drive me."

Outside, I heard Debbie shouting. She was far away, probably calling to her friends still on the bus. That meant Lydie and I had about three minutes left in private. "What about George?" I asked. "Don't you think he might want to take you? I can watch the boys, for however long you want. You need to stay overnight in the city, it's no problem."

"I don't want George to take me. That's why I'm asking you."

"But why?"

"Because I'm not planning on telling him. I don't want him or the boys to know anything about it. And Hazel," she added, leveling me with a gaze, "I just need you to agree."

What else could I do? I picked up her coffee cup and went to refill it, and as I was pouring the coffee, I heard her say thank you, so softly I almost missed it. Because I'd agreed—of course I had. And when I came back to the table, she looked at the coffee like it was something she'd never seen before, and then she said she'd see me on Monday morning. She got up and went to the door, and I drank the cup of coffee I'd poured her, sip after sip, staring out the window at her car as it rolled down the drive, and Debbie waving eagerly after.

*　　*　　*

George hadn't been up on my property that day. The next afternoon, driving home from work, I saw him out in one of his and Lydie's fields south of the house, and I pulled off the road and got out and waved him over. It was that time before seeding began, and George had been busy all week, draining the sloughs and picking rocks. The week before, he'd been waking up all the machinery from its winter slumber, taking it all out from the barn to check the hoses and pipes and shanks and clamps, and soon it would be time for tillage. I never saw much of him during the month of March, and it wasn't a time for neighborly talk. But when he saw me waving, he came right over. He had on a cap that was partly covering his face, and he tipped the bill as he got close, then settled it firmly again on his head.

I hadn't planned what to say. My head was full of the news Lydie had given me the day before. She was sick, and she wasn't planning on telling George. She was sick, and she'd only told me because she needed me to drive her over the river to the hospital. I couldn't say anything about it, and I'd needed to see her husband up close so I could determine whether he had a sense of things going wrong. "How're the fields looking?"

He nodded at the bare earth behind him. "Full of rocks the size of my head. I'll probably end up breaking that new blade I put on the tiller." Of course, I couldn't see a single rock like that, but this was how he always answered questions about the farm; he wouldn't ever say that things were easy or looking good. Karol had used to come in every day complaining about how dry the soil was getting. Or how wet. Or he'd warn me that one of our cows was showing signs of fog fever, but by the next day when the cow wasn't coughing anymore, he wouldn't dare admit that he was wrong. "I don't need to see God's bicep to know He can throw a punch," he'd liked to say.

George was the same way. Superstitious. But just now it was clear he was waiting to see why I'd called him over. He scratched his arm and squinted at me.

I couldn't talk to him about Lydie, which meant that I needed some compelling reason for this chat. I told him I wanted to see him. "This evening," I added. "After supper."

He made a sound with his tongue on his teeth. "Not the most convenient time, is it?"

"Maybe not. But"—I thought quickly—"I'm taking the kids into town to stay with Iris overnight. So I figure: there's an opportunity, we better take it."

"What am I supposed to tell Lydie?" His tone was light; he wasn't taking me seriously.

"Tell her—I don't know, tell her I've been having trouble with my television and you offered to give it a look."

"That's what you came up with? Joe's down at our house every day, talking about this and that he saw on the TV." He shook his head. "I wouldn't be so bold, Hazel. We've been too smart to get stupid now."

"Okay, then," I said, "not my television. Something else. My fridge, maybe, or—" I stopped because he was laughing. He twisted his head to glance again at the field, waiting to get back to it. I felt relieved, suddenly, that he hadn't taken me up on my offer. I hadn't made any plans for Iris to take Joe and Debbie, and it would have been a lot of trouble to work out now. And I wasn't sure how it would feel being with George when I had information about Lydie that he didn't have.

"I've got to get back to work," he said. "Me and J.B., we'll probably be up your way tomorrow, working on the back acres. You need anything then, just holler." He stopped, scratched his neck. "Anything within limits." If he were a man like Karol, he would have winked. But charm didn't come naturally to him, and he just walked away.

* * *

I was supposed to take Lydie to St. Louis on Monday, and in the three days that passed before then, we didn't see each other or talk at all. I didn't see George, either, except from afar. Usually we all met at church, but every few months Iris and Walt would invite Joe and Debbie and me into town, and we'd attend service with them instead of at our own country church, where Lydie and George went. That's what we did that Sunday. My sister and her husband were Methodists rather than Presbyterians. Despite this fact and the size of the church and congregation, the services weren't all that different. We sang hymns, and the liturgist read passages, and the preacher made his sermon. This week the reading was from Ephesians 4. I perked up when I heard the line: "Therefore, putting away lying, 'Let each one of you speak truth with his neighbor,' for we are members of one another." Considering what was at the front of my mind, I might well have considered this a message, but the matter wasn't a simple one. Because I had to wonder: Which neighbor? Which truth? And what if one of those truths isn't yours to speak?

At the end of the service, the preacher read out the prayer list, those who were sick and those who were struggling, those who had lost some-one to disease or accident or plain old age. We had a prayer list at our church, too, and my thoughts turned again to Lydie. It seemed unlikely that she'd allow herself to be added to that list. And her own husband and boys wouldn't be praying for her if they didn't know that there was a reason to pray.

After the service, we all went over to my niece's home. She and her husband had four children under the age of eight, and they lived in a big old house on Randle Street with a front parlor no one ever sat in and a big range in the kitchen that took up most of one wall. With all of us at the house, and Edith besides, it was crowded and noisy and therefore something of a wonder that we managed to sit down for a hot dinner at one o'clock in the afternoon and fit around the table in the formal dining room. My niece's husband was an accountant, like Walt had been before he retired, and the two men were as similar as could be, which is to say, quiet and forbearing. They sat across from each other at the table and chewed thoughtfully and put butter on their rolls and took second help-ings of everything. In such gatherings, the men in the family tended to fade into the drapes and upholstery—John Charlie and Karol had always been the talkative ones—and it was Iris and my niece who led the conversation now, kept food moving down the table, laughed and teased the children.

Edith and Iris hadn't ever gotten along all that well, but living in town they were accustomed to seeing each other several times a week, and they had their running topics of conversation, as Rena and I had ours. I suppose we were like most families that way, the closest bonds depending mostly on geography. Not that I felt pitted against either of my sisters in town. I didn't have the same concerns as they did, and they didn't have mine. I was the only one in the family who still had children at home; Iris's three were all grown, and Edith had never married. And I was the only widow.

Most of the conversation was taken up by my niece, who talked continually to and about her own children. She was almost fifteen years younger than me and had relied on Dr. Spock—in particular, the second edition of his famous book—for all of her parenting ideas. When her youngest, not yet a year old, started crying from the other room, she sent the eight-year-old to change his diaper. "Davey thinks it's time to eat," she said with a shake of her head, "but it is *not.*"

That was our Sunday, and then we drove back home and Debbie fell asleep in the car, even though it was only a fifteen-minute ride, and Joe tried to convince me he didn't need to go to Rena's after school the next day. I was sending him and Debbie to my sister's place because I wasn't sure what time I'd get back from St. Louis. They'd need dinner, and I didn't want to have to worry or rush. "You'll have a good time," I told him.

"Why can't I go with you?"

"You have school."

"You do, too. And you're not going."

I'd told Mrs. Brainerd on Friday that I needed to take off Monday for a personal matter, and she'd said that would be fine—the cafeteria could function without me for one day. "Work isn't school," I said to Joe, "and I'm not taking off for fun. I've got business to take care of." I let it go at that.

It started raining while we were on the road home from my niece's, and by the time we arrived at the house, it was pouring. After the big dinner we'd had earlier, we weren't very hungry for supper, so I fixed us some BLT sandwiches and we watched Ed Sullivan and then *Bonanza.* Then I sent the children to bed because it was a school night. I meant to follow them, but I fell asleep on the sofa with the television still on and woke an hour or two later to a single clap of thunder, loud and close enough that the windowpanes rattled in their casements. I was in terror, the kind that doesn't allow you a name or history, just a heart pounding so hard in your chest that you feel it as a separate animal, a desperate thing that has gotten hold of your body. I stared around the room, blinking at the television, the piano, the record player—I took it all in without knowing what I saw. I had no idea who or where or what I was, only that I had been grabbed from sleep by a loud noise that could only mean danger.

Another second or two, and then reality floated together and held: I was Hazel Wisniewski, widow and mother of two, sleeping with my mouth open on a sofa in the house my parents had built. And it was time for bed.

The thunder was loud, and I figured Joe and Debbie must have been awakened, too, but though I sat listening, I didn't hear any noise from above. Joe was eleven and a boy, the man of the house now, but Debbie was afraid of storms, always cowering in the corner whenever the wind picked up. I went upstairs as quietly as I could, and at the top, I considered the closed door on the left. For the first several months after her father's death, I'd awoken some mornings to find Debbie curled in the bed next to me. Only then would I remember that in the middle of the night I had been startled out of sleep, not by any sound, but by a presence. Eyes flying open to see this girl with her hair tangled around her face and her nightgown hanging loose on her shoulders. Sometimes I got the feeling that she'd been standing there for a very long time. Minutes. Hours. It was all the more alarming because at the time, sleep was difficult to come, yet her presence proved that once I did fall asleep, it was as if I'd fallen off a cliff. I swam up from the depths only once she was right there, breathing on me. In the morning, I'd tell Debbie that she should shake me awake when she was afraid, but she told me she hated touching my sleeping body. I didn't seem like her mother, she said. I didn't seem like a person she knew.

I stood outside the bedroom and listened for a moment to see whether she was awake now. It was quiet, but when I nudged open the door I nearly screamed because she was sitting up in bed, arms folded around her knees, her back against the wall.

She watched me with wide eyes until I sat down on the edge of the mattress and held out my arms. Then she lunged forward and started sobbing into my neck. She was crying so hard she couldn't speak, but I understood that for several minutes she had been sitting there in terror, too afraid to move. She seemed young, terribly young, not nine years old but four or five. The room was covered in its night wash, a silvery-gray landscape where every object looked like a photograph of itself.

She sniffled and slowed her crying, and after another minute sat back, looking embarrassed. I asked if she was all right now, and she said yes. Then she rubbed her eyes and looked away.

Downstairs, I washed my face. I pinned curlers in my hair. The light in the bathroom was weak, and the image in the mirror was a grim one: my cheeks loose and puttylike, deep shadows under my eyes. I was getting old; I looked old.

The storm passed, and in the morning, I awoke to a dull, drenching rain falling outside the bedroom window. I had the memory of thunder in the night and the memory of my daughter's terror, and I continued feeling uneasy, even as I made breakfast for my sleeping children, even as I knew that the things to be afraid of had nothing to do with the night.

*   *   *

George was crossing the yard from the barn when I pulled up to the house. Lugging two canisters of gasoline, one in either hand, he nodded at me, but he was not someone who shouted hellos. Still, I lifted my hand from the steering wheel to show that I'd seen him.

I didn't want to have my clothes soaked, so I figured I'd just wait for Lydie to come outside. George walked toward me through the rain, not lowering his face but grimacing into it. The water ran off his head in little cascades and dripped off his shoulders.

When he got close, I rolled down the window an inch. "What's this about an insurance agent?" he asked, leaning down so his face was close to the glass.

"Oh, you know," I said vaguely.

"No, I don't. You didn't mention it when I saw you—when was it? Friday. You haven't said a thing about it. I don't know what to think." He ran his tongue over his teeth. When he saw my eyes dart past him, his posture changed. Lydie was coming up, shielded by a big black umbrella. She was wearing a Sunday dress and shoes, and she had a Sunday purse at her side.

"Lookit, George," Lydie said, coming up, "you're getting rain all in the car. Poor Hazel, you put that window up now."

"I'll see you, George," I mumbled, and did as Lydie said.

He disappeared around the back of the house without another word. I pulled the car back out onto the lane, and we started down the road. "So we're going to see an insurance agent?"

Lydie nodded. "You wanted to take a trip anyway, get some shopping done in the city. I said I'd go along."

"Isn't that extravagant of us."

"Sure is." She smoothed the skirt of her dress and set her purse down by her feet. "I don't think George believed a word of it. Asked me at least a dozen questions about what and who and why."

I thought for a moment. Her story didn't make much sense to me, either. I had insurance through agents in Edwardsville, just like everyone else. "Why insurance?"

"Oh, I don't know." She sighed. "The only reason anyone ever goes over the river is for hospital visits or funerals, and I was trying to stay away from either of those. Insurance popped into my mind. It could be a different kind you're getting, anyway. Could be you want to add on to what you've got now. You're getting older, you know. Don't want to leave those children with nothing."

I laughed, and so did Lydie. But when I thought about it a moment longer, it didn't seem that funny.

The fastest route to St. Louis took you right through Edwardsville. We chatted about the rain, and then about this and that as I took the turns into town. By the time we'd passed the high school, though, we'd gotten quiet, and I asked if she minded if I turned on the radio. I turned the knob to the country-and-western station I usually listened to in the car. "The Wings of a Dove" was playing, and Lydie smiled and sat back. "I do like this song," she said.

A little while later I looked over and saw that her eyes were closed. I was pretty sure she wasn't sleeping, and I wondered what was filling her mind. I didn't know whether when you were sick, you thought about the big questions, whether you faced the evil possibilities head-on, or if instead you distracted yourself thinking about smaller things: what had happened the day before on your soap opera; how many jars of tomatoes were left in the cellar; how your son had gotten a low score on his last math test, and when he brought it home and you looked over the questions you realized you didn't even know how to begin solving a single one.

The big car rumbled over the road, and I kept both hands firmly on the wheel to keep it moving down the center of the lane. I liked driving, and despite myself, I was looking forward to seeing St. Louis. Two years ago, I'd taken Joe and Debbie and the two Hughes boys to the zoo. George hadn't gone because there was too much work to do, and Lydie had stayed behind because her knee was bothering her and she didn't think she could take the car ride, much less all the walking once we got over there. When we came back, she had a big meal waiting for us, fried chicken and corn on the cob and coleslaw and pie. We loaded up our plates and went outside for a picnic, where she'd spread a few quilts on the grass, and George carried some chairs out from the shed, and we ate while the lightning bugs began twinkling over the lawn. The boys all finished quickly so they could go play. After Debbie was done, she sat cross-legged beside my chair, drinking from a bottle of Coke. Lydie asked her questions about the zoo, and Debbie answered her seriously and deliberately, as if she were being interviewed and wanted to make sure she provided an accurate report.

Nearly two years had passed since that day, but as I drove down the highway with Lydie sleeping in the passenger seat beside me, I thought about how eventually George had coaxed Debbie out into the yard with an empty jar he had on the porch. "You catch a few of them," he said, "and see if you can't take them to the zoo to sell. Last I heard, they're still short on fireflies." I remembered Debbie's look, half doubting yet wanting to believe. Ten minutes later, when she brought him the jar with four or five of the insects batting around inside, George told her he'd take them to the zoo directors the next time he had business across the river.

We hadn't gone inside even as the sun slipped away. The children were all playing, and the three of us sat watching them until at last the mosquitoes got bad, and then we did pack it up. By then none of the bugs in the jar were moving much anymore, but Lydie turned to George and said, "You promised to pay her, now," and a few days later Debbie showed up with a one-dollar bill, and I wasn't ever sure whether it was George or Lydie who had given it to her.

*   *   *

At the hospital, we took the elevator with a doctor who gazed sternly at his own reflection in the brass doors, and two nurses who were gossiping about someone named Helen. Lydie and I stayed quiet, and the nurses talked on as if there were no one else in the elevator with them. I couldn't get over the strangeness of so many white uniforms; it was like finding yourself in a neighborhood of foreigners, with their own customs and ways of speaking and styles of dress. Like the way I felt driving through the colored area of Edwardsville, when I saw the way their clothes hung differently on their bodies, the way they stood outside their houses and shops looking comfortable and at ease with one another, and I understood that among themselves they were different from when they were among white people. An island of outsiders, they turned inward, gathered in around themselves.

Lydie and I were the outsiders here, intruders into a world where bodies were laid out on tables and washed and cut open and then sewn back together, or sent through X-ray scanners with limbs frozen into odd positions. The elevator pinged its way up, from floor to floor, the little lights blinking on and off.

A sign pointed us in the right direction down the hall and we came to a door with several doctors' names on it, including Dr. Brysanski. Inside was a waiting room decorated with bright orange chairs and glass tables with curved corners made of brass. The floor was worn linoleum, yellowish with old wax, but the walls had recently been repainted, and the effect was to make you wonder how long it had been since the floor was that same bright white. There were two large ferns set down in the middle of the space and three chairs between them. No one was sitting in those chairs because it was clear that the ferns would upset your hair. They made a sort of focal point, though, something to stare at from the chairs against the wall.

Four or five other people were sitting in the waiting room, and none looked very sick. I thought they must be waiting for the people who had the appointments. Of course, Lydie didn't look all that sick, either. There was no telling what went on inside a person: we could all of us have a crust of tumors growing, or be living the last day before a heart attack. I hadn't noticed anything different in Karol the day his heart seized up and stopped working.

The people in the waiting room were all city people, wearing smart clothes that looked store-made—clothes that bunched at the shoulders or tapered at the waist an inch too high or too low, with the little refinements and decorations that gave away the proud fact that they were manufactured: piping and serge, two different fabrics miraculously dyed the same shade. All these people were women, save one, and this was a man in a loose suit with his hat set upon his knee.

After Lydie put her name in at the counter, we both took our seats. That day's *Post-Dispatch* was sitting on one of the tables, and I picked it up to give us something to look at besides those ferns. I handed the paper to Lydie, but she shook her head. "You go on and tell me what's new," she said, and glanced again at the door where the nurses went in and out.

"It's going to be all right," I said. In the car, we hadn't talked at all about our reason for going to the city, but now, sitting in the waiting room, I thought about the fact that Lydie had chosen me to come with her and reasoned that it must mean she wanted to talk. Otherwise, she would have driven over here alone. "It'll be just fine," I said, "you'll see."

"Okay."

"They've got methods. Things they can fight it with."

"Things," Lydie repeated. "Far as I know, they've just got the one." She frowned and crossed her arms protectively over her chest. "And I'm not going to do that." A moment later, she smoothed out a wrinkle in her skirt, and I knew that I'd been wrong, thinking she wanted to talk.

The door opened, and a short, boxy-looking nurse with a tall fluff of red hair announced Lydie's name. I patted her arm. She nodded and stood, and followed the nurse to the back, and I was left with the other people in the waiting room, the women in their smart dresses and the man in the ill-fitting suit, who'd glanced up with hopeless dread when the nurse came out, and then returned to looking at his shoes.

After Lydie was gone, I thought about the procedure that she couldn't bring herself to mention. When I tried to place myself in her position— wearing a hospital gown and lying flat on my back, the masked doctors coming at me with knives—it was a horrible image. They took the whole breast and lots of tissue around it. That was all they knew to do. It would be painful to endure the procedure and painful after. But it would be hard, too, leading up to it—I tried to imagine how it would feel to look at my chest for the last time, to know that when I woke up from surgery I'd be wrapped in gauze, wrapped so many times that I wouldn't know, at first, how changed my body was.

I snuck a glance down at my chest. It was not the same bosom I'd had when I was twenty. It was not even the same one I'd had five years ago. Still, some women my age were already grandmothers; though I was forty-seven, I figured my body was still worth something.

When George and I became lovers, I'd figured out for the first time in my life what it was to love without any other goal than to love, and to keep on loving in the way that felt best. With Karol, we'd lived and worked together, and had children, and tried to put up with each other's faults. But with George I understood that when it comes down to it, love is only the stuff of the body. His body, mine. In the three years since we'd begun seeing each other, I had come to love the skin and bone and muscle, the hollows and curves of my own form. My body did not look the same as it had when I was young, but he hadn't loved me when I was young. He'd loved me when I was already heading to fifty.

Lydie was back there with the nurse now, unbuttoning her dress. Don't you touch me, I'd be thinking if I were in her position. Don't you dare take away what is mine.

24

When Lydie came out from seeing the doctor, she glanced around the waiting room, and I saw her register that the man with the hat on his knee was gone. His wife had come out a while before. She was pretty and had little white pointed teeth, but she was bruised-looking, her whole body discolored like an apple turning bad. The man had stood up and his wife had said something like, "Ma's got Annie," to which her husband said, "Yeah." Then they'd walked out into the hall and were gone forever.

"Well?" I asked Lydie.

"Well, it's Bry-SAN-ski, not Brysinski. He told me I was saying it wrong." And she went up to the desk and checked with them about something or other and then came back and said all right, that was it, we could leave.

We went out into the hall and back down toward the elevators, and she didn't say anything. Then we were in the elevator, with other doctors and nurses getting on and off, as they had when we were going up, and still neither of us spoke. One of the two nurses who had ridden up with us before now stood in the corner alone, facing the shiny doors. I knew she must have gotten off the elevator not long after we had, and had done some work and then gotten on it again before us, but I couldn't help but imagine that she'd been standing there the whole time, like it was her fate to ride an elevator up and down forever.

She got off on the third floor, and then Lydie and I got off at the ground floor and went out into the day. The rain had stopped, and the whole sky was a sheet of white, all the light spread out as thin as the glaze on an angel food cake. I squinted and fished in my purse for the car keys. I wouldn't be the first to speak, I decided. If Lydie wanted silence, it was hers to demand.

While I was searching for my keys, she said, "He wants me to come back. I'm supposed to return for a—he didn't say surgery, but that's what it sounds like. They'll take a piece of, of skin or flesh, and study it, and he says that'll decide if it's cancer."

"You made the appointment?"

Lydie nodded. "It's for tomorrow morning. Normally, you've got to wait a lot longer, but the doctor has got some time tomorrow because—I don't know why. But he does. I'm supposed to come here in the morning, at nine a.m. And I'm not supposed to eat or drink anything after nine p.m. tonight. So." Her purse had slipped down her shoulder to her elbow and she pulled it back up. "We should get back, then, I guess."

I was still thinking through what she'd said. "You've got to be back here at nine in the morning?"

"That's right."

"I can take you."

Lydie gave a short nod.

"I think it makes more sense for us to find a hotel rather than drive back home, and then turn around in a few hours and drive right back here again." I started walking toward the parking garage, and Lydie followed. "I guess if we've got to wait," I said as we headed up the sidewalk beside the ramp, "we might as well save some gas."

"I'll pay you for the gas. Don't you worry about that."

"I'm not worried. And you won't be paying for it, either."

"I don't know why—"

"Because I said so, that's why."

A car came rolling slowly down the ramp toward us. As it got closer, I saw that the driver was a colored man in shirtsleeves, with a crumpled-up forehead that almost folded down over his eyes. He looked about our age, and I got the feeling that he had been visiting his wife. In the front seat beside him was his teenage son, whose hair was done in an unusual way that would later become normal, but which at the time grabbed my attention. The hair made a little ball around the boy's head, a few inches long and fuzzy. "Will you look at that?" Lydie said, her voice soft with wonder. "That boy's got a halo around his head."

I laughed. It *did* look like a halo. Though there wasn't anything else particularly angelic-looking about the boy. He had an aggrieved, unhappy look about him. He was dressed in shirtsleeves, like his father, and you got the feeling he didn't normally wear anything so nice and he wasn't happy to be wearing it now. I wondered if his mother was dying, and if it was happening slow enough that he'd had time to feel that it was not only a sad but a tedious business.

The car rolled past us to the parking lot booth. An arm extended out the car window, and another arm came out from the booth window. I could hear drifting from the car the refrains of a doo-wop song, and suddenly I wanted to go somewhere else, to be in a place I'd never been before. "Let's have a night on the town," I said. "We're in the city, we've got time to kill. Let's have ourselves a time." I tried to think of something that would surprise Lydie. "Let's get a pack of cigarettes," I said, "and smoke the whole thing. Every last one, right down to the filter."

Neither of us were smoking women. My sister Edith had taken up the habit a decade before, and Iris would take a cigarette from time to time. They lived in town, and that was the difference. Women who lived in the country didn't smoke. Our men all did, and it was normal for them, but a woman smoking a cigarette seemed strange, like something that only ladies in the movies would do.

"Why don't you call George and tell him we need to stay overnight."

Lydie was rummaging around in her purse, looking for a tissue or a compact. She didn't look up as she said, "And while I'm at it, I'll just mention to him that the pot roast is in the fridge, and it goes well with mashed potatoes and green beans, and how about he makes a cherry pie for dessert." Abruptly she took her hand out from the purse, fastened the snap, and tucked it under her arm. When I didn't say anything, she sighed. "Hazel, the boys'll be wanting to eat, and Lord knows what George would do without me there to get supper on. And what about us? What are we going to do—go out dancing?"

"Why not?"

Lydie shook her head. "I don't think I've danced since, oh, probably around the time we dropped the bomb."

"And you were living in the city then, weren't you? So you should know a good place to go. Come on," I said, taking a few steps down the path, back toward the hospital door. "We're going to make that phone call."

"I just told you—"

"You told me you haven't danced in well over a decade." I strode down the path, thinking Lydie was behind me, but I'd gone several yards when I heard her say, "Well, have *you?*"

I had danced with Karol a year or two before he died. It was in our living room. He'd put a record on and extended a hand to Debbie, formally, and asked her to dance, but she'd been too shy. Let Mommy do it, she'd begged. So he had turned to me and just as gravely asked me to dance over the carpet, over the creaking spots in the floor, with the lamps burning on the end tables and Debbie and Joe both sitting on the sofa, laughing whenever Karol spun me out and then back into his arms. Some sort of magic was in the air and we were all caught up in its spell. I felt the brush of my skirt on my legs, the calloused tips of Karol's fingers pressing my wrists and the back of my neck. I shivered when he did that, feeling suddenly happy with my body, with each bone and muscle—not in the way I would feel later with George, but in the way that I could only feel there, with my husband and our two children, in our home. And when the next song came on, I went over and pulled up Debbie and Joe and the four of us danced in a circle. Afterward, I danced with my son, and Karol spun Debbie—all she wanted to do was spin—and at the end of that song the needle lifted off the record and we all looked around at one another and the magic was gone.

"No," I answered Lydie, lying. "I don't think I've probably danced since I was sixteen. So come on," I said and began walking toward the hospital door again. "There was a pay phone in the lobby. I saw it when we came in."

"A long-distance call . . ."

"Can it, Lydie. I'll lend you the dime."

By the time we went back through the glass doors, I could tell that she was getting into the idea of it. Her eyes were shining as she turned to me. "What in the world do I tell George?"

I thought fast. "Tell him my insurance man needed some paperwork signed and he couldn't possibly get it before tomorrow."

Lydie nodded, as if this made any kind of sense. Then she asked what I was going to do about Debbie and Joe.

"I'll call Rena and tell her I can't get back tonight. She won't mind having them stay over and she can get them off to the bus stop in the morning."

The thing was taking shape, putting on substance. It was no longer a fanciful idea, instead a matter to be planned and figured out. Lydie was looking thoughtful, her eyes disappearing in a squint, but the mention of what I would do with Joe and Debbie must have made her think of the boys because she suddenly shook her head. "What about supper?"

"Haven't you got anything in the freezer?" I'd taken to freezing potpies and hamburgers and stews for those evenings when I was so tired of slopping food onto plates at the cafeteria that the thought of spending any more time in the kitchen at home made me feel sick. And I knew Lydie had a deep freeze, just as I did.

"I do have some meatloaf they could eat. It won't kill them to have a meatloaf sandwich for supper, will it?"

It was clear that she'd made up her mind. We went in through the doors to the bank of pay phones on the wall and I dug around in my bag until I found the change purse at the bottom. Picking up the phone, I called the operator, and in short order the other end was ringing. I handed the receiver to Lydie. George wouldn't know that I was there with her, listening, and it seemed unfair and somehow wrong for that to happen, so I made my way over to the glass entry and stepped out onto the sidewalk.

I stood for a minute listening to traffic on the nearby streets, tires shushing the asphalt still wet from the morning's rain. Somewhere nearby, a truck changed gears. An ambulance wailed and screamed, grew closer, stopped. I turned and saw a young woman making her way up the sidewalk, her hair pushed up under a hat, a newspaper folded under her arm. Something in her gait, grim and determined, made me think she was intent on following through with a task that wouldn't be easy. It could be she was coming to see her husband, who she knew she didn't love as she should. Or a parent who had turned her loose on the world without well wishes or grace. But as she got closer and I saw the expression on her face—pinched with worry, but angry at the same time—I thought it more likely that she was coming to visit a man she had no business visiting. As she approached, she gave me a look that seemed to dare me to ask what she was doing. If George were in the hospital, I realized, I would look the same.

She reached the door, which was propped open, and passed into the lobby, and a moment later Lydie came out. "George didn't answer," she said, "but I called Sally and asked her to pass on the word for me." Sally was a neighbor on the other side of George and Lydie's place. She was the rare woman who truly had no interest in gossip. If she stopped to wonder why Lydie was staying overnight in St. Louis, she wouldn't have asked.

I went inside and placed a call to Rena, who picked up on the second ring and told me not to worry, she'd take care of everything. She would ask questions later; for now it was long-distance, and her curiosity would have to wait to be satisfied.

*   *   *

I didn't quite know what two women could find to do in St. Louis. Years earlier, before we had Joe, Karol and I had gone to the city for a wedding and stayed overnight. It was one of my cousins who'd got married, in a church that surprised me by feeling on the inside almost exactly the same as the one we attended back home, despite the fact that it stood in the shadow of a big warehouse. Afterward, instead of a stand-up snacks-and-lemonade reception in the lobby, the couple held a luncheon at a restaurant down the street. They'd rented out the whole place and the wedding guests filled it to the walls. We were all of us dressed in our good clothes, the women in sugary pastels, the men with fresh-looking shirts and jackets that creaked when they moved their arms. I had on a dark red dress I hadn't worn since before the war. It had seemed all right that morning when Iris and Walt picked us up at the house and we'd all driven out through town, down the highway, and over the wide river until the city raised its black arms around us. Once we got to the restaurant, though, the dress seemed a bit shabby. The woman our cousin was marrying worked in the accessories department at Famous-Barr, and many of her friends at the wedding were single girls who worked with her on the floor. They all had chic haircuts that made their heads look like they were resting on a half-shell, and they wore frothy dresses in every pale shade of pink, green, or blue. They were women of a type I wasn't used to seeing in the world, women whose hands danced bird-like through the air as they spoke, women with fluty laughs and sharp glinting eyes.

Next to those women, I could practically feel the dust sifting down from the folds of my dress, which was not cut simply enough to pass for new. It had a small crocheted lace collar and loose sleeves that ended just above the elbow at a cuff. The dresses the Famous-Barr ladies wore all had straight sleeves that went to a point halfway between the elbow and wrist, and I could see plainly the beauty of this style, how it made their arms look thin, and the simplicity of the cut made the color seem expensive. They were all beautiful as butterflies, lit on their chairs at the tables spread around the restaurant. I'd looked at them and thought, I am out of my league.

I had this thought again as Lydie and I stood on the sidewalk in front of the hospital, trying to figure out where to go to have a good time. It felt like we were holding something precious and dangerous and wild, like we'd had a monkey shipped over from Africa and had to figure out what to do with it.

"I tell you what," I said at last. "Why don't we ask where a good hotel is, and a restaurant. We'll take ourselves out to dinner, have a real night out on the town."

Lydie lifted her brows. "You know better than me."

Not one hour later, we'd settled into our room at the Drake-Anders, a small place on Hickory Street. It had been two separate row houses until sometime in the 1930s, when the walls were knocked down and a few more bathrooms put in, and now it was a hotel, not too chic, not too squalid, either. We didn't have our own bathroom, but the one across the hall was reserved for ladies. The room itself had a vanity with a mirror, which was enough for our purposes: between the two of us, we had two combs and a tube of lipstick.

It was barely afternoon. We weren't in the hospital any longer, but the sense of it was still with us: the long halls with hollow footfalls. It made me think we needed to get out of that room as quickly as possible.

Out on the street in search of a place to go, Lydie started telling me a story about a time years before, when Bobby wasn't born yet and Gene was just a few months old. He couldn't crawl, not quite, though felt certain he should, so when you set him on the ground he would lunge his top half forward, again and again, until he lunged to one side and fell over. "Oh, it was funny," Lydie said. "Sometimes George and I would nearly die laughing when we saw him do it." Then they'd set him upright again and he'd topple again. And again and again. You remember, Lydie said. I was walking beside her down the sidewalk, ducking the drips of rain from awnings overhead—it had rained again while we were settling in at the hotel—and at the same time I was keeping a lookout for a bar where we could go in and get ourselves a drink. I remember, I said.

Well, George's uncle died and he had to go down to Louisville for the funeral. He took a bus and left Lydie alone with their son for three days.

It was just him and her in the house, and he'd squawk if she didn't let him down on the ground, then he'd tip over and he'd squawk at that, too. Now when he fell, though, Lydie wouldn't laugh. She'd sit him upright and move away, out of sight. He could only twist his neck around so far, and he'd end up falling again, and sometimes she left him that way and he'd cry, but he managed all right. They'd laid down some carpeting in the sitting room and though the floor was cold in the winter, it wasn't frigid.

She began leaving the room. She'd go into the kitchen and wash dishes: the sound of the running water covered Gene's cries. She'd go outside and stamp around in the frozen grass. She'd wander out to the road and keep watch for anyone coming or going.

"Then it came to me that I could just leave him like that and he'd be fine—thirty minutes, an hour. The worst he could do was cry and mess himself."

By this point Lydie and I were sitting at a bar down the street from the hotel, and this story, which was getting more detailed by the minute, no longer sounded true. I'd known Lydie for years, and she'd never said anything about it. I didn't remember George leaving her alone for three days with their baby, either. But it had the tone of a confession, and I didn't stop her from giving it.

We were sipping gin fizzes. I don't think she had ever had gin before because when she took her first drink, her whole head jerked back as if she'd been slapped. I asked her if she wanted to order something else, and she shook her head. She took another drink, this time steeling herself for the taste, her mouth set in a grim line and her eyes fixed on some point on the wall behind the bar. That wall was painted a shade of red that made you think of lipstick and fingernail polish. It must have taken ten coats. It looked like if you pressed on it, you'd leave a dent.

"Anyway," Lydie said, "one day he was squawking, so I set him down, and then I went outside and got in the car and drove off."

She had both hands around the glass in her hand and she was talking in a sort of daze, like she'd done the week before, talking about Paris. "You could've driven over to our place," I offered. "I would've been glad to see you."

"Without Gene, you would have? I show up at your house and you say, hello, and where's your baby? And I tell you I left him sitting on the living room floor? Oh, sure, I can just imagine *that*." Lydie was staring at the red wall again, and I looked at it, too, as she went on. "I drove all the way up to Alton that day. I hadn't planned on it, but once I was driving I needed a place to go, and I kept heading up the highway. After a half hour or so, I looked around and saw where I was, and I decided I wanted to keep going and drive up to see that Indian rock painting they have. You know the one?"

I had heard of it—some painting on the bluffs up north of Alton; there was an Indian myth about the magical bird that it depicted, but I was fuzzy on the details. I took another sip of my drink. It was down to the ice, and I wasn't certain if Lydie would want another. I thought I'd better take my time and swirl it around a little, make the ice cubes dance. But Lydie paused her story to call the bartender over. She ordered a sherry for herself and another gin fizz for me. "I must have read about it in the paper," she went on as the bartender began to fix our drinks. "I never had been up there or given it a single thought. But once I realized I was driving north, I figured I might as well make it my destination."

Just then, I heard the door open and turned to see three men in vests and shirtsleeves looking for a place to sit. Several small tables lined one wall and most of them were free, but we were sitting at the center of the bar, taking up room. Lydie twisted around on her stool to see what had grabbed my attention. When she turned back, her face was tight. We weren't women who drank at bars, and we weren't used to sitting close to men who weren't known to us in some way—known, at least, in the way that every farmer's wife knows a farmer when she sees one. If those three men had been dressed in blue jeans and muddy boots with bits of hay stuck to their shirts, if they'd had creased skin at the backs of their necks, then we would have known how to read them in an instant. They would have sat at the bar, all in a row, but their talk would have been quiet and slow. Whole minutes might have passed without them saying a thing, and when the bartender asked what they wanted, they'd have told him he might as well go ahead and bring them some beers.

These men were not of that type. They were speaking in the way of a swing band—all at once and fast, but somehow blending together. The shortest of the men was standing a little forward of the others, and I knew he was the one who would make the decisions. I saw his eyes slide over Lydie and me: he didn't think we were much worth looking at— too old, too weather-beaten. But he walked up to the bar, nodding toward his friends to show that they should follow, and he put both hands on the wooden surface and craned his neck forward to get a good look at the bottles on the shelf.

I leaned in toward Lydie. "You were telling me about the drive you took up to Alton."

She gave me a startled look. "Oh, why, I guess . . ." She stopped and pressed her mouth into a line. The short man was standing right behind her, asking the bartender about some particular whiskey he wanted and didn't see on the shelf.

"Don't you mind them," I said in a low voice. "Did you ever see it— the painting?"

The bartender, who was doing his best to answer the man's questions about which liquors they had in stock and to listen as he explained why the one he wanted was superior to all others, had finally finished making our drinks. He slid them in front of us and took away our empty glasses at the same time.

Lydie considered her drink. "I found it, but it's not exactly a bird they have painted there. Looks more like a dragon, scales and all. The Piasa Bird, that's what it's called."

"What's it mean?" I asked. "Piasa."

"'Bird That Devours Men.' That's what I heard," the short man interjected. "I've got a friend went up to see it." He'd turned, his shoulders steering his body toward us, and he looked like he wanted to wink. Instead he just smiled. "Sorry to jump in. I'm a nosy son of a gun."

"That's all right," I said, and Lydie nodded. This was all part of some script. We'd come to a bar to talk to some men, and here we were talking. "You haven't seen it yourself?"

"I try to stay this side of the river." He took a step away to retrieve his drink from the bar, and one of his friends grabbed the opportunity to step into the space and widen it into a circle.

"What's that mean?" his friend asked in a grinning way. "You got something against Illinois, Wendell?"

The short man shrugged. "Nothing against it. Just nothing for it much, either." He stopped to look at Lydie and me, raised one hand like a policeman, and cocked his head. "You aren't from over there, are you? 'Cause if so, I've stepped in it."

"You've stepped in it," I said.

"Now, me," the friend said, "I've got family over in your parts. In Gravois?"

Lydie explained that it was a little northward, and then glanced at me as if she thought she needed my agreement for the men to believe her. I took a sip of my drink and asked the friend if he'd ever been there.

He told us he hadn't, but he wouldn't mind going sometime. Lydie and I didn't know what to say to that. He was an unremarkable-looking man in every way, except that his ears stuck out from his head so far they looked like they could pick up radio signals from New York. Still, he was fun to talk to. He was a man and a stranger, and there was something reassuring about the fact that he looked like Dopey from Disney's *Snow White*.

"So what are you all doing in St. Louis?" This came from the short man—Wendell. He pulled two cigarettes from a pack and handed one to Lydie and one to me. She took the cigarette and rested it between two fingers; I laid mine on the bar. After Wendell had lit everyone else's cigarettes, he glanced at the one I'd laid down and put his matches back in his pocket.

"We came in to do some shopping," I said, figuring this would hold no interest for any of them. But Wendell asked where we'd been, and without waiting for an answer, proceeded to explain the best areas to go. "You've got the Famous-Barr down on Locust," he said, "but my wife, she likes Stix better for clothes. You're going clothes shopping, I guess?"

Lydie nodded, looking relieved. He'd mentioned his wife, which meant we could talk now without worrying about where any of it was heading. "I'd like to get a couple new dresses," she said suddenly, as if this shopping expedition were an actual thing. She held her cigarette out and stared at its burning end. "You wouldn't believe how long it's been since I did something like that."

"You better get yourself down to Stix, then. Don't you think that's the best place for them to go, boys?"

They were married, all three of them, and that made it easier to fall into conversation. Wendell talked the most; Dopey followed along and chimed in now and then; the third man lifted his chin whenever he was called upon to agree with something that either of the other two said. He had the air of a man who knows he's good-looking and doesn't have to do much to win approval.

Lydie and I were the audience. When asked a question, we got no more than a sentence or two in before Wendell took up the baton and off he ran. Neither of his friends got more than two words in, either.

The conversation went on that way for a while. Lydie finished her cigarette and took another when Wendell offered it. I'd polished off my second drink and needed something to do with my hands, so I picked up the cigarette he'd given me earlier and held it out to be lit.

"This isn't your brand," he said as he struck a match, protecting the flame with a cupped hand and extending it toward me. Lydie cocked her head at his tone, which suggested a certain confidence between him and me that left her out of the conversation. She turned away on her stool to talk to Dopey; his name was George, it had turned out.

"You're right," I said to Wendell, "I never smoke Marlboros."

"What do you like? What kind?"

"None of them, much."

He raised his eyebrows. "You all grow your own tobacco out there?" Lydie and I had told him we were neighbors, and then it had come out that we owned land and that land was farmed. We didn't tell him it was Lydie's husband who did it all. Somehow, Wendell seemed to think we were like those landowners you read about in old novels of the South, the two of us sitting beneath giant trees on a green lawn, batting silk fans about our faces and drinking iced tea. "You roll your own cigarettes," he went on teasingly, "just the way you want them, or what?"

I looked at the cigarette in my hand, pinched between my thumb and forefinger, the way George would hold it. I had a vision of him squinting out at the flat horizon a long way off over the honey-gold acres. There was no imagining him into the dandified clothes of a southern gentleman; it was muddy work pants and a worn shirt, the edges frayed and yellow patches under the arms. Then the image clicked over, and it was Karol standing there, shoulders sloped at a steeper angle toward the ground. He'd had a way of holding himself that looked like he was tipping forward a little, about to set off at a determined walk, even when he was standing perfectly still. I thought of him lifting the cigarette to his lips, taking a long pull of smoke into the lungs, and I did the same now. "To tell you the truth," I said, the smoke swirling around in my head, "I haven't smoked a cigarette since I was a girl."

"I guess it's a city habit. My mother, you should see her, she gets her next one started before she's ever finished with the first. Sit with her an hour, and the ashtray's filled up like a planter." Wendell shook his head. "But she's particular about her cigarettes, won't smoke anything but Chesterfields. You try to offer her a Marlboro, and the look on her face could freeze your blood."

I pictured her tall, one of those big-boned women who've learned that it's better to stand up straight than try to slouch and look smaller, and so is always looking down from a high perch at nearly everything around her. She is the type of woman who'll hold her cigarette down by her hip when she isn't pulling in smoke, the type of smoker who never coughs. And the haze around her seems to come from her very self, as if she has molten lava moving through her veins rather than blood.

Wendell tipped his chin back. "You and your friend don't look like you spend too many afternoons like this."

"Like this, how?"

"Having a drink, chatting up strangers."

"Seems to me that you're the ones chatting us up."

"All in the way you see it, I guess." He grinned, a sly grin that said, *Now we're getting somewhere.* When he wasn't smiling, he had a glint in his eye like polished steel. The grin turned it into a twinkle; it made him look boyish and daring. He kept looking at me as he took a drink from his glass. It was half full of whiskey, and suddenly I wanted to drink something like that, smooth and burning, a sort of wonderful punishment.

"Why don't you buy me a drink," I said. "Whatever you've got."

He grinned again, but let it linger past its natural end, and the twinkle in his eye turned into a blue spark that flashed bright and cold, and then was gone. "What I've got here is an Old Forester, and it's a double." He gestured to the bartender to order two more.

The whiskey came, and I took a searing drink of it. It brought me back to when I was young and loved nothing more than to go out dancing, and someone would bring along a flask to pass around. No one ever asked what it was, or cared, and though I could tell that what I was drinking now was better than that moonshine had been, it was similar enough to give me the same thrill, the same feeling that I was right up close to the line of abandon, if only I cared to step over it. I took another sip and said to Wendell, "You're particular in your choice of liquor."

"I'm particular in my choice of all sorts of things," he responded, but with a lift at the corner of his mouth that said he knew I'd expected him to say it. We were fast getting to that place of speaking on different levels at once. I took another drink and looked coolly around the bar. Big-Eared George had finally taken a seat next to Lydie, and the man he and Wendell had come in with was drawn into their circle at last. He was telling a story, and Lydie and Big-Eared George both had their faces tipped up at him like children looking to their father. Her cheeks were flushed, and she had the sort of loose smile that comes on with a few drinks and stays until a few drinks more. It's a smile that looks fluttering somehow, stretching and then contracting as a flag flaps with the wind.

I had never seen this smile on Lydie's face before. She was having fun; she was happy. And it wasn't the happiness of a mother or a wife, whose happiness is like the cold spot in a lake: something you might swim through and not quite notice. It was the kind of happiness you feel often when you're young, and rarely after you're grown, a feeling that takes over the whole body, that makes you want to kiss your own hand.

I wanted that feeling. What I had instead was sharp-edged and dangerous. I could do a mean thing, I thought, or a reckless one. The flirtation between Wendell and me didn't have to go anywhere, but I wanted it to. I wanted to put someone at risk, me or him, it didn't matter. I finished my drink and tapped the rim with my finger, and as the bartender took a clean glass from the rack and began fixing me another, I leaned toward Wendell and asked if he wanted to know a secret.

"Boy, do I ever."

Well, who has ever said no to that question?

*　　*　　*

Later, when Lydie was sick—sick in more visible ways, sick enough that she wasn't getting out of bed much anymore—she would ask me sometimes if I remembered that afternoon at the bar. I couldn't tell what she was up to. That day, with her talking to Big-Eared George and the other man, whose name I never did catch, and me talking to Wendell a few feet away, could she have heard what I said? I'd been drinking, and I might have spoken louder than I intended. It was possible, but I didn't think so. By the time I got around to telling Wendell that I was sleeping with Lydie's husband, once it got to the actual moment of revelation, a kind of sober clarity settled over me. It was as if we were all eggs in a box, each of us set down in exactly the right place, so that the mold fit over us just as it should. In other words, I'd waited a long time to let my secret fly, and when the opportunity came, I took it.

Had Lydie heard? I couldn't recall any particular clue. What I remembered was a plank of light from the front window that fell over the floor and went halfway up the legs of the nameless man. Lydie, seated on her stool, had only her feet dipped into the amber glow. The afternoon was turning to evening, and soon we would stumble back to the hotel in the violet dusk, with the streetlights winking on at the moment we turned the corner and left Lafayette Square behind. But that hadn't happened yet, and for now it seemed that this afternoon would go on forever. We'd both left our true selves behind, in the hospital or at the hotel, or maybe back over the river in Illinois, and the different women we were pretending to be existed in some other world, outside of time, like in one of those science fiction novels Debbie started reading a few years later.

I was watching Lydie and the two men, and somehow I was able to view her as if she were a stranger: a middle-aged woman with a slack middle and brown arms, laughing a little too loud. She might have been someone who came to a bar like this every afternoon to see where the evening would take her. There was a kind of nervous hilarity about her mouth, which was opened wide enough to show that the inside of her lips was a different color than the outside; her lipstick had worn away. This was the same Lydie who'd told a rambling tale of taking a drive and leaving her baby all alone for an afternoon. She'd told it because she felt guilty, I figured, but we'd never got to that part.

Now I told Wendell a shortened version of my own tale of sin, and I didn't leave out the best parts, or the worst parts, either. When I was done, he said, "I take it you didn't bring that gal over the river just to break the news. Seems like a waste of a trip, if you did." He took a sip of his drink. "And a pretty long car ride back home."

I was silent, thinking of the hospital: the doctors and nurses, the rattling carts in the hallways, the squeaky shoes on linoleum.

"So, Hazel, what *are* you doing here?"

I blinked at the invitation in his voice and then turned my face to the door. It had opened to release a few patrons out into the dusk. "That's another story."

He laughed once, sharply. "I'd bet a thousand bucks it's not."

I've made some mistakes in my time, but at least I can say this: I've told nobody's secrets but my own. If Lydie didn't want people to know she was sick, I wasn't going to be the one to let it slip. I told Wendell that it was exactly as we said before: my friend and I had come to St. Louis to buy ourselves some pretty clothes, to have a few drinks, to have a good time.

"Those last two I'd say you've done pretty well." He nodded at Lydie, who had laid her head on Big-Eared George's shoulder, and looked close to falling off her stool. "But let me give you a word of warning about those good times."

"What's that?"

He tapped two fingers on the side of his glass. "They aren't hard to come by"—we both drained the last of our drinks—"but, Hazel, they sure are damn hard to keep."

*   *   *

Two days later, George came walking up to the house. I saw him from the living room window and went outside to meet him on the lawn. Lydie and I had got back the evening before. She was sore and groggy from the procedure she'd had done, and though I'd offered to help her into the house, she'd waved me away. They'd taken a little piece of her breast, and they were going to sample it to find out if it was cancer. All the hilarity of the day before was gone. It had been gone by the time we got back to our hotel.

George had thunder in his footsteps, and his face was pinched and red. I'd never seen him this way before. "I thought it was you that was sick," he said without any other word of greeting. "That story about insurance didn't make sense at all. I thought you were sick, and Lydie was taking you to a doctor."

I didn't say anything.

"You left, and I spent all day worried. I was worried about *you*." He almost spat out the word. "Then you get back last night, and she comes in all bandaged up. I don't see it till we're getting into bed. 'What's that,' I say, and she tells me it's nothing." He had his hands in his pockets, and I suspected he might ball his hands into fists if they weren't contained that way. He shot a glance behind me at the house. Debbie was inside, watching television. Joe had gone down the road to George and Lydie's place a little while before. I figured the windows were empty, reflecting nothing but sunlight and shadows. "I thought you were sick, and it made me crazy," George said now, his voice suddenly drained of emotion. "Now I figure it's Lydie, and I don't know what to think."

I didn't speak for a moment. I'd made a promise I wasn't going to say anything about it to George or to anyone. "You better talk to her," I said at last.

"What did I just tell you?" He took his hands out of his pockets and removed his hat, smoothed his hair down, put the hat back on his head.

"George," I said in a quiet, firm voice, "this isn't my business."

"The hell it's not. You're the one that drove her over there."

"She asked me to."

He was silent for a minute, or longer. Once, he craned his neck around at the far-off bark of a dog. When he turned back again, his face looked as if all the muscles it contained had collapsed, all the strain gone out of them at once. A slug of snot was creeping from his nose, and he leaned over and blew it onto the ground. For a moment I thought he was crying, and then I wasn't so sure. When he stood up straight, he said, "She had an aunt that died of it. Her grandmom, too."

"Then you know more than me," I said.

"I don't know a thing."

He waited to see if I'd respond, and when I didn't, he tipped his cap in farewell and turned and walked away. It had been more than a week since we'd been together. I watched him go, thinking: feet, hips, shoulders, head. He was all of his parts moving off down the lane. He was a body taking itself away from me for good.

Juanlan

25

An affair, then. They meet once a week, sometimes twice, in a tiny rented room above a noodle shop near the bus station. The noodle shop is owned by one of Director Wei's friends, a cheerful half-Tibetan man named Qiang Ba. This friend is married, but his wife and two children live in a village up in Aba Zhou. There is no female presence in the shop, save a slightly faded photograph of a woman standing in grasslands covered in white and blue wildflowers. She looks full Tibetan—her cheeks stained a deep red, silver dangling from her ears, and a string of heavy beads hanging down over her T-shirt—and without ever asking, Juanlan knows this is Qiang Ba's wife, and that he loves her deeply. She looks at the image every time she comes in; it is stuck to the wall without any frame or protection, and a fine layer of grease makes it seem as if it is part of the plaster behind it. The woman might be a deity of some kind, perhaps Guanyin herself, the goddess of mercy, and her mercy extends to the little room above, and to everything that goes on there without any questions asked. Qiang Ba himself has a mistress, Juanlan knows. Director Wei informed her of this fact one day when she made a comment about how his friend must miss his wife, living far away and only going home at the New Year. Director Wei had seemed annoyed by her observation, perhaps even jealous. "He's got a second woman here," he told her, digging a cigarette out of its case and lighting it with a match. "Just some shopgirl at the Hualian Supermarket."

"Do they use this room, too?" She'd glanced around at the bare walls. The room is clean and undecorated. The only color comes from the bedspread, which has a pattern of giant red roses splashed across a yellow background.

"Of course not. I pay rent on this place. Qiang Ba has nothing to do with it."

But of course he does. The first time Juanlan showed up—following the directions that Director Wei had told her over the phone the day before—Qiang Ba gave her a friendly grin and begged her to have a seat, looking all around for the best spot, even though the whole place was empty. The best spot was a seat that allowed an easy view of the black-and-white television set on a cabinet in the corner. It was tuned to the CCTV version of *Romance of the Three Kingdoms* and the volume was off, but Juanlan watched as Qiang Ba fixed her a bowl of noodles. She'd never seen noodles like these before, little flat bits of dough that he pinched off with his fingers and dropped into the pot at a rapid pace. The broth had onions in it, and thin slices of potato, too. Juanlan felt she was far away from Heng'an.

She was grateful that he didn't ask any questions or make remarks about why she was there. He sat with her through the end of the episode, then showed her the staircase, accessible from a tiny room filled with rolls of toilet paper and empty boxes. "Next time, you can just go on up," he said. "No need to ask first."

The rented room has two separate entrances, the one through the shop and another from the alley, which means she and Director Wei never have to be seen entering or leaving together. It is the perfect place for an affair, very discreet. Of course she is not the first woman to do this.

The fact doesn't bother her much. What is between them is new, whether or not there have been others. I am a mistress, Juanlan thinks, standing before the mirror over the sink in the tiny bathroom. A second woman. She turns to the side and considers herself from that angle. Then there is a sound from the other room, Director Wei turning a key in the deadbolt, and she narrows her eyes at her own reflection and goes out to greet him.

*　　*　　*

Soon after the start of the affair, Teacher Cao leaves to take Wei Ke up to Chengdu for school. There is a farewell dinner, to which Juanlan is invited, but she feigns being sick to avoid the event: her precedence over the other woman is better enjoyed from a distance. And, too, she would rather not sit at a table with her lover's family, to hear the wife thank her for attentions to her son. The tutoring has helped, a little: Wei Ke is not quite so terrible at English as he was before, though he hates it as much

as ever. During the final few days, Juanlan made him write and then
recite a two-page essay on any topic related to the English-speaking
world, and he wrote about how the spread of English-language instruction around the globe was a sign of modern imperialism. It was
a sophisticated topic, if handled simply. Juanlan taught him words like
dominant and *colonialism*. He was unable to pronounce most of them;
nevertheless, she was proud of his progress.

The very day of his wife and son's departure, Director Wei asks
Juanlan to meet at the usual place. He has a surprise, he says, that he
hopes she will like very much.

Of course it is lingerie. She has never worn lingerie, never owned
a bra that wasn't white or pale pink and very simple in construction.
This is what mistresses do. When she goes to the flat above the noodle
shop, she finds waiting for her a red bag stuffed with tissue paper, which
weighs almost nothing. It reminds her, oddly, of the money envelopes
she still receives at the New Year from her parents and grandparents,
and it occurs to her that Director Wei went to the trouble not only of
buying it but also of coming to the flat to place it here in advance. This is
thoughtfulness, romance. It is the reward for being the second woman
instead of the first.

Inside the bag, she finds two small slips of translucent fabric in a
shade of purplish pink found only in tropical flowers and birds. Juanlan
holds them up in the light from the window, dangles them from one
finger. The wrapping on the gift suggests that it is from an expensive shop. Perhaps this contributes to the effect, because once she has
tugged the tiny panties into place and hooked the see-through top over
her breasts, she finds that she is a little excited. Turned on, as Director
Wei would say. Since he is not here, she puts her hand over the underwear and presses against her own fingers, and in this way is satisfied
more quickly than she would have thought possible. When Director
Wei arrives, she says, "I couldn't wait," and, turning onto her side,
trails her hand up over her stomach. "I got so excited, expecting you,
that I touched myself."

A look crosses his face: she has surprised him, embarrassed him. It is
good to know that she can do this. "I see it fits you."

She shifts position, glancing down at the garment, which has fallen away to reveal her bare hip. Lying this way, her waist comes into definition in a way it never does in any other position, standing or sitting or lying on her back. It shows her at her best, closer to how she would like to look all the time. Even a few weeks into their relationship, she is learning to view herself from this other perspective, and to see how it is changeable, how the image can be molded and altered with subtle movements: During sex, she is aware of how her lips part, and she tries to hold up her chin so her neck appears thin. But during those times when Director Wei touches her for her own pleasure only, she understands that abandonment is what is required. She is allowed to be ugly then, and afterward, she is not ashamed but grateful. In those moments, she thinks she may be falling in love.

Director Wei takes a step toward the bed, and then another. "Yes, it fits you well," he repeats with a look on his face that is both vulnerable and eager. "Do you like it?"

"Yes."

"You look sexy. Like a movie star."

She holds out a hand. "I didn't do a good job before. Please, come and help me."

The sex is different this time, Director Wei taking her very quickly and pushing into her with such force that she feels her pelvic bones ache. But she is ready for him, and it feels good, if only because she can tell that he wants her more than usual. It is the first time they complete the act without a condom, and there is no discussion beforehand—when he is close, she puts her hands on the backs of his thighs and keeps him inside. Afterward, he pulls away to lie on his back beside her. This is their normal position after making love, not tender but restful. She hooks her legs over his waist, waiting, because after he's been satisfied, sometimes he wants to please her, too. "Go clean yourself off," he says without looking at her. Stung, she rises from the bed, avoids touching him in any way, and heads to the toilet.

When she comes back into the room, he is dressed and seated in a chair at the small table under the window. He gives her a steady look and then busies himself with another cigarette. He's already smoked one, she notes; the butt is in the ashtray. "Have a seat," he says, gesturing toward the bed.

Something in her resists this particular demand, and she leans against the wall, arms crossed over her chest. "You're upset," she says.

"No." He shakes his head. "No, I'm not upset. But I need to know—do you wear a ring?"

He is speaking of the birth control device that is placed deep inside the body, the one that is left there. Juanlan doesn't know any girls her age who have one, and she tells him so. "That's a difficulty," she says. "I don't get the free family planning, you know."

"A difficulty? I should think an abortion would be more trouble."

"Yes, probably." She doesn't say, *You would be the one to pay for it.* "It was only this one time, though. And I don't think—it's not the most dangerous time right now."

He nods slowly. His gaze has settled on her, seemingly without any thought. He might be staring absentmindedly at a picture on the wall, if there were any to stare at. "But there may be other times," he says, and then glances up abruptly. "I haven't been sterilized. My wife was the one to do it, after Wei Ke was born."

Juanlan ignores this reference to his wife. "You'd like me to get the ring?"

"I'll give you the money for it."

Her eyes go to the window, which is opened to allow in some fresh air. She can barely make out the sound of Qiang Ba's voice, greeting a customer. "Someone might recognize me at the clinic."

"You'll go to a different place. I have a friend at Number Two People's Hospital who will perform the favor. He's very discreet."

The next day, Juanlan goes alone to the hospital on the other side of town. In the instant that the doctor places the device, she feels her uterus contract, and she squeezes her eyes shut against the pain. "You may have severe cramps for the next day or two," the doctor says, nearly the only words he speaks during the short encounter. Juanlan pays with the money that Director Wei has given her.

Back home, she tells her mother she has a stomachache and goes to lie down. She is brought ginger tea and, later, plain congee. "What have you been eating at Ting-Ting's house?" her mother asks, shaking her head. Ting-Ting is one of a number of old schoolmates Juanlan uses to explain her absences.

Director Wei doesn't call. She stays in bed, curled up around the throbbing pain at her center, and they don't see each other again while his wife is away. A week later, when they meet at the flat, she wonders if sex will be different now. But it is the same as before. The only change is that after they're done, Director Wei produces three hundred-yuan notes from his wallet. "For the trouble," he says, and she doesn't hesitate to accept them.

*   *   *

A month, then two, and in this way autumn passes, and then it is winter. On the first truly cold day, Lulu has her baby. Wearing a heavy padded jacket, Juanlan goes to the hospital and coos over her new niece. How beautiful, she says. In truth, the baby is squashed-looking and splotchy. Juanlan is surprised by the stab of feeling she has for it—her very own blood. She's never visited anyone who's just given birth and is surprised to see that Lulu, beneath the heavy sweater and blankets, still looks pregnant.

Her sister-in-law sighs. "The doctor says it may take several months before my stomach gets flat again. I'll probably be fat forever." She looks down at the baby with something like curiosity. They have not named it yet, and for Juanlan, at least, this makes it difficult to think of the child as a person.

"How do you feel?"

"Tired." Lulu yawns grandly. In her arms, the baby's whole body rises and falls with her intake of breath, but its eyes stay tightly shut. "Also, though—like I'm floating. I've barely slept in three days. She nurses all the time, so even if I fall asleep, a half hour later I have to wake up again."

"And my brother—"

"He's been very good. Zhuo is happy to be the father of a little girl."

"What about you?"

Lulu looks at her evenly. "I'm happy, too."

It's been more than two months since Rob left Heng'an. He is back in America now, though Juanlan isn't sure whether he will stay there or go out traveling again. Before he left, he promised to write with news of the travel guide. So far, he's written once, and with no news of that kind. He reported that he arrived home in late September, that the rest of his time in China was uneventful. Then he said that his father had died, and he's been busy sorting out the sale of his half of the farm to his brother. He'd never said anything about being a farmer. Though she knows that it's different in America, she can't help but picture him stooping in a field of cabbages, a basket strapped to his back. She has no doubt that he will forget them all easily. They will fade in his memory until they blend with the other Chinese he met, appearing only between the lines of the guidebook's entry on Heng'an, in the write-up of the Three Springs Hotel and the recommendation of various restaurants he visited.

As for Lulu, she says she is happy, and Juanlan believes her. Or if not happy, then occupied. That was the problem before—she was bored. She had too many lonely hours in her possession and needed to give them away.

"Come look," Lulu says, beckoning. "Her eyes are open."

Juanlan stands and looks down at her niece. In the tiny face, two narrow lines glimmer wetly. The eyes seem unfocused, and the baby's whole face is turned toward Lulu's with a searching expression. "She knows you're her mother."

"She just knows I'm the one who feeds her." Glancing up, Lulu says suddenly, "Do you know, I didn't feel afraid until we went to the hospital. That whole time—all those months—I never felt afraid."

She's telling the truth, Juanlan thinks. "How do you feel now?"

Lulu runs a finger over the features of her daughter's face. "Terrified," she says.

*   *   *

Juanlan spends part of every day at her brother and sister-in-law's flat, helping cook and clean, helping to swaddle the baby and walk her around when she's crying, though Lulu always takes her back quickly.

Not with jealousy or disapproval, but as if she's not sure how to move without her, as if the baby is an extension of her own body, an extra limb. She and Zhuo Ge have no one staying with them; Lulu's mother is unwell in some way that no one has ever explained to Juanlan, and did not even come to Heng'an for the birth. "Xiao Lu should have someone there with her," her mother has said. "How is she supposed to learn how to care for a baby on her own?" Lulu herself is satisfied not to host anyone. She welcomes Juanlan's help but doesn't seem to require it. Of the advice that Juanlan's mother gives, Lulu says, "I just nod and say, 'Ma, you're so smart, you know exactly what to do' and then when she turns around I do it my way instead."

Things between her and Juanlan are not quite the same as they were before, in those months when Lulu was pregnant and unhappy, when Juanlan was newly back in Heng'an. What is different now is that Lulu is content. She is fascinated by her daughter and likes to talk about all the little changes that occur in her. At a week, they talk about her peeling skin. At two weeks, Lulu describes her new habit of staying awake through long hours of the night. At three weeks, Juanlan and Lulu stand in the bathroom together, Lulu holding her daughter over the squat toilet and making shushing noises in her ear. "You can start anytime," she says of the toilet training. "Even if your mother thinks it's too early to try."

Juanlan has no opinion on the matter, though she likes that Lulu does. Where before, her sister-in-law was angry but passive, now she enters fights with a joyful glint in her eye. It is the difference between resistance and open rebellion. "You should do what feels right," Juanlan tells her. "What worked for my mother might not work for you."

"That's the way of all of them," Lulu says.

"Who is 'them'?"

Lulu pulls her daughter back to her chest and stands. As they leave the bathroom, she replies, "Everyone who is older than us."

A new idea. Rob was older, yet Lulu seemed to listen to what he had to say. Juanlan asks whether she considers Zhuo Ge part of this category.

"Oh, he's all right," Lulu says. Crossing to the window, she points to the decorative red knot dangling from the top of the frame. She reaches up and brushes the tassels to make them swing and then glances down at her daughter's face to see if her eyes have followed the movement. "Zhuo lets me do as I please with the baby. But your mother, my aunts, all the neighbors"—she tips her head at the door—"their advice is old-fashioned. People of that generation are terrified of anything changing from the old ways."

Juanlan thinks of Director Wei, who is between her age and that of her parents. On which side does he fall in this divide? Is he old-fashioned or does he act in modern ways? Affairs outside marriage are not a new thing, of course, but Juanlan's feeling about their relationship might be new. Only a modern woman would do as she has done and take pride in it, and this must make Director Wei a little modern, too. He has chosen her, after all. He wanted her for a reason.

She has kept the secret of their affair for three months. She could tell no one but Lulu, anyway—nobody else would understand—yet she has always hesitated to speak. From incidental comments her sister-in-law has made, it's clear that she does not like Director Wei. And there is this, too: Lulu came up to the bridge, but she never crossed it. Since Rob's departure from Heng'an, she has spoken of him occasionally without any difficulty. She has fond memories of the foreigner, she's said. It was fun having him here. Remember how helpless he was, like a little baby? How he couldn't say anything, understand anything?

She likes a person, Juanlan thinks, who is fresh to the world.

This is how she knows she won't tell Lulu about the affair. Because Director Wei is not that kind of person at all; he wrests from the world what he wants because he knows it well. He is powerful. And being the thing that he wants gives Juanlan some measure of power, too.

*   *   *

"Any news from your foreigner?" Zhuo Ge asks one day. Lulu is sleeping in the other room.

"No," Juanlan says. "Nothing."

Her brother shakes his head. He is holding the baby and smoking a cigarette at the same time. He turns to blow the smoke away from his daughter's face. "You should write and ask him about the guidebook. You have his address in America?"

"It's e-mail. He can receive the message anywhere."

"You should write him," he repeats.

She doesn't write Rob. And she is surprised when, a week or so later, Director Wei also raises the subject. It is December and the flat is so cold their breath is visible in the air. They make love beneath heavy blankets and afterward keep their limbs tangled up together, holding in the warmth. There is a smell of sex beneath the wool covers. Once, it would have embarrassed her, but she has grown accustomed to such intimacies. After all, she is not the only one made vulnerable by exposure—Director Wei is made vulnerable as well. She enjoys each new revelation: the mole on his shoulder with long hairs growing out of it, the decaying nail on his left foot. An instance of fascinated horror is quickly replaced by tenderness, relief. This is what it is to see your lover, to know who he is and to accept every flaw. Maybe this is what love itself is: the act of being laid bare. She never had any of this with Du Xian, whose response to her letter in late September was both brief and simple. *You've made the right choice. We're young and we live in different places.* No bitterness or bile—he must have been waiting for her to end things first. She spent an afternoon trying to drum up some sadness; Du Xian's image wavered in her mind like a reflection on water. She could put her hand right through him and the feeling would be gone.

She hasn't told Director Wei about the breakup, and he hasn't asked. Perhaps he's forgotten that she ever had a boyfriend. Or he assumes that they continue to write each other and doesn't bother about it because she isn't doing with Du Xian what she's doing with him.

But it's also true that Director Wei does not often ask about her life. When they talk, it is almost always about everyday topics. Which is why she's surprised when he mentions Rob. "I've been thinking about your foreign friend," he says, stroking her stomach absentmindedly beneath the covers. "The American."

"You were thinking about him just now?"

He smiles at the joke. "It occurred to me that your friend might need some assistance writing an introduction to our town. He hasn't written it yet, has he?"

"I don't think so." She pushes the covers down and breathes in the cold air. The edges of the windows are whitened with steam. "I know he collected information while he was here. I told him a lot, and he saw all the best sites."

"I'm sure you shared some very useful facts. It would be better if someone from my danwei could look at it, however. You could translate the document. Such a task would not be a problem for you."

"Yes, I could translate it, if Rob wanted me to. But I haven't seen what he wrote."

"You'll ask him, then."

"It's his work. He has no reason to show it to me for approval."

Director Wei says, "You can only do what you are willing to do. But don't forget that your friend is in our debt. He was treated as a guest, and he should be glad to have a chance to return the favor."

She turns this sentence over in her mind for the rest of the day. If Rob was treated well, that treatment had little to do with Director Wei. It was *her* time and friendship that made Heng'an a place he wanted to return to. Hers and Lulu's. And yet foreigners don't abide by the same rules that Chinese people do; if Rob helps them, it will only be because he wants to do it. She understands this, and Director Wei doesn't.

Still, she does not want to disappoint him, so one morning while she is manning the desk at the hotel, she composes a few paragraphs in English. "A beautiful town in the mountains of Sichuan Province, each traveler must visit Heng'an." She thinks back to what Rob said when she first met him, how he was interested in the fact that Heng'an was located along the ancient tea route. She adds in a few sentences about that, and about the temple they visited with Wei Ke, and the countryside they biked together the afternoon Rob first met Lulu. She is careful not to sound too well acquainted with Heng'an—this is not her voice, after all.

Once she has finished writing, she makes a fresh copy, and the next time she meets up with Director Wei, she shows it to him. "I copied it from the e-mail he sent," she says to explain why the sheet is hand-written.

He squints at the text and, with a nod of approval, hands it back to her. "What does it say?"

Juanlan translates, pausing frequently to figure out how to proceed. She created these sentences, yet finds it difficult to express them accurately in Chinese. Their meaning shifts, moving from one language to another, and in the end, the words that come out sound awkward to her ears. This must convince Director Wei of their authenticity, because at the end of her recitation, he nods again and declares that the write-up is not bad. Then he gives her some notes on how to improve it. "Your American friend will not mind the additions," he assures her, and she replies that, of course, she is certain he won't.

*　　*　　*

In December Juanlan begins working in the office of a bamboo cane wholesale company. The job is secretarial, dull, and takes up most of her time during the week. She got it not long after Lulu finished her month-long confinement and found a job working at a cosmetics store downtown. Then Juanlan's mother began urging *her* to find employment, too. She was no longer necessary at the hotel, her mother argued, as Ba's health had greatly improved. He spends most of his time with his granddaughter, Ning, bouncing and rocking her as he keeps track of comings and goings at the Three Springs. The baby sleeps much of the day, anyway, in a movable crib behind the front desk, freeing Juanlan's father to check guests in and out.

There are not any more guests now than there were in the summer. But no fewer, either. Businessmen and government officials—their schedules remain more or less the same throughout the year.

"Ba," Juanlan says one afternoon on the weekend when Ning is with Lulu, "what are you going to do about the hotel when the expressway opens?"

He looks up from the stove where they're warming their hands. Throughout the winter he perpetually smells of coal smoke, since he prefers to be outside rather than inside with the electric coil—though he is careful to keep Ning free of the foul air. "What do you mean?"

"Half the guests are from Chengdu. Once the trip is shortened, people will probably not stay overnight anymore."

"You let your Ba worry about that."

Juanlan bites her lip, wondering whether to go on. "The expressway is supposed to be completed next year."

Her father nods thoughtfully. "That's what they say."

"You don't believe it?"

"They're working quickly, your brother tells us." He sits back on his stool and puts his hands on his knees. He is one of the few men Juanlan knows who doesn't smoke, and perhaps this explains his quality of stillness; when other men would be reaching for a cigarette, he merely sits with his hands in his lap. This has always made him seem wise. But in fact it is difficult to know what he's thinking in such moments, if he is thinking at all, or instead has emptied his mind. When Juanlan was young, she and her friends would sometimes play a game where they determined which animal a person most resembled: a horse, a penguin, a mouse, a fish. The only rule was that it couldn't be the person's zodiac animal. One day, they went through their families. Zhuo Ge was decided to be a zebra, Juanlan a starfish. She can't recall which animal her mother was assigned. But she remembers her father's because she came up with it herself: "I've got it!" she'd yelled. "My Ba is an egg!" Everyone had burst into laughter at the joke, because it was both unlikely and exactly right.

Now, out of the blue, her father asks if she has a boyfriend.

"A boyfriend?" she repeats with genuine surprise. "Why would you think I have a boyfriend? When would I have time to see him, if I did?"

"I don't know."

"Did you think I had a boyfriend here," she says, attempting a laugh, "or did it start when I was in Chengdu?"

"Lan'er, I was only asking because you got that job, and—" He stops suddenly and shakes his head.

"What?"

Across the street, a neighbor steps out of the door at the bottom of his building and raises his hand in greeting. "You didn't want to be here," her father says as he returns the gesture. Then he turns and hocks a glob of spit on the ground. "And yet you're still here."

"Ma *told* me to get a job."

"And how do you like it?"

She thinks of the stale, smoky air in the office, the tablets of onion-skin receipts she fills out, sorts, and files. The benefit is that she has an hour and a half free at lunch, which allows her to meet her lover once or twice a week. "It doesn't have to be the job I have forever."

"That's right. You should look for something better. Things have improved from what they were last summer. You have more opportunities."

Long-term, she has no intention of staying in Heng'an. Things with Director Wei have made the future confusing, and made the present something she doesn't want to change for now. Of course, she can't tell her father any of this. Instead she says that surely he and her mother will need her around when they start accepting foreign guests at the hotel.

"What foreign guests?"

"When the expressway opens—"

"You can't believe everything your brother says." Her father wipes his hands back and forth over his thighs for warmth. After a pause, he says, "I'm not so sure about Zhuo'er's plans. How many foreigners do you think the new expressway will bring?"

"It's not just Zhuo Ge. Director Wei's danwei is busy preparing our town for foreign tourists."

Her father gives her an odd look. "Director Wei?"

"He spoke of it over the summer," she says lightly.

Seemingly convinced, he lets the matter drop and they sit in silence together, watching the hot brick of coal smoldering in the stove. It's not raining, but the air is damp. A mist obscures the hills that are usually visible at the top of the street. The outlines of those hills are so familiar, Juanlan thinks, she could draw them in place, if needed. And yet it's strange not to see them now. Such large things hulking, and for the moment you can't even tell that they're there.

*   *   *

A few days later, she is at the market buying vegetables on her way home from the office when she spots Teacher Cao standing over a tub of fish. The older woman is directing the fishmonger on which specimen she'd like: he grabs one out of the water and holds it up, but Teacher Cao shakes her head briskly and says, "A smaller one, please." He chooses another, and then a third, and this one she accepts. In one quick motion, the man flips a plastic bag over the fish. He weighs it and hands the bag to his customer, the creature inside flapping wildly. Teacher Cao pays, and while she waits for the man to count out her change, her eyes fall on Juanlan, who has been watching the exchange with a strange fascination, her heart slapping the bones of her chest like the fish inside the bag.

"Juan-juan!" Teacher Cao exclaims, and Juanlan is unpleasantly startled by the familiarity of the address. Only childhood friends and neighbors call her this. During the period of their acquaintance over the summer, Teacher Cao always called her by her full name.

"How are you?" she manages to ask, and the older woman says she's well, thank you, only tired of this cold. She tugs on the collar of her goose down coat as if to get warmer, even though it's already zipped up to the top. The coat is an expensive brand, likely purchased on a recent visit to the city.

It's been months since she saw Teacher Cao, not since before the trip up to Tao Xu. After her return, the few remaining tutoring sessions went on in the normal fashion, with Wei Ke's parents both away at work. Then the boy went to school in Chengdu, and of course that put an end to her visits to the flat overlooking the river, with its piano and its water cooler and its gleaming white floors. There has been no reason for her to meet Teacher Cao. And yet she has often been in Juanlan's thoughts. In fact, she has grown to resent Teacher Cao more than she ever did before, even in the absence of any interaction between them. Or perhaps because of it. Absence loosens affection when the connection is thin. As far as Juanlan is concerned, Teacher Cao is the only one who got something for nothing: she secured her son a free tutor, and from the beginning it was understood that nothing was required of her in the exchange. It's her security, the assurance that the world will provide whatever she wants—this is what grates. And what prevents Juanlan from feeling guilty about what's gone on with her husband.

"How strange to run into you," Teacher Cao is saying. "I don't usually shop here. It's really a lucky coincidence."

"This is our normal market," Juanlan answers stupidly. "Why are you shopping here?" Then, to soften the question, she adds, "What brought you to our neighborhood today?"

"Oh, just running my legs," Teacher Cao replies, meaning: errands, nothing of interest or note.

"How is Wei Ke doing? Have you spoken with him lately?"

"A few days ago, yes. He's doing quite well in his studies. And in English"—she brightens, as if now remembering Juanlan's role in her son's life—"he's improved quite a lot. His last exam, he was in the top half of his class. Just barely, of course—he still needs to study more—but this is a significant improvement over his work last year. Thanks to you, of course."

"Of course." Juanlan is surprised by her own response, and takes pleasure in seeing that Teacher Cao is surprised, too. It's unnatural to respond to gratitude so directly, to acknowledge that her own effort is in any way responsible for another's success. But it is satisfying to see the other woman unsettled.

During the time they've been talking, the bag at Teacher Cao's side has fallen still, and suddenly it begins flapping around again, the fish rousing itself for a final struggle. Teacher Cao thumps the bag against her side, but this only makes the creature thrash more. With a wry grin, she hoists it into the air and declares, "It doesn't know it's lunch."

"Or maybe it does, and that's why it's fighting."

"Well, it's too late for that." She lowers the bag to her side. The plastic hardly crinkles, as it has fallen still again. "Anyway, I should get along. I've got to boil this fish before Director Wei gets home from the hospital."

"The hospital!"

"Yes, his foot has been hurting him. It's nothing very serious." She gives Juanlan a wondering look. The injury is too minor to be troubling, the acquaintance too light to cause such alarm.

Juanlan eases the muscles in her face and wills away the shock that came unbidden. Teacher Cao looks merely amused at her response. Suddenly the other woman smiles brightly and shakes her head. "My husband will be pleased to know his health is so important to our friends."

If she only knew—but of course, she never will. Juanlan is the only one who possesses the truth. She reassures herself with this knowledge: she has gained the upper hand, and Teacher Cao is not even aware of being routed. With an exchange of good-byes they part ways, moving in opposite directions. Yet though Juanlan tries to maintain her feeling of superiority, within a minute or two, all good feeling has drained completely away. In its place is pure vinegar.

*　　*　　*

The next time she sees Director Wei, Juanlan asks him about his foot.

"It's nothing, really. My foot has been hurting me for some time, and I finally decided to go see the doctor about it."

"But you never mentioned it!"

"There was nothing to mention. It doesn't concern you." Director Wei rubs his eyes. He is seated on the edge of the bed, Juanlan beside him. She's been resting one hand on his arm, but she takes it away at this last remark. To her annoyance, her eyes are suddenly wet with tears.

"Lan," he says, using the nickname he employs only in tender moments, "my health is not something you need to worry about. If I'm dying of some disease, then I will tell you. If not, I don't want to bore you with trivial things."

She turns her eyes to the wall. Breathes in deeply and lets it out again. They have not fought before, and she had not expected to have an argument now. In reality, it is not much of an argument. But there is a physical sensation of having quarreled, a shakiness in her limbs, a quick-beating heart. She can't say what is bothering her, precisely, but it has to do with the look Director Wei gave her when she mentioned that she'd run into his wife. A look of annoyance that was tinged with blame.

"Fine," he says after more than a minute of silence. "If you really want to know." And he explains to Juanlan that his foot injury was caused by a misalignment of his pelvic bones. The doctor asked him if he'd sustained a fall. "Do you remember?" he asks, his face washed clean of emotion. He is testing her, but all she can think is that she never sees him except in this room, and he rarely tells her about his life outside it. If he's fallen in recent months, she hasn't been informed of the event. "In Tao Xu," he reminds her. "I slipped on the steps going up to the old house."

Immediately, she is brought back to that day: the rain, the slick mud, and the rough stone steps. Mayor Hu and the tense underling whose name she has forgotten. What was she feeling in that moment when Director Wei fell? They were not yet lovers. She didn't know that his body would soon matter to her, that she would come to have a proprietary feeling about it.

Then it comes to her: she fell, too. Before he slipped, *she* went down on her knees on the unforgiving stone. It was a shock, the pain shooting through her legs like a bullet. Does he recall this part of the story? Did he notice at the time?

She doesn't try to remind him of it. Instead, she listens to his explanation of some tendon on the bottom of his foot, another that runs up the back of the ankle, the connection to tissues in the leg and the hip. She wanted to know, she thinks. Now she knows.

26

A Saturday morning in early May. Juanlan's father has already strolled down to the river and by eight o'clock is back again, the birdcage swinging lightly from his fingers. He hangs it on the coatrack beside the lobby door as Juanlan watches him from the front desk, waiting for the moment he will turn and see her. She will not put a smile on her face until then.

"Have you eaten yet?" he asks.

"I had some congee a while ago. Do you want some?"

"Bring me a bowl, and I'll eat it here. It's a beautiful morning, Lan'er. You should get out and enjoy it."

Nearly every morning is beautiful now—the warm sun and the clean breeze, the streets glistening with rain that comes only at night. Spring has been almost unbearably lovely this year. Unbearable because Juanlan is miserable, and the fine weather only makes her feel worse. The streets downtown are crowded with young women buying new clothes. At night, the sidewalk tables outside the barbecue and chuanchuan'r places are filled with laughing groups of friends, but she has been seeing no one but her family.

When in early spring Director Wei abruptly ended things with her, she was almost too stunned to speak. She was sitting on the bed, waiting for him, when he came into the flat at their arranged meeting time. He closed the door quietly behind him and leaned against it with his hands crossed over his stomach. "I'm sorry, Lan," he said, looking briefly at her and then away. He seemed to think she knew what he was going to say, but she didn't, not at all. She cared for him more than he did for her—this she knew—but she required very little of him. Nothing, really, a few hours a week to touch and be touched, what could be considered a few hours only when added together from the smaller fragments of time. It hadn't occurred to her that he would want to end things between them. "Why?" she asked in a choking voice, but he didn't have a satisfactory answer. These things come to a natural end, he said. Yet if that was the case, then why didn't she feel the same? Why was the end only apparent to him?

He stayed long enough to allow her to cry, and to show her that her tears didn't move him in the slightest. If anything, her crying seemed to somewhat annoy him. He was tired of her, that was all. This was, of course, the most unspeakable explanation, and the only one.

The end of his affection was a vanishing, an evaporation. There was no mourning it properly. For weeks she was confused and angry; then she grew sad; now she feels herself brushed by the fringes of despair. During the workweek, her time at the office brings a comforting numbness, but on the weekends she finds herself teetering, a toe's length away from falling headfirst into sorrow. And it is not helped by her father's constant insistence, however well meant, that she go out and enjoy herself. Today is no different than every day. "Escape your mother," he says with a wink, "before she puts you to work."

So after fetching a bowl of congee for him from the kitchen, Juanlan retrieves her bike and goes out through the gate off the alley. Without thinking, she pedals over to her brother and Lulu's flat, but at the last moment decides not to stop by after all. She can't bear the sweet innocence of her niece this morning. She would rather be alone with her gloom. So she keeps going past the turnoff to the apartment complex and then takes the road that leads south, out of town. It follows the river and is mostly flat, but in the near distance, green mountains rise. To her left is the river and the sun vaulting down. To her right are planted fields and farmers' homes. Lulu grew up in the countryside, but it's difficult to imagine her as one of these women in cloth shoes, turning the earth with a spade. That is all in her past, or else in some alternate future that never came to be. Instead, she lives in a sixth-floor flat in the biggest town in the prefecture, has a washing machine, a husband, a child, and a job selling lipsticks and skin-whitening creams to a population that feels itself growing ever more cosmopolitan. Lulu has escaped and Juanlan has not, even if they both live in the same place for now.

Juanlan rides for an hour or more, stops to buy a bottle of green tea at a baihuodian, and then turns back. As she's coming onto the outskirts of town again, she spots an Internet bar and decides to stop in. It's been a month, at least, since she checked her e-mail.

Inside, she takes a seat among the boys playing video games with the volume turned high in their headphones. Internet bars are still a new enough thing for Juanlan to feel surprised by the legions of young men who seem to spend all their waking hours in dark, smoky rooms, staring at screens. Her usual visits last no more than a half hour. Only a few of her friends from university are on e-mail.

When she opens her in-box, however, she finds a letter from Rob. Immediately her heart begins to pound as she remembers the fake write-up that she gave Director Wei. Surely this e-mail holds news of the real thing: perhaps Rob would like to send her a copy of the travel guide and is writing for her address. Despite herself, she is excited to see it. She's eager to see what he made of Heng'an, how he will represent the place, what made it into his description and what did not. And though she was never the main champion of the idea, if he's named their hotel in the pages of the guide, then they won't have a choice but to welcome the flood of tourists that will come. The future will force itself over their doorstep, after all.

But when she opens the e-mail, there are only a few lines to tell her that he's sorry, but the Three Springs Hotel won't be mentioned in the guidebook. In fact, Heng'an itself won't be included. "My editors," he says, "wanted more space for Yunnan. Tiger Leaping Gorge is just too exciting."

He goes on to talk of other matters. Things are strange here, he writes. Has she heard about the shooting at an American high school? Of course Juanlan remembers seeing this on the news a month ago or more, not long after Director Wei broke up with her. She recalls seeing the story and not caring much about it. It was too far away. And suddenly she's angry that he has used this event to turn her attention from the real purpose of the e-mail. The real purpose was to say, *You are forgotten. I don't owe you anything, after all.*

*   *   *

Riding back into town, she has the sensation of being propelled. Her feet are light turning the pedals, her hands steady on the handlebars. She knows where she is going, though she couldn't say why. But she steers in and out of traffic without noticing how close she comes to swiping this truck or that pedicab, and it is not because her mind is on other things but rather because she can't seem to focus on anything at all. Her head is filled with a light staccato, like the low sound of gunfire in the Internet bar, as the boys in their headphones shot down enemies onscreen.

By the time she gets to the noodle shop, her face is damp with humidity and sweat. She locks her bike on a pole and goes inside. Several people are gathered at the tables, watching the television, many more than are usually there, and they are all transfixed. Qiang Ba is watching along with his customers. He stands with his arms folded over his chest, and when Juanlan greets him, he seems unsurprised to see her again but beckons her over with a shake of the head. "What's going on?" she asks.

He gestures to the television, where a CCTV newsman is speaking into the camera. "See for yourself." The sound is low, but the captions scrolling over the bottom of the screen read: ". . . in the early hours of the morning, leaving nothing but rubble and the blood of innocents on the ground. The criminal attack by American-led NATO forces is a direct assault on Chinese sovereignty . . ."

She is aware of the morning being erased from her mind: Rob's e-mail, the birdcage swinging from her father's wrist.

A man seated at a nearby table says angrily, "They bombed us, the pigs."

The story comes out in bits and pieces. The Chinese embassy in Belgrade has been destroyed, perhaps as many as a dozen are dead, some of them journalists, many more injured, the building is devastated. There is footage of smoke and rubble, then a map of Belgrade with a red star on one side showing where the embassy stood. It was an American plane, several bombs were dropped, and there are no explanations except the obvious one: the United States has made an attack on China.

As the footage loops and the newsman repeats the same information, the people in the noodle shop begin to speculate. The Americans and NATO are claiming it was an accident, but this is not to be believed. A woman seated with her son in her lap says loudly, "Everyone knows the American military is top-notch. They couldn't have bombed our embassy by accident. It's an insult to say so."

"Of course it's not an accident!"

"That fucking Clinton—"

"—just because China is coming up in the world."

Qiang Ba shakes his head and goes over to his post behind the vat of boiling water. "Who wants to order?" he asks, and the others in the shop begin calling out their requests in the midst of conversations with one another. Someone turns up the volume on the television, and the voices all grow louder in response. Juanlan seats herself shakily on a free stool and lays her hands flat on the little table. A feeling is rising inside her, a sensation of restlessness that settles in her fingers and the backs of her thighs. It might be shock's reverberations pulsing through her bones, but it's amplified by knowing that she feels exactly what everyone around her is feeling. Anger, pure and simple, as it hardens to rage. *Do something.* She almost says it aloud. A woman her mother's age, seated at a nearby table, is crying over the images on the television: an arm half buried under concrete, a young woman stumbling past the camera with a cloth pressed to her bleeding head. The newscasters are naming the dead. Among them is a married couple who were living in the embassy. "Oh, it's too terrible!" the crying woman says through her tears. "They were living a happy life. What did they do to deserve this?"

Juanlan's fingers grasp the edge of the table. She catches Qiang Ba looking at her. "You need to eat," he says, but she just shakes her head.

"Clinton should be tried for war crimes," a man seated near her declares. He taps the table; he is speaking to her.

"It was a barbarous act," she agrees, "a criminal act . . ." They are the same words the newsman was using a moment before, but they don't feel any less true because of it.

Someone has switched the television to another channel. The news is the same, but this is the provincial station, based in Chengdu, and the newscasters are talking about protests. Demonstrators are already gathering outside the US consulate, they inform the audience, and more are expected to show up throughout the afternoon. Juanlan thinks of the lectures she attended there as a student, of the expat who'd spoken about American missionaries. She thinks of the lecture room with its sound-absorbing panels, of the high walls surrounding the compound, of the guards at the gates, and she is suddenly angry with herself for having gone to listen to these talks. The people who gave them were not experts, and they were not wise. Often they looked impatient at the questions the audience asked. They were, Juanlan thinks, the same as Rob: feeling themselves beholden to nothing and no one, just messing around.

"If I were in Chengdu," the man seated near her says, "I would be down there right now. And I wouldn't just be chanting slogans, either."

"Why don't you go?" she asks. "The bus station is just around the corner."

He nods as if he might be considering it. Then he turns back to the television and mutters, "The imperialist pigs!"

Do something. Juanlan is sick of watching the news. She stands abruptly, tipping her stool onto its side, and she doesn't bother to right it before making her way to the door. "Where are you going?" Qiang Ba asks. She doesn't stop to answer him.

* * *

The man behind the ticket window shows no sign of having heard the news. "Do you know about the bombing?" Juanlan asks, and he shrugs. Then he points through the door into the waiting room and says, "You've got less than ten minutes."

It's not until the bus is pulling out of the station that she remembers her bike, parked next to Qiang Ba's shop. Immediately after, she thinks of her parents. In a few hours, they will start to wonder where she is, and she won't have a chance to call them until she gets to the city. She pictures her mother pacing angrily over the hotel lobby floor, her father standing at the door, peering up and down the street. They'll worry, but it's better that she didn't call before. What she's doing is crazy; they would have tried to talk her out of it. And she doesn't feel like being talked out of anything.

It is a small bus, and the other passengers are all abuzz with the news. They spend the next hour speaking of nothing else. Even the ticket taker and the driver join in. When at last the driver turns on some music, the conversation dies down and Juanlan turns to the window, glad to be alone with her thoughts. What she is feeling is too difficult to name. It is the feeling of a dream before you have it.

Months ago, before the baby came, Lulu mentioned that she was having vivid dreams. Falling asleep was like opening a door, and once she had gone through it she was in that place forever. In one such dream, she was crossing a wide brown river with a hippopotamus beside her. Her arms were tired from swimming, and she felt a deep sense of dread. Still, she swam and the hippopotamus stayed beside her. Juanlan asked what she thought the dream meant. "It doesn't mean anything," Lulu replied. "It's some other life I'm living." But Juanlan tried to trace its meaning, to discover the emotion that explained the action. The hippopotamus was the baby, she said. "Let's hope not," Lulu said with a sharp laugh.

The next few hours pass as if in that kind of dream. Another life. Juanlan isn't sure whether she has slept or not. Their bus bumps slowly along the road, and when the expressway comes into view, she sees that it is nearing completion. The asphalt is laid, and without the lines drawn on, it looks like a river, black and flowing. And she is in a boat sailing straight down the middle.

*　　*　　*

Then they are edging slowly through the Chengdu traffic. They move in fits and starts; the southern portions of the first and second ring roads are closed, and so they are detoured north of downtown. To the south, the giant statue of Chairman Mao towers over Tianfu Square. Squinting, Juanlan imagines she can see it between the buildings, but of course this is only her imagination. She wants to open the windows and breathe in the air of Chengdu: smog and exhaust and the dust from construction.

Her resolve has been tempered over the past several hours, in the time when she was half awake, half dreaming, and when she finally steps off the bus at Xinnanmen Station, her only thought is how to get to the consulate. She asks a policeman standing outside the station, who doesn't blink as he gives her directions: a straight shot south and then left on Jinxiu Lu. "Are you joining the protests?" he asks as she starts to turn away.

She considers lying, unsure whether they are fully authorized. But the tone of the news report suggested government sanction, and so she tells him yes, she's headed there now.

"That's good," he says. "The universities are busing students over there. Join up with them and you should stay safe."

She walks two or three kilometers before reaching Jinxiu Lu, but long before that point, she passes through the membrane of a crowd and becomes part of it. Who knows how many people are marching? She sees a little boy sitting on his father's shoulders, waving the national flag and yelling, "China, fight back!" Not far away are three women her mother's age who, on a normal night, would probably be in the nearest park doing their evening dance exercises, but are now shouting along with the rest: "Blood for blood! Blood for blood!" The chant carries on for several minutes before ebbing a little, but then another is taken up in its place: "Bomb the White House!" Some people are carrying signs with the same slogans and others, slogans mentioning Clinton and Albright, how they should be killed or fucked.

By the time they reach Jinxiu Lu, the street is too crowded to get close. The consulate is a few blocks down, and word goes out that several people have started scaling the walls around the compound, that bottles and bricks are being tossed over the perimeter and onto the grounds. There are police nearby, but none are moving in the direction of the consulate, which means that this, too, will be allowed.

Juanlan stops to look at the anonymous buildings rising overhead and at the first-floor shops, all of which have their metal doors drawn.

It is a strange part of the city—a place where it seems too few people live or work, where the buildings turn in on themselves and keep their secrets. And yet it is full of people now, full of heat, full of shiny faces screaming their frustrations into the falling dusk. It is only here that she can feel a part of it all. The anger in her chest is bruising her bones to get out.

*   *   *

She takes the policeman's advice and joins up with a group of university students. It's easy enough; no one asks who she is, and there's no need to talk because they are all shouting slogans. At first she thinks that they're from the technology institute, but then decides that they're students from Sichuan University. And they've come prepared—not only with signs but with long banners and laundry tubs that they bang like drums. The throb finds its way inside her rib cage, fury made physical. The day Director Wei broke up with her, she sat on the edge of the bed, unable to say or ask anything but *why*. Now she pictures his startled face blinking at a door that she's slammed in it. The thud of the drum is that door, slamming again and again.

For an hour or longer she stands with the students, holding up one side of a banner made from a very long piece of cloth. Directly above her are the words "Down with the imperial . . . ," and though she can't read the rest, it doesn't matter. She can guess the message, and anyway, they are shouting with all the force of their united anger.

*   *   *

Some time later—it could be nine or ten or eleven o'clock—she sees, standing beneath the awning of a music shop, an old white man bending forward like a waterbird from his perch on a step. His features are nothing like Rob's, but the similarity isn't in his looks: it is simply that he stands out, that he doesn't belong. The man is shaking his head and arguing with a group of young men and women who have gathered around him: high school students, all dressed in T-shirts and matching track pants that must be their school's. One of them, a pale fat

girl with glasses, has her fists balled in rage. Another is pointing angrily at the foreigner, his finger almost meeting the older man's chest.
Juanlan makes her way toward them, twisting and pressing herself flat
between the bodies, a sensation like nausea rising in her throat. But
she is not sickened; it is excitement that makes her spine tingle and her
heart beat fast. All around her are the shouts and chants of the crowd,
and she has the sensation of being positioned exactly on the line between safety and violence, between order and chaos. It could go either way, and she doesn't know which one she wants. She makes her
way toward the foreigner and feels the throng of other bodies moving
the same way, with the same intention. The already familiar slogan
"Blood for blood!" is shouted at a distance, and a few people closer by
take up the chant again.

Juanlan pushes against two men who are blocking her way, and miraculously, they move apart. The foreigner's back is to her now, but she
has a good look at the girl with the balled fists and sees that her eyes,
behind the glint of her glasses, are sharp as knives. The girl moves a few
centimeters to the left, and in that moment, a familiar face appears behind her. The shock of recognition precedes understanding: he is taller
than he was the last time she saw him, his shoulders broader, but there
is no doubt that the boy Juanlan sees is Wei Ke.

There is a shove, from somewhere. The foreigner stumbles. When he
straightens up again, he has a look of confusion on his face that is almost
a smile. He shakes his head and says something she can't hear. It might
be in Chinese or it might be in English. He could be speaking some
other language altogether, but it doesn't matter because she isn't listening. The girl with the glasses has moved again, and Juanlan loses sight
of Wei Ke. She tries to move to one side, but the crowd has grown and
she is wedged in between a woman cradling a bunch of bananas against
her chest and some university students trying to unfurl another painted
banner. The students are screaming about the Chinese martyrs and the
American imperialists. Some of them have tears streaming down their
cheeks. And the foreigner just keeps shaking his head, repeating the
same refrain again and again.

The girl with the glasses reaches out and hits him on the front of his shoulder. It isn't a hard blow—her fingers release from a fist even as she's hitting him—but it is the next step in whatever is happening now, and Juanlan knows there will be a next step, and then a next one after that. She is watching it, rapt, her hands clasped to her chest.

They are two blocks from the consulate, and a swelling of noise suddenly rises from that direction, a cheer covering over the chanting of slogans. She peers over her shoulder to discover the source of the noise, but nothing is visible through the crowds, the hundreds or even thousands of people cramming the street. She stands on her toes, swivels her neck. Others are looking, too. "They're breaking in!" someone says excitedly, and others start repeating the news. For a moment, the attention drops away from the foreigner.

It is enough. When Juanlan turns back, she sees his bowed shape ducking under the edge of the awning, slipping behind a stack of boxes into an alley. He will get away, and it is with the help of the boy who is even now blocking the way, telling the crowd to stand back, to just leave him be. Wei Ke raises his arms, rigid and forceful, and though the crowd could turn on him, instead it turns away. He is safe. He has made sure that the foreigner is safe, too. And when he meets her eye, Juanlan knows that he saw her there a moment before, that he saw her watching the girl who flung out her fist and knew that she wasn't going to do a thing to stop it.

*   *   *

Ten minutes pass. It might be an hour; it might be two. There is no time here inside the anger of the mob. There is only shouting and pushing, shoulder blades and elbows, sweat glistening and dripping and lying thick on the skin. There is the press of bodies, the smell of them, and then the turning of heads toward some new strange event.

The odor hits her nose as it hits those around her, and yet it takes a moment for anyone to understand what it is. And in that same instant, the crowd is alive with the news: they're burning it down. The sun has set, but the sky is a rusty color—streetlights and clouds—and when

Juanlan looks up, she sees the black smoke clear against it, spreading ugly and beautiful like an oil spill. People are running away from the smoke; others are running toward it. She doesn't stop to consider which way to go. She sets her eyes on the column of smoke and starts fighting her way toward it. She'll find a bottle to toss, a rock to fling. Anything she can put her hands around.

Addie

27

She hadn't written her family back home to let them know where she was. How was she to explain it? *Dear Louisa*—she imagined the pen tracing lines on the page—*I'm no longer in Lu-cho Fu. I've left my husband and children to be with the woman I love.* No, she would not write what she couldn't bring herself to say aloud. It was too strange to be believed. She would wait until she knew when she was going back, and then she would give her explanations for having left.

One night in December she went to sleep and awoke some time later to find that she couldn't move or speak. Her limbs were paralyzed, and a heavy weight pressed down on her chest—a creature was lying there, though she couldn't get a look at it because she wasn't able to lift her eyelids to see. The creature's evil was odorless and it made no sound, but it lay atop her like a great hand slowly crushing her. With all her strength, she tried to open her mouth and scream, but her lips wouldn't part and the scream got caught in her throat, where it made only a weak hum. And she kept on screaming inside herself, while on her chest the creature didn't shift position, didn't speak, didn't move, but was terror itself, and darkness, and not death but something worse than death . . .

Poppy had her hand on Addie's arm, shaking her. "Dear, you're having a nightmare," she said as Addie moved obscurely through the sludge of dreams and into waking. "You've been moaning and crying. There, now, hush." It was cold in the room but snug under the woolen blankets, though the warming stone by their feet had lost its heat. Poppy pulled Addie toward her, and after a time they both returned to sleep.

The next morning, as they were getting dressed to go down for breakfast, Addie said, "That was no nightmare, Poppy, what I experienced last night."

Poppy looked up from the buttons she was fastening up the front of her padded coat. Since the weather had turned cold, they'd taken to adding layers over the ones they wore to sleep, and then they went out into the world that way. They only changed this bottom layer once a week.

December was not as cold in Chungking as it had been in Lu-cho Fu, where the temperatures dipped well below freezing and the wind shot volleys of snow down the narrow streets, but there they'd had stoves in every room to keep warm, and those who lived in the laotung stoked the k'ang to spend their days sitting upon it, eating meals and entertaining and sleeping there, too. Here, it was only in the kitchen that one could ever get warm. And then the oily smoke clung for days in one's clothes and hair, and with the wet climate, it was impossible to get the heavier clothing to dry after being washed. And so, like the natives, Addie and Poppy simply wore coats and gloves at all times, inside as well as out, and learned to imagine that they were not as cold as they felt.

"What are you talking about?" Poppy said. "I don't suppose you mean to say that you were having a pleasant dream."

"Not a dream," Addie said, "but not a nightmare, either. It was something wilder than that, Poppy. It was real, what I felt."

"What was real?"

"The thing that visited me. I was lying on my back, and it sat on my chest and kept me from moving. I felt it there, I'm telling you. I was wide awake."

"That was a nightmare, Addie."

"No." She shook her head.

Poppy sat on the bench at the end of the bed to put on her shoes. "All right. And why do you suppose it came? Where did it come from?"

"You don't believe me. But I know what I felt, and I know what is real, even if I can't explain it. As for why it came, I can only think—" But she left off abruptly, not sure that she wanted to continue. To hide her confusion, she began folding the sheets back over the bed.

"Think what?"

Addie smoothed the blankets over the mattress and plumped the pillows at the head. They were lumpy things that made her neck ache. She put a hand to the top of her spine now and pressed her fingers deep into the skin. "That I've made a wrong turn," she replied.

Finished lacing her boots, Poppy stood from the bench. "That's nonsense."

"I don't know."

"Yes, you do. Tell me, Addie, what do you think you would be doing in Lu-cho Fu right now if you had stayed? Would you be washing your husband's clothes, or waiting for Julia Riddell to give you your marching orders for the day?"

"That's not fair." Addie folded her hands in front of her. She was only a few feet away from Poppy, yet she felt as if she were staring at her friend from a distance. She thought of their first trip into the mountains, when they'd hollered out into the void and their voices had come back to them in echoes.

"Isn't it fair?" Poppy shook her head. Then, all at once, something soft came into her expression. "Perhaps this is about your boys. I can understand that—I'm not a mother, Addie, but I had one, once." Poppy's mother had died when she was four or five years old. Her father had never remarried, never found her a replacement, and so Poppy had been raised by her hard Irish pa and her three older brothers, all of them rough and brash and loud, and she claimed not to have missed the maternal element in her upbringing all that much. "Your boys," she said, "have not been thrown out to fend for themselves in the world. They are surrounded by those who will care for and help them. They are not alone. You haven't left them treading water, you know." She took a step toward Addie, and then another, until she had closed the space between them and was standing close. "Tell me what you're feeling."

Addie blinked rapidly and fixed her gaze ahead, refusing to meet Poppy's eye. "I'm not sure."

"Do you miss them, Addie? Your boys?" She put her hand to Addie's chin and lifted it. "Well, they might miss you also. That is not such a bad thing, however. A boy doesn't die of missing his mother, or a mother of missing her son."

"It's not missing them," Addie said slowly. She was looking Poppy in the eye now, and figuring out what she wanted to say at the same moment that she was saying it. "I don't miss them, really, not beyond what you'd imagine. Not as much as I thought I would. I'd like to see them, Poppy, but I would almost prefer—I'd just like to see them from down the road. Freddie and Henry, walking together, hand in hand. If

I could only see them like that and know they're all right, that would be enough, I think."

Poppy took her hat from a hook on the wall. "This hat makes me feel invincible," she said, "for it has taken me through some frightening times." She pressed her lips together, and Addie figured she must have been remembering the episode on the boat a few months before. "Perhaps if you find yourself a similar talisman, you'll keep the nightmares at bay."

Addie took the hat from Poppy's hand and placed it on her own head. She stepped in front of the mirror, thinking she might make a joke about how it didn't suit her. She was stopped, however, by her reflection, which was both her and not-her. Her square face had taken on a masculine look under the wide leather brim. She straightened her shoulders, raised them an inch. She set her feet wider apart on the floor.

"Look at you," Poppy said wryly, meeting her eye in the glass, "a regular desperado."

Addie pulled the hat off her head and handed it back to her friend. No, it wasn't a desperado she'd seen in the mirror. It was herself made into a stranger. It was what she would look like if she wasn't her.

*　*　*

"You are in an unusual position," Widow Liu said to her later that afternoon.

"In what way?"

"As a widow with no children. You have neither sons nor daughters, and you say you haven't met your dead husband's parents for many years. You're an orphan, then. It is a fact."

Addie blanched at the mention of her dead husband. Though she maintained in Chungking the lie that she was a widow, it was sometimes necessary to refer to the past, and so the imaginary Mr. Baker was, in her construction, simply Owen with a different name. This meant that she was perpetually referring to him as having been dead for years, rather than still living a thousand miles to the north, with her sons, without her. And this only reminded her of the guilt she carried under her skin like a splinter. "But my parents are alive," she protested.

"That doesn't matter. A wife leaves her family and joins her husband's. His parents must have no concern for you if they don't call you to their home. In my view, this makes you an orphan."

Addie was generally intrigued by her conversations with the widow, who was both very traditional in her views while also very modern, a strange sort of anomaly—a Chinese woman with both wealth and power, who took certain customs as undisputed truths rather than cultural practices. She was not a Christian, but she enjoyed discussing Christian beliefs. She never left her home, yet seemed to know more about what was happening on the global stage than anyone Addie had met in China, either foreign or native. "Widow Liu," Addie said, wanting to challenge her, "you've lost your husband, too, and you don't live with his parents. Doesn't that make you an orphan, the same as me?"

"My husband's parents have both been lying in their graves for many years. And you forget that I have my sons." The older woman frowned. "You understand that in China, your situation is pitiful. You failed to establish a family before your husband died, and when he left this earth, from that moment on you didn't have a home anymore. You see? An orphan." She stuck a finger in her tea and stirred it around. Often Addie would sit with her for an hour or longer and never see her take a single sip. For a woman whose business was tea, she seemed to drink less of it than any other person Addie had met. On the other hand, as far as Addie knew, she didn't smoke opium, either, and that made up a good part of her business. "Do you know the term *chaiku*?" the widow asked suddenly.

Addie shook her head.

"It's a type of woman—sometimes she is divorced, more pity on her—or she is not married for some other reason. She has nowhere to go except to the monastery."

"So a chaiku is a nun?"

"Not exactly." She made a movement that reminded Addie, strangely, of the photographer who had taken her family's portrait back in Marietta years before; he'd moved his hand through the air in just such a way, something in between direction and contemplation. "No," the widow went on, "such a woman is not a nun—more like a servant. She doesn't leave her monastery to go anywhere else. She's—"

"—trapped?"

Widow Liu batted a hand in her direction again, this time as if she were swatting away a fly. "No, she is given a home. For an unwanted woman, this is a kindness."

Addie hugged herself, the chill from the room seeping in through her legs, which were not wrapped as thickly as her chest and arms. "You should drink some more tea," the widow said, gazing at her levelly. "You need a refreshment of hot water, perhaps."

"No, thank you," Addie said.

Widow Liu nodded. Many women would have called in their servants regardless of the answer, but this was another of her oddities: she seemed capable of letting a person enjoy her own discomfort, if that's what was preferred.

They talked of other things for a time, and then Addie took her leave. "You'll come see me again in a few days?" the widow asked with a roll of her neck.

"If you wish."

She responded with a fluttering of her fingers that sent Addie toward the door. Widow Liu didn't like to appear eager—others came to see her, and she saw them if it pleased her. She would never beg.

*   *   *

Addie had been going to see the widow for two or three months by then. After the first visit with Poppy, they'd gone back together one more time, and the hostility Widow Liu seemed to have for Poppy was even more pronounced on that second visit. She'd frowned whenever the American woman spoke, and frequently interrupted to keep her from finishing a thought. It might have been entertaining if the widow argued with her, Poppy said, but in fact she acted almost as if she weren't there. After they left, Poppy declared that she didn't think there was much purpose in returning to see her again. "It's clear she's not really interested in converting," she said, "and I don't believe she's ever going to give us any money for the school."

Then, several days after that second visit, a messenger had arrived at the mission house with a summons for Addie. "Do you think I should go?" she'd asked Poppy. She really did feel unsure. It was awkward that the invitation was for her alone, but then she was curious as to why she had been chosen over her friend. In every other situation, she was undoubtedly the less compelling figure of the two.

"You should do whatever you like. I just wouldn't expect much from the relationship." When Addie still looked uncertain, Poppy had slapped her arm affectionately. "Oh, go on. The old woman will probably be the source of some very good gossip."

So she'd gone. Addie was interested in the widow, and it didn't matter that she wasn't a Christian and seemed intent on remaining unconverted. She was intrigued by Widow Liu's combination of confidence and diffidence, and too, there was the appeal of being able to communicate: she could understand Addie's Chinese.

She had gone back to see the widow once, and then again, and then a third time. Soon, it became a regular part of her schedule: every three or four days she would stop by the house. She was always welcomed. It seemed she had established for the first time a friendship with a Chinese woman who was staunchly Chinese. It was something quite different to speak with a person who had no interest in becoming Christian or adopting foreign ways; it made Addie imagine that she herself was somehow more Chinese, and this was gratifying, in its way.

The widow was also well informed. She read the Chinese papers and received a constant stream of visitors, including all the foreign merchants in Chungking, to keep herself educated in global affairs. Talking to her, Addie felt more connected to the outside world than she had been for some time. The British were fighting the Boers in South Africa. US forces had defeated the Spanish in the Philippines and were now fighting the natives. "I find you to be a harmless person," Widow Liu said one day when they were discussing the Americans' pursuit of the Filipino president through the mountains of his country, "despite being a foreigner. I have no illusions, however, about your nation's government. It is clear what they are about."

"What's that?"

"Extending power. In Europe, they have been collecting colonies for a long time. But America—America was a colony itself only a little over a century ago, and now it feels itself to be the peer of Europe. It wants its own colonies, and so it is looking around the world for opportunities."

"I believe you have a better understanding of the situation than I do, Widow Liu."

"Yes, that is true," the widow said without irony. She blinked at Addie in the semidarkness. "Look here: America suddenly finds itself in possession of several islands in the Caribbean and also in the Pacific. This makes it think that it is moving toward the center of power. Clearly this is a false belief. You understand that this is incorrect?"

"I'm not sure," Addie said. Since she wasn't in touch with Louisa or her parents, she felt less qualified to speak now on the American perspective than in former times. All the same, a year earlier letters from home had made frequent mention of "those murderous Spanish" and "our brave boys"—wasn't it clear how one should feel about that? The war pitted an old corrupt empire against a brave young nation. In that context, an American victory was the obvious right outcome. "I don't know that my countrymen think very much about where they stand in the world," she ventured. "It is difficult to imagine America acting anything like one of the colonial powers, in any case."

"Your country thinks it is moving toward the center of the world," the widow repeated as if she hadn't heard her, "but in fact, this is false. And do you know why? Because China has always been the center. America is just a little dog scratching at the door."

"But surely Britain is more powerful than either America or China. If you're looking for the center, then that must be it."

"Britain possesses its colonies. It does not possess the whole world."

"If China is so important," Addie said, "then why doesn't it have its own colonies?"

"Because nothing outside the boundaries of the empire is worth having. It's a lot of trouble to maintain control over such places, and what do we need that we can't produce here? It is the rest of the world that needs something from us." The widow gave a harsh laugh. "Of course, this makes all you foreigners unhappy. 'Unfair trade practices,' you cry.

You have your president's adviser who's put out a document charging all of Europe to play fair. 'Maintain China's sovereignty'—however, I am not fooled. This has nothing to do with China's good and everything to do with what is good for *you*. But don't misunderstand me," she added after a moment's pause. "China is not as powerful as it should be, and it hasn't been given the recognition it deserves by the world. We have been run over by foreign powers for decades, and this is certainly a disgrace." She squinted at Addie, as if considering the exact shape and scale of the indignities visited upon China by those who looked similar to her.

Widow Liu often seemed torn between pride in the history of the Chinese and contempt for the weakness its government had displayed over the course of her lifetime. Foreign powers had come in and scooped up whole regions of the empire, had taken over ports, established banks and businesses and foreign concessions. Some of this business revolved around tea and opium, and this was where she had a personal concern. The widow and her family's trading company had already been engaged in dealings with foreigners for years. As she explained to Addie, she'd been forced to learn from them. "The truth is that I don't much like Americans or Europeans or anyone else, but you are here now and we must learn how to deal with you." She shook her head and yawned. "Come, now, I have something for you." And taking out a small purse, she passed it over to Addie.

She turned over the silk bag in her hand. "What's this?"

"Money for you and your work—use it as you see fit. I would be careful about it, however, going home. There are more thieves in Chungking than there are grains of rice, and I wouldn't trust you to handle such an encounter as you ought."

"What exactly is the appropriate response to a robbery, Widow Liu?"

"It depends on the situation."

This hardly seemed fair. Addie folded her arms and said, "Then why do you believe that I would handle it incorrectly?"

"Because," the widow said calmly, "you have no sense of intuition, and neither do you have a true understanding of fear."

"What gives you that idea?"

Widow Liu waved a hand over her face. "Child, it's your entire expression that tells me."

Addie opened her mouth to dispute her, but another visitor was announced and the widow dismissed her, as she often did, with a nod.

Picking her way down the stairs, Addie thought of the night when she had awoken with the creature on her chest and found herself unable to move. It was now distant enough that she could recognize it as a nightmare, but still she carried close the memory of the terror it had caused her. The widow was wrong: she did indeed understand fear. It was only that she knew that it wasn't always accompanied by danger.

The reverse, it turned out, was also true. But it would be some time before she comprehended it.

*   *   *

In the autumn, less than two months after Addie and Poppy arrived in Chungking, an article had appeared in a British newspaper describing an attack on Christian converts in Shantung. The dead were all Chinese, natives of the town, and the attackers named were the Boxers. Addie recalled the men who had stopped her and Poppy on the boat near T'ien-chin. No foreigners were involved in this recent attack, and perhaps this was why none of the missionaries gave it a great deal of concern. It was the cost of doing mission work in such a wild land as this. Over the course of her years in China, Addie had periodically heard tales of violence committed against Chinese Christians and foreigners alike. Enmity, envy, resentment, or fear led to a murder in some small corner of the empire. The incident was enough to make one uneasy for a time, but the disquiet passed. These were inevitably local affairs, and the locales were never so close to home as to merit real panic.

But then a new report came to raise the alarm. In January, the papers reported the murder of an Anglican priest that had happened on New Year's Eve. It had been snowing, the report said, and the priest had tried to run from his attackers. He'd slipped and been captured, and they'd chopped him to pieces. Once again, blame was laid on the Boxers. This latest attack had also taken place in Shantung, and reading about it, Addie felt a stab of fear in her chest. Shantung was east of Shansi, with a narrow strip of Chih-li Province between them. It was not very close to Lu-cho Fu, though it was the same general area. "I wouldn't worry," Widow Liu said when they discussed the news, "for your friends back in Shansi. Both the Empress Dowager and your foreign governments have condemned the acts. And besides, there is no leader of this group; they are a ragtag bunch. It's local troublemaking, that's all." This was more information than the British paper had given, but it gave Addie little comfort. Poppy delivered more or less the same verdict: "It's a grisly affair," she said, "but there's no use in us panicking."

Addie wasn't panicking. Rather, she felt haunted. She couldn't stop imagining a white landscape with a group of men stealing over it, all sounds swallowed up by the swirling, drifting flakes. She saw the Reverend Brooks glancing up with horror at his attackers. She saw blood spilled on the snow.

A second report added details that the first had omitted: Reverend Brooks had had a ring put through his nose before being paraded through a nearby village like an animal. In this telling, his brief escape through the snow happened afterward, when he was naked and tired and had already been tortured. The Boxers threw his body in a ditch after they were done. It was retrieved later by another mission priest to be buried.

The murder of the British man was all the missionaries in Chungking could talk about. One got a foreboding sense from the reports, from the fact that the attackers weren't bandits or robbers but members of an organization—a movement—with a violent name and a terrible cause. The Boxers hated Christians and they hated foreigners, which was all that the missionaries stood for, after all.

"What had that Brooks fellow done," Mr. Wickford asked sadly over dinner one night, shaking his head, "but bring light to the dark? What have we any of us strived to do here but make better the lives of a miserable populace?"

"We've all had the best of intentions, I'm sure," Poppy said with a firm nod. "This will all die down soon, just you watch."

Later, after they had gone to bed, Addie asked Poppy how she could feel that confident. "What could possibly make you think this isn't serious?" she asked. She recognized a petulant tone in her voice that belied her fear.

"Of course it's serious. It's only that I know how news spreads here—the Chinese are terrible propagators of exaggeration. The only ones worse for it are missionaries. Look," she said, laying her hand on Addie's arm in the dark, "we're a long way off from all this. Who's to know—it might all have passed over already, and we're only keeping fear alive here because we don't know any better."

"But how do you *know*?" Addie asked again, her eyes open to the darkness. Pale light leaked in through a small window over the door and made vague shadows on the ceiling. She felt as if she were swimming, and Poppy's hand on her arm was either pushing her down or trying to pull her up to the surface.

"I don't, dear. But wouldn't you rather think the best than the worst? We're here now, anyway, and there's nothing we can do, since travel would be particularly unwise at this time."

We're here now, anyway. This was the truth, as hard and plain as a fruit stone. And it was comforting, too. This was what Addie tried to ignore: that she felt glad to be far away, even while Owen and the boys were nearer to the danger. She worried for them, yes—she felt sick whenever she imagined Owen traveling alone near some village like the one where the Reverend Brooks had met his fate—and yet she could convince herself that this worry was out of proportion to the situation. Owen was not being led through their town like a donkey, to be jeered at and scorned; he was known there, they were all known there. Didn't they have Li K'ang and Wei-p'eng to vouch for their goodness? And besides, Lu-cho Fu was two hundred miles or more from the place where the Anglican priest had been killed. That whole part of China was not accountable for a single murder, however ghastly and terrible.

The fact still remained: *I'm here now, anyway.* Not up north, where the thing had happened. Here. And she could feel relieved that she was safe.

*   *   *

Several weeks passed. Then one day when the weather was particularly cold and damp, as Addie sat shivering on her bench in the widow's reception room, the Chinese woman suddenly asked if she were making any plans to return to the States. Addie thought she might have misunderstood. They had been speaking of the widow's business; she wanted to send her middle son, she'd said, on an expedition into the mountains to the west, to a place where they had established business with the local tea growers. In such remote places, she said, it was necessary from time to time to send an envoy from civilization, for the people there were awed by everything that was foreign to them, "and more apt to abide by the terms we set." The widow had paused, and it was then that she asked if Addie were planning on returning to the States. Addie had to ask her to repeat the question. "I wanted to know whether you are planning to return home," she said.

"I have no such plans," Addie replied, sitting up a little. "I hadn't thought of going home."

"Now, or ever?"

"Certainly not now. Perhaps not ever. I have no such plans," she repeated.

The widow folded her hands in her lap. A moment later she unclasped them to smooth the wrinkles from her robe. "Few people enjoy revising their previous intentions."

Addie said nothing, waiting for her to go on.

After a half minute of silence, Widow Liu cleared her throat. "You have said nothing to me about this business, and I am not sure whether the foreign news has carried it yet: the Empress Dowager has issued a statement with regards to the Boxers. She has taken back her previous condemnation of the group and put out what amounts to a letter of support. You understand what this signifies?"

Addie blinked at her, comprehension slow to follow.

"It is a warning," Widow Liu went on. "Tsu Hsi almost certainly means to encourage further attacks on foreigners. In light of this news, it struck me that you may want to make plans to return home, where you will be well out of the path of danger. I can be of assistance, if you require it."

Unlike most houses in Chungking, the widow's house seemed to swallow all sound. Within its walls, you might feel that you were afloat upon the sea, that when you stepped outside, you would find in every direction a great nothingness, a wide swath of empty gray. Now, though no sound accompanied it, Addie felt the reverberations of many fists knocking on the doors, of a great many feet stampeding through the streets. And yet she felt calm as she asked Widow Liu if she really believed that the movement would spread to Chungking.

"Who's to tell? We are a large empire, and the problems that afflict one area may not affect another at all. There is a drought in the north now; meanwhile, here in the south we are well watered. People grow angry when they are hungry. Only give them an enemy, and they will turn their anger in that direction." The widow tipped her head to one side. "So they are angry in the north because of the weather, but in the south we have both rain and sun. In this way, you might feel comfortable remaining in Chungking. And yet I am not certain that the Boxers are no threat to you here. The T'ai-p'ing Heavenly Kingdom may have begun way down in Kuang-hsi, but within two years they had nearly captured Peking. In a decade and a half, they marched through nearly every corner of China. In that case, of course, the Christians were the aggressors; here it is the reverse. The lesson remains."

The rebellion to which the widow referred had ended a quarter century before Addie's arrival in China. She had never been clear as to why it was fought in the first place, but she knew that the missionaries universally renounced the insurrectionists, whose leader claimed to be the younger brother of Jesus Christ. These people were not real Christians; they were mystics, fanatics. And yet Addie felt that she would rather meet a T'ai-p'ing fanatic than she would a Boxer. "So the lesson is that a rebellion can spread farther than one expects?" she said. "However, if the Boxers should come down to Chungking, I think they would find a population that is more amenable to foreigners here than they are in the north. Look at our friendship, Widow Liu—yours and mine. I never spoke with anyone so freely in my previous mission, and I had been there a much longer time than I've been here."

The widow smiled in the manner that was common to her. It was shrewd and ironic; rarely did it have much to do with real joy. "You cannot believe that I am typical of the population here," she said, "or anywhere else. I am a rare treasure." Her mouth turned down at one corner: this was closer to a real smile for her, Addie had learned over the course of their acquaintance. "While you are correct that you have made a friend in me, I cannot agree that all of Chungking might follow my example. Tell me, child, have you made any other friends here?"

Addie admitted that she hadn't. "Still, the people seem more open than those I knew in Shansi. I would say that the"—she paused, searching for the word in Chinese—"the temperament here is warmer."

"And yet even in our friendship—which I have acknowledged to be real—there is a certain expectation that one owes the other."

Addie sat up in her chair. "Do you believe that I owe you, or is it the other way around?"

Widow Liu paused a moment before asking in an even tone what Addie thought she, the widow, gained from their relationship.

"Friendship, I suppose." Addie blinked at the widow. "Isn't that enough?"

"But what is friendship except an agreement that one will help the other whenever possible, whenever asked? And sometimes even when not asked at all?"

Addie thought of the money the widow had given her, which she had turned over to Mr. Wickford for use in the school. She considered for the first time that the widow's donation was a debt to be repaid, but without any resentment of the implication of this form of friendship. The more she thought about it, the more it made sense. What could she say of any of her relationships that did not depend, in some measure, on one person helping the other? Perhaps one did not tally up favors; that might be taking it too far. But as she watched the widow, seated across from her in the dim light of her richly appointed visiting room, Addie wondered what she could possibly offer the Chinese woman in return for both the donation of money and the donation of time: Addie enjoyed her visits, perhaps much more than the widow did.

Widow Liu did not seem to require an answer to her previous question. "Of course, the very best situation is when one friend can help the other in a manner that helps herself at the same time. A double benefit—that is the very best outcome."

"And have you thought of such a scheme?"

The widow shrugged. "I am always considering it. Let us see how the present situation unfolds."

*   *   *

After returning from the widow's house, Addie went into the library in the mission house to clear her mind. The best method, she'd discovered, was to fill it with words. She would sometimes pluck a volume at random from the shelves and read a few lines, a page or two, until she had pushed out every troubling thought. Today she found a book that bore the name of Evan Wickford as its author. It was called *Prayers from the Middle Kingdom*, and had been printed in the year 1893 by the Missionary Board's press in Boston. Inside were many pages of poetry interspersed with short works of prose, the latter of which resembled the Dispatches one might find in a local newspaper back home. The poems had titles like "An Old Grandmother Counts Her Coins" and "Incense Smoke Hovering O'er the Heathen Temple." The meter in the lines was unremitting, the rhymes landing as heavily as a stack of wood.

The poems were not very good, but still Addie found herself moved by the book. She recalled the conversation she and Poppy had once had with Mr. Wickford about the need for a published account of the Chinese missionary's experience. Here he'd already written something of the kind and said nothing. Either it was modesty or a strange kind of hidden pride. Either way, he'd been motivated to filter his perceptions through art—and to go through the trouble of getting his art out into the world.

She stood paging through the book for a few minutes before seating herself at the table. She'd begun coming here every now and then to write letters addressed to Owen or Louisa or her parents that she later put straight into the stove in the kitchen. It was a sort of compulsion, she supposed: she wrote down the memories that visited her during the day and then deposited the paper in the flames. It helped with the feeling of anxiousness that had been building in her over the past few months. The present situation only gave it direction.

Today she sat down without any paper or pen, only running her fingernail over the surface of the table, which was smooth and glossy. She had the urge to carve something into it—not her name, as children did, but a feeling, a word, a message whose permanence would be a testament to its truth. Yet when she searched her mind, it was such a jumble of impressions that she wasn't sure what she would write, even if she had a knife in her hand right now.

Poppy found her still seated at the table when she returned from her own round of afternoon visits. She sat herself down in the opposite chair and put out her hands. "Addie," she said, "what are you doing?"

Addie stretched her hands over the table and linked her fingers with Poppy's but didn't speak for some time. At last she said, "I visited Widow Liu today."

"And how is the dear woman?"

"The same as ever. She had some news. The situation up north, Poppy—it's grown rather grave. The widow told me that the Empress Dowager has changed her position with regards to the Boxers. She's thrown her support behind them."

"Yes, so I heard."

Addie pulled her hands away. "You heard? Why didn't you tell me? When did you hear it?"

"Yesterday, I suppose—yesterday or the day before. The papers have all reported it. I supposed that you had already learned of it from someone else."

"From someone else—who would that be?"

"The widow, apparently."

Addie felt the reply as a rebuke. She sat quietly for a moment, staring at her hands, which she had placed in her lap.

"Look here, it's all very far away, and I am still convinced that it will remain that way."

"Far from us, you mean."

"Yes." Poppy's eyes were clear and hard as she said, "There's nothing to be done about the past, Addie. Even if, moving down the scroll as the Chinese do, it is hovering right above us."

She was referring to Addie's decision to leave, of course. Addie could not go back and change that decision or the journey that followed it. She could not return to Lu-cho Fu. Her and Owen's and the boys' fates had once all been bound up together, as threads in a single spool of yarn. Then hers had unraveled. She had not understood how completely until now. They were there and she was here, and whatever would happen to them, she had no control over it.

Poppy would leave it at that, but she had to take it further: Addie was not responsible for the violence galloping over the north, but neither was she an innocent. None of them were. They'd come to China to spread the flame of Christian faith, to shepherd all the sheep that didn't even know they were lost, but the truth was that they had failed. The people did not want them here. As Widow Liu had pointed out, the foreigners as a group had taken much more than they had given. And so, the Boxers, who hovered over them now as a shadow.

Surely Owen would know what to do. Even now, she hoped—she trusted—he and the boys were on a ship back to America.

She looked across the table at Poppy. "We must decide what our own course of action will be."

"With regards to what?"

"The rebellion. Poppy, you truly don't feel we're in any danger here?"

"I don't. But evidently you do."

"I think it's worth considering our options."

"All right, then, I'd say there are two: first, we pick up our skirts and run as fast as we can to the nearest port so we can flee; or second, we remain here and continue our work."

Addie stood and went to the wall of books. She saw the volume by Mr. Wickford but didn't take it down from the shelf. She only wanted something to busy her while she thought, and ran her eyes over the titles. There were the many volumes of missionaries' accounts from all different parts of the world; there were the religious tracts; there were the map books and prayer books and books of common Chinese words and phrases that had been compiled and edited and expanded by a succession of missionaries to Chungking, of which she and Poppy were only the latest. And suddenly she found herself thinking of the sitting room in her sister Louisa's house, where she had spent a few weeks during the only trip back to America that she had taken since coming to China. It was the room where she and Owen and the boys had slept: the whole house encompassed only a kitchen on one side, and a small bedroom on another. But almost the first thing Louisa had done upon Addie's arrival was to take her into the sitting room to show her the shelf that held jars of fossils and arrowheads, and beside them, a collection of four or five books. There was a Bible and an almanac of the world, as well as two or three novels. "If you knew," Louisa said fiercely, "how I had to fight to get every last one of these. We don't get the newspaper here very often, you know." Addie had nodded and said with a laugh that they didn't take a paper in Lu-cho Fu, either.

She hadn't understood then why her sister so needed to show off this meager library. There were so many other things to see, to discuss: the changes that had occurred in both their lives were too great to be numbered. Two weeks was too little to go through even a small part of it.

She understood now. Remembering how, as they drove up the lane that day, Bert, previously a stranger to them all, had shaded his eyes with his hand and said, as if it were the most ordinary thing in the world, "There she is. There's Louisa." Addie had squinted at that lone figure standing in front of a small house, a few small buildings—she would come to find out that they were the barn and the henhouse—and seen nothing else but that figure and the great immensity surrounding it. Her sister, pointing at the books a few minutes later, had been telling her that you couldn't get further from the world than where she was. Not even China was further. No place was further from the world than where you were.

I have all your letters, Louisa had told her later. *I've kept every last one.*

Addie turned from the wall of books and said to Poppy, "Tell me they aren't in danger—Owen and the boys. Tell me they'll be all right."

Poppy tipped back her hat so she could look her in the eye. "They aren't in danger. They will be all right."

Addie nodded. If it was a lie, then she'd choose to believe it for now.

Hazel

28

When Lydie got sick—real sick, I mean: those last months when she wasn't able to move around very much—I was in and out of their house two or three times a day, bringing food and helping with the laundry. It was summer and because I didn't have my work at the cafeteria, I had time to help. Sometimes I brought Debbie over. She didn't like to be inside the house with Lydie and me, but she'd find things to do outdoors when I didn't have any chores for her. She was almost ten, and every pail of standing water still had the potential to become a magic potion. Sometimes she sat in the yard drawing faces on rocks. She did the same thing at our house—I'd find whole families of them lying there when I walked to the mailbox or to the clearing where we burned trash. I avoided stepping on those rocks with their faces either grinning or surprised-looking, the same as I'd avoid stepping on a baby chick.

Debbie would have been fine at home on her own, but I brought her over to the Hughes's house as a sort of protection because I knew she'd be a warning bell for when George was coming. He always stopped to say hello on his way to the door, and sitting inside with Lydie, I'd hear them talking through the open window.

I didn't want to be around George because I didn't like having to pretend we didn't have things to say to each other, to speak like we were neighbors and nothing more. What were we by then? Former lovers, I guess. But only recently former. And we were angry with each other: he was angry with me because I'd kept Lydie's secret, and I was angry with him because—I wasn't sure why. Because I had to be. Because he had let it be easy between us for so long, and the truth was that no matter what we felt for each other, it had never been right to take up together as we did. I was angry with him because he'd ended our affair, and I was angry with him for not ending it sooner.

I came to the house in the morning, late enough that George was sure to be out in the fields. Sometimes I'd see him from a distance as I drove down the lane, sitting way up on his John Deere, tending the land that had my name on the deed. I always drove down to their place because I was loaded down with the food I brought each day: meatloaves, roasts, pots of chicken and dumplings. Every night I fixed the next day's dinner for George and the boys so I could spend the morning doing other chores. Come dinnertime, I'd set the food out on the table and say good-bye. Then I'd collect Debbie from the yard and Joe from the fields, and drive back home before George and his sons came in to eat. Twelve years old, my son had decided he was going to be a farmer, just like his dad had been, but I made him come home to eat dinner at our house because mealtimes were sacred. Even though Lydie could barely eat anything more than applesauce, it was her house and her family and I wasn't going to preside over her table or have my family intrude on hers.

In my own kitchen at dinnertime with Debbie and Joe, I'd imagine George and the boys sitting down to the meal I'd left out for them in the kitchen, the table set, knives and forks lined up on either side of the plates, glasses waiting to be filled with milk or water. This routine was repeated for supper, except that I didn't heat up the meal myself. I left casseroles on the counter, Tupperware containers packed with chicken salad in the fridge. Fresh Parker House rolls in the bread bin. Cobs of corn in a pot of water on the stove, needing only a ten-minute boil. I always left a note on the counter with careful instructions and arranged it so the food wouldn't sit for more than an hour or so because it was summer and anything would spoil if left out for too long. I always included that in the instructions, too: *Meat and vegetables go in the fridge when you're done.*

The next morning, the first thing I'd do after going in to see Lydie was to open the fridge and see what was left. I started to learn what they liked and what they didn't. Lima beans were never more than half eaten, whereas large quantities of spaghetti would have disappeared completely, the platter washed clean and waiting for me on the counter. I knew without being told that it was George who did it. I always looked for a note slipped under the base, but there never was one.

*   *   *

As much time as I spent in their house, I didn't spend all that many hours with Lydie, at least not while she was still well enough to have guests. When someone was visiting, I tried to stay out of the way as much as possible, even if I knew the person well. My sisters all stopped by at various times, and even then I made myself scarce. I figured that Lydie had her friendships without me, and I had no business butting in on them. I wasn't fooling myself: I knew I'd gotten in the middle of the one relationship that mattered more than any other, and I guess I was trying to make amends, even in the smallest of ways. I couldn't ask Lydie to forgive me, so I did my penance through deeds. Which meant that I spent a lot of hours in the kitchen, peeling potatoes and boiling beans and frying hamburger patties, and down in the cellar with the washer, and out in the yard hanging wet clothes on the line. I did some light cleaning, too—a little sweeping, a quick wipe with the dust cloth—but I tried to get this done when Lydie was taking a nap, because whenever she caught me at it she told me to stop, she wasn't paying me enough for all that.

My own house was going without cleaning, my own garden growing weeds, the vegetables all rotting on the vine. No matter. It was only in the mornings that I had any free time, and though it wasn't much, I spent it with Lydie. Sometimes I turned on the television and we watched the morning programming, but most of the time she preferred to lie quietly listening to the birds singing and the flies slamming up against the screens. I'd read to her then; I read aloud parts of the newspaper and we discovered together how dull most of it was: tips on summer gardens, reports from the statehouse. Nothing competed with Lydie's sickness. And why would she care, anyway, about a bill being debated, when she wouldn't be around to hear how it turned out? This was the first time I'd been present for the long process of dying, and I was learning how it took you out of time, how it turned the world inside out.

Usually Lydie preferred to hear one of her Agatha Christie novels instead of the paper. We started with *The Body in the Library*, and when that was finished we went on to *A Murder Is Announced*. A few chapters into the book, Lydie declared that she was tired of Miss Marple. "I've got a few Poirots," she said. "Any one of them is fine."

I set down the paperback and went over to take a look. She and George didn't have a large library, but they had a few shelves of books behind a glass-fronted door. One shelf held the staples that every household kept: dictionary, family Bible, church cookbooks, world atlas, and a decade's worth or more of the Farmer's Almanac. But they also had three full shelves of novels, one of them nothing but Agatha Christies. I ran my eyes down the row and plucked *Murder on the Orient Express*. I'd read it myself years before but didn't remember anything except that there were a lot of deaths in the backstory—a whole family, I thought I recalled. One murder had set in motion several other deaths by grief and suicide. I didn't remember much about the lead character, though. "Why not Miss Marple?" I asked.

"Oh," Lydie said, "I think I'm just tired of women."

It was an odd thing to say for someone who was married and only had boys. It was true, though, that all her visitors were women. Lydie's mother had died years before, but George's mother came down from Wood River on the weekends and bustled around. There were sisters-in-law, too, and the endless procession of neighbors and friends. Somehow only women seemed able or willing to venture near. I wasn't sure if it was the nature of Lydie's disease or some more elemental law: only the female of the species can minister to the sick.

I thought this must be what Lydie was referring to. But then I saw her staring out the window, where at that particular moment you could see the tractor in the distance, and I realized that her words meant something more: it wasn't only that she was tired of women, but that she missed the company of men. Her husband and boys were out working from dawn to dusk, and she stayed in her sickroom staring out a window at empty fields and sky, waiting for the rare instance when one of her boys came into view.

"Let's see what our man Hercule Poirot is getting up to," I said, and opened the book and began to read.

I read until it was time to get dinner ready, and then Lydie closed her eyes and said she thought she might just take a rest. I went to the kitchen and started readying the steak and onions for George and the boys. I'd bought the steaks the day before with the money George had begun leaving for me; every few days I'd find a five-dollar bill tucked under the serving dish. The first time I saw the bill lying there, I thought maybe it was a note he'd left, but the money was probably a better discovery. I didn't mind the cooking, but I'd been wondering how to handle the expense. George and the boys ate twice what Joe and Debbie and I did. I was reminded of years before, when my mother and sisters and I would prepare giant dinners for the men on days when they were baling hay on our land, or when neighbors came over to help with slaughtering the hogs. I remembered wondering at the amount they could put away, each man taking two or three plates of food. Whole quarts of gravy would have been dispensed of by the end of the meal. Dozens of potatoes. Six or seven pies.

I trimmed the steaks and was slicing up an onion to fry with them when my eyes started watering. That onion must have been particularly powerful because I couldn't keep my eyes open, and after a minute or two I had to set down the knife and walk away. I went out onto the porch where I'd left Debbie cutting up green beans a little while before and found her reading one of her science fiction novels, one sandal swinging from the big toe of her left foot, the other sandal lying on its side on the floor. "I'm all finished," she said guiltily before I could ask what she was doing, and gestured to the pile of trimmed beans in the pail.

"Why didn't you say so?" I asked. "I've got plenty more you could do."

Debbie closed the book on her lap, holding the place with her finger as she waited for me to tell her what new chore she should tackle. I had to think a minute. The truth was that there was more to do than I could keep in my head at one time, and all the inessential tasks I'd pushed to the back burner. There wasn't any point having Debbie pick tomatoes if I wasn't going to get around to canning them. Finally I told her to go collect the dirty laundry from the floor of the bedrooms upstairs. It had been a few days since I'd done any washing for the family.

"But those are the *boys'* rooms," she said.

"That's right, and those boys are busy working all day. The least you can do is help me get some clean clothes for them to change into when they're done."

"But—"

"Debbie."

She laid her book down on the chair and went past me through the door.

After she'd gone, I went down the steps into the yard. It was blazing hot in the house and even hotter outside in the bright sunshine. How long had it been since Lydie was out in the daylight? If there ever came a break in the heat, I decided, I would take her out to sit on the porch. But today was too uncomfortable: it was one of those days when the sky curved over the landscape like a giant eggshell, dull and white, and the heat seemed to rise off every blade of grass.

I was standing there sweating in the heat, wiping eyes still filled with onion tears, when Bobby came up from around the barn. He was a little younger than Joe, but taller and had more muscle since he'd been doing farmwork alongside his father for the past several summers, and this made him seem older than my son, more mature. He was a quiet boy, gentle and pliant. Or he had been, anyway, until all this business with Lydie began. Since then, I hadn't seen too much of him, and when I did, he always seemed to duck his face to avoid looking at me, as if I was the cause of embarrassment or pain. It had to do with my taking care of Lydie: it was hard to pretend that his mother was still well when I was in the house nearly every day.

He darted a quick look past me to determine whether he could go inside without attracting my notice. But I called out to him and he was forced to walk over the grass toward me. "You finish up your work early?" I asked.

"No, Mrs. Wiz." That was what all my children's friends called me, the name Wisniewski too cumbersome. "I was just coming in to get a Band-Aid." I saw for the first time that he was holding one hand in the other. He seemed to notice at the same moment the tears in my eyes because he quickly glanced away again. No point explaining that I'd been cutting onions—there was plenty to cry about without them.

"You cut yourself?" I asked, and he lifted his right hand to reveal a smear of blood. I asked what had happened.

"Scraped it on the hitch, somehow. It ain't deep, anyway."

I took his hand and examined it up close. He was right; it was a shallow cut, but there was plenty of blood, and dirt and machine oil getting all mixed up with it. "Come on inside. Let's get you washed before you get an infection."

In the kitchen, I turned on the tap and washed both Bobby's hands in my own, making sure to scrub at the lines of dirt and digging around the fingernails. I was gentler with the injured hand, but it must have hurt. Still, he didn't make a sound or even a grimace; he was watching the drips of blood falling into the sink with a kind of pride. Once I was satisfied that his hand was clean, I went to retrieve some bandages from the bathroom cabinet and on the way peeked my head into the living room to see whether Lydie was sleeping. She was.

When I got back to the kitchen, Debbie was standing by Bobby at the sink. I hadn't heard her come down, but a basket of dirty laundry sat on the floor, disregarded. She turned when she heard me and made a face. "Bobby's bleeding," she said, as if the fact might have escaped my notice.

What was it I saw on their faces in that moment? Nothing that should have been too surprising—two children exhilarated by the sight of blood. They wore identical expressions of guilty excitement, a sudden shared charge moving through the air. Debbie hadn't been party to Bobby's injury, but coming upon him alone in the kitchen with blood dripping from his hand, she had stumbled into a scene already in action and none of the explanations immediately evident. It was something different, a whiff of drama. After the long quiet of a morning spent snapping the ends off a pile of green beans, anything approaching an emergency was sure to interest her. Her eyes were bright with it, as were Bobby's.

I shouldn't have been surprised, yet for a moment I felt something close to alarm at their stance, the two of them facing me together from the other side of an invisible line. It was that first instance when you understand that your children have already become something separate from you, that there are unknowable parts of them you didn't even know to wonder about, or fear. The future standing up, overshadowing the present.

It was only a moment. Then I crossed the room to stand beside Bobby at the sink. Taking his hand, I blotted the fresh blood with some tissues I'd brought with me from the bathroom. Then I began wrapping it up with the bandage and tape. Debbie stood watching me, biting her fingernails, and when I was done, she asked if Bobby was going back out to work.

I glanced at the clock. It was a quarter to eleven, and I always had dinner ready by eleven thirty. "Why don't you stay in here and rest up," I told him. Turning to my daughter, I said, "You go run and tell Mr. Hughes that Bobby's going to stay here till dinner."

Once Debbie had left, Bobby thanked me and then leaned against the counter, looking uncomfortable. I knew he'd rather go back out and help his father, but I had told him to stay, and he was waiting now for me to tell him what to do next.

"Get yourself a glass of water," I said, "and let's go see how your mother's doing."

"She's probably sleeping. She sleeps a lot."

I stepped past him to grab a glass from the cabinet and then handed it to him to fill. "That's true, but I know she'd be glad to spend a little time with you. Go on and get a drink and let's go see if we can wake her."

In the living room, Lydie was sitting up partway with several pillows at her back. It wasn't a very comfortable position; her lower back was hurting so badly she thought it might be that the cancer had spread to the bones. "What're you doing coming in so early?" she asked Bobby.

"Cut myself," he said, not moving from the doorway.

I'd already taken several steps across the carpet and my presence made it all the clearer how far Bobby was staying from the sickbed. I wanted to go over and draw him physically into the room, but I stayed where I was. After a pause, Lydie spoke: "Come over and let me take a look at it."

Her tone was almost harsh, much more so than usual. She hadn't ever been the sentimental type, but her voice was naturally soft. Now all that softness was gone, leaving a hollow scrape in its place. I tried to think whether it was that way when she was speaking with me alone and decided that it wasn't; this was some other way of talking that I hadn't heard from her before.

Bobby waited a second or two before following her orders. When he came up to her at last he was cradling the injured hand and he held it out for her inspection, gingerly, as if afraid she might grab it and squeeze.

Lydie turned her eyes on the bandaged hand. "You washed it good?" Bobby nodded.

"And you thanked Mrs. Wisniewski for wrapping it up for you?"

"Yes, ma'am."

She leaned back a little and looked at him. Her eyes were flat. "How'd you get yourself hurt?"

He explained to her about the tractor. "I was going to go back out—" He stopped abruptly and glanced at me. Then he looked down suddenly and blushed because it sounded as if he were blaming me for keeping him back.

"I thought he might sit here with you and rest awhile before dinner," I said to Lydie. "It's already getting on to eleven."

She nodded without looking at me. It was quiet for several seconds, and then in the same instant Lydie reached out to take her son's hand and Bobby turned to look at me. He gave me a pleading look, as if I was the only one who could make this torture end. And because he'd turned away, he didn't see his mother's effort. She dropped her hand without touching his. "Go on," she said sharply when he had turned back to her again. "You go out and help your dad until dinner is ready. And be careful you don't hurt your hand any worse."

Bobby breathed out quickly and took off without shooting another glance at me.

Once he was gone, Lydie slid down so she was lying flat with her head on the pillows. She closed her eyes and said in the voice she hadn't used with her son—the tired one—that she'd be grateful if I would go fix dinner for the boys. Of course, I told her, and walked into the kitchen to start frying up the steaks.

*   *   *

There came a point when Lydie's dying could no longer be considered a background event. She'd been stationed on the sofa in the living room for more than a month, and with help, she was still able to get up to go to the bathroom. What she needed help with was the standing part. The bathroom was right next to the living room, so she could walk to it on her own by using the arm of the sofa and then the wall for support. But standing up was difficult—the cancer was making her bones weak, and she was afraid of falling and breaking something. So I'd help her swing her feet onto the floor and then I'd sit beside her on the sofa. I'd reach my arm behind her back to grab hold of her waist and she'd lean her shoulder against mine, and then I'd lift with that whole side of my body. I was afraid of hurting her, but she knew how to protect herself; she held her arms in such a way as to shelter her chest.

This was how things went for a time. I knew that George was the one to help her up and down in the evenings after I'd gone home, though Lydie never spoke of it. Then one morning after I'd been sitting with her awhile, she told me she had a favor to ask. She was lying half-reclined with her eyes raised to the top of the window, which showed a view of green leaves, perfectly still. "It's been over a week since I had a bath," she said.

"That long?"

She turned to look at me. "You've got to have noticed, Hazel. I'm starting to smell."

I had noticed. For the past two or three days I'd had to will myself not to breathe through my mouth whenever I helped her up from the sofa. I'd seen no reason to mention it. I figured she must know and that it was none of my business to tell her if she didn't.

"George has been helping me," Lydie went on. "That little stool in the bathroom—he sets it in the tub and then helps me to sit. I've managed, up to now. I send him out of the room and I've been able to—to wash myself. I don't think I can anymore. Last time I almost fell off the stool."

I stood from my chair. "How about I go run the bath now?"

Lydie nodded. She'd gone back to staring at the top of the window, and I left her like that. While the tub filled, I retrieved a towel and washcloth and a fresh nightgown from the linen closet. I'd been putting her nightgowns there after I took them down from the line because I didn't want to set foot in George and Lydie's bedroom. Most of the time, I had Debbie take the laundry upstairs when it was done.

When the tub had collected a foot or so of water, I set the stool inside it and then went back to get Lydie. The leaves outside were moving a little now and I felt the breeze coming in through the screen. "All set," I said.

"You got a different gown for me to put on?"

"Sure."

"A towel?"

"That, too. And a washcloth," I added.

"There should be a glass on the side of the tub—"

"I saw it."

"All right, then," she said, but she still didn't move.

I waited half a minute. Then, "Lydie," I said, and she turned to look at me. "It's all right if this bothers you. But it's just a bath, you know. You tell me what you need, and we'll get it done. It's as simple as that."

She stared back at me without responding, her eyes fixed on my face with an expression I'd never seen before, one that had a whole bundle of emotions mixed up in it: shame and gratitude and fear and sadness. Or maybe it was only the flicker of understanding that this was the next stage, and surprise that I was going to be the one to take her through it.

I helped her into the bathroom and got her seated on the stool, but her feet were still out of the tub. "Why don't you hold on to my shoulders," I said as I pulled off her socks, "and I'll help you swing your legs around." I was leaning over, half crouching, and I twisted toward her so she could get a firm grasp on my shoulders. When she lifted her arms the smell got worse, and it wasn't just the odor from not washing for a week, but a smell like rotting meat. She groaned a little. "Does it hurt?" I asked, and she said yes, it did, like hell.

Once we'd gotten her feet inside the tub, I tugged her nightgown up from under her backside and then began peeling it off her as gently as I could. I knew it hurt to move her upper body in any way, but there was no avoiding it. And I saw what was causing that smell: there were dull red lesions all over her chest. The spots were mostly small and dusty-looking, but in one area they were larger. There were two bandages on her left breast and they didn't look as if they'd been changed for some time. "Should we take those off while you wash?" I asked after I'd pulled the gown all the way off and dropped it onto the floor behind me.

"Yes, I think so."

As I peeled the bandages off, I forced myself to talk. I talked about how hot it was and wondered whether we'd get any rain. I talked about how the summer seemed to be stretching on forever and I couldn't wait for it to end, and though this was a thoughtless thing to say to a woman who might not live to see another turning of the seasons, Lydie didn't say anything because of course I didn't mean it that way. I talked and I was careful to make my voice as even as I could. But my heart had started pounding because it was suddenly clear to me that despite the many hours I'd spent in Lydie's house for the past month, and the many mornings I'd sat reading and talking with her, I hadn't really known what the cancer was doing to her body. I'd seen her grow thinner and more tired, seen her skin take on an odd luster and her eyes grow dull. But those symptoms could have belonged to any number of illnesses, and the truth of the matter was that I'd been thinking of the cancer as something contained inside her, hidden away in the dark and never to be seen. Now here it was to prove me wrong, and it was angry and evil-looking, breaking out of her skin like some sort of demon. Beneath the bandages were red mounds and craters crusted yellow, bleeding fresh at the edges.

The quicker we got through this bath, I figured, the better. I kept up my steady stream of nothing-talk while I half lifted her from the stool to take off her underwear, and then I took the glass from the side of the tub and began pouring water over her shoulders. She gasped when the water ran over the open wounds, there was no helping it. I asked if she wanted me to do her hair. "It looks something awful without setting it," she said, "but I guess I don't need to worry too much about that."

I put shampoo in her hair and then soaped the washcloth to wash her face. It was peculiar to be looking at her from such a close distance, rubbing the washcloth around her nose and over her cheeks and forehead.

Her family used Ivory, like we did, and the smell of it was comforting. Lydie had closed her eyes when I started on her hair and she kept them closed while I was doing her face. But when I stopped to dip the cloth in the water, she opened her eyes and stuck her tongue out at me. That made us both laugh.

I washed her neck, and then her arms and legs. I washed her back and her shoulders and even her hands. At last, there was nothing left but her chest and between her legs. The prospect of washing her chest scared me more because I didn't know how to clean the wounds. I figured I shouldn't get soap on them, so I wrung out the cloth in fresh water from the faucet and just tapped gingerly around the red areas on her skin. It made me think of Edith, of her time in the WAC during the war. Surely, she'd washed wounds worse than these—and yet I found it hard to imagine her taking on such a familiar role with anyone. Edith wasn't the comforting type. Then again, maybe a businesslike temperament was better suited to the task.

I hadn't stopped talking this whole time because I was too afraid of silence. I'd gone through the weather and what was happening in *Murder on the Orient Express* and on *As the World Turns*. I was running out of topics when Lydie remarked that this was the first time someone had bathed her since she was a child. How strange, she said. "Was it your mother who used to bathe you?"

Usually it was Iris or Rena, I said.

"And now, see, I only had brothers"—she sighed—"so my ma was always the one responsible for me."

I was standing Lydie up now so I could wash between her legs, and it was better to have her talking of things long ago or far away rather than have to focus on that. But the topic of mothers long departed was a dangerous one, and I tried to turn the conversation to baths and how different they were now than they had been a few years ago, explaining how I still found myself thinking I needed to drag out the big tub when it came time for baths at night; we'd finally gotten our indoor plumbing.

"I remember when we got this bathroom put in," Lydie said dreamily, "and I took that first bath in a tub with clean water. I felt like a queen. There wasn't any grit at the bottom and no hairs floating around.

I don't believe I ever got to sit in water that clear before. When I was young I always bathed after my brothers, and then I got married and I always went after the boys."

As I listened, I ran the cloth quickly along the folds at the top of her legs. I'd never been this close to another woman's privacy before, but it wasn't so strange. I was reminded of when my children were young, how they didn't know to be ashamed of anything, and how I'd had to teach them that shame—I remembered slapping Debbie's hand away from her business when I was giving her a bath. She might have been three years old.

Lydie fell quiet all of a sudden, absorbed in her own thoughts. We were just about finished with the bath, anyway, and I went to help her back down onto the stool to rinse off. That's when I saw that she was crying. It seemed to have come on quickly, and I asked what was wrong.

She gave me a look like I was a fool, and of course I was. "It's so ugly," she said, squeezing her eyes shut and shaking her head. She was a taller and a bigger woman than me, but she looked at that moment as small as a child.

"What is?"

"All of this. I wish I'd come up to it quick instead of day by day getting worse."

Droplets of water were dripping down from her wet hair onto her shoulders, and I wanted to dry them but didn't dare move. All the same, I wasn't sure what to say, so I just kept my hands on her arms, keeping her upright.

Lydie was quiet, soft sobs making her body shake. Then she looked at me and said, "Joe and Debbie are all right."

It took me a second to figure out what she was saying: it was that my children had lost their father and they were still carrying on. In fact, four years after his death, they barely seemed to be grieving at all. How could I tell her that this made me glad even while it broke my heart? That I imagined them growing older, and their father meaning less and less to them with every year that passed? I wasn't sure if this was what she wanted to hear, but she'd spoken as if she were asking a question, and I felt compelled to answer: "Yes, they are."

"That's good. It's what I want for my boys. I don't want them to miss me long. They're old enough to take care of themselves, but still young enough to get over it. That's good," she repeated.

"There's no getting over it, Lydie." I was going to go on, to tell her I thought Gene and Bobby could handle more than she was giving them right now, but she interrupted me with: "Help me dry off, will you?" And that was that.

I patted her dry, and then I got some fresh bandages from the cupboard and taped them on. Lydie stayed quiet throughout the process, and it was only after I'd helped her into a fresh nightgown and led her back to the sofa in the living room that she spoke again. She was out of breath, and as soon as she lay down, her eyes fluttered closed. But I heard her say my name as I pulled the sheet up to her chest and tucked it under her arms. I'd brought a fresh sheet in the day before, but already it smelled off, and I was thinking that tomorrow I'd trade it out for a new one. "Hazel," she said as all this was going through my mind. "I've still got a little ways to go."

I pulled the sheet so it wasn't too tight. "Of course you do."

"But I don't want them going there with me."

"Don't want who?"

"My boys," she said, her eyes moving a little, as if she was trying to hold my gaze and it kept slipping away. "And George," she added. Then she explained that she didn't intend to let her family see her die. "I need you to stay here with me. And I need you to send them away."

All the air left the room. I dropped onto the edge of the sofa, the little strip of cushion that wasn't taken up by her body. My hands were still grasping the sheet at her sides. "Where?"

"I don't know. I'll leave you to figure that out."

I released my grasp on the sheet and sat back. Now I was viewing her from a little distance and I saw that her eyes were still searching my face, but the expression in them was something different than I had thought up close. It wasn't pleading or scared or soft or uncertain. It was clear and it was hard. "When?" I asked, and I could feel my shoulders shaking.

She blinked and then turned her eyes from mine. She was gazing up at the ceiling when she answered: "Soon."

29

When Karol died, time stopped working as it should: a day stretched into a year, a week passed in a blink. Space changed, too. Before, there was the solid fact of him everywhere—his razor in the bathroom cabinet, his jacket on the hook, his laughter and his cold sweat, his weight on the other side of the bed—and then he was nothing; less than ether, he was gone. The atmosphere in the house had shifted. Every day I had to consider different options and choose the best one and this might have been what life looked like all along, but I'd never realized it before, and when I did, it was exhausting. I was a widow, but otherwise my roles were the same—mother, sister, neighbor, friend—and yet they didn't *feel* the same; they didn't come naturally to me anymore, the actions were no longer automatic or easy. I became a mechanical doll that moved a dozen muscles to make a smile. Sometimes it worked. Often, it didn't.

Those first few weeks, I felt sick to my stomach. Then it changed to a sharp pain in my chest, then an itching, then an ache. Grief took over my whole body so I felt it in every organ and limb, except when I was numb, which was much of the time. After a while the ache went away, and I discovered that I still had my arms, my ankles, my liver, my spleen. Eyes blinking in bright light. Lungs filling and emptying.

My heart had been beating the whole time, I realized, without skipping a beat.

A recovery of some kind. Grief stretches on to the horizon, but you keep moving through it. I knew this because Karol's death wasn't my first tragedy. There was my brother Junior disappearing: word came that he'd hopped a train going east, and that was all we ever learned. And then there was Herbert, who'd passed the year before Karol did. My parents' death was a cruel joke—killed in a car accident during the only vacation they ever took in their lives, pursuing that classic dream of every midwesterner, to see the ocean, just once. The police said my father wasn't wearing any shoes, and the mystery of this detail haunted me still. And then there were the family tragedies that happened before I was alive, or at least before I could remember. The brother I only ever met as a baby, a sister who died of sickness years before I was born. The family's losses become part of you, become your own. My mother never spoke of the children she grieved over, but my father would remind us on the occasion of an anniversary: "Be kind to your ma today. She's remembering your brother." The anniversaries were always those of their deaths, never their births. My mother was certainly one for endings.

What I'm saying, then, is that I wasn't inexperienced in loss when Karol suddenly left me all on my own. But one tragedy in no way prepares you for the next. I mourned Karol, and there was a sort of pleasure in the mourning because I was certain that it was the worst I'd ever suffer. A wife loses her husband; her children lose their father. No one has a greater claim on devastation. No other loss can compare to this.

I continued to believe that right up until Lydie died.

*   *   *

In the end, I spent a little over three weeks living alone with her in that house. Twenty-three days altogether, but it might as well have been a year, a decade, a lifetime. It was like something from one of Debbie's science fiction novels: a whole civilization rises up, thrives, collapses, and turns to dust—and on the last page you find out that it all took place in the blink of a god's eye. Not *the* God but a god. Those books have to invent everything, starting right at the beginning.

During that time, I sent Joe and Debbie to stay with Rena and John Charlie. Joe was angry with me because he no longer got to help George and the Hughes boys with the farm, but what could I do with my son's anger over something trivial when I had Lydie's orders to follow? And I had no doubt that they were orders. She had made it clear that she wanted me to be the one to lead her down those last few steps toward death, and this wasn't a directive I would have refused anyone, much less someone from whom I'd taken so much.

Did she know what I'd taken? Was this the reason she felt she could ask me—tell me, more like it—to nurse her at the end? I didn't know. I couldn't ask. Even if she knew or had somehow guessed about George and me, staying with her was nothing so simple as a punishment. It was something else: a pact, maybe. An agreement. It was her bonding me to her memory while she was still breathing, while her heart continued to beat. It was an assurance that when she was gone, I would honor our friendship better than I'd done when she was alive.

George was living in my house with Gene and Bobby. I tried not to think of them there—him, especially. I assumed he was sleeping in the bed where we had often made love. His head was on the pillow, and I both looked forward to and dreaded the time when I'd return to the house and find evidence of him there: stray hairs, a lingering scent, a sock kicked under the bed. He and the boys were eating at my kitchen table; Rena told me she dropped some food there every other day, and others of our neighbors and friends were doing the same. They were all curious, of course, about this arrangement that exiled George and his sons from their home, and me and my children from ours. Why Hazel? they might be asking. Why not one of Lydie's sisters-in-law? And in fact, George's sisters did call the house; they were about the only ones, aside from his parents. Everyone else figured they had no claim, I guess, but family could insist. I gave them updates on Lydie, and each time I had to repeat her instructions that no one come to see her. Somehow or other, they all obeyed. Whether they resented me or were thankful that I was the one chosen to take on the nursing duties and not them, I didn't know. My guess is that it was some mixture of both. In any case, both family and neighbors stayed away from the Hughes's house, and if anyone bothered George with inquiries, at least they were keeping him and the boys fed at the same time. You could count on neighbors to buy their gossip with casseroles.

Meanwhile, George was there, inhabiting the rooms I'd lived in my whole life, and I was here, in the home he'd made with Lydie these past two decades. He was a ghost haunting my house, and I was a ghost haunting his.

And what was Lydie? The god of all this. Everything happening in the blink of her eye.

*   *   *

I didn't see much of anyone, but I called George every evening to give him an update on his wife. We never talked long, and I spoke with the certainty that other ears might be listening. I told him how the day had gone—how long she had been awake, whether she'd eaten at all—but I left out the worst of it. After all, the whole reason Lydie had wanted her family to leave was so that they might be spared the difficult and messy end. And the truth was that I felt some protectiveness over her dying. I was watching her fight a losing battle, and I was a part of the fight, too, even if I was only the equivalent of a flag-bearer. The real fight was all hers. But it was also true that I knew the struggle better than anyone but her, and I was possessive of my role as first and only observer. Talking to George on the phone each night, I kept my updates short and vague. I left out all that mattered.

The only time I saw him was a few days before Lydie died. It was at my house; Rena had brought my children to see me, just for an hour or two. I didn't feel comfortable leaving Lydie alone any longer than that. I didn't want to go far, either, so we met at the house. This was the second time—the first had been the previous week. It didn't seem right to absent myself completely from Joe and Debbie when in reality I was staying just down the road from our house. But I also couldn't give them much time because Lydie was in no place to care for herself. If she needed to move, I had to be there to help her. If she wanted water, it was me that fetched it.

Both times I saw my children, we met when George and his sons were out working. We sat on the porch and talked as if we were ac-quaintances. The first time, Debbie cried. The second time she pouted. Joe looked out at the fields with open longing and talked only when Rena asked him a direct question, trying to coax him into talking to me. For my part, I didn't try very hard. I was nearly exhausted with the emotional labor of nursing a dying woman who was both my best friend and the person I'd most wronged in my life, and I couldn't worry about anyone else, not even my children. They were with Rena; they were fine. This would all be over soon.

That second meeting, however, George came up to the porch unex-pectedly, and when he saw me, he gave me a look like I might be on fire.

It was clear he didn't know what to say, so he talked to Rena and the children and he ignored me. He'd come to the house for some water, and after a minute or two of small talk, he went past us into the kitchen and we all listened to the sound of the tap running. Then he came back out onto the porch and asked if he could have a moment's private talk with me.

We went down the porch stairs and walked around the side of the house in silence. At the back was the fence with blackberry bushes, and I saw that the berries were full. Beyond them, on the other side, was the garden where I would normally be spending my mornings this time of year. I didn't want to see the state of it—overripe tomatoes blackening on the ground, weeds crowding out the carrots and beets—so I stopped and said I thought this was far enough to put us out of earshot of the others, and asked what he wanted to talk to me about.

"What do you think I want to talk about, Hazel? You think I brought you out here to chat about the weather?"

I straightened my shoulders and looked him in the eye. "If you brought me out here to shout at me, then I won't bother to stay. You go on and yell at the wind if you want to yell."

"Never heard me shout before, did you? 'Mild-mannered George, never raises his voice.'" He said this last in a strange tone, high and affected. Then he shook his head and frowned. "Lydie used to say that. It made her so angry that I wouldn't get upset when we fought. Me, I always figured there wasn't much to get worked up about. What do you think we fought about?"

He looked at me as if I might want to answer him, but I had folded my arms and sealed my lips tight. If he wanted to deliver a monologue, I'd let him, but I wasn't going to participate in any other way.

"The kids and money," he went on, "that's all. How much are we going to have and what're we going to spend it on. How much do we put aside. But that's all shared business, so why'd I want to get angry at her over something we're trying to solve together? Never made sense to me. Not one bit. And still it made her mad that I stayed even-keel. She wanted to ruffle my feathers, and they wouldn't be ruffled. Well, I've got a reason to scream and shout now, and she won't even see it. Won't even let me show her how upset I can get."

He was moving as he spoke—not pacing, exactly, but taking a little step to the side and then back again, like the ground was so hot it was burning the soles of his feet. It almost looked like he was dancing, and I pictured him at one of the stomps I'd gone to when I was young. He'd have been among the men who stayed close to the wall, building up the nerve to ask a girl to take a spin on the floor. There were certain kinds of men who couldn't keep their feet from moving: all that nervous energy had to come out somehow. Those were the ones you wanted to dance with. You had to try extra hard to send the right signals, though, because most of the time they weren't good at reading them.

George paused to take out a cigarette and light it. He blew the smoke out in a sharp cough. "What am I supposed to do, Hazel?" he asked. "Family's not supposed to split up this way. I've got two boys who know their mother is dying, and we're none of us allowed to get anywhere near her. Gene and Bobby don't say nothing, but I know they're thinking about her. Bobby gives me a look sometimes. What am I supposed to say to him?" He took another pull on his cigarette and blew out a cloud of smoke. "Paralyzed, that's what I am. I'm no better than an army vet who's lost his legs."

He was going in circles, saying the same thing four different ways, none of them quite right. I'd have let him go on for a while if I thought it would do him some good, but I could tell it was doing the opposite. He was a man; he needed to go throw or hit something, to act out his emotion through some physical act. I glanced back at the house to make sure no one had ventured off the porch in search of us, and then I walked past him a few steps toward the barn. "Come with me," I ordered.

The barn door slid open without much noise; George had oiled the slides sometime recently. I saw that the tractor was gone now, which meant that Gene or Bobby was out somewhere riding it. I saw, too, that the barn was deserted. Once inside, I took George's hand and led him over to the butchering table, which we hadn't used for years. It was thick with dust and bits of hay. A quick wipe with his gloves made it clean enough.

What is there to say about what followed? I held on to him tight and put my face to his shoulder, and though I didn't feel like crying, it was the right position for a woman to take comfort from a man. He had his face pressed to my neck, and that felt right, too. We were quick about it, and quiet; it was a great heavy table made of wood, and it had handled heavier bodies than ours.

When he was finished, George breathed heavily into my neck for another half a minute and then he suddenly pulled away, pushing me from him almost with violence. And this let me know in an instant that I'd been wrong: our making love hadn't solved anything. George turned toward the wall to zip up and I heard him say, so quietly I almost didn't hear, "Getting too old for this."

Without looking back, he slid open the door and went out, leaving the door open behind him. I gazed at the slanted rectangle of light on the ground and thought about what had just happened. It had been an act with only physical dimensions, almost a reflex. We hadn't talked during or after; we hadn't even kissed. His face buried in my neck and my face pressed to his shoulder, this had kept us separate the whole time.

Searching my conscience, I came up with only the old guilt, nothing new added to it. I put a hand to my hair and smoothed my dress over my hips, and then I went out through the barn door into the bright light of another nearly endless summer afternoon.

*　　*　　*

Before heading back to Lydie's house, I sat awhile longer with Rena and the children on the porch and talked about cattle and trucks. Though Joe was upset with me for taking him from his work with George and the boys, he'd started helping out at Rena and John Charlie's dairy farm, since he was staying there now for what might be the whole summer. It wasn't really farming he was interested in but machines, and the machinery on a dairy farm was, in its way, just as impressive as a tractor. John Charlie had started giving him driving lessons down the roads out their way, too, and driving a car had been Joe's greatest dream for at least two years. I was glad he had something to be excited about. As for Debbie, she remained sullen the whole time.

After they left, I went inside the house to grab a few things. I was getting tired of wearing the same three dresses I'd brought with me to Lydie's and wanted to refresh my wardrobe. When I entered my bedroom, I saw that the bed was neatly made, and George had left no traces other than a suitcase that lay closed on top of the cedar chest. I had no interest in examining the bed for his head print on the pillow. I opened the closet and chose a few of the summer dresses hanging near the front, and then I closed the door again and left the room.

I had one other errand to complete at the house. When I told her I was going over to the house to see Debbie and Joe, Lydie had asked me to pick up some books; she'd gotten tired of the selection at her house and could no longer bear the television. So I climbed the stairs, the heat opening up with every step, and once upstairs I went right to the corner closet, where the boxes of books were stored. The closet held an odd assortment of things: a handleless pot I'd never got around to having mended, a box of mason jar lids, Karol's paintings. There were too many of those paintings, and they all looked the same; I would have to get rid of some of them when I had the time to think of such things. In the closet there were two boxes of books, one near the front and the other near the back, but the first one held mostly Debbie's space alien novels, and I didn't figure Lydie would be too interested in those. I moved some things out of the way and dragged out the one from the back. It was bigger than I'd counted on, too heavy to carry easily down the stairs, loaded down as it was. I took out about half the books and left them pushed against the wall by the closet, and then I carried the box downstairs and out to my car. I glanced back as I drove away and thought how unnatural it felt to leave my house like that, how lonely it appeared in the rearview mirror.

At Lydie's, the smell of dust and old paper tickled my nose as I carried the box inside, my arms aching from the weight and the angle. I went right into the living room and found Lydie awake but bleary: it was clear she had been sleeping only a moment before I arrived.

"What's that you've got there?" she asked with what sounded like suspicion.

"I brought over some books from my house. You asked me to, remember?" Lydie and I seemed to fall into this way of talking from time to time, in which she acted doubtful and, in response, I pointed out that I was only looking after her interests. She had sent away all those who loved her, and she was stuck with only my company. Things were bound to get testy sometimes.

I crossed the room and set down the box on the chair beside the bed. Before they left, George and the boys had replaced the sofa with a mattress on box springs, but there wasn't a headboard and this meant that now Lydie spent all her time lying down. She turned her head just an inch to peer at the box out of the corner of her eye, but then she returned to her previous position, face tipped to the ceiling. She'd told me that she had mapped the whole thing—all its watermarks, its minor dips and hills—so that she could have described the terrain even with her eyes closed. It had become a strange sort of landscape for her, she said, and any time a June bug or a spider went crawling over it, she'd watch its passage with such keen interest that even if she fell asleep, as soon as she awoke she'd scan her eyes over the ceiling in search of it.

As I lowered the box onto the chair now, I was standing close to her head, and she sniffed at me and narrowed her eyes. My heart leaped into my throat, thinking that she must have detected George on me, the smell of our sex. But she shook her head and said, "Old books," and asked me to show her what I'd brought.

We spent some time going through the contents of the box. I pulled out the volumes one by one and read the titles aloud, and if she recognized one she'd make a comment about it, and if it was something she hadn't heard of, she'd ask me what I knew. But I didn't have any more information than she did; there were books near the bottom that I'd never heard of or even laid eyes on before. They were my parents' books: things they'd either forgotten to take or else decided to leave behind when they moved into town. There was an old hymnal, a First Communion book, a couple of Western novels, including *The Trail of the Lonesome Pine* and *The Prodigal Judge*—Lydie said she thought she'd heard of those two, maybe—and there were several autobiographies by soldiers who'd fought in World War I. I wasn't sure who would have bought those, since my brother had died over there and it was something that was never talked of in our family for fear of upsetting my mother. The books might have been Herbert's; he was the only one besides Edith who'd liked to read, and I figured Edith was far too young to have been buying those accounts when they were first published. But it seemed a strange thing, too, to imagine my brother, the minister, reading about poison gas and trench warfare—

Lydie yanked me from this reverie with a command to continue going through the box. I reached in and pulled out the next layer, which consisted entirely of old editions of the *Saturday Evening Post*, all their covers tearing off at the spines, and I thought of how my mother had read those magazines cover to cover each week, even in her darkest times, when she wouldn't do much of anything else. I told Lydie about this, how she'd slap away our hands if we tried to take a look at one before she'd gotten the chance. "She said it was her one and only prize for getting through another week," I explained.

"Is there a prize? I never did hear about that."

"No, me either. I'm not expecting any thank-yous from Joe or Debbie, not anytime soon." I flipped open one of the magazines and read a headline aloud.

Lydie was quiet for a moment. "How are they? Joe and Debbie."

"They're fine. John Charlie's got Joe working the milking machines. Debbie's probably under Rena's foot most of the day, but that's all right."

Another pause. Then: "You see my boys while you were over there?"

I flipped another page, scanning the print. "They must have been off working somewhere. So much for us mothers being the only ones."

"And George? You didn't see him, either?"

I turned another page, trying to ignore the way my chest felt as if it had been filled with vinegar and baking soda, fizzing away and making breathing difficult. "He came in just for a minute, while we were sitting on the porch."

A fly thwapped the window by Lydie's head, and her hand twitched in response, as if to swat it away. By now it was too painful for her to move her upper body, and so both hands remained at her sides. "He want to talk to you?"

I closed the magazine now and set it down on top of the others. If Lydie wanted to follow this line of talk, I figured it wouldn't do me any good to pretend I was too distracted to pay attention. There was a little space at the foot of the bed, and I sat down now and said, yes, in fact, George had asked to speak with me in private.

Lydie had her eyes closed, and I couldn't tell her reaction. After a moment, she asked what he'd said.

"What do you think? He wanted to know how you're doing."

"The phone reports aren't enough," she said, more a statement than a question.

"He's your husband, Lydie. It's breaking his heart not to be here."

She opened her eyes now and looked down the bed at me. Her eyes were bright—not glowing, exactly, but almost as if they might be putting off heat. "That's not true."

"You don't think it's hurting him to be away from you right now?"

She ran her tongue over her teeth and made a sucking sound. Her mouth got dry sometimes, and I thought of going to the kitchen to pour her a glass of water, but I was half afraid she'd reach out and grab my wrist to keep me from leaving. "I do think it's hurting him," she said. "Him, and the boys, too. I imagine they all feel bad enough when they think about me over here." Her eyes wandered back to the ceiling. "But I don't think they're getting their hearts broken," she said. "That's the whole reason I sent them away, to keep that from happening."

"And you're not rethinking that decision?"

"No."

I waited a minute and then left the room to get that glass of water—with a straw, since it was easier for her to drink that way lying down. When I came back, she lifted her head from the pillow and took a small sip. It went down the wrong pipe, though, and in a moment she was coughing violently, her whole body seizing up with the effort. It was half a minute or longer before she had done. Then she lay breathing hard, her face tight with pain. "Can I get you anything?" I asked.

She shook her head.

I watched her breathing in and out, her chest rising and falling beneath the sheet. When I last bathed her a few days before, I'd had to turn away when I saw her left breast; the skin had broken across an area several inches around. "I can't look at it myself, anymore," Lydie had said. "Just clean up as quick as you can, and if you need to look away, you go ahead and look away."

After her coughing fit, I left Lydie to rest and went into the kitchen to fix myself some coffee and a snack. I was drinking coffee all throughout the day now, not just mornings, and eating bits and pieces of things while standing up at the counter: saltine crackers and slices of cheese, tuna from the can, a hard-boiled egg. Every couple of days I'd make a pot of plain chicken soup, and that was about all that Lydie ate.

I decided to make myself some toast, and while the bread was in the toaster I got some butter and preserves from the fridge. I was nearing the bottom of a jar of blackberry preserves that had the year 1959 scrawled on masking tape stuck to the lid, and every time I looked at it I'd find myself meditating on this date, on the oddity of eating blackberries picked during a completely different era of my life. The summer of 1959, when these preserves were canned, was the first summer after Karol died. It was the year I'd begun my affair with George. We might have been in bed together at the exact moment Lydie was plucking berries from the vine. Back then, I'd occasionally thought of what I did with George as a kind of salvo I was firing against the judgment of the world. It had seemed a bold thing; it was my secret act of defiance.

That was all done now. I was bound to Lydie—though I didn't know whether it was anger or love that did it, whether it was an honor or a punishment that she was bestowing upon me.

What did she know?

I turned over this question a hundred times a day. But I could never find a way to ask it.

*　　*　　*

When Lydie woke again, I heated up a little soup on the stove for her to eat. It was afternoon, neither dinnertime nor suppertime, but that didn't matter. Time was a strange thing in that house, bendable. It would double back on itself so that one afternoon felt so similar to another that I wasn't at all certain that they weren't one and the same. But then, too, I'd realize that a whole week had passed, and though not a single event had happened during the course of those seven days to make it stand out, if I compared one Sunday to the last, I knew that her health was going downhill fast.

I brought the soup into the living room and pulled up the footstool to sit beside her. As I dipped the spoon into the bowl, she said she didn't feel like eating.

"You haven't had anything all day."

"Haven't I?" Her eyes swam past my face. "I could've sworn I ate this morning."

"No, you didn't." I ventured to dip the spoon in again, but this time she spoke more forcefully: "I said I don't want it."

"Fine," I said, standing. "I'll put it back in the fridge for later."

"I'm not going to want it then, either."

I stood looking down at her and waited for more: an outburst, an explanation. When nothing came, I said, "You might change your mind," and then went and put the soup away again. Afterward, I went out on the porch and sat awhile on my own. Not a sound came from the living room, and though I wondered if Lydie wanted me to come in and talk with her, or read to her, or turn on the radio, I didn't move for a long time—an hour or more—during which I sat listening to the whine of the summer cicadas and slapping at mosquitoes that landed on my arms, and feeling sorry for myself, and angry at myself, wondering how I'd managed to get tangled up in the business of another woman's dying, and wanting it all to be over, and then hating myself most for what that wanting meant.

*   *   *

That evening, I read to Lydie from some of the old *Post*s. The earliest one was from 1913, two years before I was born, and the latest one was from 1930. My parents must have stopped subscribing around that time, and never picked up again after the hard times ended. It had taken long enough for those times to go, and then it was the war, and then it was the trouble with Junior, and then it was my parents moving into town. The world got close enough then, I guess, that my mother didn't need the magazine to tell her about it anymore.

I read about the first bird known to have crossed the Atlantic and an old opera singer named Clara Louise Kellogg, and Lydie drifted in and out. By the time it was dark, I was ready for bed myself, and I roused her to take her to the bathroom one last time and then I went into the other room.

Though I was feeling tired, it took me a long time to fall asleep. Hours, maybe. I floated, moving between thinking and dreaming. A memory came of Lydie before she got sick, sitting at my kitchen table with a lit cigarette and talking about Mamie Eisenhower. A phrase—not even a complete sentence—echoed in my ear: ". . . prune whip and canasta in the White House!" Cigarette waving through the air, smoke curling up toward the ceiling. This all came to me as clearly as if caught under glass, but then I remembered all of a sudden that the only time I ever saw her smoke was in St. Louis, at the bar. Parts of that memory might have been true, but not all of it was. Maybe I was asleep, after all.

It wasn't until the next day that we finished going through the box of books I'd brought back from my house. In the morning, after I'd made myself some eggs and had some more toast—Lydie still wouldn't eat anything, and I didn't fight her on it—she asked if I'd read to her some more.

"You want the *Post* again? More on men's fashions for Easter? Or the question of whether women should get the vote?"

"That sounds all right," Lydie said with a smile that turned into a grimace of pain. I noticed it and stayed quiet, since she'd made clear to me that she didn't want to talk about how she was feeling anymore.

I went to grab a new magazine, but we were at the bottom of the box and instead of more *Post*s, I found a book. It had a plain cloth cover with the title *Prayers from the Middle Kingdom, Vol. IV.* The paper inside had gone yellow and was mildewed around the edges. I figured it was a religious book, something that Herbert had brought home when he was studying to go into the ministry. Paging through, I saw that it was filled with poems. I flipped the pages, reading out titles. Some had titles that were Christian in nature; others seemed more like nature poems. Still others had words I didn't recognize: "When the Chih-fu Hears a Plea" and "Midnight Fog on the Ch'ang Chiang." Reading them aloud, I stumbled over the strange words. "What do you think they are?"

"Foreign, I guess," Lydie said. "Why don't you read a few."

So I recited the one about fog and another about cooking rice over an open fire. It was only once I was reading them aloud that I remembered about my mother's sister, who had gone to Asia as a missionary many years before I was born. She and her family had been murdered by the Boxers, and like the other tragedies my mother suffered, it was something she never talked about. I don't believe she ever even mentioned her sister's name in my hearing. But Edith and I had heard the story from somewhere (probably Rena, who was older than us and seemed to know everything we didn't), and it had caught our curiosity. For years as children, whenever Edith and I had a spare playmate and were away from any listening ears, we'd play a morbid game of "Boxers and Christians," which was just like tag except that the one playing the Boxer got to carry a stick and, if she caught the ones playing Christians, got to stab them in the heart.

"Goodness, I *remember* that game," Lydie cut in as I was explaining. "You do?"

"Sure I do." Her eyes were open, but because she didn't turn her neck, it looked like she was talking to the ceiling. "First, I remember being confused by the name because it seemed that it should involve fighting with fists. And then, too, I used to hate it because Edith was so *vicious* playing the Boxer. She'd raise that stick like it was a long sword, and I'd fear I was going to lose my head."

"The one playing the Boxer was supposed to aim for the heart," I said, laughing. "Edith should have known that. I never played with you, I guess?"

"You were so much older. Seven years at that age is an ocean of time."

"What an awful game," I said after a moment. "Especially since it was my aunt who really did get killed."

We speculated on where the book had come from—whether it was my mother who'd bought it, or whether it was given as a gift ("A strange sort of gift," Lydie said in a wry tone)—and how it had ended up at the bottom of this box. But there was no figuring it out. My mother had been dead for more than a decade. "A mystery," Lydie declared, "that's better than any Agatha Christie novel. Let's hear another and see if we can solve it."

I flipped to a page and read aloud:

FORGIVE ME (LORD GOD, IN WHOM ALL GRACE RESIDES)

Two words carved with a knife so sharp
Into this table o' wood
But, Lord, I will speak true to Thee:
I did whate'er I could.

Forgive me, then, I beg You, Lord,
For that which gives me Shame—
For Selfishness and Secrecy
And crimes without a name.

'Tis only through Thy Grace, O' Lord,
My soul's great Hope be met:
To be washed clean, to be made whole;
All Sins, like blood, be let.

A silence rose after I'd read the last line. I felt pinned, pointed to, outlined in red. For a moment, I had the strange thought that Lydie had instructed me to read that particular poem on purpose—that she was telling me that she knew, after all, that she knew everything. But then I remembered that I was the one who had chosen it.

"I believe," she said at last, "I've heard recipes written better than that."

"Not a great poet, this Mr. Wickford."

"No, he isn't. Wasn't." She blinked at the ceiling and said, "I guess you'll be reading prayers over me soon enough."

"Lydie!" I said.

She frowned and shook her head. She was forty-one years old and marching quickly toward death while the rest of the world went on as if it didn't matter. In a month I'd be back at work, serving Gene when he came through the cafeteria line; Bobby would come around the house to see Joe; even George I'd see often enough to talk over the business of the farm. I'd be seeing them all soon, and for years to come.

But for now, the dew was burning off the grass and the bees were flying through the clover, and a squirrel, ignorant of it all, was hopping branch to branch with its big tail quivering in the air like a question mark. Lydie's eyes were closed. A soft breeze moved the curtains. Down the road, I thought, her boys were coaxing the corn up out of the soil, and in a month, it would be as tall as either of us, or taller.

Correspondence

30

July 1, 1900

Dear Louisa,

Lately, I have been thinking very much of the past. I am remembering a certain day some eighteen or nineteen years ago, when you and I were walking out the high road near the house. Flora was with us, but we weren't walking with her. She was already so stiff and proper—you know. Twelve or thirteen, she must have been at the time, but already as elderly in her behavior as old Mrs. Bly. She was behind us, I think, not walking as quickly as we were, taking her time in those silly shoes she liked to wear. Anyway, as I recall, we came to the top of the open hill, and you and I looked at each other and then we looked back at Flora, and "Oh, please, you two, don't" was all she said, but it was too late because we were already running down. It was much too steep, I knew that before we began down. You might have, too, or maybe not—you were perhaps seven years old, and not as wise as my nine years. In any case, we most certainly would have run it before then if it weren't just this side of dangerous.

Do you remember, Louisa? Do you remember the exhilaration, the wind, the clouds streaming past, the blur of grass and those little purple flowers all around? It was exquisite, for what might have been only a brief moment but felt like an endless time—I know I lost track of you and would have forgot you altogether, except for your voice screaming in glee somewhere a little behind me, a little ragged shout—but anyway, it was pure joy and wonder, and then I tripped. I went tumbling head over foot, down and down, and I knocked my head on a stone or a root, and great God, did it hurt. By the time I got to the bottom I was seeing stars. And you came tumbling after. Later, when I asked whether you tripped at the same time, you told me you fell on purpose. "I saw you go down," you said, "and thought I should do it, too."

This is all too metaphorical, isn't it? We two, the ones that went out into the world, wanting something different, wanting exhilaration. Me going first, and you following just after. Yet, dear, this isn't why I remember that tumble down the hill. It's because when we got to the bottom and were lying there, panting and giddy, we both heard a terrible noise, a sort of screaming. There was a house cat with her insides torn out. She was lying not three yards distant from us. I suppose she must have been attacked by a fox or a dog—something that got disturbed by the noise we were making and ran off before we arrived at the bottom of the hill. Oh, God, that poor cat, I can still remember her: an orange tabby, slender and sleek, no doubt she had been a good hunter herself before she met that fox or that dog. She wasn't looking at us, no doubt she was half out of her mind with pain. You started crying, "What do we do? What do we do?" and you looked at me with round eyes because I was the elder and should have known the answer. But I didn't know, either. So we ran. Back up that hill, scrambling, hands grabbing at whatever bush or stone we could use to make it quicker, fast, fast, as quick as we could away from that cat and her devastating misery. When we got to the top, Flora was angry with us for taking such a risk. You and I looked at each other and somehow agreed without words that we shouldn't tell her about the cat. As I recall, the three of us went on our way, sobered and shaken, Flora by our behavior and you and I by our encounter with the cat, which was an encounter not only with death but with violence and suffering. Nature red in tooth and claw. I don't believe we ever spoke of it between us. It was as if it never happened—

—except that in my mind, that cat is still there, in all her wretchedness, forever dying. And we are forever running away from seeing it.

This is what I remember: we ran first for joy, and then later for fear—as I said, it's all highly metaphorical. I take comfort, Louisa, from imagining you snug in your farmhouse now, out there under the great open Illinois skies. You will stay there forever—or I hope you do, anyway. I understand that after a certain point, staying is the brave and virtuous act, whereas leaving is the cowardly one, and selfish.

All the north of China is dissolving into violence and chaos—do you know this? Have you heard? I don't know what kind of news reaches you in America, but here the stories are worse every day. I say stories because they are too horrible to be believed, and because I am not there to witness them. I will not explain myself, except to say that I am not a good woman. I left my family and now they are in grave danger and I am safe. That is all there is to know—

I won't stay to hear what will finally break me. And if all is well, if they've gotten out safely and are even now sailing home, then it's better that they believe I was not likewise spared.

You, who know me better than anyone, can already guess what happens next: I am leaving again, and this time for good. Months ago, when the situation seemed grave, when I was entertaining fear without knowing what it really was, when the true horror of all this had not yet even begun—Poppy articulated two options: to return home or to stay. But there was a third one, hiding, and that is the one I'll choose. This is my great disappearing act, Louisa. I am going where no news will reach me, and where news of my presence will not ever go out into the world. China has such places—I have a friend here who knows them and has agreed to help. Or I should say that we will help each other, for it seems that my appearance still holds some magic for those who have never seen a foreigner before, and therefore she thinks I can be put to some use.

She will help me, I think, only because she does not know the truth. She thinks I am a widow and cut off from my family. Well, and perhaps I am—

Forgive me for writing this—and also for the fact that you will never get to read it, for I mail it through the flames. Forgive me, forgive me. I find myself asking pardon again and again, though I know I don't deserve it, from you or from anyone. I deserve nothing but still I ask for one more thing, which is that you remember—not with compassion or pity—but with love,

Your sister,
ADDIE

Driving, 1951

Like an ocean. In autumn, that's the only fitting description: all the colors of the corn with the light bouncing off the leaves, wave after wave of it coming at you from all directions, and the tractor—out there, to the west or the south—the only ship in sight.

Hazel and Karol have signed the papers; they own the farm. This is their house. And this is their land, and those are their fields stretching out this way and that. At a certain point, they become someone else's, but from a distance you can't see the dividing line and so all that corn out there waving and waving, it could all be theirs. An ocean of it, theirs. In the same way two fish own the deep black sea.

*   *   *

It's the second harvest since Bert and Louisa moved into town, and Hazel's sisters are talking of sending their parents on a trip to the coast. "Do they even want to travel?" Hazel asks.

"Sure they do," Iris says. "Every human deserves to see the ocean once in their life. All that mass of sameness puts the soul in a new frame of mind."

Their parents are doing well enough in their old age. Louisa's memory has grown patchy, but she is untroubled by the fact or by much else, even if their father is querulous. After a lifetime of hard work, they are owed a vacation, it seems. "Sameness," Hazel repeats, dipping another beet out of the pot and putting it straight into a tub of ice water. Iris and Rena are helping her can every last vegetable from the garden. Their hands are all stained a beautiful red. "If you want them to feel bowled over seeing a lot of the same thing, why don't you bring them back out here for the day?"

"They've had enough corn for a lifetime," Iris says. "Let them see the ocean, for a change."

"That's right," Rena agrees. "Them and me both. I'd get away if I could, but those cows don't take a break, it turns out, and I don't get to take one, either." She slices a beet, revealing circles inside like a sawed-through tree. "*You* know what I mean, Hazel. We can't just up and go."

Hazel hasn't told her sisters about the baby yet; at her age, it's too ridiculous to get all gushy. It's enough having the farm that makes her too busy to leave. "Who's taking them, then?" she asks, glancing at Iris.

"Oh, we'll figure it out," her sister says. "This is Daddy's fondest dream, you know, and he and Ma both deserve to live it."

The beets are canned: that's autumn. Then winter comes with its scraping winds and its snow, which melts a little and refreezes into ice. Walking to the henhouse and back, Hazel puts her arms out for balance and feels like she's dancing. The view is all variations on white, beige, and black. Cans of vegetables are brought up from the cellar most days for dinner. Beets are lucky they have such a pretty color, Karol says, because they sure do taste like dirt.

In the spring, Edith is suddenly among them again. Back from Chicago—for good, she says. Hazel gives her a room at the house, no questions asked, even though her younger sister comes down for breakfast most mornings with a look like she's taken a hard punch to the gut. Red eyes from crying, but if she doesn't want to say anything, that's her business. There's Edith for you, Hazel thinks: a perpetual mystery.

*   *   *

Biloxi is the closest big water, and so it wins out over the Carolina coast. Anyway, it's on the gulf; there will be a sand beach and soft waves; there will be seagulls. All this has been debated and settled without Edith's say, though it doesn't really matter to her where she goes. "You don't have to do it," Hazel says when Edith tells her she's going to be the one to drive their parents down south. Hazel looks her in the eye as she speaks. "Iris and Rena hatched this plan, you let them figure it out."

But Edith doesn't mind. She's got nothing else going on. "It'll be fine," she tells her sister. "Change of scenery and all that."

Two weeks she's been back now, staying at the old home place with Hazel and Karol. Everything is familiar and also strange: they've rearranged some of the furniture and added a few things; the dairy cows are gone; her sister's on stork watch. Hiding heartbreak has turned out to be harder than she'd counted on. Sleeping in the bed she once shared with Hazel, she's reminded of how as children they'd whisper together before going to sleep. They used to tell each other everything and now she can't tell and Hazel can't see the most important fact about her: that she has loved, and loved hard, and now it's all done. About a thousand times a day, Edith closes her eyes and is back on Orleans Street, walking home from the bar, with Moira suddenly spinning away from her and declaring that she can't do this anymore. "I want kids," Moira keeps saying, raising her hands to her head and grabbing her hair in two handfuls. "I wanna get married and have a husband and kids. I want a life."

Their life in Chicago is the one that Edith wants back. The third-floor walk-up with the rattling radiators, burned spaghetti, and hangover headaches. After the WAC, on the GI Bill's dime she went to Harvard on the Rocks, the place so crowded she had to share a locker with two other students. When classes let out, the single long hall was so packed she could hardly turn her head, but out of that crowd came Moira, and that was it. After two years, they went down to Urbana together to finish their degrees and then they moved back to Chicago. Edith got a job as a secretary in an insurance office on the near south side. Moira taught elementary school. She'd thought they would stay there forever, but after her girl said good-bye, Edith knew she had to go.

So now she's back with her family. Eventually, she knows, she'll make a life of some kind. She'll move into town, get a job, a place of her own. But for the moment, all she wants is to be moving again. Give her the open road and a destination. Give her something to keep her mind off the thing that hurts.

* * *

Bert's feet aren't working right. They go tingly and then numb and no amount of pushing on them makes the feeling return. Lou used to try—she'd sit on the side of the bed and haul his legs up into her lap and beat at the soles of his feet the way, years before, she'd beat the rugs she'd dragged out from the house and slung over the fence—but a few months ago she stopped doing it. One morning she got out of bed and padded off to the kitchen, and he waited a few minutes to see if she'd come back before he finally gave up and struggled to his feet with only the aid of his cane. The next morning was the same; it's as if all of a sudden she forgot about his feet. Maybe forgot about him. She forgets a lot.

It could be worse, though—yes, by God, it could be much worse. Lou's seventy-seven, and he's seventy-nine. Who would have ever thought they'd make it this old? Either of them alone, much less the two of them together? His own pa at seventy-nine had been dead a quarter century. And with how hard he and Lou worked all those years, you'd think their bodies would've gave up a long time ago. Every day was a struggle, fighting weeds, fighting the weather, fighting to get a hog onto the butchering bench, to rake a whole field of hay into bales. Fighting sick children and sick cows and fighting years and years of not nearly enough. Up before dawn and falling into bed so bone-tired at the dark end of a day that he never felt any poverty of light in those years before the electrical wires came out to reach them. God said let there be light, but He still kept half the darkness for sleeping, didn't He.

Yes, considering all that his body has been asked to do, Bert considers himself lucky that the worst of it now is his feet going numb. He only hopes he's dead before they give out on him completely. In the meantime, he can walk; he can drive. He can do all the things a man's required to do.

Edith doesn't agree. "Daddy, your feet," she says with a shake of her head when he asks for the keys.

It's morning, early. He's been up for two hours, sitting with their packed suitcase inside the house, waiting for Edith to pull up in her sister's car. Too filled with anticipation to eat more than a slice of buttered toast when Lou called him in for breakfast. She'd looked down at the suitcase and asked where he was going. "You know we're going to Biloxi," he'd said, angry that she couldn't remember. Confusion spreading over her face like a cracked egg. Then she'd started nodding slowly and said that's right, Biloxi, the ocean, it must have slipped her mind.

"You can't drive with your feet like that," Edith says now, "if they've got no feeling in them."

"Of course I can."

She makes a fist over the keys and crosses her arms, as if he might lunge out and grab them from her. The Coronet's not hers, anyway. It belongs to Iris, who's been giving him and her mother rides in it ever since they moved into town. Not that they have much need for motor travel: there are stores the next street over, and their new church is only a few blocks away. But he knows this car well, could drive it all the way down to Biloxi, no problem. He'd planned on having his daughter take the wheel only when he got tired, and now here she is, standing by the driver's side with crossed arms and a narrow gaze, looking like a policeman or a schoolteacher. "Daddy, I'm a real good driver, you know that."

"I know that? Who told you I know that?" He leans harder on his cane and throws a fierce glance at his wife for support, but she just opens the backdoor of the car and climbs in.

He's throwing a tantrum, Louisa thinks. Look at him there: old man acting like a little child. He wants his toy. Old man with his floppy mouth and white eyebrows, saying no no no. Never thought her own daddy would get so ornery, so old. Where's Mother to put him right? Where's Mother to play "Oh, Promise Me" on the piano, and Daddy to sing with his hand on her shoulder, chin lifted, nose lifted? You sing not with the nose, Louisa, my love. That's why you must get the nose up and out of the way. The front door opening and there he is setting his hat on the table by the front door, there he is asking, "What dinner delicacies doth my nose detect?"

"Roast," Louisa says. "We're having roast for dinner."

Edith leans in the open window. "What's that, Ma?"

"Roast."

Edith squints and shakes her head. When she straightens up again, her father has already opened the front passenger door. He lowers himself into the seat and thrusts his cane at her to stow in the back. Then he sets his gaze firmly on the windshield and spends the next several hours staring at it—not through it, but at it—as if glass is the most interesting substance he's ever laid eyes on. As if it would never occur to him to look at the things beyond it.

*   *   *

They stop at a Red Fox in Chester to relieve themselves. Bert buys a pack of Camels and smokes one while he's standing on the porch, then immediately lights up the next once they're settled in the car again. He doesn't try to get in the driver's seat, and Edith chooses not to draw attention to her victory.

Two hours later, he says, "You planning on letting us stop to eat some dinner?" It's the first full sentence he's spoken since they started out in the morning.

"I figured we'd stop awhile in Cairo."

Her father sniffs. "I don't know where we'll eat there."

"They'll have places, Daddy. Cairo's no small town."

"Your ma's not used to eating in restaurants. She fixes us some chicken on bread, and that's what we eat."

Hands on the wheel, Edith concentrates on the gray tongue of the road wagging ahead. "You must've figured we'd be eating out while we're gone." She steals a quick glance at the backseat and is startled to see her mother looking right at her. Louisa narrows her eyes and says, "I could eat half a heifer."

At the diner, they sit and a waitress appears to take their order. Bert orders for Louisa. She likes what he likes, which makes it easy. They'll have one pork chop each. "There's two in an order," the waitress says and flicks her pen in the direction of the sign. Are they thin? Bert wants to know.

"Get two orders," Edith says. She turns to the waitress and says wearily, "They'll each have an order. Daddy, you want sauerkraut and mashed potatoes on the side? Ma, is that okay?"

Louisa turns a mournful look upon Bert. "Don't they have fried apples?"

The business of ordering finished, Edith is nearly exhausted. This is day one, and they've planned on eight. In her suitcase out in the car are two bottles of bourbon, carefully wrapped in a nightgown. She was never a drinker before she went to Africa, but the war practically required it, and just because they were women didn't mean they wouldn't demand their fill. War drinking was done with a grimace. It was many different lips leaving marks on the rim of a bottle. Then, in Chicago,

Edith discovered the bar. She and Moira would order Rusty Nails, Manhattans, Stingers, Old-Fashioneds. Edith loved the names almost as much as she loved the taste, almost as much as she loved the way the drinks made her feel—like she was Amelia Earhart in the cockpit, looking down on the world.

Her parents don't drink, except on Easter when they buy a bottle of wine sweet enough to make your teeth ache, and everyone at the table gets a glass containing exactly two sips. What would they say if they knew their daughter has packed not one, but two bottles of bourbon? Nothing, probably. They would cover their eyes to keep from seeing it, plug their noses to prevent the odor from entering their nostrils. Her parents have led the smallest of lives, which is why that first glimpse of the ocean is worth all this: the long drive down, her father's anger, the way her mother's whole face collapses when the pork chops arrive with catsup, and no fried apples to be seen.

*   *   *

Just before they reach Tennessee, Edith steers them off 51 and onto 45. There's a Highway 45 up near Effingham, but Bert isn't sure if it's the same one. He and Karol went through Effingham that day when they went looking for Junior. Can't remember the town, just that 45 went right through it. He has a distinct memory of crows: a whole flock of them perched in a tree that only had leaves on the bottom branches. Bert had known it was a lost cause driving to Terre Haute, that if Junior had jumped a train coming out of Edwardsville there was no way he'd get off so soon. Why not take it farther east, into new states and territories? Junior's disappearance was the last straw for Lou, the last tragedy she'd allow herself to suffer, but Bert doesn't think of it like that. The way he sees it, wandering was the only thing that kept their son from real trouble. The war screwed him up in the brain—whether it was from seeing gruesome things, or doing them, who's to say. Maybe it was all the noise. In any case, Junior came back from Europe touched in the head, and after that he just had to keep moving. And surely he's still out there, walking around.

Now they take 45 down into Mississippi. They stop in Tupelo for the night, nearly four hundred miles under their tires, and Edith gets them a room with two beds. She lies beneath a pane of moonlit glass and stares at the shadows on the ceiling. Her father is snoring loudly and this yanks her back to her childhood when her sisters would try to come up with the funniest description of the sound traveling through the walls and ceilings from their parents' downstairs bedroom. "It sounds like a bear choking on a mouthful of frogs." ". . . a saw rubbing over a washboard." ". . . a tractor mowing nails." She'd wondered how it was possible for her mother to sleep right next to this sound; then one day she thought of their friend, whose family lived a few dozen yards from the railroad tracks. Whenever Edith visited their house and a train went through, the noise was enough to make her put her hands over her ears, but her friend didn't seem to even notice. That was the answer, then. You can get used to anything.

Edith's not sure she believes it anymore. Maybe the ear can get used to rude noises, but the body as a whole seems incapable of accepting new realities. Edith feels the loss of Moira even now, in this motel room, with her parents sleeping a few feet away. Lying on her side, she feels a tightness in her spine that goes all the way down to her tailbone. Her very wrists register the absence; they feel flimsy and brittle. Moira used to curl herself around Edith, and they'd fall asleep that way. The physical memory has ruined sleep. She hates to lie on her side because of it, but it's the only position in which she can ever drift off.

After what must be at least an hour listening to her father's snores, Edith flings back the sheet. Her suitcase is open at the foot of the bed, and in the moonlight she plunges her hands in among the clothing to search for the bottle. The smell, when she removes the cap, is so sharp she fears that it will wake her parents. But no, they continue sleeping. She sits in bed with her back against the wall and takes small sips, counting snores in between them, waiting for ten and then fifteen and then twenty snores to pass before she allows herself another drink. In this way she gets through another half hour or longer. Once a dancing warmth has settled into the soles of her feet, she replaces the cap on the bottle and hides it in the sheets beside her, then slides down so her head is on the pillow.

At some point she's awoken by someone shoving her shoulder. Her eyes flip open to see the shadowy form of her mother hovering over her, not quite spinning but not staying still, either. "Ma," Edith says, heart racing, cutting through the haze. "What are you doing?"

"You think you can sleep all morning? Your father needs his breakfast. Up two hours already, milking and—"

"Ma, I don't think—" Edith puts a hand to her head, trying to steady it. "Daddy's right there." She points to the other bed.

"Don't you back talk." Her mother slaps her swiftly on the cheek. It makes a flat sound in the three seconds of silence in between her father's snores. "You get out of bed and come help. I was down in the kitchen just now and couldn't find the big skillet. You put it somewhere it doesn't belong. You or one of your sisters. How many times have I told you, you've got to rub grease on it, and now it's got all rusty. You come on."

Edith sits up, one hand to her cheek, which is hot and stinging. It was a pretty good hit, considering the darkness and the angle. Her mother isn't looking at her, and she's glad for the chance to assess her own condition. A light drunk, but nothing too severe. She can keep her words straight, though what does it matter if her mother isn't even in the same reality? And Louisa is now glancing worriedly around the room. "It's so dark out," she says. "Gonna be a storm before long."

"That's fine," Edith says after a moment. "We need the rain."

"That's right, we sure do. I'd forgotten about that. A good rain will do us good. I don't care for lightning, though."

"But we'll be inside the house. Why don't you sit down here by the window and watch?" Edith stands a little unsteadily in the narrow space between the beds and helps her mother to sit down on the mattress next to Bert. He's still sleeping, though his snoring has temporarily quieted.

"But there's breakfast—"

"Hazel will help. You just rest here, Ma. It's going to be a busy day."

"Yes, all right."

Edith crosses to the door. Now that she's awake, she's got to use the toilet, and the shared bathroom is down the hall. At the door, she glances back at her mother, whose face now shows a kind of patient embarrassment; she doesn't see any rain, but doesn't want to admit it.

Out in the hall, Edith doesn't feel the regret she'd expected. Diving into someone else's delusion—she's done that before but always regretted it after. Sometimes when Moira was drunk, really drunk, right up at the edge of passing out, she'd mumble to Edith about places and things that had nothing to do with them or their life together. A classroom, a chalkboard. Bleachers. Slurring her words, she'd make Edith blush with talk about tongues and fingers, but it was all taking place somewhere else, in her past. She'd had an affair when she was in school. A fellow student, or a teacher. Fifteen or sixteen years old, and she'd been doing things that Edith at her age wouldn't have even known to wish for. All those years later Moira was still going back to it, remembering, yes, and also slipping into the past, and sometimes when it happened Edith would feel so jealous of the person her girl was moaning for that she'd pretend to be her. She'd whisper that Moira was a real sexpot, a Sheba in schoolgirl's clothes. She'd say they had to be careful they didn't get caught. Even while she was speaking the words, Edith would feel ashamed, imagining a witness who would call her on the charade.

When she gets back to the room, her mother is still sitting on the edge of the mattress. The bedside lamp is now burning, and she turns at the sound of the door. "Let me see you," she says, and Edith feels nervous as she crosses the room, afraid that her mother is back in her senses and has smelled the bourbon on her breath, or found the bottle in the sheets. "I know I know you," she says slowly. "But the strangest thing is, I can't think who you are."

Edith sits down on the bed across from her. "I'm Edith. I'm your daughter."

"Oh, yes," Louisa says, though she still looks unsure. Then she glances over at the sleeping form beside her. Bert's turned on his side, facing away from them. "And *that*," she says, turning back to Edith, "must be a sack of potatoes." Which could be another delusion, except that she winks.

*   *   *

Bert wakes to the sound of a door slamming. His eyes fly open, and the first thing he sees is a sheet of rain. Then a concrete wall. "Lou?" he says, trying to keep the panic out of his voice.

"We're here," she says from somewhere behind him. He turns and finds her in the backseat of the car. A car, Iris's car, but where's Iris? He blinks and scratches his stomach, thinking. Looks out the rear windshield behind his wife's head and through the rain sees three palm trees, all in a row. Vacation, Biloxi, palm trees. They're here.

The door beside him opens, and he turns around to find Edith handing him his cane. In her other hand she clutches an umbrella. "Let's go get checked in. We'll drive the car around closer to our room, once we know where it is. It's raining to beat the devil."

The place the travel agent booked for them is called the Oceanview Motel, but there aren't any ocean views. Across the street, in the direction of the water, a stand of trees crowds the landscape, blurry in the rain. One block down is a filling station. In the other direction is a line of souvenir shops. Edith, trying to hold the umbrella over the three of them, shepherds her parents into the motel check-in office and up to the desk, where a large man with a goiter on his neck greets them in an accent so thick she only manages to understand the words because they're the expected ones. She gives him their name, and he pages through the reservations book.

"That's two beds, you say, ma'am?"

"Yes, two."

The man shakes his head. "You're in a one-seater, says right here." He points to his book as if the upside-down scribble of words proves, beyond the shadow of a doubt, where the blame doesn't lie. "But that's all right, I've got a room'll do the trick for you folks. Down the end, second floor."

"We can't stay on the second floor," Edith says impatiently. "The stairs—" She glances at her father, but it's clear he hasn't managed to keep up with the exchange. Edith lowers her voice. "He can't handle stairs very well."

The man glances at Bert and makes a noise from the throat.

"What's taking so long?" Bert demands. "Didn't you make a reservation?" He gives Edith a reproving stare, then turns and gives the man behind the desk the same look.

Edith sighs. "I'm afraid we'll have to go somewhere else."

"Now, look," the man says, shifting in his chair, "I don't know how it happened that you didn't get a two-seater, ma'am—miss?" He glances at her left hand lying atop the counter.

"Miss," Edith says stoutly.

"Miss, then. The name's Baumann, isn't it? Like I was saying, Miss Baumann, I don't know how this happened. Could be the fault lies on this end, could be it lies on yours." He pulls another book across the counter and flips it open. "But how about we look at our options and work out something that pleases every last one of us—even you, mister." He smiles and shoots a finger gun at Bert.

Ten minutes later, Edith helps her parents settle into a small room on the first floor, just a few doors down from the office. A fine unit with a single bed and a desk, a small radio, even a private bathroom. All in all, a better place than she'd originally expected. And she has the key to another room on the second floor. Suddenly she feels the rush of her good fortune: the nights will be her own—no more of her father's snoring, her mother's waking in the dark hours of the morning. "I'm going upstairs just to set down my things. Then why don't we head out? I don't know if we want to try the beach today—" She glances out the window at the rain pouring off the roof in sheets.

"I need to eat a hot meal," Bert says.

"And souvenirs," Louisa puts in. "I want to bring back something for Iris and—and her sisters."

"Sure, Ma," Edith says. "You told Hazel you'd send her a postcard."

"I told who—"

"Did we pack the address book, Lou?"

Louisa looks at Bert, wide-eyed. The address book—is it in her purse? Surely it would be too big to fit in there. As large as they make them now—last time she used one it was the size of a record machine. They used to be the size of a deck of cards. But here's her purse, and it does feel heavy. She sets it down on the bed and begins riffling through. "Surely," the woman is saying, "you don't need to look up Hazel's address."

"I've never been there—"

"Hazel's?"

Louisa blinks at the woman, whose face is so like her daughter's but whose manner is not. This woman is—well, meddling would be the word. Telling her, Louisa, where she's been and where she hasn't. And meanwhile the hinge on the door isn't staying put. That door, behind her. It's sliding, somehow, the hinge is—moving down when it should stay still. Louisa abandons her purse and steps quickly over to the door.

"Lou, what do you think you're doing?"

Bert's angry with her for something, probably having to do with the door, but was she supposed to just stand there and watch the hinge slide off? "It's fine," she says. "It's all fixed now."

"Wasn't broke to start with," he says.

Edith looks from one parent to the other. "She's in and out sometimes," Hazel had warned her. "You won't always know what she's talking about." Of course people start to drift when they're as old as her mother. Stranger to Edith is the way Bert and Louisa seem to have exchanged personalities. Her father, who was always so steady and grave, has gotten tetchy. Whereas her mother, who used to descend into periods of darkness that lasted for weeks, who would accuse you of stealing from her (once it was a spoon; another time it was an arrowhead from the jar full of curiosities she kept on display in the living room), who would go chasing you across the yard and slap you silly if you forgot to close the cellar door—now she's mostly pleasant, only occasionally upset, and even then the cause is something buried deep in the past, visible only to her.

In other words, there are some things worth fighting over and many more that aren't, and for the present Edith is happy to leave her parents on their own to sort out their version of what's happening. Report back, she wants to say, whenever you're done. Just let me know what you decide on, and that will be fine.

*　　*　　*

The door to Room 208 is open, so Edith goes right in. But a moment later, a woman peeps her head out from the bathroom. "Just finishing up here, ma'am," she says. "Come on in, if you like. Watch out for the cart."

Edith glances at the cleaning cart and then at the woman. "I can come back if I'm troubling you . . ."

"You won't bother me, ma'am. Give me three minutes, and I'll have the place spick-and-span."

She disappears into the bathroom, and Edith stands looking after her before lifting her suitcase onto the bed. Her dress suddenly feels tight across the chest, and her heart is thumping hard. It's the maid being there in the room when she had expected it to be empty. And it's her voice, too. It came out the voice of a Negro, but the woman looks white. It boggles the mind to hear one thing and see another. The maid has got auburn hair and—Edith would swear she saw freckles. Of course, there are light-skinned Negroes living all over the country, but this is something else; this is a decision. Surely, the woman could pass if she wanted to, yet here she is talking that way, not hiding a thing. And in Mississippi, no less. The only Mississippian Edith ever met before coming here was another nurse in the WAC, a fat girl with the most beautiful eyes and the most terrible teeth, who explained, the first night Edith met her, why Arabs, though dark-skinned, are superior to Negroes. "Just look at them noses. Closer to Roman than nigger"—as if that answered all questions one might have about the matter.

Edith begins pulling out the dresses she's packed and shakes out the wrinkles, listening to the sounds from the bathroom, the swishing and scrubbing, the running of the tap. If she closes her eyes, she's back in Chicago and that's Moira moving through the background, cleaning their apartment on a Sunday morning. They never went to church; in Chicago, where there were so many churches of all types and denominations—a steeple on every corner—it was possible not to attend because you could always lie about where you went and no one could prove any different. All kinds of things are possible in the city that aren't in a town like Edwardsville. Or in Biloxi, Edith is willing to bet.

The maid comes out from the bathroom toting a little carton of cleaning supplies and the trash can. "I'll just dump this, ma'am, and you're all set."

"Thank you." Edith watches her collect the other trash can from the room and take them both out into the hall. If she could only get her to speak again. If she could just get a good look at her face. She glances down at her suitcase, willing her hands to busy themselves with unpacking. There's a feeling bubbling up inside her, a kind of happy excitement. By the time the maid comes back in, Edith's heart is pounding, and she looks up from the pair of stockings she's pulled from her suitcase to give her a smile so big it surprises them both.

"Oh," the maid says, crinkling her eyes with what might be amusement. Then she grasps the handles of the cart, backs out into the hall, and is gone.

*　　*　　*

They've come a long way from home. Not since he was a young man, a new husband, has Bert traveled this far. But he knows what's what: he doesn't have many years left on this earth, and there are things that are possible now that never were before. He hadn't known he wanted to see the ocean until Louisa started to act strange, and then suddenly the desire came over him to experience, with her, something totally new. Something that wouldn't send her straight into the past. More and more, that's where her mind goes, and there's never any warning; she's suddenly somewhere else, seeing people who aren't there, talking to the dead. The worst of it is that he doesn't always realize when it's happened. Only last week, he and Lou were sitting on the porch watching the birds and the people who came trooping by on the sidewalk carrying paper bags from the store, and the occasional car rolling down the street, and they were commenting on all of it, just chatting. It was such a pretty day. Bert took his wife's hand and she smiled and told him how glad she was that he was here. Me, too, he told her. And she said: I wasn't sure you'd find me. He thought of how he *had* found her—that was exactly it—he'd found her all those years ago in the parlor of her father's house in Marietta: this pretty girl that reminded him of a dragonfly, her stillness full of movement. I found you, he said. I was one lucky son of a gun. Yes, you were, she said. And then, not two seconds later, she looked over and said, Well,

Junior, we're glad you're home now, but we sure wish you would've told us where you were going.

After lunch at a diner, they open their umbrellas against the downpour and head down the sidewalk in search of souvenirs. It's not necessary to look far: every place that isn't serving food is selling postcards, painted shells, collectible plates and glasses and ashtrays and spoons. Bert takes them past the first shop, and the second, until he sees that they're all selling the same things. "I like the look of this place," he says when they arrive at the doorway of a third store, identical to the others. Edith raises her eyebrows, but Louisa's whole face lights up. There it is, that excitement. He hopes this turns out better than the shrimp sandwiches he'd ordered for both of them at lunch. At the sight of those little critters spilling like ants out of the bread, Louisa had given him a wild look. "Bert, what *is* this?" she asked, and he'd had to pretend it didn't alarm him, that it was exactly what he expected. He'd taken a giant bite and almost gagged at the texture. But hidden it, for her sake.

Inside the shop, Louisa turns over a plate and finds that it costs two dollars. That's enough to buy a tank of gas for the car. That's the cost of their motel room. You could buy a horse for not very much more than that, couldn't you? At some point, maybe. Not now, no one rides a horse anymore. And if you did, you would have to spend more than two dollars to buy one. Two dollars would buy you—what? A bridle.

But it's an awful lot of money to spend on a souvenir plate that one of her children will set in a china cabinet for show. Bert will know best what to do about all this. She beckons him over and shows it to him.

"Who were you thinking we'd give that to?" he asks, and Louisa is ready to tell him, but when she opens her mouth, no name comes out; the answer is gone. "Lou?"

"I—well, I can't seem to remember." She turns the plate in her hand, considering. It has a painting of some big old famous hotel on it, and there are palm trees in front, and at the very bottom are blue ocean waves and the name of the hotel and the year, 1951. But that can't be right because it's 1910, isn't it? Maybe a year or two later, but surely no more than that. Time hasn't gotten so far away from her yet.

"Why don't we give it to Iris," Bert says. "She's got that cabinet to put it in."

"Sure," she says uncertainly. "But how about this one with the lighthouse? Mrs. Moeller might like something like this."

Bert levels her with a steady gaze. "Mrs. Moeller's dead, Lou, and you know it."

She blinks at him, wide-eyed. After a moment she starts nodding slowly, but he can tell she's faking it: she doesn't remember anything about their old neighbor dying. "Poor Mrs. Moeller," she replies. "She sure was a help when Joseph was ill."

Does she remember about Joseph? Does she know that her favorite child has been dead even longer than Mrs. Moeller, that they never got to bury him because he died of an infection all the way over in Europe during the Great War? When they got the news, Lou sank into one of her spells, the longest ever, up to that point: for nearly half a year she hardly said a word, forgot to wash herself or the children, hurt herself with the sewing needle so often that at last he had to take away every needle and pin that he could find in the house, put them all in a box that he hid in the barn. She was so racked with grief that her milk dried up and Hazel, less than a year old then, had to drink cow's milk like the rest of them. Iris and Rena kept Hazel alive; their mother might not have noticed if she disappeared altogether.

Louisa's holding up an ashtray now, a bright blue enamel one with sculpted waves and, on the bottom, where the cigarettes get stubbed out, the words *Beautiful Biloxi!* "Hazel might like this," she says.

He decides to test her: "Who's Hazel?"

She gives him an incredulous look. "Why, she's our daughter, Bert. What in the world is wrong with you?" Then she calls to Edith, who's standing at the door of the shop, looking out at the rain, to come over and see what they've chosen. "Just look what we found for Hazel." She hands the ashtray to Edith, then adds, almost as an afterthought, "Of course, she won't ever see the ocean any other way."

"Why's that?"

"Because she's not like you." She pats her daughter's cheek. "She's no brave adventurer."

When she steps away to examine some other items in the shop, Bert puts his face close to Edith's and says, "I wouldn't feel so proud. You ask your mother who she thought she was talking to just then, and I'd bet five dollars it ain't you."

* * *

Edith's no bull dyke. There were a few of them in the WAC: short-haired women who wore stiff white shirts and smoked Marlboros, who walked with their legs two inches farther apart than was normal. The first one she met was a woman who went by Elroy. Edith assumed that this was her last name—it was common practice in the Corps to call strangers by their surnames—but it turned out that the woman's last name was Deveare. "How'd you come by Elroy, then?" Edith asked, and the woman, though shorter by six inches, tipped back her head as if she were looking down from a great height. "I came by it honest," she replied in a voice so husky Edith might have thought it was a man speaking to her. "How'd you come by yours?"

She'd never met a woman like that before, but she had met what she was. What she, Edith, understood herself to be. When she was nine, a lady had come to the house and given her a book. She had no idea how the meeting came to be, unless the woman was an Amazonian angel sent down from heaven with the sole purpose of showing Edith she wasn't the only one of her kind in the world. The woman wore a cowboy hat and had a long gray braid down her back, and she towered from a moun-tainous distance as she considered Edith. "Dr. McBride," she said.

"Who?"

"I'm Dr. McBride. Who are you?"

Edith stood with her shoulders back and tried to look magnificent. "I'm Edith Baumann."

The woman asked her age, and Edith replied to the month. "And your mother?" she asked. "Is she at home?"

"No." Edith squinted up the road to where her mother had gone two hours before to help a neighbor tend to a sick pig. "Are you a cowgirl?" she asked, staring at the woman's head.

The woman laughed. "I'm sorry to tell you I am not."

"Then where did you get your hat?"

"I bought it a long time ago to replace another that I had." She peered up at the trees and frowned.

Edith waited for her frown to fade before asking, "Do you doctor people or animals?"

"Neither, and you do ask a lot of questions." She cleared her throat. "I'm a doctor of philosophy, which means that I tend to our collective brain and to our many ways of understanding." She reached down and grabbed a twig out of the top of her boot, snapped it in two, and tossed it into the grass. Then she put the book into Edith's hands and uttered the mysterious sentence: "This is for you." Or at least that's what Edith decided she'd said. Really, the woman had spoken in a foreign language, one she couldn't recognize. And yet, she understood. When the woman turned and walked back down the road toward town, Edith watched her until she disappeared behind a stand of trees a half mile distant.

She'd thought the book would hold a message especially for her, but it turned out to be filled with religious poetry. That was all right. It wasn't the book; it was the woman. The woman was the message.

And the message sustained her. From nine to twenty-three: that's fourteen more years Edith lived at home, never meeting another woman like her or another girl like herself. But knowing that they must exist in the world. And when the opportunity came to leave home with a place to go (the posters reading "This is my war, too!") and a mission to accomplish ("Are you a girl with a star-spangled heart?"), she took it; she jumped in with both eyes open. Not looking for love, not even thinking it was possible that another woman could love her, just wanting to meet people from different places, to see all the different variations of a woman that were possible in the world. Her first kiss was with a fellow nurse, who laughed good-naturedly afterward to hide her own embarrassment. It wasn't until Edith met Moira after the war that she learned that friendship wasn't a necessary step in the process. The first time they were alone together, Moira took a curl of Edith's hair and put it between her lips. She liked a girl who looked like a girl, she said, but who went after what she wanted, like a man.

Edith had been so high on nerves in that moment, she didn't stop to wonder if that's what she liked, too. She took her cue and played the role that was assigned her.

The maid is down the hall when Edith returns; her cleaning cart is parked in front of the door of a closet. How to talk to her without some flimsy excuse—the need for a fresh towel or a new roll of toilet paper? Every option is a request, and inevitably the wrong one. What she really wants is for the woman to speak to her. To come fill up the space in Room 208 with her presence.

Edith walks past her own room to the cart. The maid is rummaging in the closet and doesn't see her, but when at last she steps back with a stack of towels in her arms, Edith says abruptly, "Could I get one of those?"

"Sweet Jesus on the cross!" the maid yelps, dropping several towels. "You scared me."

"I'm sorry. Let me help—" Edith quickly squats down to collect them and is finished before the other woman has the chance to join her.

"Just set them right there on top of the cart," she says when Edith is standing again. "You said you need one?"

Something about the exchange feels different, and it takes Edith a second to realize that it's the lack of a "ma'am" or a "miss." Every southerner she's met—at filling stations, at the hotels, in the shops and restaurants—has tacked on this form of address as a matter of course. Especially the Negroes, who seem to put it at both the beginning and the end of every sentence, and sometimes sprinkle it in the middle, too. She's not sure what to make of its absence now. "Yes, if you would," she replies when she sees the maid peeling one of the still-folded towels from the stack. "That is, if you have any extras."

"Oh, sure I do." She grins suddenly, a brief flash of brilliance that shows her dimples and also reveals that she's missing her back teeth on the bottom. "I've got dozens of them. Thousands."

Edith laughs and is grateful that the woman doesn't ask why she needs it. "What's your name?"

"Mabel," she responds. A second later, her eyes dart away, as if suddenly regretting that she's revealed this information.

"Mabel," Edith repeats. "That's a nice name. I had a friend—," she begins, but then breaks off. Moira and Mabel really aren't similar names, after all, and there's no reason to bring up the past. After a moment, she says, "I'm grateful for the towel, Mabel." She's started to turn away when the maid asks for her name. Glancing back over her shoulder, "It's Edith," she replies.

"How nice. That's a very pretty way to be called."

The woman's voice contains something it didn't before. Something in the tempo of the syllables, the soft fall at the end of the sentence. The way that last word conjures up the image of her hovering over Edith and saying her name again and again.

"Mabel," Edith says, turning back fully now, "I was hoping you might help me with something else."

"What would that be?"

Edith takes a quick breath. "I want to have a nightcap later, and it would help to have a glass to drink from. Do you have any idea where I could find something like that? A glass?" She tilts her head. "Or better yet: two?"

A few seconds pass, enough time for Edith to nearly be felled by nerves. She worries that a line of sweat is forming over her lips and eyebrows, that her hair is coming unpinned at her temples. Mabel looks and sounds nothing like Moira, but the feeling in Edith's stomach is similar to the first time she spoke with her girl in Chicago. It's hopefulness combined with fear. And she finds herself wondering if her legs will give out beneath her, if blackness will blot out her vision. She holds her breath until Mabel says softly that she supposes she could find two glasses lying around somewhere. "I could drop them off later tonight," she offers. "How's ten?"

"Ten would be grand," Edith says, letting out all the air in her lungs in a little explosion.

The maid laughs as she pushes her cart away down the hall, repeating the last word—*grand, grand*, as if she has never heard it before.

* * *

"Edith, give me the keys." Bert holds out his hand, palm up, and wags his fingers.

"We've been over this, Daddy. You know we decided that it's better if I do the driving."

"We? Who's 'we'?"

"I don't want to fight about this again. It's raining cats and dogs, and you've already slipped twice today—"

"That's not the rain, it's my feet."

"Daddy." She looks at him, and he turns away, harrumphs.

They drive to an Italian restaurant that the motel owner recommended when Edith asked where they could go that was a little farther afield. "We'll get tired of eating at the same places every day," she explained to her parents. After the experience with the shrimp, Bert's wary of eating even stranger food—he's never had Italian, doesn't know what it looks or smells or tastes like—but Lou's eyes got bright when the motel owner suggested it. Why not humor her, he figures. But the place sure does seem strange. At the restaurant, he squints at the menu for thirty seconds, not recognizing a word. "You order for us, Edith," he says with a frown.

His daughter calls the waiter and then rattles off some dishes she says she's sure they will like. All this is old news to her: after Chicago and as a war nurse in Africa, Bert figures she's been acquainted with people even odder than the little man hovering over their table, whose thin mustache and dark eyes make Bert feel uneasy. The man is probably an anarchist, a spy. His face looks like it belongs in a newspaper.

The waiter disappears and returns a moment later with a bottle of wine and three glasses. Edith gives her father a staunch look. "I thought we'd celebrate a little tonight," she says as the man upturns the glasses with a flourish and pours. Then, quickly, before either of her parents can protest: "If you don't like it, you don't have to drink it, you know."

Once the waiter has gone, Louisa leans forward and puts her nose over the glass. It's a very pretty color, but the smell is mostly vinegar and a little bit chalk. A strange smell, if the tiniest bit familiar. Not very, though. She's not sure she wants to try it at all, but then—she's had it before, hasn't she? "Bert?" she says. "Haven't we tried something like this?"

"We have a sip every Easter," he says, "just to honor the Lord. But you and me, Lou, we ain't drinkers. We don't drink wine or anything else much like it."

"But won't you try it tonight?" Edith asks. "Daddy? Ma? Just a little sip, that's all. I'd like to make a toast, is why." She raises her glass, and Louisa picks up her glass, too, and waits. There was a wedding, she remembers, and a celebration at their house. One of their daughters was getting married, and Bert gave a toast. None of their other children had a party at the house, but this one had, and Bert said a few words and it was very nice.

After a pause of several seconds, Bert puts his hand on his glass and gives a little nod.

"All right," Edith says, raising her glass higher. "What I wanted to say was that tomorrow we're going to see the ocean—or the gulf, anyway—and neither of you has ever done that before. I first saw it when I was going overseas, and I haven't seen it since I came back home. It's not like anything else I ever saw in my life. It's big enough to remind you how small we are, but it's a grand thing, and what I wanted to say was that it makes me glad to know you're going to have that same experience. I'm happy to be on vacation with you both. So here's to you, Daddy." She drinks from her glass. "And here's to you, Ma."

Louisa takes a small sip of the wine, barely lets it touch her lips. She doesn't much care for the taste, but it's the polite thing to do. "Thank you," she says. And there's Bert, sitting across the table, gazing right at her with water in his eyes, tears on his cheeks. He's moved, the silly thing. She could almost cry, too, seeing him moved like that. Really, she could.

Back at the motel, Edith says good night and is ready to head up to her room when Bert asks her to come in and sit awhile. "We've got a radio," he says.

She glances at her watch, the car keys jangling in her hand. It's close to nine o'clock. She's got the time. "All right," she says.

Inside, she sets her purse on the bed and goes over to switch on the radio. It's a large one, with several large knobs. Edith drops the keys on the desk and fiddles with the dials until a station comes in. There's Nat King Cole singing "Mona Lisa." She stops, remembering a dark theater and *Captain Carey*. Moira beside her in the dark, their fingers laced beneath the armrest.

"That's a nice song," her mother says behind her. "I'd like to hear it through."

Edith turns from the radio. Her parents are seated side by side on the edge of the bed, like they're sitting in church, concentrating on the sermon. The song ends, and another begins, and Edith pulls the chair out from the desk and lowers herself into it. Half an hour, she decides.

But after ten minutes, she's getting impatient. What if Mabel comes early and she isn't in her room? What if she left her bed unmade, or forgot to put away her stockings? After the fourth song ends, Edith pushes back her chair and stands. "I'm beat," she says, faking a yawn. Then she kisses her parents, takes her purse from the bed, and bids them good night.

*　　*　　*

Bert is brushing his teeth when he hears a door close. "Lou?" he calls out, and at the same time pokes his head out from the bathroom. The room is empty.

Cursing to himself, he rinses his mouth quickly and then crosses the carpet to the door. He stumbles once—this darn room, tight as a cigarette box—but catches himself on the chair that Edith was sitting in earlier. Then he opens the door and steps out into the hall.

Louisa is standing a few doors down, her back to him. With her is a woman wearing a red hat tilted at such a steep angle it's a wonder it doesn't slide off onto the ground. "—think your father and I don't know where you're going—," Bert hears his wife say in a hissing voice. At the same moment, the woman glances at him over Louisa's shoulder. She has an ironic expression, as if she's used to dealing with strangers like this.

"Come on now, Lou," Bert says, coming forward. "Don't you bother this lady with your nonsense."

At the sound of his voice, Louisa turns, her eyes burning and her forehead creased in rage. "You tell her," she spits. "Your daughter here thinks she's going driving with that boy she's so stuck on, that Harvey

Ascher, dressed like a rich lady, thinks she's a real egg wearing that hat." Turning back abruptly, Louisa reaches for the red hat, but the other woman is too quick for her; she knocks Louisa's hand away with a swift, efficient flick of her wrist. "No, *thank* you," the woman says, straightening her shoulders.

Bert puts one hand on his wife's back and with the other gently turns her away, back toward their room. "Lou," Bert says, "you leave her alone now. I told her she could go." He glances back over his shoulder and nods once at the woman. The polite thing would be to apologize, but Louisa is protesting, and he doesn't have the energy to deal with niceties. It's as much as he can do to get his wife calmed down, to remind her where she is, who she's talking to, who's not there.

Funny thing, though: he hasn't thought of that boy Harvey for twenty, thirty years, probably. Nice young man, lived over on the other side of Fox Road. Wanted to date one of his daughters, and darned if Bert can't even remember which one.

*　　*　　*

Three knocks. Edith pinches her cheeks for color, takes two deep breaths, and smooths her dress over her hips. Then she opens the door. "Good evening," she says very formally, and stands aside to let the other woman in.

Mabel walks past her into the room, then stops and turns her head from side to side. "It's a spooky feeling," she says, glancing back at Edith. "Usually, I'm in here, it's with my cleaning cart." She gives a nervous smile before reaching up to unpin her hat.

"That's a lovely color," Edith says. "Do you like wearing red?"

At this, Mabel looks amused and glances at the hat, now dangling from her long fingers. "Well as I like any color, I guess." She drops it on the bed and then, perhaps rethinking the familiarity, picks it up again.

"I'll take that." Edith places the hat on the desk and busies herself fiddling with the radio. What kind of music do Negroes enjoy? she wonders. Is it the same as what she likes?

She pauses on the station she was listening to before, with her parents. There's a pang of regret that she left them early, but a moment later it's gone. Tony Alamo is crooning out "Harbor Lights," the sway of whatever instrument—guitar?—cradling his voice like a rocking hammock. She turns back to find Mabel holding out two glasses. "I brought these," she says.

Edith fills both glasses halfway with bourbon. Enough to do the trick. Mabel is already raising the glass to her lips when Edith touches a hand to stop her. "Wait, we should make a toast." She pauses a moment, thinking. "To new beginnings," she says, raising the glass.

"Oh, no," Mabel says, laughing. "That's not how you do it. I've got this way of toasting. It's something I learned way back when. Here." She raises her own glass to Edith's mouth, letting it hover there. "Now you." And she guides the glass in Edith's hand toward her own mouth. Edith can smell the bourbon sending its happy message up into the air between them. "To life and love and having a damn good time."

They both take a sip, carefully. Then another, and another, slowly draining the glasses with arms threaded into a strange kind of knot. On the last sip, Mabel sloshes a little of the bourbon down Edith's chin, and then carefully, slowly, unlinks their arms. "That was on purpose," she says softly, taking a step to close the gap between them. Edith feels the bourbon on her skin and thinks she should lick it away. But Mabel leans close and does it first.

*   *   *

Louisa is dreaming of boats on the water. She's swimming among them, all the boats of various sizes floating around her. Too close. She's bobbing softly at first, but then, quickly, she's getting tossed in the waves. No, she's in a bed and the bed is shaking. It's Bert, sitting on the edge of the mattress, beating his own feet. "Go on and get dressed, Lou," he says. "We're heading out in a minute."

"Where are we going?"

"To see the ocean."

She doesn't argue, doesn't ask. Somehow, she knows it's just him and her going. Last night, they had dinner with Edith. They ate noodles with red sauce, and Louisa had a sip of wine, and Bert nearly cried. Then they listened to the most beautiful songs on the radio. She remembers all of this, and though she doesn't remember making any plans for today, Bert is rising shakily to his feet, his cane having appeared as if by magic to help him. She watches him cross to the desk and lean one hand heavily on the edge. He takes something up in his hands. Then he turns and gives her a grin. "Let's go, Lou," he says, and tosses the keys around to make them jangle.

*   *   *

Though he's looking out for the first sight of the gulf, somehow he misses it. After they've been in the car a few minutes, Louisa points a shaky finger at the windshield and asks if that's the ocean, there. "You can't see it yet," Bert replies. "We're still a few blocks away." But then he realizes she's right; the water lies against the sky like a bank of gray snow. He's been looking at it for a while and didn't realize what it was, piled up high in the distance. He figured it was clouds. "There it is now," he says, and Louisa peers through the glass as if for the first time. "Golly, it's a big old thing," she says.

They park on the shoulder of the road that runs parallel to the beach. There's not much of a shoulder, just a strip of tall, unruly grass, and then on the other side of it the sand begins. A little path made of wooden planks cuts through the scrub, and Bert starts over to it, leaning on his cane. He makes it along the path just fine. Once he gets to the sand, it's a different story. "Give me your arm, Lou," he says, and she's there before he finishes the sentence, firming the muscles of her arm and letting him lean his weight on her. That's his girl—looking out for him the same way he looks out for her. He pauses, and sensing it, she turns her face up to him and grins. Got a smile like a sun shower. He meets her eyes and she's there, all there; she knows just who she's looking at. "Let's go," Bert says.

The sand is uneven, but Louisa leads him without too much trouble. They take it slow. Twice, Bert stumbles and rests his weight harder on her arm, but she's ready for it. He'd walk on his own if he could, she knows, but his feet worry him so. That's all right: she can be feet enough for both of them. The way they're walking now, it's like they're in a three-legged race. Years ago, she watched such a spectacle: two pairs of boys, each pair tied together with thin rope. There was a field with purple wildflowers and quilts laid out with people eating sandwiches on them. Fifty yards off, a girl in a bonnet stood with her arms raised straight in the air, a dog at her side. Her sister? Anyway, when she lowered them, the boys started toward her and everyone cheered.

Strange, but Louisa could swear that's the girl right there. Off in the distance, raising her arms. It doesn't make sense, though, because they're at the ocean. That scent on the air is of fish and brine. Someone's pressing her arm, leaning heavily on her, and when Louisa turns her head she sees that it's Bert right beside her. Bert, her husband. They're walking on sand toward the ocean, and this is the first time she's been here. Glancing back where she was looking before, she sees a fisherman standing a little ways down the shore. At his feet is a bucket.

When they get to the strip of wet sand that borders the water, Bert shakes off her arm. "I'll be all right now," he says, and glances down. "The sand's firmer here. I'll be all right. Let's go get our feet wet."

"We're wearing shoes," Louisa says sensibly.

Most times her mind is a balloon drifting ten feet above everyone else, and he's constantly tugging it back down to earth. But then she opens her mouth and comes out with something like this that proves she's clued in to the present moment and knows exactly what's going on. Because it's true: they're still wearing their shoes. He stands there a minute, unsure how to proceed. There's no bench or anything else nearby to sit on. He should've thought about this. Should've planned better. They're standing less than a yard from where the waves are lapping up, but they can't go any closer without sinking into the wet sand. He glances down the shore at the fisherman and watches him cast out the line. When he turns back, Louisa is already standing ankle-deep in the water.

"What do you think you're doing?"

Louisa glances over her shoulder and laughs. "Oh, it's warm." A wave comes up and breaks over her shins. She half-turns back to Bert, squats down quicker than he'd have thought possible, and scoops up the surf in her palms. For a moment, he thinks she's going to throw it at him. Instead, she dips her face to the water and splashes it over her head. Then she rises. "Look, I'm baptized."

He shuffles forward, planting his cane in the wet sand with each small step. The water washes up over his feet, and he shouts. He'll have to take off his shoes when they get back to the car so they don't slip off the pedals.

Louisa is looking out at the water now. In the near distance, a fish jumps out of a wave and disappears beneath the gray surface. "This is the first time I've felt the ocean," she says.

When Bert reaches her, he puts his hand on her arm. She accepts his weight easily, without even looking at him. "*You've* seen it before," she says simply.

"No."

"Oh, yes, you have. You're the one that told me what it's like. Ocean Beach, that's where you saw it. San Francisco. I might have it on me . . ." She starts patting her sides. When she looks up, her glance slides over him as if there's no firm place for it to land. "I guess I must've forgot my purse. I always put it right there in the inside pocket."

"What is it you put in your purse, Lou?"

"Your letters."

Bert fixes his gaze on her profile. "What did I write you about? I can't remember."

"About China, mostly. All those places you saw over there."

"I saw a lot, did I?"

"You bet you did. More than me, by about a million miles." She looks over at him, and her eyes are clear now. She gives him a smile full of love. "You can't remember it?"

He breathes in and then breathes out again. "I'm starting to forget things, Lou."

She nods sympathetically. "You're getting on in years, aren't you?"

"I am. But not you."

"No." She glances down and pulls at the sides of her dress with disinterest. The fabric is damp from the baptism she gave herself a few minutes ago.

Bert presses her arm. "Tell me what I wrote." And when she doesn't respond: "About the ocean, I mean."

She still doesn't answer him. She's staring out at the water. It's so still, not at all like she'd thought it would be. She'd expected waves ten or twenty feet high, crashing surf, white foam. What she sees is so calm and flat it could be the farmland that spreads out from the house in every direction. North, south, east, west. Everything in between: an infinity of cardinal directions, each last tick around a full circle.

What did the letter say? She remembers reading it to Bert; he was standing by the stove in the old house, the little house that was their very own. Oh, she loved him in that tiny house. Just try to find it if you can. Such an immensity of nothing around them: they are tiny dots on a nearly empty map. Over there is their narrow bed. Across from it two chairs at a table. There is the window and beneath it the cupboard not half filled with their things. A rug on the floor. There is the shelf of treasures she dug out of the dirt when she first arrived. There is the stove, and the chimney that sends smoke out into the open air. Here are the letters in her hand as she shoves them into the stove. Here is the smoke pouring out the chimney and testing the open air.

Acknowledgments

I bear a debt of gratitude to a number of people and organizations, too many to name, but here is a partial list:

Thanks to Ellen Levine and Alexa Stark at Trident Media Group for being the first two people outside my family to believe in this book, and for their indefatigable advocacy on my behalf.

Deep gratitude to Laura Brown at HarperCollins for her passion and commitment, for her vision, and for her very keen eye. May every writer be lucky enough to work with an editor like her.

Great thanks to Jonathan Burnham, whose enthusiasm changed the life of this book, and to everyone at HarperCollins who helped bring it out into the world.

I am truly grateful for the various organizations that have provided support and guidance throughout my writing career:

The Writers Studio in San Francisco, for teaching me how to stretch and grow.

My friends and fellow writers at Ohio State, and the faculty I was lucky enough to work with there: Lee K. Abbott; Lee Martin; Michelle Herman; Andrew Hudgins; Brenda Brueggemann; and especially my mentor and dear friend, Erin McGraw.

All the great people at St. Albans School, in particular Donna Denizé and Vance Wilson.

And my students, colleagues, and friends at UWEC.

Thanks to the Alumni Graduate Grant for Research and Scholarship at Ohio State, and to the University Research and Creative Activity Grant at UWEC, for financial assistance on this project.

Thanks to the many, many books, letters, journals, newspapers, and other research materials I consulted along the way, especially Nat Brandt's *Massacre in Shansi* and Eva Jane Price's *China Journal: 1889–1900*. Thanks to the Oberlin scholar whose name I've unfortunately forgotten, but to whom I owe the detail of an organ being installed in a

Chinese mission house. Thanks to Josh Bauer, Winnie Khaw, and Alex Long for their research assistance.

For the love and support of everyone I am lucky enough to call a friend, from every place I have lived, I am beyond grateful: from St. Louis, Carleton, San Francisco, Columbus, DC, Wisconsin, and, of course, Ya'an. Special thanks to Dai Ou, Bao Shuang, She Hongxia, and all the Shimian crew, and with love and gratitude for my "Ya'an family": Luo Xinping, Jiang Hong, and Jiang Yiling.

Thank you to all the women writers who have meant so much to me, as both a reader and writer, at various stages of my life, most especially: Maya Angelou, Jane Austen, Maxine Hong Kingston, George Eliot, Muriel Spark, Zadie Smith, Alice Munro, and Louise Erdrich.

Thank you to all the smart women, the difficult women, the women who fight and take up space in the world. Now more than ever.

Inexpressible thanks to my family—Pattersons, Butterfields, Borhams, and Gershmans—for their faith through the years, for their belief, encouragement, and love. The support we give one another is beyond measure.

Finally, with every bit of my heart, all gratitude to Brett Beach, for whom there are no other words but you, you, you.

About the Author

MOLLY PATTERSON was born in St. Louis and lived in China for several years. The winner of a 2014 Pushcart Prize, she was also the 2012–2013 writer-in-residence at St. Albans School in Washington, DC. Her work has appeared in several magazines, including the *Atlantic* and the *Iowa Review*. *Rebellion* is her first novel.